SOCCER:
THE WORLD CUP
1930-1998

by John Robinson

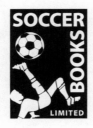

SOCCER BOOKS LIMITED

ACKNOWLEDGEMENTS

I would like to thank the many journalists and authors whose articles and publications on all aspects of football have provided much of the essential background information for me to write this book. In addition, I wish to thank all of those who were involved in the preparation of the manuscript and artwork.

Last, but not least, I must thank the footballers themselves, the 'Peles', the 'Fontaines' and the 'Eusebios' – all the great and not so great names whose efforts have combined over the years to make each World Cup so unique and (often) so enjoyable.

John Robinson

British Library Cataloguing in Publication Data

A catalogue record for this book is available from the British Library

ISBN 1-86223-023-4

Copyright © 1998, SOCCER BOOKS LIMITED (01472 696226)

72 St. Peter's Avenue, Cleethorpes, N.E. Lincolnshire, DN35 8HU, England

Printed by The Cromwell Press

CONTENTS

INTRODUCTION

The FIFA World Cup

The very first meeting of FIFA (Federation International de Football Association) took place in 1904 when representatives of the seven original member countries – Belgium, Denmark, France, Holland, Spain, Sweden and Switzerland gathered together in Paris to establish FIFA's constitution. One of the privileges then endowed upon it by those members was the exclusive right to organize a world soccer tournament. However, it was 16 years before there was any further progress in establishing the competition. Then, at a meeting in Antwerp, FIFA's Congress, prompted by two Frenchmen (Jules Rimet, the president, and Henri Delaunay, the secretary), accepted in principle the idea of such a tournament.

In 1924 the FIFA meeting was held in Paris concurrent with that year's Olympic Games, and more details were then discussed. Two years later, M. Delaunay summed up the then current situation when he declared that 'In the Olympic soccer tournament, many countries are no longer represented by their best players' (who were professionals). Clearly a truly representative world soccer tournament could no longer be confined to the Olympic context so, at the 1928 FIFA Congress, it was resolved to take immediate steps to begin a four-yearly 'World Cup'.

Five countries aspired to stage the first series: Holland, Italy, Spain, Sweden and Uruguay; and, meeting at Barcelona in 1929, FIFA selected Uruguay as the first hosts. Given that Uruguay (a tiny country with a population of only two million) was a three-week steamer journey from Europe, this may seem to have been a surprising choice until one takes three other factors into consideration:

- Uruguay were the reigning Olympic champions and had been so since 1924.

- Uruguay undertook to pay all the entrants' travelling and hotel expenses in full.

- Uruguay agreed to build a new stadium in the centre of Montevideo specifically for the final games.

Regardless of the merits or demerits of the choice of such a distant venue, the World Cup was at last under way. A solid gold cup was designed by the French sculptor Lafleur, and the date was fixed for the start of the first series – 13 July 1930.

FIRST WORLD CUP

Uruguay 1930

BARELY two months before the first World Cup was due to commence not a single European country had entered the competition. Holland, Italy, Spain and Sweden, the disappointed aspirant hosts, declined en bloc, as did Austria, Czechoslovakia, Germany, Hungary and Switzerland. The four Home Countries – England, Scotland, Wales and Northern Ireland – were all ineligible as they had withdrawn from FIFA in 1928 after a disagreement over 'broken-time payments' to amateur players. Belatedly, after the slighted South American federations had threatened to withdraw from FIFA, both France (under pressure from Rimet, the FIFA president) and Belgium (under pressure from Seeldrayers, the Belgian vice-president of FIFA) agreed to compete.

Yugoslavia also entered and, strangest of all, the Rumanians entered on the instructions of their monarch King Carol who even selected the Rumanian team! Despite the absence of the cream of European football, the competition at last assumed a truly 'world' flavour as the USA and Mexico joined the South American countries, Argentina, Brazil, Chile, Paraguay, Peru and the hosts Uruguay, to complete the contenders for the first World Cup.

The format for the series prescribed a first-round competition on a 'pool' basis with three pools of three countries and one pool of four countries. Each country played the other pool members and the winner of each pool progressed to 'straight' knock-out semi-final and final matches.

Four countries were seeded, Argentina in Pool 1, Brazil in Pool 2, Uruguay in Pool 3 and USA in Pool 4, and on 13 July 1930 (a Sunday afternoon) France met Mexico in the very first World Cup match. Despite an early injury to their goalkeeper, Thepot, France gained a fairly easy 4-1 victory, but in their next game (a fierce confrontation with Argentina) were unable to overthrow their seeded components and lost 1-0. In fact, only Yugoslavia managed to upset the seedings when they defeated a skillful but disorganized Brazil 2-1 and went on to top Pool 2 with two wins.

Thus Argentina, Uruguay, USA and Yugoslavia progressed to the first semi-finals, each with a 100% record. Argentina faced USA and Uruguay met Yugoslavia. Combining skill with strength, the South Americans hammered

9

home their superiority with a brace of 6-1 wins.

Oddly enough, then, the first World Cup Final became a re-run of the 1928 Olympic Final with the champions, Uruguay, facing their neighbours and arch rivals Argentina. Thousands of Argentinians who crossed the River Plate to support their team were searched for weapons outside the stadium, and before the start there was even a heated argument about which match ball to use. Should it be a Uruguayan ball or an Argentinian ball? – ludicrously that was the question. Some reports suggest that diplomatic resourcefulness finally prevailed and that two different balls were used, a Uruguayan ball in one half and an Argentinian ball in the other!

It is uncertain that this was true but, as this was truly a 'game of two halves', one would like to think that the Argentinian ball was used in the first half and Uruguay's in the second. The game itself was surprisingly good-tempered. Uruguay's Pablo Dorado gave his country a 12-minute lead but goals by Peucelle and Stabile left the home side trailing 2-1 at half-time. In the second half, Pedro Cea scored a 55-minute equalizer and although Santos Iriarte put Uruguay ahead ten minutes later, the game was evenly balanced until Castro (Anselmo's one-handed understudy) scored a fourth in the dying seconds.

The 4-2 victory for Uruguay was ecstatically acclaimed in Montevideo with celebrations deep into the night and a national holiday was proclaimed for the following day. Meanwhile, in Buenos Aires, the Uruguayan consulate was stoned by an angry mob fuelled by reports of biased refereeing and brutal play. The World Cup had well and truly arrived!

POOL 1

	P	W	D	L	F	A	Pts
Argentina	3	3	0	0	10	4	6
Chile	3	2	0	1	5	3	4
France	3	1	0	2	4	3	2
Mexico	3	0	0	3	4	13	0

POOL 2

	P	W	D	L	F	A	Pts
Yugoslavia	2	2	0	0	6	1	4
Brazil	2	1	0	1	5	2	2
Bolivia	2	0	0	2	0	8	0

POOL 3

	P	W	D	L	F	A	Pts
USA	2	2	0	0	6	0	4
Paraguay	2	1	0	1	1	3	2
Belgium	2	0	0	2	0	4	0

POOL 4

	P	W	D	L	F	A	Pts
Uruguay	2	2	0	0	5	0	4
Rumania	2	1	0	1	3	5	2
Peru	2	0	0	2	1	4	0

SEMI-FINALS

Uruguay 6   Yugoslavia 1
Argentina 6   USA 1

FINAL

Uruguay .... (1) **4**   **Argentina** .... (2) **2**

Dorado, Cea, Iriarte, Castro   *Peucelle, Stabile*

Team: Ballesteros, Nasazzi (Capt.), Mascheroni, Andrade, Fernandez, Gestido, Dorado, Scarone, Castro, Cea, Iriarte

Team: Botasso, Dela Torre, Paternoster, Evaristo (J), Monti, Suarez, Peucelle, Varallo, Stabile, Ferreira (Capt.), Evaristo (M)

SECOND WORLD CUP

Italy 1934

ITALY, one of the unsuccessful applicants for the honour of staging the 1930 series, were chosen as hosts for the second World Cup by the FIFA Congress of 1932. The first series had been a profitable venture for the host nation, but the prospects of the second series being financially viable were not great. Nevertheless Mussolini's Fascist government underwrote any potential losses and the stage was set for a greatly enlarged competition.

The holders, Uruguay, returning a little of the snub given to them in the previous series, declined to defend their title – the only reigning champions ever to do so. To reduce the 32 initial entrants to a more manageable 16, a qualifying tournament was staged in which, ridiculously, even the host nation was required to compete. No doubt the organising committee breathed a sigh of relief when Italy beat Greece in that tournament!

The finals were played on a straight knock-out basis (dispensing with the 'pool' system employed in 1930) and no seeding was used. Whilst such a 'sudden-death' arrangement had its merits, the inevitable outcome was that half of the entrants only played a single game. Indeed, Mexico, who travelled all the way to Rome to play their qualifying eliminator with their neighbours, the United States, did not participate in the Finals at all!

Twelve of the 16 finalists were from Europe: Austria, Belgium, Czechoslovakia, France, Germany, Holland, Hungary, Italy, Rumania, Spain, Sweden and Switzerland; one from Africa: Egypt; one from North America: USA; and only two from South America: Brazil and Argentina.

Both South American countries were eliminated in the first round. Argentina, fearing more 'defections' from their ranks, left all their stars at home (several of their 1930 squad were signed by wealthy Italian clubs and one, Monti, was actually in the 1934 Italian squad), and, not surprisingly, lost 3-2 to Sweden. Brazil went down 3-1 to Spain in Genoa. In fact, only European countries proceeded to the next round, with Egypt losing 4-2 to Hungary and USA going down 7-1 to the hosts, Italy. The other games in the first round provided no surprises with Czechoslovakia beating Rumania 2-1, Germany coming back from 1-2 at half-time to beat Belgium 5-2, and

Switzerland defeating Holland 3-2. Austria beat France, as expected, but were extremely lucky to be awarded a dubious winning goal in extra-time.

The second round provided two particularly interesting ties, Italy against Spain and Austria against their neighbours and old rivals Hungary. In Florence, Italy, a hard if not downright violent team, shrugged off a first-half goal by Spain's Regueiro and drew 1-1 in a bruising encounter which left their right-half Pizziolo with a broken leg. Proving that they could give better than they received, when the game was replayed the following day, Italy used just three reserves whereas the battered Spaniards fielded seven. This gave Italy the edge and they won the replay 1-0.

Meanwhile, in Bologna, Austria and Hungary fought out their own violent tie. Hungary's right-winger Markos was sent off shortly after his team-mate Sarosi had put them back in the game with a penalty when 2-0 down, but his countrymen were then unable to overcome the deficit. In the best match of the round, the elegant Czechoslovakian team were harried all the way by Switzerland before winning a thrilling end-to-end game 3-2. Germany beat Sweden 2-1 in the other tie of the round.

The semi-finals brought together Hugo Meisl's Austrian 'Wunderteam' and the uncompromising Italy, in a game which was played on a quagmire of a pitch. The Austrians were favourites to win after Italy's rugged second-round marathon, but Meisl would have none of it, believing his team to be the underdogs. The combination of a heavy pitch and hard opponents proved his point as Austria went down 1-0 to a goal scored by Italy's Argentinian winger Guaita. In the other semi-final game, Czechoslovakia had little trouble in beating the well-drilled but uninspired German team 3-1. A third-place match was played for the first time and Germany, after taking a 30-second lead, won the game 3-2.

The Final between Italy and Czechoslovakia was played in Rome which, with a smaller than standard pitch and an attendance somewhat less than capacity, was hardly the ideal setting for an Italian victory. Both sides were captained by their goalkeepers, Italy by Combi and Czechoslovakia by Planicka, and big-match nerves were very much in evidence. There was no score until 20 minutes from the end when, to a stony silence, Puc scored for Czechoslovakia. Italy looked to have lost their chance of victory but, eight minutes from time, Orsi unleashed a 'bender' which curled into the Czechoslovakian net and took the Final into extra-time. To the delight of the home crowd Schiavio shot a 97th-minute goal which gave Italy victory and Mussolini a great boost in popular acclaim.

FIRST ROUND

Italy	7	USA	1
Spain	3	Brazil	1
Hungary	4	Egypt	2
Austria	3	France	2
Germany	5	Belgium	2
Sweden	3	Argentina	2
Switzerland	3	Holland	2
Czechoslovakia	2	Rumania	1

SECOND ROUND

Italy	1	Spain	1

Play-off

Italy	1	Spain	0
Austria	2	Hungary	1
Germany	2	Sweden	1
Czechoslovakia	3	Switzerland	2

SEMI-FINALS

Italy	1	Austria	0
Czechoslovakia	3	Germany	1

THIRD-PLACE MATCH

Germany	3	Austria	2

FINAL

(After extra time)

Italy .... (0) 1 **2**   **Czechoslovakia** .... (0) 1 **1**

Scorers: Orsi, Schiavia

Scorer: Puc

Team: Combi (Capt.), Monzeglio, Allemandi, Ferraris, Monti, Bertolini, Guiata, Meazza, Schiavio, Ferrari, Orsi

Team: Planicka (Capt.), Zenisek, Ctyroky, Kostalek, Cambal, Krcil, Junek, Svoboda, Sobotka, Nejedly, Puc

THIRD WORLD CUP

France 1938

THE THIRD World Cup was played as the war clouds gathered throughout Europe. Civil War raged in Spain, and Hitler's Germany had proclaimed the Anschluss and gobbled up Austria – drafting the best Austrian players into the German team. FIFA offered Austria's place to England (the four Home Countries had still to rejoin FIFA) but, to no one's surprise, their generosity was declined.

France was chosen as the venue by the 1936 Berlin Congress of FIFA and, once again, the other aspirant hosts, Argentina, refused to take part, in complete disregard of the wishes of the soccer-mad Argentinian people.

As in 1934 the tournament was played on a 'sudden-death' knock-out basis, but with only 16 countries left following Austria's withdrawal Sweden were given a bye to the second round. Eleven other European countries took part: Belgium, Czechoslovakia, France, Germany, Holland, Hungary, Italy, Norway, Poland, Rumania and Switzerland. South America's sole representative was Brazil with Cuba and the Dutch East Indies making up the numbers.

In the first round, the holders, Italy, took an early lead against Norway, but the Scandinavians came back strongly with a second-half goal to level the score at full-time. Piola, Italy's centre-forward, scored the winner in extra-time and the champions breathed a sigh of relief. Meanwhile, in Strasbourg, an extraordinary game was being played between Poland and Brazil. Brazil took a 3-1 lead at half-time thanks to a hat trick from Leonidas, but Poland's inside-left Willimowski scored a hat trick himself to level the score 4-4 at 90 minutes. In extra-time, both Leonidas and Willimowski increased their goal tallies to four, but the gallant Poles finally went down 6-5.

In Paris, Germany were shocked to be held to a 1-1 draw by Switzerland and even more surprised in the replay, when the Swiss overcame a 2-0 half-time deficit to win the tie 4-2. Hungary walloped the Dutch East Indies 6-0 and the host country easily defeated Belgium 3-1, but the real shock of the round came in Toulouse. There, Cuba (who were mere stand-ins – Mexico had withdrawn) fought a thrilling 3-3 draw against Rumania and then went on to win the replay 2-1.

The second round brought together the host country and the champions in a game that was played at the Colombes Stadium, Paris. A 58,000 crowd saw Italy take a sixth-minute lead, but France immediately levelled the score. The tie swung from end to end and it was not until the second half that two goals by Piola secured a win for Italy. At Bordeaux, Brazil and Czechoslovakia played a notorious match which ended 1-1 in goals, 2-1 to Brazil in sendings-off and left Czechoslovakia minus two players with broken bones. The replay was a sedate affair, aided by nine different Brazilians and six different Czechs and Brazil went through to the semi-finals with a 2-1 win.

The Cubans' dreams of a further shock result against Sweden were quickly crushed and they were fortunate to lose by 'only' 8 goals to nil. The Swiss, still drained by their hard tie against Germany, lost 2-0 to Hungary in Lille.

Thus, the semi-finalists were decided and Italy faced Brazil in Marseilles. Brazil fielded only three of the team that had beaten the Czechs in the quarter-final and struggled to control the lively Italian forwards – especially the centre-forward Piola. By half-time the Italians were 2-0 in the lead and, although Romeo scored an 87th-minute consolation goal for Brazil they never looked able to equalize.

In the other semi-final, Sweden shocked Hungary with a first-minute goal but Hungary soon hit back and a hat trick by Svengeller and goals from Titkos and Sarosi saw them comfortably through to their first Final.

In the third-place match Leonidas of Brazil, appropriately captain for the day, scored two goals bringing his tournament total to eight and helping his country achieve a 4-2 victory over the Swedes.

The Final was played on 19 June, the hard, physical Italians facing the skilful ball-playing Hungarians. After only six minutes Italy went into the lead through Colaussi, their speedy left-winger, but the Hungarians equalized through Titkos within a minute. After 15 minutes the Italians again took the lead through Piola, and Colaussi added his second, ten minutes before half-time. In the second half, despite Sarosi pulling a goal back for Hungary, Italy were never seriously troubled and ten minutes from time Piola scored his second and Italy's fourth goal. Italy deservedly retained the cup 4-2 and, with the onset of the Second World War, actually kept it for another 12 years.

FIRST ROUND

Italy	2	Norway	1
France	3	Belgium	1
Czechoslovakia	3	Holland	0
Brazil	6	Poland	5
Cuba	3	Rumania	3

Replay

Cuba	2	Rumania	1
Switzerland	1	Germany	1

Replay

Switzerland	4	Germany	2
Hungary	6	Dutch East Indies	0

Sweden received a bye

SECOND ROUND

Italy	3	France	1
Brazil	1	Czechoslovakia	1

Replay

Brazil	2	Czechoslovakia	1
Sweden	8	Cuba	0
Hungary	2	Switzerland	0

SEMI-FINALS

Italy	2	Brazil	1
Hungary	5	Sweden	1

THIRD-PLACE MATCH

Brazil	4	Sweden	2

FINAL

Italy .... (3) **4**   **Hungary** .... (1) **2**

Scorers: Colaussi 2, Piola 2   *Scorers: Titkos, Sarosi*

Team: Olivieri, Foni, Rava, Serantoni, Andreolo, Locatelli, Biavati, Meazza (Capt.), Piola, Ferrari, Colaussi

Team: Szabo, Polgar, Biro, Szalay, Szucs, Lazar, Sas, Vincze, Sarosi (Capt.), Szengeller, Titkos

FOURTH WORLD CUP

Brazil 1950

IN 1946 the four Home Countries rejoined FIFA and the stage was set for Britain to participate at last. Brazil's late entry into the Second World War ensured that it was little affected by the hostilities and its selection as the venue for the fourth World Cup served to fire the Brazilian people's fanatical enthusiasm even further.

Once again controversy surrounded the preliminary stages. The British Home International Championship was designated as a qualifying group with the top two countries guaranteed a place in Brazil. The Scottish FA ungraciously announced that Scotland would go as British champions or not at all and steadfastly refused to budge when they finished runners-up. Nor were they the only country to pull out: Argentina, at loggerheads with Brazil, repeated their 1938 performance; Czechoslovakia, still understrength after the ravages of war, pulled out amidst a welter of bitter recriminations; Turkey withdrew after qualifying, and then France, having agreed to take their place, withdrew when they realized how unfairly the competition had been organized. Even Portugal refused to take Scotland's place and only 13 countries participated in the finals.

The organization greatly favoured Brazil who played five of their six games in Rio, whereas the other countries were forced to travel thousands of miles to stage their games in various parts of the country. Additionally, the competition was arranged in a quite ludicrous manner, with two groups of four, one of three and one of only two leading to a final pool of four countries. Extraordinarily there was not even a final game although, ironically, the last tie of the competition provided a superb 'final' in all but name.

The European contingent was much depleted by the Second World War, and only England, Italy, Spain, Olympic champions Sweden, Switzerland and Yugoslavia made the trip. South America was represented by Bolivia, Brazil, Chile, Paraguay and Uruguay while the USA and Mexico made up the numbers. The pool groupings were as follows:

Pool 1: Brazil, Mexico, Switzerland and Yugoslavia,
Pool 2: Chile, England, Spain and USA,

Pool 3:   Italy, Paraguay and Sweden,

Pool 4:   Bolivia and Uruguay.

The competition in Pool 1 opened at the still uncompleted Maracana stadium with huge traffic jams and rubble and scaffolding everywhere. A 21-gun salute welcomed the Brazilian team onto the pitch and an ecstatic crowd roared them on to an easy 4-0 victory over Mexico. Brazil's next game in Pool 1 was against Switzerland and there was consternation in Brazil when the game ended 2-2, as Yugoslavia had meanwhile beaten both Switzerland and Mexico. Facing Brazil the elegant Yugoslavs threatened to topple the host country when, although one goal down at half-time, they pressed strongly for an equalizer. However, the opening was missed, Zizinho linked his way through for a second goal and Brazil were through to the final pool with five points.

In Pool 2 the opening two games ended in predictable wins for Spain (3-1 over the USA) and England (2-0 over Chile), but the third tie provided the biggest surprise of the competition. England, widely expected to win the series, faced the least fancied team of all, the USA, on an arid, bumpy pitch in a ramshackle stadium at Belo Horizonte. Fielding a side containing most of the great footballing names of the day (including Alf Ramsey – their manager in 1966) England cantered through most of the first half pinning the Americans in their own penalty area until, in the 37th minute, the unthinkable happened – the USA scored. In the second half, England pressed with increasing desperation, but the harder they tried the worse they fared and, at the final whistle, they were still behind. The world's press had a field day, exalting the victorious Americans, but the result was greeted back home with disbelief by the astonished English fans.

Spain beat Chile 2-0 and the 'fat was really in the fire' when England faced them in their last game of the pool. England's Jackie Milburn headed what seemed to be a perfect goal in the 14th minute but the Italian referee ruled it offside although a Spanish defender was clearly between Milburn and the goalkeeper. Spain scored in the second half to put England out of the competition and to progress to the final pool.

Pool 3 started in Sao Paulo with the holders, Italy (sadly understrength after the Superga air crash the previous year, in which the superb Torino team were annihilated) meeting the Olympic champions Sweden. Managed by an Englishman, George Raynor, Sweden had an outstanding team but, urged on by a partisan Italo-Brazilian crowd, the Italians took an early lead.

Unperturbed, Sweden were soon back in the game and led 2-1 at half-time with goals from Jeppson and Andersson. In the second half Jeppson added a further goal and although Italy pulled a goal back, Sweden won 3-2. The second match in the group brought together Paraguay and Sweden and, after Sweden were comfortably in front 2-1 at half-time, the Paraguayans performed very creditably to achieve a 2-2 draw. In the last match of the pool, Italy faced the humiliating prospect of finishing bottom whereas Paraguay were in with a real chance of reaching the final stages. Fielding a much more balanced side, Italy took a first half lead through Carapellese with Pandofini adding a second-half winner to ensure their own respectability, as well as Sweden's passage to the finals.

Pool 4 consisted of a single match between Uruguay and the complete outsiders, Bolivia. Shiaffino notched four goals and his team-mates scored another four as Uruguay strolled through to the final pool.

Thus the stage was set for the six matches of the final pool. In Rio, Brazil set off at a gallop against Sweden and were in the lead 3-0 at half-time thanks to two goals from Ademir and one from Chico. During the second half they ran riot over the Swedes with a breathtaking display of footballing genius and, with Ademir increasing his personal tally to four goals, ran out 7-1 winners.

Meanwhile, in Sao Paulo, Uruguay were struggling against Spain in a fiery match. Down 2-1 at half-time, they pulled back to 2-2, 18 minutes from time and held on for a draw. Nor did Uruguay impress in their next game (also in Sao Paulo) when, playing Sweden, they were again 2-1 in arrears at half-time and looking anything but happy. The Swedes were then reduced to ten men for a while by a bad Gonzales foul on Johnsson and drained by their long journey from Rio, went down 3-2.

Back in Rio, Brazil thrashed the weary Spanish side 6-1 and, with four points and thirteen goals, faced the prospect of their final game against Uruguay with some relish. Uruguay had struggled to obtain three points and Brazil, on the crest of a wave, looked certain to take their first championship. Both Sweden and Spain were out of the hunt already when they met in Sao Paulo, while the home country squared up to Uruguay in the championship decider. Sweden, no doubt assisted by the fact that Spain were obliged to travel from Rio, took the game 3-1 to finish in third place overall.

Although the Brazil v Uruguay match is often referred to as the '1950 Final', in fact it was merely the 'Final Pool decider'. However, a finer final would have been hard to envisage and, before an official attendance of 199,854 (the highest ever), Brazil looked to be certain of victory. In fact, defeat seemed inconceivable to the ebullient home crowd and the State Governor in his pre-match address referred to Brazil as 'champions to be' and 'without equal'. Clearly this was a case of counting one's chickens before they had hatched, and although under immediate intense pressure from the superb Brazilian attack, Uruguay defended resolutely and, by half-time, were beginning to show their own teeth. Soon after the restart, Friaca scored a goal for Brazil and the huge crowd howled in delight. Undeterred, Uruguay streamed into the attack and were soon putting Brazil under pressure themselves. Their commanding centre-half Varela pushed forward and, half-way through the second half, started a right-wing move which culminated in Schiaffino scoring a deserved equalizer. Now the Brazilians were forced to defend and, ten minutes later, Uruguay took the lead through their winger Ghiggia. Brazil fought back to exert such intense pressure that, in the final minute, their whole team except the goalkeeper Barbosa were in their opponents' area.

To the dismay of the home crowd Uruguay held on to their lead and, for the first time since 1930 the cup was on it way back to Montevideo.

POOL 1

	P	W	D	L	F	A	Pts
Brazil	3	2	1	0	8	2	5
Yugoslavia	3	2	0	1	7	3	4
Switzerland	3	1	1	1	4	6	3
Mexico	3	0	0	3	2	10	0

POOL 2

	P	W	D	L	F	A	Pts
Spain	3	3	0	0	6	1	6
England	3	1	0	2	2	2	2
Chile	3	1	0	2	5	6	2
USA	3	1	0	2	4	8	2

POOL 3

	P	W	D	L	F	A	Pts
Sweden	2	1	1	0	5	4	3
Italy	2	1	0	1	4	3	2
Paraguay	2	0	1	1	2	4	1

POOL 4

	P	W	D	L	F	A	Pts
Uruguay	1	1	0	0	8	0	2
Bolivia	1	0	0	1	0	8	0

FINAL POOL

	P	W	D	L	F	A	Pts
Uruguay	3	2	1	0	7	5	5
Brazil	3	2	0	1	14	4	4
Sweden	3	1	0	2	6	11	2
Spain	3	0	1	2	4	11	1

THE FINAL POOL DECIDER

Uruguay .... (0) **2**   **Brazil** .... (0) **1**

Scorers: Schiaffino, Ghiggia   *Scorer: Friaca*

Team: Maspoli, Gonzales (M), Tejera, Gambetta, Varela (Capt.), Andrade, Ghiggia, Perez, Miguez, Schiaffino, Moran

Team: Barbosa, Augusto (Capt.), Juvenal, Bauer, Danilo, Bigode, Friaca, Zizinho, Ademir, Jair, Chico

FIFTH WORLD CUP

Switzerland 1954

THE SELECTION of Switzerland as the venue for the fifth World Cup competition was perhaps a wise choice in terms of accessibility but, in the event, the organization was poor and the Swiss police prone to unnecessary, unjustified excesses. The 'Iron Curtain' was raised sufficiently to permit the entry of a number of Eastern bloc countries. Germany, now divided into East and West, was in the throes of rebuilding its economy and morale and, establishing a pattern for the future, met little difficulty in qualifying over Norway and the Saar. Once again the British Home International Championship doubled as a qualifying group but this time Scotland (although once again runners-up to England) agreed to participate in the finals. The white-hot favourites were Hungary who, in November 1953, had crushed England 6-3 at Wembley and had then repeated the treatment 7-1 in Budapest in May 1954.

The 16 participants, sieved by a qualifying tournament, were each obliged to play only two first-round matches although they were divided into four pools of four. The logic behind such a decision is difficult to follow but this arbitrary seeding of two countries in each group (to prevent their meeting in the first round) had a profound effect upon the ultimate destiny of the cup. The top two teams in each pool progressed straight through to the quarter-finals whereon the competition was played on a knock-out basis. There was no provision for goal difference to decide between teams achieving the same number of points – in that event play-offs were used to decide.

South America was represented by the holders, Uruguay, and the beaten 1960 finalists, Brazil. Mexico flew Central America's flag and Asia's first representatives were South Korea. In addition, Austria, Belgium, Czechoslovakia, England, France, Hungary, Italy, Scotland, Switzerland, Turkey, West Germany and Yugoslavia represented Europe.

The seeds were Brazil, France, Hungary, Turkey, Uruguay, Austria, England and Italy and they were pooled as follows:

Pool 1: Brazil, France, Mexico and Yugoslavia.

Pool 2: Hungary, Turkey, South Korea and West Germany.

Pool 3: Austria, Czechoslovakia, Scotland and Uruguay.

Pool 4: Belgium, England, Italy and Switzerland.

The competition began in Pool 1 with the seeded French facing the youthful and potentially outstanding Yugoslavs. Trailing 1-0 at half time, France were held by the Yugoslavs in the second half and went down by that single goal. Brazil, the other seeds, cruised to an effortless 5-0 victory over Mexico, who then lost 3-2 to France in their next game (by courtesy of a disputed penalty). The last game in Pool 1, between Brazil and France, looked set to ensure a play-off for the second quarter-final place, until Yugoslavia, having weathered much Brazilian pressure, took a 1-0 lead late in the first half. Brazil levelled the score 1-1 at full-time and extra-time was played at a most pedestrian pace – both teams being thus assured of a quarter-final place.

In Pool 2 Hungary trounced the outclassed South Koreans 9-0 with Kocsis scoring a hat trick and Puskas and Palotas notching up a brace apiece. West Germany were little troubled by the weak Turkish side (who had, fatuously, been chosen as seeds along with Hungary) and won their first match 4-1. Facing Hungary in their next game, Sepp Herberger, the wily West German manager/coach, deliberately fielded an understrength team knowing that a defeat would ensure a play-off against Turkey for the second place which, if attained, would give an easier quarter-final tie. In the event, he was probably embarrassed by the 8-3 annihilation that the Hungarians handed his team, yet the ultimate outcome went precisely according to plan. Cynics claim that his tactics went beyond planning for a quarter-final place, as Puskas, the brilliant Hungarian inside-left, was so severely injured by a deliberate West German foul that he became a virtual passenger for the remainder of the competition.

In the final game of the pool, Turkey crushed the South Koreans 7-0 to earn their play-off against West Germany for the second quarter-final place which, predictably, ended 7-2 in favour of the Germans.

Meanwhile in Pool 3, Scotland fought well against Austria in Zurich and were unfortunate to go down by a single goal. However, feeling himself to be hamstrung in his job, manager Andy Beattie resigned. The consequences of this move, yet another example of the Scots' self-destructive capacity, were to emerge in their next game. Dispirited and argumentative because of the departure of Beattie, Scotland faced the towering Uruguayans in the first international game to be televised live in Scotland. Uruguay had beaten Czechoslovakia 2-0 in their first game but their uninspired performance had lulled the Scots into a false sense of security. Right from the kick-off Uruguay's superb inside-forward Schiaffino dominated the whole field and handed Scotland a humiliating lesson in how to play football. Nor was he alone: Varela, although 39 years of age, was a pillar of strength at the centre of the Uruguayan defence and the Scots never looked like scoring. Leading 2-0 at half-time, Uruguay moved into overdrive in the second half and romped to a 7-0 victory with a super hat trick from Borges and two more from Abbadie. The other quarter-final place from Pool 3 went to Austria who had little difficulty in defeating Czechoslovakia 5-0 with Probst scoring a deserved hat trick and Stojaspal grabbing the other two goals.

Finally, to Pool 4. Fielding a number of well-known players, England had their recent thrashing by Hungary in mind when they met Belgium. Although fairly strong up front, the English defence was unbalanced and pedestrian with no real replacement having been found for Neil Franklin, their centre-half of earlier years, while there was a shaky backstop in goalkeeper Merrick. After cruising to a comfortable 3-1 lead, England looked set for victory until the Belgians exposed the weakness of the English defence, to level the score at 3-3 after 90 minutes. The extraordinary rules of the series demanded extra-time in the event of a tie and this was duly played – the game ending all square 4-4. In their next match, England met the host country, Switzerland, and with Billy Wright superb at the centre of a restructured defence, achieved a comfortable 2-0 victory to ensure a quarter-final place against the destroyers of the Scots – Uruguay.

Italy, the other seeded country in Pool 4, were shocked in a particularly rough match against Switzerland, losing 2-1 thanks to a second-half goal from the Swiss centre-forward Hugi. In this volatile game, the Brazilian referee Mr. Viana failed to control the excesses of the robust Swiss defence in the first half or the almost homicidal Italians in the second half, and was fortunate to avoid the mass clashes which were to follow in one of the later games in the tournament. Italy pulled themselves together to beat Belgium 4-1 in their other match in Pool 4 and were faced with a play-off against Switzerland for the quarter-final place. The discipline of the Italian squad was then reported to have gone haywire and this was reflected in peculiar team selections for their play-off. Several of the leading players were left out and others were played totally out of position. The net result was one of humiliation for the Italians who were unable to find any cohesion whatsoever, yielding the game 4-1 without a fight.

Thus the quarter-finalists were decided, with the host country drawn against their neighbours, Austria, while England faced Uruguay, Brazil were to play

Hungary and West Germany met Yugoslavia.

England's game against Uruguay was a far different affair to that of their old rivals Scotland in the previous round. In an entertaining game the English defence resisted stubbornly under the inspiration of Billy Wright, and the attack (coaxed and prompted by the commanding Stanley Matthews) put the Uruguayans under immense pressure. Unfortunately, poor goalkeeping by Gil Merrick once again let England down when (England having pulled back to 1-1) he misjudged a long shot by Varela. Early in the second half, Varela was allowed to drop-kick a free kick and England's defence were so astonished that they allowed Schiaffino to run through, Merrick again failing to prevent the goal. Still undismayed, England fought back and Tom Finney scored in the 67th minute to make it 3-2. Merrick slipped up once more 13 minutes from the end and Uruguay were through to the semi-finals with a 4-2 win.

In Berne the game between Brazil and Hungary ended in Hungary's favour with a similar scoreline but the game was a very different affair. So notorious was this match to become that it has since acquired the title 'The Battle of Berne'. Starting in their own typical style, Hungary galloped into the attack from the opening moments and, within minutes, were 2-0 up. Without Puskas, who watched the game from the touchline, Hungary allowed Brazil to come back into the game and the mercurial Brazilian forwards were subjected to a whole series of irritating fouls which culminated in a 17th-minute penalty for a foul on Indio. This was duly converted by D. Santos and by half-time temperatures were rising.

The second half began with more aggravating fouls and obstructions and, before long, Hungary were awarded a penalty which Lantos slammed home to lift the score to 3-1. The niggling play continued and, in the 72nd minute, shortly after Brazil had pulled a goal back, the English referee Arthur Ellis sent off Hungary's Bozsik and Brazil's N. Santos for fighting. Still the Brazilians pressurized the Hungarian defence but, just one minute from the final whistle, Kocsis headed Hungary's fourth goal from a Czibor cross to put the game beyond doubt. In the final seconds Brazil's inside-left, Tozzi, was sent off for a vicious kick on Lorant.

Although the match ended 4-2 to Hungary, the action did not end with the final whistle. The Brazilian centre-half Pinheiro was struck in the face by a bottle as he entered the dressing room (some say by Ferenc Puskas) and the Brazilian team then attacked the Hungarians in their own dressing room. In the minutes that followed, only three players – Castilho of Brazil and Kocsis and Hidegkuti of Hungary – refused to become involved in a disgraceful brawl. Afterwards, neither country reprimanded its players and FIFA's Disciplinary Committee then toothlessly swept the whole debacle under the carpet.

In the third quarter-final, Switzerland faced Austria at Lausanne and roared into a 3-0 lead in the opening 20 minutes, but then conceded five goals in seven minutes and, by half-time, were trailing 5-4. Nor did the scoring end there. The Swiss captain Bocquet, who was suffering from a serious illness, disregarded his doctor's advice to play but, as the heat rose, placed his team-mates at a severe disadvantage. In the second half Austria scored twice more and Switzerland once to settle the contest 7-5 – one of the highest scores in any World Cup finals match.

The next day, in Geneva, the tie between West Germany and Yugoslavia ended in a comparatively tame 2-0 victory for the West Germans who, whilst lacking in flair, were nonetheless immensely fit and determined.

In the semi-finals Austria were hot favourites to see off their West German neighbours. They were renowned for their superior skill and technique and, having scored seven in the quarter-final, looked destined for their first Final. Unfortunately for them they made a grave mistake by bringing back their renowned but off-form goalkeeper Walter Zeman and this gamble proved decisive. Totally unnerved, Zeman created panic amongst his own defence by his dreadful performance as Austria crashed 6-1.

For the other semi-final the Swiss authorities, fearing a repetition of the vicious 'Battle of Berne', ringed the pitch with steel-helmeted troops for Hungary's clash with Uruguay, despite Uruguay's promise that there would be no violence. However, the South Americans kept their word and the Lausanne crowd was treated to an absolute classic of a match, played in a thrilling end-to-end style. Hungary took a 1-0 lead through Czibor and held it until just after half-time when Hidegkuti made it 2-0. Uruguay fought back gamely, and in the last 15 minutes Hohberg scored twice to level the score at full-time. In extra-time Kocsis headed two memorable goals to win the tie for Hungary and their manager, Mandi, declared Uruguay 'the best team that Hungary had ever met'!

The third-place play-off was, as usual, something of an anti-climax and Austria (having dropped Zeman again) won a comfortable 3-1 victory over Uruguay.

Everyone who had seen Hungary decimate the hapless West Germans in the first round were convinced that the Final would be a repeat of that game. The burning question was 'would Puskas be fit to play?'. The answer: 'not really', but he did anyway! As usual Hungary began the game with a virtual cavalry charge and within eight minutes were two goals up (scored by Puskas and Kocsis) and pressing for more. The West Germans, however, did not yield under the onslaught and hit back with a Morlock goal inside three minutes and, after sixteen minutes, were level at 2-2.

By this time Puskas's injury was becoming a real burden although he played bravely on. In a wonderfully open game he was twice denied in the second half by brilliant saves from Turek as Hungary besieged the West German goal. Time and again the Hungarians came close to scoring but on every occasion either Turek or a post or an outstretched foot saved them. Then, seven minutes from the end, Rahn scored for West Germany, and the frantic Hungarians threw everything into the attack. Two minutes from time Puskas scored what seemed to be a perfect equalizer but Mervyn Griffiths, the Welsh linesman, ruled it offside. Still Hungary attacked, and in their final drive Czbor hit a cracking shot which Turek somehow managed to clear. Then, to the delight of the 30,000 West German fans who were present, it was all over.

After a formidable run of victories, the 'Magical Magyars' had registered their first defeat and West Germany had pulled off a quite remarkable comeback to crown an exceptional World Cup competition.

GROUP 1

	P	W	D	L	F	A	Pts
Brazil	2	1	1	0	6	1	3
Yugoslavia	2	1	1	0	2	1	3
France	2	1	0	1	3	3	2
Mexico	2	0	0	2	2	8	0

GROUP 2

	P	W	D	L	F	A	Pts
Hungary	2	2	0	0	17	3	4
Turkey	2	1	0	1	8	4	2
West Germany	2	1	0	1	7	9	2
South Korea	2	0	0	2	0	16	0

Play-off
West Germany .... 7 Turkey 2

GROUP 3

	P	W	D	L	F	A	Pts
Uruguay	2	2	0	0	9	0	4
Austria	2	2	0	0	6	0	4
Czechoslovakia	2	0	0	2	0	7	0
Scotland	2	0	0	2	0	8	0

GROUP 4

	P	W	D	L	F	A	Pts
England	2	1	1	0	6	4	3
Italy	2	1	0	1	5	3	2
Switzerland	2	1	0	1	2	3	2
Belgium	2	0	1	1	5	8	1

Play-off
Switzerland .... 4 Italy 1

QUARTER-FINALS

West Germany .... 2 Yugoslavia 0
Austria .... 7 Switzerland 5
Uruguay .... 4 England 2
Hungary .... 4 Brazil 2

SEMI-FINALS

West Germany .... 6 Austria 1
Hungary .... 4 Uruguay 2

THIRD-PLACE MATCH

Austria .... 3 Uruguay 1

FINAL

West Germany .... (2) **3**   **Hungary** .... (2) **2**

Scorers: Morlock, Rahn 2   *Scorers: Puskas, Czibor*

Team: Turek, Posipal, Kohlmeyer,   **Team**: Grosics, Buzansky, Lantos,
Eckel, Liebrich, Mai, Rahn, Morlock,   Bozsik, Lorant, Zakarias, Czibor,
Walter (O), Walter (F), Schaefer   Kocsis, Hidegkuti, Puskas, Toth (J)

SIXTH WORLD CUP

Sweden 1958

IN 1948 Sweden won the Olympic soccer title with a team of outstanding players but, because of the Swedish Federation's great antipathy towards professionalism, by the 1950 World Cup many of the stars had been signed by rich Italian clubs. The 1958 World Cup was staged in Sweden at a time when these archaic attitudes towards the professional footballer were at last shelved in that country and, for the first time some of those brilliant exiles were able once again to don their national colours.

After two World Cups in which the British Home Championship had doubled as a World Cup qualifying group for two countries, murmurs of protest from other members of FIFA had resulted in all four Home Counties being placed in different qualifying groups. Ironically, the net result (contrary to the initial beliefs of those FIFA protesters) was that all four qualified for the Finals. It would be fair to point out that this was a little lucky as, although England, Scotland and Northern Ireland qualified on merit, Wales only did so by good fortune. Uruguay, who, like Wales, had been eliminated in the preliminary group, were offered the opportunity to play Israel (whose opponents had all withdrawn) for a final place, but their refusal gave Wales another chance. Thus Wales, winning 2-0 both home and away, qualified for their first (and so far only) final series.

Besides Uruguay the other notable absentee was Italy who had been unexpectedly eliminated by the gritty Northern Ireland team captained by Danny Blanchflower and under the managership of Peter Doherty.

In addition to the host country Sweden, and the champions West Germany, fourteen other countries participated in the Finals. Argentina, Brazil and Paraguay represented South America and, once again, Mexico represented Central and North America, while Austria, Czechoslovakia, England, France, Hungary, Northern Ireland, Scotland, USSR, Wales and Yugoslavia provided the European challenge.

The countries were grouped into four pools of four (as in 1954) but this time the controversial seeding arrangement was dropped and each country played three games. Once more the top two teams in each group progressed to the quarter-finals which were played on the basis of a 'sudden death' knock-out as were the later rounds. In the event of two countries tying for second place on points, goal difference was disregarded and play-offs were used as deciders. The countries were pooled as follows:

Pool 1:   Argentina, Czechoslovakia, Northern Ireland and West Germany.

Pool 2:   France, Paraguay, Scotland and Yugoslavia.

Pool 3:   Hungary, Mexico, Sweden and Wales.

Pool 4:   Austria, Brazil, England and USSR.

Pool 1 began with the champions, West Germany, playing Argentina who found themselves denuded of three of the players who had earned them the 1957 South American title – Maschio, Sivori and Angelillo. Not for the first time were Argentina's chances shaken by the wealthy Italian clubs (who had scooped up this brilliant trio) and the opening game was to emphasize their difficulties. West Germany themselves were experiencing problems and little had gone right for them since their victory in 1954. Almost immediately after winning the world title, many of their squad had been taken ill with an outbreak of jaundice which prompted widespread insinuations of drug-taking, and they had recently been struggling to regain their top form.

Argentina took an early lead but the West Germans kept their heads and by half-time were ahead by 2-1. Although down to virtually ten men in the second half, West Germany were little troubled by the Argentinians and ran out deserved 3-1 winners. In their first game in Pool 1 Northern Ireland faced the useful Czechoslovakian team and played well to win 1-0 with a solid header from Wilbur Cush. Their next game, however, proved to be something of a disappointment as, seemingly unaware of the dangers posed by Argentina, Northern Ireland lost control of midfield almost from the kick-off. Lacking any real bite up front they struggled to remain level 1-1 at the interval and, bowing to Argentina's superior skills, conceded two second-half goals to go down 3-1. Meanwhile, West Germany were labouring against the lively Czechoslovakians and were fortunate indeed to earn a 2-2 draw thanks largely to a dubious goal by Schaefer who charged the Czech goalkeeper over his line.

These results had left the pool wide open and, in Malmo, Northern Ireland fought hard to gain a splendid 2-2 draw against West Germany with Harry Gregg superb in goal and Peter McParland grabbing both the Irish goals. This left both Argentina and Czechoslovakia still in the hunt for a quarter-final place as they met each other at Helsingborg. This game is said to have been the turning point after which Argentinian football, previously renowned for its skill and attacking artistry, became a dour, defensive and at times destructive force. Certainly, whatever the historical significance, the Czechs simply annihilated Argentina, running in six goals to Argentina's one, and, as a result, went on to face Northern Ireland in a play-off for the second place in Pool 1. Argentinian fans meanwhile turned on their heroes when they returned home, pelting them with rubbish and souring their footballing style for 20 years to come.

Without their injured goalkeeper, Harry Gregg, Northern Ireland faced up to the ebullient Czechs in the play-off. Uprichard the replacement goalkeeper was himself injured, as was Peacock, but, nevertheless, the Irish pulled back a one-goal deficit to earn extra-time and McParland scored the winner (his second) in the 97th minute. Northern Ireland, as had been predicted by Peter Doherty, reached the last eight.

In Pool 2 the superb goalscoring combination of Raymond Kopa and Just Fontaine exploded onto the World Cup scene against Paraguay. Fontaine scored a hat trick to give a hint of what was to follow and Kopa scored one goal in France's 7-3 trouncing of the South Americans. Scotland earned their first-ever World Cup point with a 1-1 draw against the exciting and skilful Yugoslavs in their first game in Pool 2. Facing an absolute deluge of Yugoslavian attacks in the first half, Scotland showed great determination to keep the deficit down to 1-0 at half-time – a super goal by the Yugoslav right-winger, Petakovic. In the second half Scotland broke quickly after another Petakovic shot had hit their post and Murray headed in a deserved equalizer after a mix-up in the Yugoslavian defence.

The next two games in Pool 2 both ended in 3-2 victories for the underdogs. Firstly, France lost to Yugoslavia despite two more well-taken goals from Just Fontaine, and then Paraguay (who had unexpectedly eliminated Uruguay in the qualifying competition) surprisingly beat the weary Scots 3-2 at Norrkoping.

So it was that all four countries approached their final games in the pool still in the hunt for a quarter-final place. Yugoslavia, who were the best placed of the four countries, came very close to throwing away their chance because of inept goalkeeping by Beara. Thanks to his errors, Paraguay levelled the score to 3-3 and, driven on by Parodi (their dominant inside-forward), looked capable of winning, although the Yugoslavs held on to ensure their own quarter-final berth. The Scots meanwhile faced the French goalscoring machine and went in at half-time 2-0 down after goals by Kopa and Fontaine. Down, but not out, Scotland hit back in the second half with a fine goal by Baird, but were unable to equalize, going down 2-1. France were through to the quarter-finals and, once more, Scotland finished bottom of their first-round pool.

Pool 3 began with an easy 3-0 victory for the host country Sweden over the mediocre Mexicans. Wales met Hungary at Sandviken and played well to draw 1-1, the Welsh goal coming from John Charles, their formidable centre-forward who played for Juventus. Post-revolution Hungary without Puskas, Kocsis and Czibor, who had not returned to their country after the 1956 uprising, looked a very ordinary side. Indeed, rumours abounded of a demoralizing search by the Hungarian secret police of the players as they were about to leave Budapest, confiscating money which they had gathered to buy Swedish goods. Whatever the cause, the Hungarians looked and remained a nervous and uninspired force for the whole of the competition and in their next game went down 2-1 to Sweden, despite the emergence of their one bright asset – the powerful right-footed shooting of Lajos Tichy. Wales, meanwhile, playing their worst football of the competition, led the lightweight Mexicans by a single Ivor Allchurch goal, only to concede an equalizer in the dying minutes.

Sweden then went into their last pool game against Wales, already assured of a quarter-final place and Hungary faced Mexico needing a win. In a dreary game against the hosts, Wales held on for a goalless draw to secure a play-off. Hungary, meanwhile, whilst still very subdued, made light work of beating the Mexicans 4-0 thanks to Tichy's powerful finishing. In the play-off against Hungary, Wales went behind to another Tichy goal, but came back strongly in the second half to level the score, necessitating extra-time. The Hungarian defender Sipos was sent off in the added time and Terry Medwin scored the winner to get Wales into the quarter-finals.

In Pool 4, England, cruelly deprived of the likes of Duncan Edwards and his team-mates by the Munich disaster, faced the USSR in their first game. Why only 20 players were selected (instead of the permitted 22) remains a mystery as does the incredible omission of Stanley Matthews and Nat Lofthouse who were then both at the peak of their form. The selectors' short-sightedness was soon emphasized when England's one remaining forward of real stature, Tom Finney, was injured during the first game. The other England forwards of note, Johnny Haynes and Bobby Robson, looked decidedly jaded after an exhausting league season and despite his injury, which was to keep him out of the remaining games, Finney was the one who turned the tide after the Russians had gone two up early in the second half of that opening game. After 65 minutes Billy Wright hit a free kick into the Russian goalmouth and Derek Kevan headed in to make the score 2-1 and, six minutes from the end, Finney converted a penalty to give England a 2-2 draw.

Brazil defeated Austria with consummate ease, running in three goals without reply, and moved on to face England in their next game. Brazil were confronted with a re-organized English defence intent on closing down their attack by employing Don Howe alongside Billy Wright at the centre of the defence, with Bill Slater marking Didi tightly. These tactics proved successful as Brazil were unable to find the net and, although the final score was 0-0, England could well have snatched a second-half victory with a little more luck up front.

Playing their second match, Russia beat Austria 2-0, putting a serious question mark over England's quarter-final chances, but then were fortunate to lose only 2-0 to Brazil (now fielding Pele for the first time in the World Cup). This left England requiring a win or a draw against Austria in their final game in Pool 4. Played at Boras, this game proved to be a tedious affair with England struggling against the unglamorous and unimpressive Austrians to such an extent that they looked to be in serious danger of defeat. Twice they went down to long-range shots from the Austrian forwards until first Haynes and then Kevan struck back to earn a face-saving 2-2 draw. Tying on three points each, England and Russia met at Ullevi in the play-off and, once again, the toothless English attack made little impact on the game. MacDonald, England's goalkeeper, who had had a superb series, was unfortunate to give Russia their chance to score with a sloppy clearance and Ilyin, striking the ball hard in off the England post, was overjoyed to give his side the winner. To be fair, England should have won comfortably, and one can only speculate upon the difference which Bobby Charlton (had he been included in the team – he was in the squad) might have made.

So the quarter-final line-up was Wales versus Brazil, Northern Ireland against France, Sweden to face USSR and West Germany against Yugoslavia. The Swedish team had received surprisingly little support from their own fans during their first-round matches and their quarter-final tie against Russia again highlighted the incredulity of the Swedes that their team could do well. This game, however, proved to be the turning point and Sweden besieged the Russian goal before winning a semi-final place with a 2-0 victory. Without John Charles, Wales nevertheless performed with great determination against

Brazil with their stalwart defence holding steady against the formidable South American attack. To their credit, Wales held out until the 65th minute when Pele struck a shot which was deflected past the Welsh keeper Kelsey to clinch a semi-final place for his country.

The Northern Irish were ill-prepared for their quarter-final against France having only the day before undertaken the 210 mile journey to Norrkoping by coach. Understrength because of injuries to Gregg and Peacock, the Irish struggled to restrain the French goalscoring threat and held out until just before half-time when Wisnieski scored. In the second half, Fontaine struck with two goals and Piantoni scored another to give France a 4-0 victory. West Germany beat the elegant Yugoslavs in the other quarter-final, their uncompromising, no-nonsense play snuffing out their opponent's flair. A lucky shot by Rahn in the 12th minute secured for the Germans a victory which they did not deserve.

The semi-finals brought together Sweden against West Germany, and Brazil against France. Sweden's match, played in Gothenburg, heralded an amazing change in the attitude of the home crowd. Apparently sceptical of their team's worth Sweden's fans had been, to say the least, subdued during the opening Pool 3 games, and it was not until the quarter-final defeat of USSR that the Swedish scepticism evaporated. In the semi-final, nationalistic fervour, whipped up by cheerleaders on the pitch, gripped the Swedes who responded with quite astonishing enthusiasm, disdaining the West German supporters and creating some doubts that the tie would be played. However, played it was, and, to thunderous chanting, the Swedes pressurized West Germany from the outset. Then, much against the run of play, West Germany took the lead through Schaefer with a cracking long-range shot. Within five minutes Sweden had equalized – a dubious goal scored by Skoglund by courtesy of a Liedholm pass after a blatant hand-ball. After 12 minutes of the second half, Juskowiak, West Germany's ruthless full back, was sent off for retaliating against a Hamrin foul, and Sweden gained the upper hand. In the 75th minute West Germany's Walter was injured by a vicious Swedish tackle and, virtually down to nine men, West Germany crumbled under the relentless pressure and lost the game 3-1.

France, starting uncertainly against Brazil, went down to a superbly worked goal (finished off by Vava) in only the second minute. Within ten minutes Fontaine had equalized and the French were very much in the game for the next 30 minutes, prompted by their superb attacking strategist Raymond Kopa. Then, late in the first half, France's central defender Jonquet was hurt and Didi put Brazil into a half-time lead. After the interval Pele turned on his brilliance and decimated France with a superb hat trick, Piantoni managing a late consolation goal.

In the third-place play-off, Just Fontaine secured a place for himself in the World Cup record books by scoring four of France's six goals against the Germans to achieve the all-time scoring record of 13 goals. Raymond Kopa, who masterminded so many of those goals, scored a penalty himself in a game which France dominated to earn third place.

The stage was set for Sweden to play Brazil in the Final in Stockholm and the volatile Brazilians were so in awe of the sort of emotion that the Germans had faced in Gothenburg, that they prompted the World Cup organizers to banish the Swedish cheerleaders from the pitch. Without such incitement, the Swedish crowd were unexpectedly quiet. George Raynor, Sweden's British manager, predicted that an early Swedish goal would throw Brazil into panic but, after Liedholm had put Sweden ahead in the fourth minute, was soon forced to eat his words. Within six minutes Vava had equalized and then Brazil really turned on the magic with Pele thundering a shot against the Swedes' post. In the 32nd minute Vava scored his second goal and despite further pressure the score remained 2-1 at half-time. Ten minutes into the second half Pele scored one of the greatest goals ever seen in a World Cup Final when he took a high ball on his thigh, hooked it over his head and, spinning round, volleyed into the Swedish goal. This effectively demoralized the Swedes who went 4-1 down in the final quarter hour to a goal by Zagalo. Sweden pulled a goal back through Simonsson but then the magnificent Pele soared to a Zagalo centre to make the final score 5-2.

At last Brazil had achieved their dream and as they ran excitedly round the pitch waving first the Brazilian and then the Swedish flag, the crowd applauded them – for once the best team in the competition had won the title!

POOL 1

	P	W	D	L	F	A	Pts
West Germany	3	1	2	0	7	5	4
Czechoslovakia	3	1	1	1	8	4	3
Northern Ireland	3	1	1	1	4	5	3
Argentina	3	1	0	2	5	10	2

Play-off

Northern Ireland .... 2 Czechoslovakia 1

POOL 2

	P	W	D	L	F	A	Pts
France	3	2	0	1	11	7	4
Yugoslavia	3	1	2	0	7	6	4
Paraguay	3	1	1	1	9	12	3
Scotland	3	0	1	2	4	6	1

POOL 3

	P	W	D	L	F	A	Pts
Sweden	3	2	1	0	5	1	5
Hungary	3	1	1	1	6	3	3
Wales	3	0	3	0	2	2	3
Mexico	3	0	1	2	1	8	1

Play-off

Wales .... 2 Hungary 1

POOL 4

	P	W	D	L	F	A	Pts
Brazil	3	2	1	0	5	0	5
England	3	0	3	0	4	4	3
USSR	3	1	1	1	4	4	3
Austria	3	0	1	2	2	7	1

Play-off

USSR .... 1 England 0

QUARTER-FINALS

Brazil .... 1 Wales 0
France .... 4 Northern Ireland 0
West Germany .... 1 Yugoslavia 0
Sweden .... 2 USSR 0

SEMI-FINALS

Brazil .... 5 France 2
Sweden .... 3 West Germany 1

THIRD-PLACE MATCH

France .... 6 West Germany 3

FINAL

Brazil .... (2) **5**   **Sweden** .... (1) **2**

Scorers: Vava 2, Pele 2, Zagalo   *Scorers: Liedholm, Simonsson*

Team: Gilmar, Santos (D), Santos (N), Zito, Bellini, Orlando, Garrincha, Didi, Vava, Pele, Zagalo

Team: Svensson, Bergmark, Axbom, Boerjesson, Gustavsson, Parling, Hamrin, Gren, Simonsson, Liedholm, Skoglund

SEVENTH WORLD CUP

Chile 1962

IT IS remarkable that Chile was ever chosen to stage a World Cup competition. That enormously long, narrow, impoverished strip of a country up the western side of South America was devastated by severe earthquakes just as it pleaded its case to host the finals. The hard-working President of the Chilean FA Carlos Dittborn pleaded, 'We must have the World Cup because we have nothing else'. FIFA were impressed by the Chileans' determination and realizing that, after two successive European finals a South American venue must be chosen, agreed to Chile's request.

Nor did Chile let FIFA down, as they quickly set about building one superb new stadium in the capital Santiago and another, smaller but nevertheless impressive, at Vina Del Mar. True, one group were based at the ramshackle Braden Copper Company's stadium at Rancagua and another thousands of miles to the north at Arica, but these disadvantages did not detract from the series.

England were the sole British representatives in 1962, qualifying against Portugal and Luxembourg without losing a game, whilst Scotland, Wales and Northern Ireland all failed to make the grade. Northern Ireland, in the same qualifying group as West Germany and Greece, never looked like qualifying after losing their first game 4-3 to West Germany at home and finished with only two points to West Germany's eight. Wales were unfortunate to be drawn in a group where they needed to overcome Spain to progress to further games and did well (although not well enough) to hold out for a 1-1 draw in Spain after losing 2-1 at home. Scotland, drawn against Czechoslovakia and Eire, scored an impressive six points (which would have won them most of the qualifying groups) but were unlucky to lose the play-off against Czechoslovakia 4-2.

The holders, Brazil, were once again the favourites (particularly in view of the venue), and Argentina, Chile, Columbia and Uruguay also represented South America while Mexico, having played a gruelling eight games to reach the Finals, represented North and Central America. Europe was represented by Bulgaria, Czechoslovakia, England, Hungary, Italy, Spain, Switzerland,

USSR, West Germany and Yugoslavia.

The format was the same as 1958 with four groups (no longer called 'Pools') of four countries, each playing one another and the top two of each group progressing to the quarter-finals. Unlike all previous competitions, in the event of a tie (with two countries scoring the same number of points), goal difference was to be used to determine the qualifiers. The countries were grouped as follows:

Group 1:   Colombia, Uruguay, USSR and Yugoslavia.

Group 2:   Chile, Italy, Switzerland and West Germany.

Group 3:   Brazil, Czechoslovakia, Mexico and Spain.

Group 4:   Argentina, Bulgaria, England and Hungary.

Shortly before the competition began Carlos Dittborn, whose impassioned plea had secured the series for his country, died of a heart attack and it was with great sadness that many watched the opening match in Santiago remembering his determination. His two young sons raised the flags of Chile and Switzerland (the competing countries) and a minute's silence was observed before battle commenced. 'Battle' was not really the right word for it (although Switzerland scored in the sixth minute) and it was not until Chile struck a post in the 23rd minute that they really got into their stride. L. Sanchez scored the equalizer on the stroke of half-time and within ten minutes of the restart Chile were 3-1 up and cruising to a comfortable victory, much to the appreciation of the crowd. The next match in the group, the following day, featured West Germany and Italy before another big crowd – 65,440. Quite unjustified criticism of Chile by two Italian journalists had served to enrage the Chilean public to such an extent that the Italian team were greeted with jeers and catcalls wherever they went, and in this atmosphere West Germany held on for a goalless draw.

The next game in Group 2 has, like a number of its predecessors, assumed great notoriety under the title of 'the Battle of Santiago'. The match, between Chile and Italy, was poisoned by the continuing bad blood resulting from the slur of the Italian journalists, and once again a large crowd howled their disapproval as the Italians took the field. In such inauspicious circumstances English referee Ken Aston had to control an increasingly violent contest. In only the seventh minute Italy's Ferrini was sent off after kicking Landa but refused to leave the pitch until, eight minutes later, he was escorted off by police. Italy packed their defence and held on, though increasingly incited to violence by Chile's provocative tactics. Five minutes before half-time the Chilean L. Sanchez retaliated to a hard tackle by Mario David with a punch which knocked him senseless. The referee was unsighted and his two linesmen, Goldstein of the USA and Elcaz of Mexico, both appeared to see nothing. Sanchez remained on the pitch but David, who in the 46th minute kicked Sanchez on the neck as they clashed for the ball, was less fortunate and was sent off. This reduced Italy to just nine men and they continued to pack their defence with only Altafini staying up occasionally supported by Umberto Maschio (whose nose had been broken in an earlier collision with Rojas). It was not until the 74th minute that the deadlock was broken when a Chilean free kick from a foul by Maschio was cleared to Ramirez who headed Chile into the lead. In the 88th minute a second goal, by Toro, secured a 2-0 victory for the hosts but matters did not end there. After studying a film of the game, a FIFA commission suspended Ferrini for one game and delivered 'severe admonishments' upon both David and L. Sanchez.

Group 2 proceeded with West Germany taking on Switzerland and both managers were determined to show the world that Europe could produce good, exciting and, above all, sporting football. They succeeded in an entertaining game which was marred only by an injury to Switzerland's Eschmann, who hobbled on determinedly for the rest of the first half despite a fractured ankle. Right on the stroke of half-time, West Germany took the lead through Brulls. In the 60th minute Seeler scored a second German goal and although Switzerland pulled a goal back in the 75th minute they thus lost any interest in making the quarter-finals. When Chile met West Germany in the next game in the group, their four points already assured them of a quarter-final place and this, no doubt, removed much of the edge which would otherwise have emerged. The game itself was to become the most enjoyable in Group 2 as West Germany took a 22nd-minute lead from the penalty spot in the midst of remorseless Chilean attacks. In the second half the pattern remained the same and it seemed to be merely a question of time before Chile scored an equalizer until Seeler broke away to score a second German goal in the 82nd minute. This victory secured for West Germany the right to remain in Santiago for their quarter-final whilst Chile had to fly off to Arica. The remaining game in the group between Italy and Switzerland, whilst well supported with the enmity towards Italy now forgotten, proved to be a thoroughly enjoyable game which swung Italy's way after the Swiss goalkeeper had been injured. Although the final score was 3-0 to Italy, Switzerland still finished the series earning a respectful ovation from the home crowd.

Group 1 was the only one which had two South American countries and Uruguay met Colombia in the first game on the opening day. Colombia were appearing in their first-ever World Cup having, as a result of their roguish policy of enticing the world's dissatisifed players to play without transfer fee, been expelled from FIFA from 1949 to 1957. The game was played in Arica at the renamed Carlos Dittborn stadium and Colombia took an 18th-minute lead through a Zuluaga penalty after they had weathered much early Uruguayan pressure. Although Uruguay attacked hard, Colombia came close to scoring a second goal later in the first half when Coll hit a post. In the second half Uruguay began to 'cut up rough' and they conceded a series of free kicks. Nevertheless, it was Uruguay who scored via Cubilla in the 57th minute and, in the 73rd minute, Sasia made it 2-1 for Uruguay who held on to the lead with little difficulty. Then came the all-East European clash between USSR and Yugoslavia, and it proved to be an uncompromising affair. Yugoslavia had the ability to play superb flowing football and the Chilean spectators showed their appreciation as, in the first half, they hummed along like a well-oiled machine (although Russia never really looked to be in danger). In the second half the Slavs temperament let them down as they went a goal down in the 53rd minute and excitedly pressed for an equalizer. When this did not come, they crumbled and an 85th-minute goal by Ponedelnik secured a 2-0 victory for Russia.

Yugoslavia's second game, against Uruguay, started with Uruguay dominating the first 20 minutes and scoring in the 19th minute. However, a Skoblar penalty in the 26th minute followed quickly by a Galic goal enabled Yugoslavia to go 2-1 ahead at half-time. Four minutes into the second half Yugoslavia scored again and then closed the game down with a dour seven-man defensive display. After 71 minutes the Yugoslav Popovic and the Uruguayan Cabrera came to blows and were sent off as the game degenerated into increasing violence.

The next game in Group 1, when Colombia met the USSR, reads like a script from Roy of the Rovers. Within 13 minutes Russia had taken a 3-0 lead and looked to be ready to bury Colombia, until, in the 22nd minute, Aceros pulled a goal back. There followed a period of increasing pressure by the Colombians but it was not until the 57th minute that another goal was scored – again by Russia. With less than 25 minutes to play and 4-1 down, the situation seemed hopeless for Colombia until they stormed back in the 68th minute and in an eight-minute spell were back in at 4-4. Indeed this fightback was so demoralizing for the USSR that they were fortunate indeed to hold on for a point.

So it was that the USSR met Uruguay in their last match needing at least a point to be sure of a quarter-final place. When Uruguay were reduced to ten men by injury, Russia took the lead and, although Uruguay drew level again, scored a late winner in the 89th minute. This left Yugoslavia needing a point against Colombia to make the quarter-finals. Exhausted from their exertions against Russia, Colombia nevertheless started gamely but, after they had gone a goal down in the 20th minute, were given a 5-0 trouncing by the skillful Yugoslavs.

Group 3 started with Brazil facing Mexico who (as usual) were being acclaimed by their press as the potential champions. As they had participated in four previous series without so much as a single win, this enthusiasm was greeted with due scepticism by the Brazilians, who launched themselves against Mexico's packed defence from the start. Mexico held out until the 56th minute when Zagalo gave Brazil the lead. In the 72nd minute Pele scored a wonderful goal (beating five bemused Mexicans before unleashing an unstoppable shot) to ensure victory for Brazil. The next match brought together two other sides, both of which had been tipped as potential champions – Czechoslovakia and Spain. Spain fielded Ferenc Puskas who had been such a force for Hungary in 1954, but Czechoslovakia had a solid and dependable defence. Furthermore, Alberto Di Stefano, the most accomplished goalscorer of the day, was sidelined with an injury and without his presence Spain struggled to make much impact on the game. In the 79th minute the Czech Stibranyi scored the only goal of the match after Scherer had rounded Santamaria (who had played for Uruguay in 1958) before laying on the perfect pass. Spain faced Mexico in their next game and applied relentless pressure throughout but were held off until Peiro scored the winner a minute from the end.

In what was to be a rehearsal for the Final, Brazil met Czechoslovakia in the next Group 3 game but, despite dominating the play were unable to score. Pele, who was injured in the first half, was little more than a passenger for most of the game and was unable to play again in the series. Brazil's last game in the group was against a Spanish side reorganized beyond belief by the Spanish coach Helenio Herrera. Making no less than nine changes from his original eleven, his gamble seemed to be working as Spain clung to a 1-0 lead from a 35th-minute Adelardo goal. Then Amarildo, Pele's replacement, proved himself with a well-taken goal in the 72nd minute and followed up with the winner four minutes from time.

The last match in the group was of no significance so far as the quarter-finals were concerned as Czechoslovakia had already secured their place, but the Mexicans still had a surprise up their sleeves. Inspired by their goalkeeper, Carvajal, Mexico shrugged off a first-minute Czechoslovakian goal and were 2-1 up at half-time. Two minutes from the end Mexico scored a third goal from a penalty to register their first World Cup win.

England meanwhile were drawn in Group 4 which began with a bruising game between Argentina and Bulgaria. Argentina opened well with a goal by Facundo after only four minutes but then closed the game down with a tight defensive display. Any Bulgarian flair was quickly snuffed out and, although they achieved the required result, Argentina earned themselves no friends at all. The following day England faced Hungary in undoubtedly the finest game in Group 4. Regaining something of their previous enthusiasm, Hungary mounted attacks with a fluidity and verve to which the English defence responded admirably. Unfortunately the English forward line, with the exception of Bobby Charlton, was again found to be lacking with Johnny Haynes (as he had been in 1958) a shadow of his true self, Bryan Douglas completely off form, and both Jimmy Greaves and Gerry Hitchens particularly quiet. Clearly such lack of inspiration from the forwards spread to the English defence, and in the 16th minute Lajos Tichy, whose shooting had provided the one bright spot in Hungary's 1958 performance, shot his country into the lead. England fought back as Charlton hit the side-netting and Bobby Moore saw his magnificent 30-yard drive turned over the bar, yet still Hungary seemed to be more dangerous. It fell to the England half-back Ron Flowers to score the equalizer with a 58th-minute penalty but even this did not lift the English attack. Twenty minutes from the end Alberto scored the second goal for Hungary and England were finished. Without doubt the better team had won.

England's second game was against Argentina and, realizing that a defeat would end their chances, England were determined to win. Having watched the spoiling tactics of Argentina against Bulgaria, England were prepared for their opponents and, in the event, played much better than they had against Hungary. Flowers put England into the lead in the 17th minute from the penalty spot and, three minutes before half-time, Charlton made it 2-0 with a cracking low shot. In the second half Jimmy Greaves put his side three up in the 65th minute and, although Argentina pulled one back (a gift of a goal 12 minutes from the end) England's chances of reaching the quarter-finals were resurrected. The following day Hungary really hit form against Bulgaria and, with Albert scoring a super hat-trick, won 6-1 to put themselves in pole position for a quarterfinal place. In the next game Hungary faced Argentina and were forced on the defensive in the 12th minute when their inside-right Gorocs was iniured by a kick from behind. This unbalanced the Hungarians who, nevertheless, held on for a 0-0 draw to move into the last eight.

So England went into their final game against Bulgaria knowing that a draw would see them through to a quarter-final tie against Brazil. Perhaps it was this daunting prospect which moulded the English approach but, whatever the reason, the game was described, with some justification, as being the worst of the series. The meagre crowd chanted Malo, Malo (terrible) as England left the field at half-time but as both sides settled to defend for a goalless draw the second half petered out into complete paralysis – terrible was the word!

For the third consecutive series, West Germany met Yugoslavia in the quarter-finals (the Germans won the first two), while England faced Brazil, Chile confronted the USSR, and Czechoslovakia played Hungary. First that West German game – would it be third time lucky for Yugoslavia? The Yugoslavs attacked straight from the kick-off, and almost went into the lead; then West Germany themselves almost scored. However, despite the huge crowd (63,324), the two sides soon began to feel themselves to be isolated as, listening to the radio report of Chile's tie in Arica, the Chileans burst into rapturous applause when their own country took the lead several hundred miles away. The play swung from end to end and both countries came close to scoring although the Yugoslavs were playing with the greater fluency and skill. Just five minutes from the end Radakovic gave Yugoslavia the lead and they held on for a richly deserved victory – at last!

Meanwhile, in Arica,the USSR faced eleven Chileans on the field and a seething, chanting seventeen thousand off the field. Unlike the Swedes in 1958, they needed no encouragement from cheerleaders to prompt them to support their country! Chile took an eleventh-minute lead to the delight of their fans but, a quarter of an hour later the Russians equalized to deathly silence. Two minutes after that Rojas put Chile in front again and pandemonium broke out as he hugged first the Russian goalkeeper and then the referee! Chile held on to their lead and touchingly dedicated their victory to the newborn son of the late Carlos Dittborn whose widow had given birth on the very morning of the match.

In Vina Mel Mar, Brazil, playing England, came on song for half an hour and showed the world their true greatness. Until then England had held them level at 1-1 and, with Bobby Charlton in fine form, were beginning to press. Although Springett, the England goalkeeper, was not entirely blameless for the Brazilian's second and third goals in the 53rd and 59th minutes, they nevertheless deserved their lead and their fluency increased as the match progressed. Victors by 3-1 at the final whistle, Brazil looked set for another championship.

The last quarter-final was very much an Eastern bloc affair as Czechoslovakia faced Hungary with a Russian referee and a Bulgarian linesman! In only the 13th minute Scherer put Czechoslovakia ahead from a breakaway and the Czechs then put up their shutters. Hungary turned on a fine display of football, outplaying the static but solid Czechs in all departments but they were unable to beat the opposition's goalkeeper Schroiff. So it went on as the red-shirted tide of Hungarian attacks foundered on the Czechs defence until, at the final whistle, the score remained 1-0 to Czechoslovakia.

The semi-finals brought together Chile and Brazil in Santiago while Yugoslavia faced Czechoslovakia in Vina Del Mar. Chile's match was played before the biggest crowd of the series (76,594) and was the culmination of two whole days of riotous celebration in the capital. Brazil proved to be by far the better team and Garrincha set about winning the game single-handed with two goals in the 9th and 32nd minutes. Further goals followed as Chile reduced their deficit to 3-2 with a 62nd-minute penalty, only to concede a fourth goal 12 minutes from the end. Then, as desperation spread within the Chilean ranks, their centre-forward Landa was sent off and then Garrincha kicked Rojas and was ordered off too, to howls from the crowd. As he made his way to the dressing room he was struck on the head by a bottle in an unsavoury end to an exciting match.

The other semi-final was a great anticlimax with a mere 5,890 watching the game at Vina Mel Mar. Czechoslovakia surprised Yugoslavia by combining a hitherto unseen attacking flair with strong defensive work and were unlucky not to be in the lead at half-time. Early in the second half Czechoslovakia at last took the lead which the Yugoslavs wiped out with a 68th-minute goal by Jerkovic, only to be crushed by two goals from Scherer later in the game. The third-place play-off ended in a deserved victory for the host country although Rojas left it until the very last kick of the game to score the winner!

The Final started with Brazil (established as the firm favourites to win) facing Czechoslovakia who had been the underdogs in both the quarter-finals and semi-finals. Not in the least overawed, Czechoslovakia went ahead in the 16th minute through Masopust but Brazil struck back just two minutes later with an Amarildo goal. Had the Czech keeper Schroiff maintained the brilliant form of previous matches, the outcome might have been different but, in the second half, he floundered twice more and Brazil attained the title for a second time with a 3-1 victory. At the end the Chilean crowd hushed for a moment as Czechs hugged Brazilians, then sang their Anthem before both teams ran a lap of honour with the flag of Chile held aloft.

GROUP 1

	P	W	D	L	F	A	Pts
USSR	3	2	1	0	8	5	5
Yugoslavia	3	2	0	1	8	3	4
Uruguay	3	1	0	2	4	6	2
Colombia	3	0	1	2	5	11	1

GROUP 2

	P	W	D	L	F	A	Pts
West Germany	3	2	1	0	4	1	5
Chile	3	2	0	1	5	3	4
Italy	3	1	1	1	3	2	3
Switzerland	3	0	0	3	2	8	0

GROUP 3

	P	W	D	L	F	A	Pts
Brazil	3	2	1	0	4	1	5
Czechoslovakia	3	1	1	1	2	3	3
Mexico	3	1	0	2	3	4	2
Spain	3	1	0	2	2	3	2

GROUP 4

	P	W	D	L	F	A	Pts
Hungary	3	2	1	0	8	2	5
England	3	1	1	1	4	3	3
Argentina	3	1	1	1	2	3	3
Bulgaria	3	0	1	2	1	7	1

QUARTER-FINALS

Brazil	3	England	1
Chile	2	USSR	1
Yugoslavia	1	West Germany	0
Czechoslovakia	1	Hungary	0

SEMI-FINALS

Brazil	4	Chile	2
Czechoslovakia	3	Yugoslavia	1

THIRD-PLACE MATCH

Chile	1	Yugoslavia	0

FINAL

Brazil .... (1) **3**   **Czechoslovakia** .... (1) **1**

Scorers: Amarildo, Zito, Vava   *Scorer: Masopust*

Team: Gilmar, Santos (D), Mauro, Zozimo, Santos (N), Zito, Didi, Garrincha, Vava, Amarildo, Zagalo

Team: Schroiff, Ticky, Novak, Pluskal, Popluhar, Masopust, Scherer, Kvasinak, Kadraba, Jelinek

EIGHTH WORLD CUP

England 1966

ALTHOUGH England (as hosts) participated in the 1966 series, it is perhaps interesting to note that this was the first time since the Home Countries had been eligible, that not one 'qualified' as such for the final stages. Events went on to show that England would certainly have done so but the absence of Scotland, Northern Ireland and Wales was a sad blow for their supporters. Scotland were unfortunate to have drawn a tough qualifying group which contained Italy, Poland and Finland. After losing to the Poles at Hampden Park they could only field an under-strength side against Italy in Naples and, losing 3-0, were effectively out of the competition. Wales too were in a strong group containing Greece, Denmark and the USSR and were eliminated by the latter although they had managed to beat them 2-1 in Cardiff. Northern Ireland were perhaps the most unfortunate of all, winning three and drawing two out of their six qualifying games (against Holland, Albania and Switzerland) to be eliminated by Switzerland after managing only a draw in Albania. Their eight points would have been sufficient to win any of the other fifteen qualifying groups.

The competition was played in precisely the same format as the 1962 series with four groups of four leading straight to the quarter-finals. Brazil, the reigning champions, together with Argentina, Chile and Uruguay represented South America, while Mexico once more represented Central and North America and, surprisingly, North Korea represented Asia and Australasia. European nations predominated with England, Bulgaria, France, Hungary, Italy, Portugal, Spain, Switzerland, USSR and West Germany making up the 16 finalists. The participants were grouped as follows:

Group 1 – (Played at Wembley & White City):
England, France, Mexico and Uruguay.

Group 2 – (Played at Villa Park & Hillsborough):
Argentina, Spain, Switzerland and West Germany.

Group 3 – (Played at Goodison Park & Old Trafford):
Brazil, Bulgaria, Hungary and Portugal.

Group 4 – (Played at Ayresome Park & Roker Park):
   Chile, Italy, North Korea and USSR.

The series opened with the hosts, England, facing the Uruguayans at Wembley in Group 1. With the stadium only three-quarters full, the 'Wembley roar' was curiously muted as the ruthless South Americans defended dourly. Employing 'blocking', tactics with tackles around knee-height and obstruction used as a second line of defence when beaten, Uruguay clinically closed the game down. The two wing men, Connelly and Charlton, were unable to make any impression on play and, in the centre of the attack, both Greaves and Hunt were also kept out of the game. Neither side came close to scoring in just about the most arid goalless draw that the World Cup had seen.

The next Group 1 game was between France and Mexico. Full of confidence, the French expected to be able to exploit their greatest asset, 'the speed of their players', but it was the Mexicans who began the game with the more apparent flair. Within five minutes, the Mexican striker Borja put a Chaires cross just over the bar and ten minutes later was unlucky to be ruled offside after putting the ball in the French net. The passing and cohesion of the French team was astonishingly poor and, four minutes into the second half, Borja put Mexico 1-0 into the lead. This goal signalled an uplift in the pace of play with Mexico pressing harder and looking good for a win until Herbin, busily chasing around the field, encouraged his team-mates to greater efforts. The equalizer came on the hour (an unspectacular goal by Hausser) and, although the Mexicans fought hard, the game ended 1-1.

Two days later France met a very different Uruguay at the White City stadium. The difference was in the approach rather than the players, as the Uruguayan defence found themselves near to panic whenever the lively French forwards attacked. Eventually the Uruguayan Manicera pulled his defence together but then paid the ultimate price when his rugby tackle on the French forward Herbert (which appeared to be outside the penalty area) was rewarded with a penalty kick. De Bourgoing drove the ball into the South Americans' net but, far from sinking Uruguay, this gave them the impulse they needed. By half-time, goals from Rocha and Cortes had given Uruguay the lead and, in the second half, the French were unable to break down the re-established Uruguayan defensive barrier.

England's next obstacle was Mexico, and another dreary match it proved to be. Packing their defence with nine and ten men, Mexico denied England's attack until a Bobby Charlton 'special', seven minutes from half-time, gave them the lead. In the second half Charlton, again, sent Greaves through and his well-struck shot rebounded to Roger Hunt who made the score 2-0. Mexico never looked capable of scoring although England had still to establish a proper pattern to their play.

Mexico's final game against Uruguay unexpectedly saw the recall of their veteran goalkeeper Carbajal, who had taken part in four previous series. After a shaky start he gained his stride and was not seriously troubled by any of the infrequent Uruguayan attacks. Neither too (after an early Mexican onslaught) was Mazurkieviez in the Uruguayan goal and the game petered out into a rather lifeless 0-0 draw which was enough to ensure a quarter-final place for Uruguay.

France meanwhile entered their final game against England knowing that they required a clear four-goal victory to reach the final stages. Within minutes of the start Herbin was injured and moved to the centre-forward spot to try at least to tie up an English player and this clearly gave England the impetus they sought. Playing much better than in either of their previous games England took the attack to the French and were rewarded with two Roger Hunt goals, one in each half. Nobby Stiles, incited by French provocation, had a wretched game but despite this the English defence was little troubled. The 2-0 victory secured England's quarter-final place, but an injury to Jimmy Greaves effectively ended his World Cup run.

In Group 2 West Germany began in devastating style against a Switzerland side depleted by the exclusion of Leimgruber and Kuhn for disciplinary purposes (they had broken a curfew). After clearing a dangerous Swiss cross in the opening seconds of the game, the West Germans were troubled only once more by the Switzerland attack as they asserted their authority on the game. After a quarter of an hour Held put them into the lead sweeping home the rebound from a Seeler shot, and five minutes later Haller made it 2-0. Just before half-time Beckenbauer scored a third and, with two further goals in the second half, West Germany easily swept aside the Swiss.

The second Group 2 match provided perhaps the greatest surprise of the first week of the series when Argentina beat Spain. Facing such stars as Gento, Suarez and Mel Sol, a hard and efficient Argentine side looked to be the most likely ultimate victors when they went in 0-0 at half-time. Sure enough, two second-half goals from Artime ensured them victory by 2-1 but even at this early stage their sometimes brutal tactics were earning them few friends.

The Swiss, smarting from their 5-0 drubbing by West Germany, faced Spain in their next game. Right from the kick-off Switzerland defended in such depth that Spain were forced to rely on long-range shots and made little impression on the Swiss defence. Indeed the Swiss themselves soon began to attack and, in the 28th minute, Quentin put them into the lead. Then, in the 67th minute, Sanchis won the ball on the halfway line and rode tackle after tackle before smashing a superb equalizer into the roof of the Swiss net. This stirred the Swiss and Quentin had a goal disallowed soon afterwards. The final outcome of the game was decided by another brilliant goal – a devastating header by the Spaniard Amaro, which robbed the hard-working Swiss of a point.

West Germany then met Argentina and were subjected to a barrage of remorseless, provocative fouls. Constantly under threat from the skilful Onega, West Germany were unable to make any impression upon their brutal opponents as the game degenerated into little more than a kicking match. The Argentinian Albrecht (who had already been cautioned for a rugby tackle on Haller) was sent off in the 65th minute for yet another bad foul. Argentina held on for a goalless draw but were reprimanded afterwards by FIFA for their vicious play.

In their next appearance at Hillsborough, the English crowd, augmented by many West Germans, wasted no time in showing the Argentinians what they thought of their brand of football. Facing the Swiss, Argentina were booed relentlessly from the outset despite tempering their play because of the FIFA warning. Switzerland, however, had little to offer, and repeatedly lost possession until, in the second half, Artime and Onega gave Argentina a 2-0 victory. Thus, when West Germany and Spain met at Villa Park the following day, both knew that Argentina were through to the quarter-finals. While West Germany needed only a point to qualify, Spain required a victory. Tacticians to a man, West Germany seemed intent on achieving a draw and played accordingly until Spain took a one-goal lead in the 28th minute. West Germany then had to attack and Emmerich, chasing a ball practically into the photographers, loosed a tremendous shot which flew into the roof of the net. In the second half the game remained evenly balanced until Seeler scored the winner for West Germany, six minutes from the end.

In Group 3 the holders and favourites, Brazil, began what was to prove an unhappy defence of the cup with a game at Goodison Park against the unglamorous Bulgarians. With an incredible 5,000 Brazilians amongst the 47,308 crowd, the chants were for Pele (Pelly!). The game was an uncompromising affair with Bulgaria intent on snuffing out the Brazilian flair and it soon became very violent. Brazil took the lead midway through the first half when Pele (a foul on whom had created the free kick) hit a magnificent 'bender' into the Bulgarian net. Pele and Zhechov conducted a personal feud throughout the first half which, in the 28th minute, threatened to break out into 'lynch law' as a number of angry Bulgarians advanced on Pele after a particularly bad foul on Zhechov. Still the conflict continued and, after Pele was injured by Zhechov, the referee made clear his intent to expel the next offender. In the 64th minute, Garrincha, like Pele in the first half, swerved a thunderous free kick into the Bulgarian net after he had been fouled. The stubborn Bulgarians fought doggedly on but were unable to breach the Brazilian defence, going down 2-0.

At Old Trafford, Hungary faced Portugal and were unlucky to have their goalkeeper Szentmihalyi injured early in the game. This was the last series before the introduction of substitutes and Szentmihalyi's injury clearly gave Portugal an advantage. Although the skilful Hungarian forward-line caused the Portuguese defence much anguish, Portugal took the lead through Augusto after Szentmihalyi had been unable to gather a corner kick. Bene gave Hungary a deserved equalizer in the 61st minute but their goalkeeper was again at fault when Augusto scored his second six minutes later. Towards the end of the match Portugal increasingly wasted time, content with their lead, but ironically scored a third goal through Torres in the time which was added on for stoppages.

The next match in Group 3 provided one of the greatest games that the World Cup has ever seen: Brazil (without the injured Pele) against Hungary at Goodison Park. Emulating their eminent predecessors from 1954, Hungary swept into the attack from the outset and were 1-0 up after only three minutes, a superb goal by Bene. In the 15th minute Brazil equalized, much against the run of play, and so the score remained until the second half when the Hungarian mastermind, Albert, prompted a magnificent goal. His exquisite pass sent Bene on a run which culminated in Farkas volleying his cross into the Brazilian net. Ten minutes later Meszoli scored a third Hungarian goal from the penalty spot and Brazil had lost their first World Cup match since 1954.

Portugal's next two games proved just how underrated they had been. In the first they played Bulgaria who inexplicably gave them a fifth minute lead with a ridiculous own goal by Vutzov. Eusebio grabbed a second in the 35th minute and the Portuguese, barely troubled by the Bulgarians, scored a third goal seven minutes from the end. Next, they played Brazil who, in the aftermath of the resounding defeat by Hungary, had made no less than seven changes to their side. Clearly this was not the calibre of the Brazilian side of the last eight years, even though Pele (obviously unfit) was recalled. After 25 minutes Portugal, assisted by sloppy goalkeeping by Manga, were two goals up and well in command when Morais perpetrated a vicious foul on Pele. This kick, which left Pele a limping passenger for the remainder of the match, sealed Brazil's fate and, although they pulled a goal back in the 64th minute, Portugal's victory never seemed in doubt. Five minutes from the end the brilliant Eusebio scored Portugal's third goal to hammer the final nail in Brazil's coffin.

The last game in Group 3 between Hungary and Bulgaria ended in victory for Hungary despite their being a goal down and under pressure for much of the first half. By half-time, though, they were 2-1 up and, once they were ahead, turned on a delightful display of soccer skills, easily winning 3-1.

Group 4, meanwhile, got off to a predictable start as the USSR brushed aside the uncertain North Koreans with a deserved 3-0 victory and the Italians defeated Chile 2-0 (albeit with an uninspired display). This beginning gave little hint of what was to follow.

Chile met North Korea in their next game and the English support for the underdog soon manifested itself in overwhelming backing for the little Koreans. After 28 minutes Chile took a deserved lead from a Marcos free kick and, despite the urging of the now fanatical Middlesbrough crowd, the Koreans seemed doomed to defeat. However, just two minutes from the final whistle, Pak Seung Zin equalized to the delight of the crowd.

The following day the USSR took on Italy at Roker Park. Selecting a strangely unbalanced team, Italy never settled down against the Russians whose splendid right-winger, Chislenko, ran through their defence at will. His second-half goal settled the match and Italy were beginning to look vulnerable. In their next game, with North Korea at Ayresome Park, Middlesbrough, Italy's team selection once again looked inappropriate. Against a team whose only real assets were speed and stamina, the Italian manager, Fabbri, picked his slowest defenders and then capped this odd choice by fielding Giacomo Bulgarelli (who was struggling with a knee injury) in midfield. The Middlesbrough crowd willed on their North Korean favourites who ran at Italy from the opening whistle. After half an hour Bulgarelli fouled Pak Seung Zin but, in the process, tore his knee ligaments so badly that he was stretchered off the field, leaving Italy with only ten men. North Korea harried Italy for every ball and, in the 42nd minute, scored with a searing shot from Pak Doo Ik. Increasingly desperate, Italy were simply unable to pull this goal back and, in the biggest shock since England lost to the USA in 1950, crashed out of the tournament.

In the final Group 4 game, Russia maintained their 100% record by beating Chile 2-1 and, effectively, gave North Korea their ticket to a quarter-final tie against Portugal. England met Argentina, Uruguay faced West Germany and USSR lined up against Hungary in the other games.

Firstly, that infamous England versus Argentina encounter at Wembley. Brazil had already departed for home, criticising European refereeing for allowing over-physical tackles on their stars, and the rift between Europe and South America seemed to polarize around this. From the very first kick of the match Argentina embarked upon an infuriating series of fouls which totally suppressed the English attack. Herr Kreitlein, the German referee, set to work cautioning player after player in an attempt to defuse the situation but, at every turn, he found his decisions protested by the argumentative Argentinian captain Rattin. Shortly before half-time matters came to a head when the referee could take no more of his dissent and, after more vehement protests over the booking of another Argentine player, Rattin was ordered off. For ten minutes pandemonium reigned as he argued and appealed against the decision and then finally refused to leave the field. At last, after furious touch-line rows with FIFA officials, he reluctantly went and, as play resumed, made the long trek to the dressing room, stopping to exchange insults with the crowd as he went. Still the determined Argentinians held on and it was not until 13 minutes from the end that England at last snatched the only goal of the match through a superb header from Geoff Hurst.

Controversy also reigned at Hillsborough when West Germany faced Uruguay. Uruguay started well and could have notched up an early goal but instead were unlucky to fall quickly behind when a shot by Held was diverted into the net by Haller. Throughout an open and exciting first half Uruguay pressed for an equalizer. In the second half, however, the whole atmosphere altered when the West German Schnellinger escaped a penalty appeal after apparently handling the ball on the goal-line. This prompted the Uruguayans to forget about football and, whenever possible, they played their opponents instead of the ball. Neither were the West Germans blameless and their aggression culminated in an unfortunate incident which altered the course of the match. Just after half-time Emmerich blatantly kicked the Uruguayan captain Troche who repaid the assault with an immediate kick in Emmerich's stomach. For this he was sent off and, for good measure, slapped Seeler's face on the way off! Minutes later another Uruguayan, Silva, was also (somewhat harshly) dismissed and, down to only nine men, Uruguay crumbled to a 4-0 defeat in the last 20 minutes.

The match between Hungary and Russia emphasized the greater physical strength of the Soviet team as they pressured the lively Hungarians into mistake after mistake. In only the fifth minute the Hungarians handed their opponents a gift when Chislenko scored after Gelei the Hungarian goalkeeper had dropped an easy ball. From then onwards, fierce tackling and the threat of fierce tackling subdued the Hungarian attack and, two minutes into the second half, Gelei fumbled another cross (this time from a corner kick) and Porkujan scored Russia's second goal. Although Bene scored for Hungary later in the half, the Russians ran out worthy 2-1 winners.

The other quarter-final proved to be the most exciting of them all as North Korea met Portugal. In Eusebio Portugal had the outstanding player of the competition, as skilful as Pele but far more determined in his pursuit of goals. The game was played at Goodison Park and a number of Middlesbrough fans travelled over to support North Korea, their adopted favourites. North Korea began unbelievably well, scoring in only the first minute and following up twice more within 20 minutes. The Koreans themselves seemed as startled by their 3-0 lead as the Portuguese and, still playing fast, enthusiastic football, looked capable of pulling away even further. Eusebio, however, displaying a flair and urgency scarcely seen in any World Cup, had other plans and he scored two goals before half-time. After 60 minutes he sprinted past the North Korean defenders to score the equalizer and, minutes later and still not satisfied, looked certain to score when he was hacked down in the Korean penalty area. Taking the penalty himself he gave Portugal the lead and later Augusto scored a fifth to complete a remarkable victory for the Portuguese.

The semi-finals brought together West Germany and the USSR at Goodison Park and England and Portugal at Wembley. It was perhaps unfortunate for the Merseyside fans that they were not given the opportunity to see England play and the relatively meagre crowd (38,273) reflected local feeling on the matter. In the event the semi-final between the USSR and West Germany was a really dreadful affair enjoyed by few but the German fans who were present. The match soon became more of a demonstration of the skills of unarmed combat than of soccer, as the Russians crunched into the Germans from the kick-off. The Germans responded in kind as one bone-jarring tackle followed another in a travesty of a game. Lev Yashin, the veteran Russian goalkeeper, provided the one bright spot with his outstanding sportsmanship capping a superb goalkeeping display, to keep his country in the game. It was clear that, sooner or later, a serious injury would result and, sure enough, Sabo injured himself in attempting to foul the German midfielder, Beckenbauer, and limped through the rest of the first half. Worse was to follow as, just before half-time, the Russian star, Chislenko, was injured by a Schnellinger tackle which won the ball and led straight to a West German goal. Smarting with indignation and frustration, the hobbling Chislenko came straight back onto the field and, within seconds, was sent off for a bad kick at Held. Down to only nine men in the second half, Russia held on grimly conceding just one more goal and actually pulled one back in the dying minutes. West Germany had reached their second Final via a game best forgotten.

England and Portugal met at Wembley the following day in a game which was the complete opposite to the first semi-final. Bobby Charlton played his finest-ever game for his country and scored the first goal after 20 minutes. Portugal's talented forward-line foundered on the rock of England's superb defence which elevated its play beyond all recognition. Nobby Stiles, too, played his finest game as he completely stifled the superior talents of Eusebio, making him seem very ordinary indeed. After the interval Portugal pressed remorselessly for an equalizer but were thwarted by Gordon Banks, his handling faultless once again. Bobby Charlton sealed matters eleven minutes from the end when his thunderous shot tore into the Portuguese goal. Portugal still refused to yield and were rewarded minutes later when Jackie Charlton was forced to concede a penalty with Banks beaten. Eusebio scored from the spot, and for the remaining few minutes England defended resolutely against the vigorous Portuguese attacks to earn their first Final place.

The third-place play-off between Portugal and the USSR attracted a surprisingly large crowd of 70,000 to Wembley. This fixture is always an anticlimax but this time, although the urgency and enthusiasm were missing, the game itself was not without quality or action at both ends.

Eusebio opened the scoring with yet another penalty kick but Malafeev hit back to level the score at half-time. In the second half Torres scored the winning goal to earn third place for Portugal – a just reward for their entertaining contribution to the competition.

On the following day, Wembley was packed for the Final. Alf Ramsey had been torn between bringing back the now-fit Jimmy Greaves in place of Roger Hunt but decided against doing so. The game began nervously and, after 13 minutes, a bad clearance by Ray Wilson resulted in West Germany opening the scoring through Haller. Within six minutes Geoff Hurst headed England's equalizer from a Bobby Moore free kick and the crowd hummed with excitement as the play swung from end to end. First Tilkowski, the West

German goalkeeper, then Gordon Banks saved goalward shots and, three minutes from half-time, Roger Hunt missed an easy chance. The second half started during a brief downpour of rain and continued to the same pattern as the first half with the irrepressible Alan Ball, in particular, making probing runs down the right of the field. Still there was no score until just 12 minutes from the end when Peters thumped a half clearance into the German net. Four minutes from full time, as the West Germans pressed for an equalizer, England had the opportunity to put their lead beyond recovery when Ball sent Hunt and two others clear in a three-to-one attack. Once again Hunt wasted the opportunity as he passed too soon to Charlton who was then unable to score. In the final minute Herr Dienst the Swiss referee awarded West Germany a contentious free kick on the edge of the English area and, from this, in the dying seconds, Weber scored the equalizer. As extra time became necessary for the first time since 1934, the tension in the stadium became unbearable. Alf Ramsey boosted his team's morale by pointing to the exhaustion of the Germans and within two minutes England had twice come close to scoring. Ten minutes into extra time Ball crossed for Hurst to rocket a furious shot onto the underside of the West German bar and out again and Hunt, in elation, threw his arms aloft. Had the ball crossed the line or not? In the confusion that followed Herr Dienst consulted his Russian linesman Bakhramov and, to the ecstasy of the crowd, awarded a goal, a decision which will always remain contentious. Once more the Germans threw everything into the attack but England held firm. In the final minute Hurst broke away and scored again with a terrific left-footed shot, making him the first player to score a Final hat trick. West Germany barely had time to restart play before the whistle blew for the end, and the cup had returned to the land where football began.

GROUP 1

	P	W	D	L	F	A	Pts
England	3	2	1	0	4	0	5
Uruguay	3	1	2	0	2	1	4
Mexico	3	0	2	1	1	3	2
France	3	0	1	2	2	5	1

GROUP 2

	P	W	D	L	F	A	Pts
West Germany	3	3	0	0	9	2	6
Argentina	3	2	1	0	4	1	5
Spain	3	1	0	2	4	5	2
Switzerland	3	0	0	3	1	9	0

GROUP 3

	P	W	D	L	F	A	Pts
Portugal	3	3	0	0	9	2	6
Hungary	3	2	0	1	7	5	4
Brazil	3	1	0	2	4	6	2
Bulgaria	3	0	0	3	1	8	0

GROUP 4

	P	W	D	L	F	A	Pts
USSR	3	3	0	0	6	1	6
North Korea	3	1	1	1	2	4	3
Italy	3	1	0	2	2	2	2
Chile	3	0	1	2	2	5	1

QUARTER-FINALS

England .... 1 Argentina 0
Portugal .... 5 North Korea 3
USSR .... 2 Hungary 1
West Germany .... 4 Uruguay 0

SEMI-FINALS

England .... 2 Portugal 1
West Germany .... 2 USSR 1

THIRD-PLACE MATCH

Portugal .... 2 USSR 1

FINAL

(After extra time)

England .... (1) (2) **4**   **West Germany** .... (1) (2) **2**

Scorers: Hurst 3, Peters   *Scorers: Haller, Weber*

Team: Banks, Cohen, Wilson,   **Team**: Tilkowski, Hottges, Schulz,
Stiles, Charlton (J), Moore, Ball,   Weber, Schnellinger, Haller,
Hurst, Hunt, Charlton (R), Peters   Beckenbauer, Overath, Seeler,
                                     Held, Emmerich

NINTH WORLD CUP

Mexico 1970

INITIALLY, it had been expected that the ninth World Cup would be staged in Argentina but, at the 1964 FIFA Congress which was held in Tokyo, during the Olympics, Mexico petitioned for the series. Although the Mexican FA's claim was aided by the preselection of Mexico for the 1968 Olympics, opposition to the staging of the World Cup there was fierce. Several European delegations had already experienced the debilitating effects of heat and altitude in that country and were decidedly against the venue. Unfortunately Argentina's previous erratic support for the tournament coupled with the precarious state of her economy proved to be the deciding factors, and Mexico won the nomination.

For the Home Countries, the qualifying competition once more proved to be an insurmountable problem and only England as champions travelled to Mexico. The ludicrous system of geographical grouping again ensured that the stronger footballing nations of Western and Eastern Europe were pitted against one another while Third World sides faced equally unaccomplished opposition. Nor could FIFA's arguments – that geographical groupings were for financial reasons – be accepted. How on earth could Australia's games against Rhodesia and Israel, have been arranged to save them expense? In the qualifiers, Scotland, who faced West Germany, Austria and Cyprus, were given an unenviable task and lost their last two games to both West Germany and Austria. Wales too had a stiff fight in Group 3 where their opponents were Italy and East Germany and they failed to win a single point. Northern Ireland, yet again, came closest to qualifying when they came second to the USSR in Group 4, losing their final game in Moscow without their key player, George Best (who was injured while playing for Manchester United just two days earlier). Other notable absentees were Hungary, Austria, Argentina, France and Yugoslavia, the 1968 European championship runners-up, who, together with Spain were put out by Belgium.

The competition was played in precisely the same format as the eighth World Cup with four groups of four, leading straight to the quarter-finals, but, for the first time, substitutes were allowed. Mexico appeared as hosts and, because of this, El Salvador did not need to beat them in the qualifying competition and they, too, represented Central America. South America was represented by Brazil, Peru and Uruguay, while Morocco (who had progressed towards the finals after drawing lots with Tunisia) represented Africa. Europe was represented by Belgium, Bulgaria, Czechoslovakia, England, Italy, Rumania, Sweden, USSR and West Germany, and Israel made up the numbers, representing the rest of the world. The groupings were:

Group 1 – (Mexico City): Belgium, El Salvador, Mexico and the USSR.

Group 2 – (Toluca & Puebla): Israel, Italy, Sweden and Uruguay.

Group 3 – (Guadalajara): Brazil, Czechoslovakia, England and Rumania.

Group 4 – (Leon): Bulgaria, Morocco, Peru and West Germany.

The climatic difficulties in Mexico cannot be emphasized too greatly and the decision to begin many of the games at noon seems, in retrospect, to have been ludicrous. This peculiar decision (which ensured that most games were played in temperatures approaching 100°F) underlined once more the degree to which the game was becoming prostituted to commercial interests and the media which packaged the World Cup for a worldwide television audience.

So it was that the opening game in Group 1 between Mexico and the USSR kicked off at noon on 31 May 1970 in the cauldron heat of the Azteca Stadium in Mexico City. A capacity crowd of 112,000 saw the game which, in the best traditions of the previous series, ended in a goalless draw. Many blamed the referee Herr Tschenscher for stifling any initiative by his heavy-handed control of play but the truth of the matter was that neither side was prepared to risk defeat. The Russians could rightly feel aggrieved that four of their players were booked for relatively innocuous fouls and the Mexicans could argue, with some justification, that they deserved to win but, nevertheless, a draw was a fair result for such a tedious match.

The next game in the group pitted the surprise qualifiers, Belgium, against the complete outsiders, El Salvador. Skilful and composed though they were, Belgium found it difficult to impress against an El Salvador team which had no right to have reached the Finals. Van Moer gave Belgium the lead after twelve minutes and although Belgium then practically encamped in the El Salvador half of the field, it was not until ten minutes into the second half that they scored another (also by Van Moer). Ten minutes before time Lambert added a third from the penalty spot to conclude this dreary game. Facing Russia in their next game, Belgium never really got into their stride as their opponents took control from the kick-off. After a quarter of an hour Bishovets put the USSR into the lead with a powerful 30-yard drive which, aided by the high altitude, sped under keeper Piot's diving body. Belgian counter-attacks foundered against the strong Russian defence ably marshalled by Shesternev, and the Soviet attack took increasing control of the game. In the second half, Russia took Belgium apart as Asatiani, Bishovets and Khmelnitski all found the net with well-taken goals. Lambert scored a late consolation goal for Belgium, who now faced the task of beating Mexico in their last Group 1 game if they were to progress into the quarter-finals.

Mexico, meanwhile, played El Salvador, the country which had gone to war with its neighbour, Honduras, as a result of a clash in the qualifying competition. After a promising start in which they won three corners within the first five minutes, Mexico became increasingly erratic as their attacks failed to score a goal. Then, shortly before half-time, El Salvador were given justification for embarking upon another war as perhaps the most ridiculous refereeing error of any World Cup resulted in their falling a goal behind. The Egyptian referee, Aly Kandil, awarded El Salvador a free kick on the touch-line but, as they were preparing to take it, a Mexican player did so instead and from it Valdivia scored for Mexico. Mr. Kandil gave a goal and absolute pandemonium broke loose as the El Salvador players jostled and intimidated him in their exasperation. Two players were booked and it became apparent that a sending-off would have ended the game there and then. El Salvador refused to restart the game and, when ordered to do so, simply booted the ball into the crowd and the referee then prudently blew for half-time. In the second half, demoralized El Salvador simply lost heart and Mexico won 4-0.

El Salvador's final game, already a lost cause, was against the USSR. After the body blows of their Mexico game, they pulled themselves back well and held on bravely until Bishovets sunk them with two second-half goals. The last Group 1 game between Mexico and Belgium was played the following day with Belgium needing a win and Mexico a draw to progress to the next round. Before a packed house, it was Mexico who unexpectedly went for goals in a thrilling, hard-fought game yet, as in their previous match, a goal came from an awful refereeing error. In the 15th minute, Valdivia ran into the prostrate Belgium defender Jeck (who had just cleared a free kick) and, to the astonishment of the Belgium players, was awarded a penalty. Pena scored from the spot but, unlike El Salvador, Belgium fought back with a determination and venom which incited the Mexican crowd to fever-pitch and the game became steadily rougher. If the Belgium team had been able to control their emotions better they may have found it possible to overcome Mexico but in the fervent atmosphere of the Azteca stadium they at least went out fighting – literally!

Half of the Group 2 matches were played in Toluca which, at 8,792 feet above sea-level, was the highest of all the venues, but the first game in the group was played at Puebla. This was between Uruguay – much the same dour physical team that had played in 1966 – and part-timers Israel, and, as expected, resulted in a win for Uruguay by a 2-0 margin which belied their complete control of the game. Next in Group 2 Italy faced Sweden in Toluca and neither side were able fully to adjust to playing in such rarefied atmosphere. In the first half Italy played impressively but were lucky to score when a shot from Domenghini deceived Hellstrom in the Swedish goal. Although the Swedes tried to hit back in the second half, the altitude overcame both sides and the exhausted players settled for a 1-0 scoreline. Italy's next game was against Uruguay and, with two points already under their belt, they went out for a draw. Packing their defence Italy strolled through the game as the Uruguayans persistently lobbed hopeful crosses into their goalmouth, without causing any danger whatsoever. The 35,000 crowd groaned audibly throughout as they saw the tie peter out into a crushingly boring goalless draw.

Sweden faced Israel in their next game and were shocked to find that this was not to be the easy win for which they had hoped. Instead Israel matched them in all departments and, 13 minutes into the second half, equalized the goal which Sweden had scored minutes earlier, with a superb shot from Spiegler. From then onwards the game swung from end to end as frantic attackers were repelled by equally determined defenders and Sweden saw their chances of a quarter-final place become increasingly remote. The game ended in a 1-1 draw leaving Sweden with the task of defeating Uruguay by two clear goals in their last Group 2 match. As a target, two goals may not now appear to be that great but, with Uruguay as the opposition, Sweden had quite a fight on their hands. Before the game began there was controversy as rumours of attempted bribery of the proposed referee De Moraes of Brazil necessitated his replacement at the last minute. Uruguay protested vehemently about the change, feeling this to be an indictment of them, and played the game under protest. Nor was the task of the replacement referee, Mr. Landauer of the USA, a simple one, as Uruguay's renowned iron defence set about closing the game down. Over the years, Uruguay have been notorious for their spoiling cynical tactics and against Sweden they excelled themselves. Determined to prevent Sweden from playing football, Uruguay held out until the closing seconds when Grahn scored the only goal of the match. This effectively meant that, in the last Group 2 game, Italy would need to lose to Israel by 1-0 to enable Sweden to progress further. Such a result seemed highly improbable but, with their 1966 nightmare against North Korea still fresh in their minds, Italy could be forgiven for starting the game shakily. With such a fine attacking forward-line Italy should have done better but Vissoker in the Israel goal played so brilliantly that he began to look unbeatable. In the event Israel held out for a draw and Italy topped the group with four points but just one goal from their three matches.

Group 3 contained both the champions England and the favourites Brazil and began with a game between England and Rumania. England's 1969 tour of Mexico had been intended as a public relations exercise to win the friendship and support of the Mexican people in addition to introducing key players to the climatic problems which they were to face. In the event it proved to be a debacle as Alf Ramsey, never at ease with the media, repeatedly rebuked and annoyed the Mexican press. Indeed in 1970 the arrival of the English team aroused such fury that they were described in the newspapers as a 'team of thieves and drunks' – no doubt a reference to Bobby Moore's arrest in Bogota on trumped-up theft charges and Jeff Astle's arrival in disarray because of a horror of air travel. This ill-feeling manifested itself in the spontaneous jeering and whistling of the English flag during the opening ceremony, and created an unwelcome backdrop to England's game. Rumania had eliminated Greece, Portugal and Switzerland in the qualifying competition and were in no way overawed by England in their first game. With their centre-forward Dumitrache sparkling up front Rumania held on for a 0-0 half-time scoreline and threatened to do even better in the second half. Early in the second half, the Rumanian full-back, Mocanu, whose tackling throughout the early stages had been ferocious, scythed down England's Keith Newton who was injured so badly that he had to leave the field. Tommy Wright came on as substitute and he, too, received the same brutal treatment. Mocanu escaped so much as a caution for his excesses but, strangely, this physical assault only served to stiffen England's resolve and in the 67th minute, Geoff Hurst shot them into the lead with a well-taken goal. Rumania were unable to get back into the game and England achieved the opening victory which they so greatly needed.

Brazil began in fine style against Czechoslovakia in the next Group 3 match. From the start Brazil's defence looked decidedly below par and the Czech striker Petras put his country into the lead after only 12 minutes. Then the exciting and immensely skilful Brazilian attack took control of the game and, in the 24th minute, Rivelino equalized with a beautifully-struck free kick which swerved around the Czech defensive wall into their net. Pele and Gerson then got into their stride, and the shakiness of the Brazilian defence seemed to become irrelevant. Next, one of the most memorable moments of any World Cup game emphasized the brilliance and alertness of Pele, still at the height of his powers. Taking possession of the ball in his own half, Pele spotted that Viktor, the Czech goalkeeper, was off his line and from over 60 yards unleashed a soaring goalward shot which flashed within inches of Czechoslovakia's post as the goalkeeper scrambled frantically back. In the second half, although the Czechs came close to scoring on several occasions, Pele demonstrated further brilliant ball control before shooting Brazil into the lead and, on the hour, Jairzinho scored their third after taking the ball in what seemed to be an offside position. As Czechoslovakia tired, Jairzinho scored Brazil's fourth and final goal to cap a splendid performance.

The next game in the group saw Petras once more give Czechoslovakia an early lead, this time against Rumania, and again this was thrown away. In the 54th minute Neagu equalized with a smartly taken goal which, cutting in from the left, he slotted neatly between the keeper and his near post. Dumitrache scored a penalty-kick winner for Rumania 13 minutes from the end after Neagu had been rugby-tackled in the box. This result left both Rumania and Czechoslovakia with difficult tasks in their last Group 3 matches – victories over Brazil and England, respectively.

For many observers the next game in Group 3, bringing together as it did the champions and the champions-elect, England and Brazil, was the true World Cup Final. Indeed this was undoubtedly the finest game of the series but, from England's point of view, was preceded by a sort of personal vendetta which could have been avoided. England had chosen to stay at the Guadalajara Hilton which was situated in the centre of the town, and from early evening on the day before the game this was besieged by a rabble of hostile, noisy Brazilian supporters. Driving around, honking their car horns and chanting 'BRA-zil' throughout the night, this army of cheats made sure that the English team were unable to sleep. Thus England kicked off in the 98°F heat of the Jalisco stadium, Guadalajara, already tired and, seemingly, anxious only to avoid defeat. Brazil on the other hand only knew one way to play – to win! England's excellent defence, marshalled by Bobby Moore and backed by the finest goalkeeper in the world, Gordon Banks, faced undoubtedly the best attack in the world, but in the first ten minutes it was England's attack which dominated play and came close to scoring. Then at the other end Banks made one of the most memorable saves ever when he performed a minor miracle diving and twisting to scoop a superb Pele header from the line. At half-time England went in 0-0 and were beginning to look as if they could win the points, and the second-half started with the same mixture of attack and defence. After a quarter of an hour Tostao dribbled through the England defence, pushed aside Bobby Moore and passed to Pele who teed the ball up for Jairzinho to thunder a shot into the net. England fought back, brought on Jeff Astle and Colin Bell instead of Francis Lee and Bobby Charlton, and put pressure on the Brazilian defence. Then the chance of the game fell to Jeff Astle who was renowned for his powerful right-footed shooting but unfortunately went to his left foot! If anything ever emphasized the difference between England and Brazil, this was it – the inability of so many of the English players to kick with both feet. He missed, England lost 1-0 and faced a much stiffer quarter-final draw – if they won their last Group 3 game.

Before that was played, Brazil met Rumania who once more fielded the hacker of the series, Mocanu. Four times he committed vicious fouls which warranted explosion, yet his theatrical manner of raising his arms in feigned distress when approached by the referee, prevented it. (This all sounds a bit familiar – doesn't it?). Pele, however, scored two goals and Jairzinho another and, although Rumania hit back with two goals of their own, Brazil ran out worthy if somewhat roughed-up winners. England did manage to win their last Group 3 game against Czechoslovakia but, fielding a reorganized team, played absolutely terribly. Even Gordon Banks showed his fallibility and England were rather fortunate to win 1-0, thanks to a first-half penalty by Clarke. It was clear that changes would have to be made for the quarter-final.

Group 4 began with a game between Bulgaria and Peru which was preceded by a minute's silence for the victims of the Peruvian earthquake which had occurred since the Peruvian team had left for the World Cup. Although all the Peruvian players were relieved to learn that their families were safe, this seemed to unbalance Peru who quickly went two goals down. However, after bringing on two substitutes, Gonzalez and Sotil, Peru fought back and ran out worthy 3-2 winners. The next day West Germany met Morocco (the first African country to reach the finals since Egypt did so in 1934) and were shocked when Houmane Jakir put the Africans ahead in the 22nd minute. Morocco fielded a team of surprisingly skillful players and West Germany gradually began to realize that they had a fight on their hands. The first half ended with Morocco still in the lead but then the Dutch referee, Van Ravens, preposterously started the second half before all the Moroccans had returned to the field. Although the small crowd was amused by the incredible spectacle of Allal, the Moroccan goalkeeper, racing onto the pitch just in time to palm away a shot, clearly this was not a just way to restart a game. After 56 minutes West Germany equalized and then, just 12 minutes from the end, Muller snatched an undeserved winner.

In their next game, against Peru, Morocco once again played above themselves in the first half and held on to a 0-0 half time score. A quarter of an hour into the second half Cubillas shot Peru into the lead and, in a devastating ten-minute spell, made one goal and scored another – one of the greatest World Cup goals of all time. Both sides continued to play superb attacking football but the score remained 3-0 to Peru. Bulgaria faced West Germany in the next match in the group. Libuda was brought into the West German team and he played with such speed and flair that West Germany never looked like losing. From the kick-off West Germany pinned down Bulgaria in their own penalty area but, completely against the run of play, Bulgaria took the lead in the 12th minute. Eight minutes later Libuda scored the equalizer and, by half-time, Bulgaria were 2-1 down. In the second half West Germany took complete control and deserved their 5-2 win when the final whistle blew.

Three days later Peru and West Germany, both of whom had already earned a quarter-final place, met to decide who would travel to Guadalajara and who would remain in Leon. Both sides went flat out for goals in an entertaining game and, for the first time in the series, West Germany took an early lead (through Muller, who had scored a hat-trick in their previous game). By half-time Muller had notched up another hat-trick and West Germany were leading 3-1. There was no score in the second half although the game continued in exactly the same vein as the first with a display of end-to-end soccer which was a credit to both sides. The final game in Group 4 matched Morocco with Bulgaria and, with the group already won, attracted a very small crowd. There was nothing really to play for, so the spectators could be forgiven for their lack of interest and, with both sides playing half-paced football, the game ended 1-1.

The quarter-finals threw up an interesting re-run of the 1966 Final with West Germany against England in Leon. The other ties brought together USSR and Uruguay in Mexico City, Italy and Mexico in Toluca, and Brazil and Peru in Guadalajara.

First that game in Leon. West Germany were intent upon exacting revenge over England for their defeat in the 1966 Final and had just run into peak form. England on the other hand were without Gordon Banks who had been taken ill (Peter Bonetti took over) and many say that this was the deciding factor of the game. On paper at least, West Germany were the favourites as England's performances had been far from impressive but, confounding their critics, Alf Ramsey's side began very well. Bobby Charlton and Martin Peters played deeper than previously and this quickly neutralized West Germany's wingers. England were playing splendidly and, on the half-hour, Alan Mullery scored with a rasping shot from eight yards out, a terrific ending to a move which he had started back in his own half. Five minutes after the interval, Peters scored a second from a Keith Newton cross and England seemed to be cruising to a comfortable victory. In the 57th minute the West Germans made perhaps the most decisive substitution of the game by bringing on the lithe, skilful Grabowski in place of Libuda. Grabowski's freshness soon emphasized the problems which Terry Cooper was having (both heat and exhaustion) and it became obvious that he must be substituted. Before this could take place Beckenbauer scored with a seemingly innocuous shot which Bonetti misjudged, and England began to look vulnerable. When the substitution was made Colin Bell replaced Bobby Charlton who, although tiring, still posed a great threat while Cooper, by now practically on his knees, played on. Nor did the strange tactics end there, for ten minutes later Peters was replaced by the dour defender Norman Hunter. Ramsey evidently hoped to save two key men for the semi-final. So it was that England elected to defend but, without the energy to do so, yielded up midfield and began to struggle in the heat. Then Uwe Seeler, beating the English offside trap, headed a tantalizing curling ball which spun over the head of Bonetti (who was out of position) into the goal. This necessitated extra-time and, after England were denied what appeared to be a perfect Hurst goal, West Germany scored the winner with the ineffectual Bonetti once more floundering out of position. The champions were thus beaten as much by the team changes and tactics as by the opposition – but it was still so close.

Brazil, firm favourites with the Mexican crowd, met Peru in an open and thoroughly exciting game at Guadalajara. With the ex-Brazilian wizard Didi in charge, Peru's style of play closely resembled that of Brazil and the resulting confrontation was a joy to behold. In the first 15 minutes Tostao masterminded a goal for Rivelino, then scored the second himself as Brazil surged into the lead. Peru hit back in the 28th minute and it was not until the second half that another goal was scored – Tostao making it 3-1 to Brazil. Still Brazil played wonderful attacking football and this left enough space for Peru to pull a goal back through Cubillas. Undaunted, Brazil turned the screws once more and Jairzinho scored a fourth goal to complete a thrilling victory – both for Brazil and for the game of soccer.

At the highest location of all, in Toluca, Mexico faced Italy who had won only one of their group games and had scored a single goal. Doubtless they would have preferred the gigantic Azteca Stadium in Mexico City where 100,000 fanatical Mexicans could have intimidated the opposition into all kinds of mistakes. Nevertheless almost all of the 30,000 crowd were behind Mexico, and when Italy went a goal down in the 27th minute they began to seem very vulnerable even though Domenghini equalized later in the half. After half-time Italy replaced Mazzola with Rivera and, together with Riva, he began to tear the Mexican defence to shreds. First Riva and then Rivera scored past the unnerved Calderon in the Mexican goal and Riva grabbed his second and Italy's fourth goal to seal Mexico's fate.

In the Azteca Stadium the USSR confronted Uruguay in the fourth quarter-final. After 90 minutes there was no score, Russia having attacked bravely and Uruguay having shown their talent for defending. As extra-time was played Uruguay took the upper hand and scored the only goal of the match just three minutes from the end. The Russians protested long and loud that the ball had crossed the line for a goal-kick before Gubillas had centred for Esparrogo to head in, but the goal stood. Once again a controversial decision had decided the game but, this time, television replays vindicated the decision of Mr. Van Ravens, the Dutch referee, and Bob Davidson, the British linesman.

In the semi-finals Brazil took on the defensive might of Uruguay at Guadalajara and Italy met West Germany at the Azteca Stadium. Brazil and Uruguay, who were old rivals, could scarcely be described as friendly, and Uruguay felt rightly aggrieved to be facing Brazil at what had become virtually their home ground. All the same Uruguay stifled Brazil's attack with their renowned rugged defence work and, in the 18th minute, unexpectedly took the lead through Cubilla. The test of a great team comes when it is faced by such adversity and, on the stroke of half-time, Clodoaldo scored a glorious equalizer. This timely goal inspired Brazil and in the second half they shrugged off Uruguay's increasingly violent tactics so that, with goals from Jairzinho and Rivelino, they ran out worthy 3-1 winners.

The other tie between West Germany and Italy could hardly be described as a classic – hardly that is, until the 91st minute. Italy took the lead early in the game through Boninsegna and then yielded up midfield as they defended in depth. West Germany, durable and persistent as ever, equalized through Schnellinger in the final minute of the game and the stage was set for an extra-time thriller. Gerd Muller shot West Germany ahead but Burgnich equalized almost immediately and Riva gave Italy a 3-2 lead at the turnaround. Nor did the thrills end there as Muller scored his tenth goal of the series to level the score at three all. Franz Beckenbauer injured his shoulder but refused to leave the field, playing on with his arm strapped to his side. This factor above all others turned the remaining few minutes Italy's way and Rivera scored the winner to earn Italy their first Final appearance for 32 years.

Before the Final, the third-place play-off supplied its usual blend of anticlimax and apathy at the start but after West Germany had taken the lead through Overath everything changed. Uruguay, no longer needing to use cut-throat tactics, came out of their shells and the game came alive. No further goals were scored though, as West Germany, meeting attack with counter attack, held onto their lead in what proved to be one of the most thrilling games of the tournament.

So it was that Italy met Brazil in the Azteca Stadium, both knowing that a win would give them permanent custody of the Jules Rimet trophy. In essence this was Pele's swansong – he had sworn never to play in another World Cup in 1966 but Brazil became the beneficiaries of his change of heart. Italy played unattractive man-to-man defensive football from the start and never really got to grips with the Brazilian style of play. Gerson dominated the midfield for Brazil and Carlos Alberto cruised up and down the right wing creating all sorts of problems for Italy. After 18 minutes Pele rose spectacularly above the Italian defence to head in a Rivelino cross. Seven minutes before half-time Boninsegna scored an undeserved equalizer after Clodoaldo had carelessly backheeled into his own half but Italy failed to hammer home their psychological advantage. In the 66th minute Gerson shot Brazil back into the lead and five minutes later Jairzinho made it 3-1 after Pele had touched on a Gerson free kick. Now the pressure was really on Italy and six minutes from the end they made an extraordinary substitution, replacing Boninsegna (the only forward who looked capable of scoring) with Rivera. Clearly, team politics played as great a part in this decision as tactics but, whatever the reason for the substitution, it did not help Italy one bit. Three minutes from the end Brazil 'killed' Italy off with a fourth goal scored, fittingly, by skipper Carlos Alberto and the Jules Rimet trophy was on its way to a permanent home in Brazil.

GROUP 1

	P	W	D	L	F	A	Pts
USSR	3	2	1	0	6	1	5
Mexico	3	2	1	0	5	0	5
Belgium	3	1	0	2	4	5	2
El Salvador	3	0	0	3	0	9	0

GROUP 2

	P	W	D	L	F	A	Pts
Italy	3	1	2	0	1	0	4
Uruguay	3	1	1	1	2	1	3
Sweden	3	1	1	1	2	2	3
Israel	3	0	2	1	1	3	2

GROUP 3

	P	W	D	L	F	A	Pts
Brazil	3	3	0	0	8	3	6
England	3	2	0	1	2	1	4
Rumania	3	1	0	2	4	5	2
Czechoslovakia	3	0	0	3	2	7	0

GROUP 4

	P	W	D	L	F	A	Pts
West Germany	3	3	0	0	10	4	6
Peru	3	2	0	1	7	5	4
Bulgaria	3	0	1	2	5	9	1
Morocco	3	0	1	2	2	6	1

QUARTER-FINALS

Brazil	4	Peru	2
Uruguay	1	USSR	0
West Germany	3	England	2
Italy	4	Mexico	1

SEMI-FINALS

Brazil	3	Uruguay	1
Italy	4	West Germany	3

THIRD-PLACE MATCH

West Germany	1	Uruguay	0

FINAL

Brazil .... (1) **4**   **Italy** .... (1) **1**

Scorers: Pele, Gerson, Jairzinho, Carlos Alberto

Scorer: Boninsegna

Team: Felix, Carlos Alberto, Brito, Piazza, Everaldo, Clodoaldo, Gerson, Jairzinho, Tostao, Pele, Rivelino

Team: Albertosi, Cera, Burgnich, Bertini (sub. Juliano), Rosato, Facchetti, Domenghini, Mazzola, De Sisti, Boninsegna (sub. Rivera), Riva

TENTH WORLD CUP

West Germany 1974

IN 1972 West Germany won the European Championship with a quite exceptional display of the hard-running, interchanging style which came to be known as 'total football'. With this as a backdrop, the world cast its eyes to the Federal Republic as it was chosen as the venue for the 1974 World Cup.

A completely new trophy was commissioned to replace the Lafleur original (won outright by Brazil in 1970) which had been presented by Jules Rimet himself in 1930. The new 'FIFA World Cup Trophy', weighing eleven pounds and almost 20 inches in height, was tastefully cast by an Italian sculptor and paid for by FIFA, who had declined Brazil's generous offer to provide the replacement.

The changes did not end there. For the first time since 1950 the concept of 'groups' was extended beyond the first-round games. The Final itself was retained but the semi-finals were entirely dispensed with, the finalists and third-place play-off teams being the winners and runners-up respectively of the two second-stage groups. As before 16 nations competed and these were divided into four first-round groups of four, the top two of which progressed to two second-round groups of four countries.

For the first time since rejoining FIFA after the Second World War, England failed to qualify for the Finals and, with Wales and Northern Ireland also going out, Scotland, qualifying for the first time since 1958, were Britain's only representatives. Once again, the preliminary competition had proved to be the insurmountable obstacle as Wales were drawn in the same group as England along with Austria and Poland. England drew their Wembley fixture with Wales and their other performances left them with the task of beating Poland at Wembley to qualify. The Poles weathered unrelieved second-half pressure to gain a 1-1 draw, and England and Wales were thus out of the 1974 series. The one bright spot for the Home Countries was Scotland's elimination of Czechoslovakia and their consequent qualification. Elsewhere there were the usual justifiable grumbles about the failure to 'dezone' the weaker Third World teams. This resulted in some second-grade footballing countries qualifying with comparative ease while considerably stronger

European and South American teams eliminated one another. The justification for these grievances was emphasized by the grossly unfair insistence that the winners of one European Group and one South American group must play-off for a single place. In the event this particular contest drew together the USSR and Chile and, after a 0-0 draw in Moscow, the USSR refused to play the return match in the Santiago National Stadium where, following the military coup, a number of political prisoners had been executed. Undoubtedly FIFA's handling of the whole preliminary competition was insensitive and unreasonable; fortunately, however, the organization of the Finals themselves was beyond criticism.

West Germany as hosts and Brazil as champions were automatically included in the final 16 teams together with Argentina, Chile and Uruguay who represented South America while Bulgaria, East Germany, Holland, Italy, Poland, Scotland, Sweden and West Germany represented Europe. Additionally Australia became the first Oceanian country to reach the Finals, and Zaire became the first Central African country to do so, while Haiti made their first appearance representing Central and North America. The countries were grouped as follows:

Group 1:   Australia, Chile, East Germany and West Germany.

Group 2:   Brazil, Scotland, Yugoslavia and Zaire.

Group 3:   Bulgaria, Holland, Sweden and Uruguay.

Group 4:   Argentina, Haiti, Italy and Poland.

After the appalling terrorist massacre of Israeli athletes in the 1972 Olympic Games in West Germany, the security for the series was thorough and extensive with a noticeable presence of soldiers and armed police within and without the stadiums. In this rather forbidding atmosphere the tenth World Cup began in Frankfurt. The opening game provided the almost customary spectacle of an arid goalless draw, in Group 2 of the series. Brazil, brilliant winners in 1970, met Yugoslavia and were so surprised by the Slavs' enthusiasm that they almost allowed Katalinski to take an early lead. The South Americans' lack of incisiveness up front underlined their need for a centre-forward in the mould of Tostao or Vava. In the absence of any alternative, Jairzinho was obliged to fill the gap and Brazil struggled in vain to settle to any pattern, so that the game petered out into a tame draw. The next match in the group brought together Scotland and Zaire. As usual there had been dissension in the Scottish camp: both Billy Bremner and Jimmy Johnstone were disciplined for non-footballing incidents and manager Ormond had to intercede on their behalf to avoid their being sent home. The Scots needed to run up a big score against Zaire to give them some margin for error in their other games, but they struggled to score at all. Indeed, although they could be forgiven for underestimating the Africans – who played some quite exhilarating football – Scotland's lack of power in the area was more than evident and it was not until Lorimer scored midway through the first half with a fierce right-foot shot, that they began to relax. Jordan headed a second from a Bremner free kick later in the half and Zaire braced themselves for a second-half onslaught. This did not materialize and, struggling in the heat, Scotland seemed content with two goals and played half-pace possession football until the final whistle.

The Scots next faced Brazil in a game memorable for Billy Bremner's superb display of footballing skill. For the first 20 minutes, Brazil turned on the sort of display which, had it been maintained, would have won them the cup, and it was only Bremner's inspiration that kept Scotland in the game. Later in the game, although the Scottish defence struggled to contain the brilliant Brazilian forward-line, Bremner, Jordan and Lorimer all missed chances to score. Just as Yugoslavia had been, Scotland were let off the hook because Brazil lacked a goal-scoring centre-forward, although Harvey in the Scottish goal (playing probably his best game for his country) was called to the rescue on a number of occasions, and the game ended with a 0-0 scoreline. The inconclusiveness of this confrontation meant that both Brazil and Scotland were in danger of missing the later stages of the competition, particularly after Yugoslavia took Zaire apart. They drove in goal after goal as the Africans failed to settle in the same way as they had against Scotland. By half-time the Slavs were 6-0 up and looked capable of doubling that score. In the second half they eased back somewhat but still ran out easy 9-0 winners, equalling the World Cup goal-scoring record for a single game.

This result left Scotland requiring a win or draw against Yugoslavia in the last Group 2 game – although a draw would only suffice if Brazil did not beat Zaire by more than one goal. Such was the tense situation as both Scotland and Yugoslavia and Brazil and Zaire kicked off at the same time. Scotland were unfortunate to go a goal down to a second-half Karasi header and it was not until the closing stages that substitute Hutchinson (who had replaced the largely ineffective Dalglish) finished a glorious run with a pass to Jordan who scored the equalizer to make the final score 1-1. All eyes turned to the Brazil vs Zaire game where Brazil, like Scotland, had struggled to find the net. Brazil led 1-0 at half-time, and 2-0 soon after, but could not add a third until later in the game when Valdomiro rather luckily squeezed a shot under the keeper's diving body. Thus Scotland were eliminated (although with great credit) on goal difference and, in the process, they became the first country to go out of the World Cup without losing a game. They paid a heavy price for failing to destroy the weakest team in the group.

West Germany faced Chile in the first Group 1 game which was played in Berlin. Demonstrations on the terraces by Chilean left-wing activists provided a hostile atmosphere as West Germany struggled to beat the South Americans. Chile's defence was remarkably solid and the West Germans made little impression until the full-back, Brietner, scored with a tremendous long-range shot in the second half. Once again, as the score ended 1-0 in their favour, West Germany demonstrated their doggedness and tenacity by overcoming an indifferent performance to win a game. Next East Germany and Australia took the stage. Australia, a team comprising largely of immigrants under the managership of the Yugoslav Rale Rasic, soon showed their determination and East Germany struggled to get into the game. At half-time there was no score and either team looked capable of winning the points. In the second half the Australian defence faltered as Curran gave away an own-goal and Streich scored a second to give East Germany a 2-0 victory.

The next game was played in Hamburg and, this time, Australia's opponents were West Germany. Once more the Australian defence proved equal to most attacks as West Germany, too, found Australia a tough nut to crack. Nor were the home crowd enamoured by their team's performance as, more than once, Franz Beckenbauer exchanged insults with their critical supporters. Nevertheless, the West German resilience won through and in the end they won comfortably enough by 3-0 although Australia deserved at least a couple of goals.

East Germany, who had been held to a 1-1 draw by Chile, now moved on to the first encounter between both sides of divided Germany, which was the next tie in the group. West Germany with four points were already assured of a second-round place and East Germany, too, could be reasonably certain that their three points would enable them to progress but, nevertheless, the game certainly provided tension. There was tight and very evident security as a helicopter circled above the Hamburg stadium and armed police seemed to be everywhere. The game itself proved rather less intense as East Germany settled down to a well-drilled tactical defence and counter-attack style of play. West Germany seemed most likely to score as Cirabowski and Muller both went close but Kreische of East Germany had the miss of the match when he failed to net a first-half sitter. After the interval the West Germans completely dominated the game but, with the scoreline still 0-0, East Germany's Sparwasser scored the winner just eight minutes from the end to top Group 1. Australia and Chile played out a 0-0 draw in the last game of the group. In the event West Germany's defeat led them to an easier second-round group but, for once, this had not been a tactical ploy by their manager. Indeed there was something like England/Scotland rivalry as Helmut Schoen was slated by a West German press indignant that their country had been defeated by their East German neighbours!

In Group 3 Holland played delightful football against a poor Uruguayan team. With Cruyff displaying masterful control of the midfield, the Uruguayans found themselves utterly outclassed. For once even their notorious terror tactics failed as Johnny Rep put Holland into a half-time lead and scored another goal in the second half. Castillo summed up his team-mates' frustration as he punched Rensenbrink in the stomach – an offence which earned him a dismissal. The score remained at 2-0 but this flattered Uruguay who were beginning to look as if they should have stayed at home.

Sweden had struggled to qualify, requiring a play-off win over Austria, but, in the next game in the group, against Bulgaria, they showed that they had come to play football. Bulgaria, however, had other ideas and closed the game down by closely marking the twin Swedish threat of Sandberg and Estroem, the excellent Atvidaberg forwards. The game ended goalless as, surprisingly, did Sweden's next tie against Holland. Indeed, relaxed and with nothing to lose, Sweden played with such enthusiasm and determination against the Netherlands that they came close to obtaining a result. Had Cruyff not been in such devastating form that day, matters might well have gone differently.

The next game in the group could hardly be described as a classic with both protagonists, Bulgaria and Uruguay, renowned for their tactical sterility. Bulgaria have often been referred to as Europe's Uruguay and matching bone-crunching tackles in kind, they were determined not to lose at all costs. The score ended 1-1, honours and bruises more or less even. Facing Holland in their next game, Bulgaria must have wondered what had hit them as the great Cruyff literally took them apart. Dour defence culminated in Neeskens scoring twice from the penalty spot as Holland ran amok. At half-time the score was 2-0 and Holland scored twice more in the second half to ensure that they topped the group with five points. Even Bulgaria's sole reply was by courtesy of Holland – an own goal by Krol.

Although they were undefeated, Sweden had failed to score a single goal and, in the last game in the group, were anxious for a good result to progress to the next round. Once again their opponents Uruguay were negative and destructive in their approach to the game and at half-time the score was still 0-0. But in the second half the Swedish forwards came into their own and Edstroem with two goals and Sandberg with another ensured their country's victory and progression to the next round.

Group 4 provided the highest drama if not the best football of the series. The opening game was between Haiti and Italy whose goalkeeper Dino Zoff had, at the start of the game, played over 1,100 minutes of international football without conceding a single goal. At half-time there was no score but in the second half Sanon put the surprisingly good Haiti team into the lead before Rivera, Benetti and Anastasi made the final score 3-1 to Italy. Unfortunately, the matter did not end there as, the following day, a routine dope test on Ernst Jean-Joseph, the Haitian centre-half, proved positive and he was barred from further participation in the series. Then the sinister nature of the Haitian regime became distastefully apparent as he was dragged from his team's quarters, beaten up by his own officials and held incommunicado awaiting a flight back to Haiti. Justifiably terrified he telephoned two neutral officials who realized his plight and vainly attempted to intercede on his behalf. Incredibly the upshot was that the officials were reprimanded by FIFA's World Cup organizing committee while Jean-Joseph was flown back to Haiti. The effect of this brutality upon the morale of the Haiti team can only be guessed at but suffice it to say that, in their two remaining games, their performances were abysmal. Their next opponents, Poland, barely had to break into a sweat to win 7-0 and, although the 4-1 scoreline of their other game against Argentina was an improvement, the commitment was well and truly lacking – a sad end to a sad series.

Poland met Argentina in the second game in the group, an exciting end-to-end encounter which probably heralded Argentina's rehabilitation back into the footballing arena after a prolonged spell as the cynical 'bad boys' of soccer. Right from the kick-off the game was full of flair and excitement and although Kempes could have put Argentina ahead in the opening couple of minutes, Lato and Szarmach both scored within ten minutes to put Poland firmly in the lead. So it remained until the second half when Heredia pulled one back for Argentina but Lato then capitalized upon a goalkeeping error to grab a third goal for Poland. The final score was 3-2 to Poland and the stage was set for an epic confrontation between Argentina and Italy in the next game in the group. For once a clash between the two countries proved to be a footballing delight which Argentina richly deserved to win. In the event, with a final score of 1-1, Argentina had to be content with a moral victory but, after their 4-1 victory over Haiti in their next game, they were still pushing the Italians for a second-round qualifying place. Poland's 7-0 victory over Haiti had ensured their progress to the next round but the last game of the group found Italy needing at least a point from them. Italy lost 2-1 and complained of unfair refereeing decisions but, in reality, were fortunate not to lose more heavily.

The second-round groups were designated as Group A and Group B with Argentina, Brazil, East Germany and Holland in Group A and Poland, Sweden, West Germany and Yugoslavia in Group B.

Group A began with East Germany facing Brazil at Hanover. The East Germans defended stoutly, containing the Brazilians' attacking flair until Rivelino scored from a second-half free kick. This was a well-rehearsed and executed manoeuvre with Jairzinho joining the East German defensive wall to make the gap for Rivelino's shot, and although Brazil were unable to score any more goals, they thoroughly deserved their victory. The next Group A game brought an understrength Argentina (without Babington who was suspended for three cautions) against the on-song Dutch. With Cruyff at his brilliant best, Argentina were simply not in the game with a chance and had no answers as Holland ran out worthy 4-0 victors. Neither could East Germany hold Holland in the next Group B game (although Weise succeeded in marking Cruyff comprehensively) and the Dutch again won comfortably. And then, in the first-ever World Cup meeting between the two nations, Brazil were fully tested by Argentina in the next Group A game. At half-time the score was level at 1-1 but Brazil snatched victory with a second-half goal by the ebullient Jairzinho.

Both Holland and Brazil had four points each and so when the two faced one another in their next Group A game, Brazil needed a victory and Holland a draw to progress to the Final – a promising scenario. Such a confrontation could and should have provided the game of the series but it turned out to be just about the reverse. From the outset the Brazilians handed out a barrage of brutal treatment to the Dutch who were quick to respond in kind as the game became peppered with free kicks and stoppages. Neeskens in particular was in the wars, first knocked unconscious by Marinho and then violently kicked by Pereira who was sent off for his trouble. Yet Neeskens had the last laugh as he put Holland into the lead by way of a Cruyff pass. Cruyff himself then scored the deciding goal, volleying a Krol cross superbly into the Brazilian goal to put the fine Dutch side into the Final. The final Group A game brought together Argentina and East Germany who, without a point between them and little to play for, could hardly be blamed for the boring 1-1 draw that resulted.

Meanwhile, in Group B. Poland were very fortunate indeed to overcome the battling Swedes who threatened early in the game to overwhelm them. A goal by Lato gave Poland victory but Sweden could have sewn the game up earlier when Hahn and Tapper both scorned easy chances. Then West Germany faced Yugoslavia and, to the delight of the home crowd, began at last to emerge as a force to be reckoned with. With the magisterial Beckenbauer dominating the field of play Breitner and Muller scored West Germany's goals. Next it was Poland's turn to play Yugoslavia and, as they had been against Sweden, were somewhat fortunate to win. Deyna opened the scoring for Poland converting a penalty stupidly conceded by Karasi who then atoned for his error by scoring a superb equalizer. Lato grabbed the winner for Poland in the second half. Throughout the tournament Sweden had been an inspiration. They had gone out to play exciting, attacking football and, in the next Group B game, against West Germany, they excelled themselves. The lively Edstroem and Sandberg had once more combined to provide the drive up front as the Swedes took a 1-0 half-time lead, and began to seem poised for victory. True to form, West Germany crept rather than stormed back but, nevertheless, at the end, were worthy 4-2 winners. Sweden gained some consolation against Yugoslavia, albeit somewhat academically, when they deservedly achieved a 2-1 victory. As in Group A, this left two countries with a 100% record facing one another and the clash between West Germany and Poland delivered less than it promised. Before the game started a cloudburst rendered the pitch unplayable and the kick-off was delayed while the surface water was drained away. The game itself could not be described as outstanding but, nevertheless, was not uninteresting as it swung from end to end. At half-time the game was finely balanced at 0-0 although West Germany were indeed fortunate that their goalkeeper, Maier, had been able to pull off an incredible save when Lato seemed certain to score. Muller's second-half goal clinched victory for West Germany and with it a place in an all-European Final against Holland.

Before the Final, the third-place match proved to be the usual dreary formality. Poland, commanded by the midfield general Deyna, won with a second-half goal by Lato, but the absurdity of playing a pointless tie was once again clearly emphasized.

The 1974 World Cup Final began with an incredible situation. From the kick-off, Holland went into the attack for a full minute of possession play and, as Cruyff linked his way into the area, Hoeness tripped him, giving away a penalty. Neeskens thundered his spot-kick past the diving Maier and Holland were in the lead before any West German player had even touched the ball! This was a classic example of the 'total football' ethos. Incredibly, although this was the tenth Final, it was the first in which a penalty had been awarded! Much has been written about the resilience of West Germany in the face of adversity and this set-back was the acid test of that quality. Holland, seeming to savour their ascendancy over their old antagonists, stroked the ball about for fully 20 minutes while the West Germans struggled to find an answer to their torment, but crucially the Dutch failed to find the net again. West Germany were themselves awarded a penalty when Jansen tripped Holzenbein and Breitner had no difficulty in levelling the scores. This gave the hosts the impetus that they required and, a little before half-time, the lethal finishing of Muller put them into the lead for his 68th international goal. In the second half Holland were weakened by injuries to Rensenbrink and Rijsbergen and were denied an equalizer thanks to superb goalkeeping from Sepp Maier. Much to the delight of the home crowd, West Germany won the championship with a determined rather than brilliant performance and the best team in the competition, Holland, had to be content with second place.

GROUP 1

	P	W	D	L	F	A	Pts
East Germany	3	2	1	0	4	1	5
West Germany	3	2	0	1	4	1	4
Chile	3	0	2	1	1	2	2
Australia	3	0	1	2	0	5	1

GROUP 2

	P	W	D	L	F	A	Pts
Yugoslavia	3	1	2	0	10	1	4
Brazil	3	1	2	0	3	0	4
Scotland	3	1	2	0	3	1	4
Zaire	3	0	0	3	0	14	0

GROUP 3

	P	W	D	L	F	A	Pts
Holland	3	2	1	0	6	1	5
Sweden	3	1	2	0	3	0	4
Bulgaria	3	0	2	1	2	5	2
Uruguay	3	0	1	2	1	6	1

GROUP 4

	P	W	D	L	F	A	Pts
Poland	3	3	0	0	12	3	6
Argentina	3	1	1	1	7	5	3
Italy	3	1	1	1	5	4	3
Haiti	3	0	0	3	2	14	0

QUARTER-FINALS GROUP A

	P	W	D	L	F	A	Pts
Holland	3	3	0	0	8	0	6
Brazil	3	2	0	1	3	3	4
East Germany	3	0	1	2	1	4	1
Argentina	3	0	1	2	2	7	1

QUARTER-FINALS GROUP B

	P	W	D	L	F	A	Pts
West Germany	3	3	0	0	7	2	6
Poland	3	2	0	1	3	2	4
Sweden	3	1	0	2	4	6	2
Yugoslavia	3	0	0	3	2	6	0

THIRD-PLACE MATCH

Poland .... 1 Brazil 0

FINAL

West Germany .... (2) **2**   **Holland** .... (1) **1**

Scorers: Breitner (pen), Muller   *Scorer: Neeskens (pen)*

Team: Maier, Beckenbauer, Vogts, Schwarzenbeck, Breitner, Bonhof, Hoeness, Overath, Grabowski, Muller, Holzenbein

Team: Jongbloed, Suurbier (sub. De Jong), Haan, Krol, Rijsbergen, Jansen, Neeskens, Van Hamegem, Rep, Cruyff, Rensenbrink (sub. R. Van Der Kerkhof)

ELEVENTH WORLD CUP

Argentina 1978

MISGIVINGS about the selection of Argentina as the venue for the 1978 World Cup were not confined to Europe. Military dictatorships are never renowned for their tolerance and the junta which then ruled in Buenos Aires was notable for its repressive brutality. In the two years between the take-over by the military government and the start of the Eleventh World Cup, literally thousands of their opponents had been murdered and tortured, and thousands more had simply disappeared. Add to this the rampant 'mega' inflation, the poor condition of the stadiums and the extremely violent nature of the Argentine crowds, and one can understand the misgivings of the other countries.

However, the Argentinians began in a businesslike manner, and set up a new body (the Ente Autarquico Mundial) to speed up the reconstruction programme. The fact that the leader of the new body was assassinated en route to its first press conference did nothing to mitigate the world's scepticism, and neither did it reduce the immense task with which it was faced. Even after the preparations had begun, rumours abounded that the series would be moved to Holland or Belgium and these were supported by additional stories that Holland would otherwise withdraw. By giving Argentina the World Cup at this time, FIFA seemed to give moral support to the junta and, by implication, its policies; from a purely football point of view, the overriding question, which was never satisfactorily answered, was whether or not the safety of the players could be guaranteed. In the event the answer to that question was 'yes' – off the field at least. Most of the fears regarding the stadiums and organization also proved unfounded although, as we will see, few of the participating countries were entirely happy when the tournament was over.

The format was precisely as in 1974 and, once again, England failed to qualify. This time, unlike 1974, there could be few English complaints as, under the 'leadership' of Don Revie, the standard of English football at international level had plunged to an all-time low. Italy won England's qualifying group and Revie's departure for a hugely lucrative post in the Middle

East added insult to injury. Northern Ireland were unlucky to face the omnipotent Dutch in their qualifying group and also failed to qualify. Wales were eliminated by Scotland thanks to a grossly unfair goal which arose as a result of a Jordan handball and, for the second consecutive series, Scotland were Britain's sole representative. Certainly, the standard of the Scottish players at that time was far superior to any of the other Home Countries but the ineptitude and naivety of the Scottish manager, Ally MacLeod, posed serious problems.

Apart from Scotland, West Germany as champions were automatically through to the Finals and Austria, France, Holland, Hungary, Italy, Poland, Spain and Sweden also represented Europe. For South America, the hosts Argentina joined Brazil and Peru, with Mexico, Tunisia and Iran filling the other places. The countries were grouped as follows:

Group 1:   Argentina, France, Hungary and Italy.

Group 2:   Mexico, Poland, Tunisia and West Germany.

Group 3:   Austria, Brazil, Spain and Sweden.

Group 4:   Holland, Iran, Peru and Scotland.

Although the stadiums were just about ready for the start of the tournament it had been a near thing. Playing surfaces were questionable – the River Plate stadium, for instance, was completely returfed because it had been watered with sea-water; others were not much better. Shortly before the tournament began a bomb killed a policeman at the Buenos Aires press centre and the publication of an Amnesty International protest against the Argentine junta signed by dozens of the players increased the sense of forboding. Nor did the absence of two of the footballing giants of the period, Franz Beckenbauer and Johann Cruyff, augur well and Holland, although potential favourites, found themselves without several other leading players who also declined to participate.

So it was that the Eleventh World Cup began on 1 June 1978 with a Group 2 tie between West Germany, the holders, and Poland. True to the now well-established pattern, the game was a crushingly boring 0-0 draw. Time and again the system of subjecting two teams to the scrutiny of the whole world after a flamboyant and drawn-out opening ceremony has proved to be self-defeating, and this was no exception.

The next Group 2 game was between Tunisia and Mexico and was the first game to be played at the New Rosario stadium. Although they began somewhat hesitantly and were trailing 1-0 at half-time, Tunisia surprised everyone by playing some really admirable football and ran out 3-1 winners over Mexico, thanks to goals from Kaabi, Goummidh and Dhouib. Facing Poland in their next game, Tunisia began as they had ended against Mexico and pressed the Poles very hard. But for an unfortunate slip just before half-time, which let Lato in to score for Poland, the Africans would have at least held Poland to a draw as they dominated most of the remainder of the match. In the event they were most unfortunate to go down 1-0.

The West German camp, meanwhile was experiencing its usual spate of insubordination as the players protested about the manager's tactics, the coaches complained about his indecisiveness, and everybody grumbled about the boredom at the team's training camp. Helmut Schoen, the West German manager, answered the criticism by altering the formation and was gratified to see his decision bear fruit as his side thrashed the weak Mexicans 6-0. Poland faced Mexico in the next Group 2 game and, not before time, brought the mercurial Boniek back into their side. This had an immediate effect on the Poles' play and he scored two of their three goals as Poland cruised into the second-round group with a 3-1 victory. The concluding game in the group provided one of the biggest surprises of the tournament as West Germany struggled to hold the Tunisian team. The Tunisian midfield general Dhiab completely outclassed his West German counterparts and Tunisia never looked to be in danger of losing the game. West Germany were fortunate to hold out for a scoreless draw and, finishing second in the group, qualified for the next round of the competition.

Group 1, in the meantime, had begun with the sort of violent game that has earned the World Cup many rebukes over the years. The protagonists were Argentina and Hungary, and the intimidatory effect of the hugely partisan home crowd soon manifested itself upon the unfortunate referee. The game began promisingly enough, and without excessive unpleasantness, as Csapo gave Hungary a 12th-minute lead which Luque equalized three minutes later. Then the match deteriorated into a violent shambles as the Argentinians handed out very rough treatment to the Hungarians who were quick to respond in kind. Argentina took the lead in the last quarter of an hour and Toroscik, the Hungarian centre-forward, who had taken a tremendous amount of stick from the Argentinian defence, at last retaliated against a Gallego foul and was sent off. Tibor Nyilasi, Toroscik's midfield link-man, was also subsequently dismissed whilst the brutal play of the Argentinian defenders went largely unpunished.

In the next game in the group France shocked the defensive Italians by scoring a goal in the first minute and, for once, the Italians were forced to attack. Paolo Rossi, at last included in the Italian side, equalized in the first half and Zaccarelli scored the winner after half-time. Before the competition began there had been pessimism, if not downright dismay, in the Italian camp and this victory raised morale immensely. Next, Argentina went on to meet France and that they won 2-1 was an absolute travesty of justice. France played well but, in the dying seconds of the first half, found themselves behind after Argentina, incredibly, had been awarded a penalty when a Frenchman had fallen on to the ball. Platini equalized in the 62nd minute but Luque scored the winner later in the second half with a long-range shot. In the 80th minute another appalling decision by the referee deprived France of a penalty when Didier Six was blatantly pulled down in the area and play was waved on. Clearly, the Argentinians were benefiting from the sort of weak refereeing which so strongly favoured the home side.

After their victory over France, Italy were at last beginning to believe in themselves and brushed aside with consummate ease a Hungarian team which lacked the attacking flair previously provided by Nyilasi and Toroscik (both suspended). Rossi again opened the scoring and further goals by Bettega and Bonetti gave Italy a 3-1 victory. So it was that Italy and Argentina met in the next game in the group, both already assured of places in the second round, but with Argentina seeking a win to top the group and remain in Buenos Aires. Thanks to some fine goalkeeping by Dino Zoff, Italy were able to hold on for a 0-0 score at half-time and, in the second half, Bettega put them ahead. This time Argentina suffered from poor refereeing and Italy held on to their lead to top their group with six points out of six. The final game in the group ended in a 3-1 win for France over Hungary, who thus finished bottom without a single point.

Group 3 began with a match between Austria and Spain. Austria proved quite a handful for Spain as goals by Schachner and Krankl gave them a 2-1 victory. There was much discord within the Brazilian camp for various reasons, prominent among which were the unenthusiastic adoption of manager Coutinho's methods which seemed at odds with all the best aspects of Brazilian football. Sweden clearly outplayed Brazil in their first game and deserved more than a 1-1 draw, although Brazil protested because referee Clive Thomas had blown for half-time just as they put the ball into the Swedish net. In their next game, Sweden faced Austria and, after going behind to a Krankl penalty in the first half, were unable to claw their way back into the game. The veteran

Rivelino had been voicing dissatisfaction with his manager, and so was omitted from the Brazil side to play Spain. This threw their midfield into disarray and they were very lucky to scrape a 0-0 draw. Cardenosa, the Spanish midfielder, should have won the game for his country in the second half, but he hesitated when presented with an open goal and let Brazil off the hook. Spain met Sweden in their last game in the group requiring a win to pressurize Brazil for the second qualifying place. In a tremendously tight game, Cardenosa atoned for his miss in the previous match with an inspired second-half performance and his team-mate Asensi scored the only goal. The last game in the group, between Brazil and Austria, was crucial for Coutinho the Brazilian manager who was under attack from all quarters. Austria's four points already assured their second-round participation but, with only two points, Brazil desperately needed a result. Again Brazil were lucky and, although they played without conviction or, frankly, much flair, the Austrian defender, Pezzey, misjudged a cross and allowed Roberto to score the only goal of the match.

Scotland were faced with Peru in the first game in Group 4, a game which they approached with confidence bordering on the suicidal. Ally MacLeod appeared genuinely to believe that he had a potential cup-winning side and his apparent euphoria was unaffected by stories in the world's press about discontent amongst the Scottish squad. Reports of heavy drinking, too, were ignored as he set out to select his 'cup-winning' side. Quite why he left out Graeme Souness, why he included at least two grossly off-form players, or why he forgot to make provision for the marking of Cubillas – one of the most outstanding players of the day – will never be known. Whatever the reasons, history will be the judge. Although the game began quite well for Scotland with Jordan scoring a 15th-minute goal, by half-time Peru were level. In the second half Cubillas moved into a higher gear and scored two superb goals to give Peru a 3-1 victory. Scotland's discomfort did not end there as Willie Johnston, their dynamic little left-winger, then failed a routine dope test. Packed off home, Johnston's career was in ruins. The spirit in the Scottish camp by this time was at an all-time low.

Holland had found no difficulty in disposing of Iran 3-0 thanks to a Rensenbrink hat-trick and, in their next match, the demoralized Scots themselves faced the Iranians. The Scottish performance that day could best be described as an embarrassment as Iran showed the disjointed and argumentative Scots how to play football. The final result was 1-1, with Scotland needing an Iranian own-goal to gain the point. Holland could only manage a 0-0 draw with Peru in their next game and confronted Scotland in their last match of the group.

By this time, Peru had already beaten Iran 4-1 and were assured of a second-round place, so the battle was between Scotland and the 1974 finalists Holland for the other place. At long last Souness was brought into the Scottish side and the Dutch, who were also very much at odds with themselves, soon found themselves in trouble. At half-time the score was 1-1 after a Dalglish goal and that tigerish competitor Archie Gemmill scored two more in the second half to give Scotland a 3-2 victory. Yet, for the second consecutive series, Scotland went out on goal difference, humbled by the lowly but raising their game against the favourites.

The second-round groups fell quite strangely insofar as Group A, based in Buenos Aires, was solely made up of European teams, Austria, Holland, Italy and West Germany, while Group B comprised the three South American countries, Argentina, Brazil and Peru plus Poland.

In Group A Holland began to find some form and turned on a devastating display against Austria. Brandts was brought into the Dutch defence and after only five minutes headed the first goal from a free kick. Rensenbrink excelled, too, scoring Holland's second goal from the penalty spot and making others for Rep and Van Der Kerkhof as Holland powered to a 5-1 win. Italy met West Germany in their first Group A game and this time it was the Germans who put on a defensive display. Playing with virtually a ten-man defence, they hoped for and very nearly achieved a breakaway goal in the first half but were brilliantly denied by Zoff the Italian keeper. Although Italy twice came very close to scoring, West Germany held on for an undeserved 0-0 draw – a result which neither country wanted. Italy then met Austria and, with goal difference so important, went all out for a high score, mindful of Austria's hammering by Holland. They began well and after 15 minutes were in the lead through a superb Rossi goal but then, as so often before, were found wanting in stamina. Austria crept back into the game and by the second half were effectively in control and looked capable of winning. Fouled and obstructed whenever they attacked, Austria looked unlucky to be denied two well-justified penalty appeals and, losing 1-0, saw their chances of progress to the Final disappear.

In a rerun of the 1974 Final, Holland then faced West Germany in a game which proved to be one of the outstanding matches of the tournament. West Germany took an early lead through Abramczik but Haan equalized midway through the half with a thunderous 35-yard drive. After 70 minutes the Germans regained the lead and Holland threw everything into the attack which finally paid off in the 83rd minute when Van Der Kerkhof scored the equalizer. The 2-2 final score was a fair reflection of the play and the quality of football. Austria met West Germany in their last game and, with nothing to lose after their previous two results, the Austrians stormed back in the second half after going behind to a first-half Rummenigge goal. Vogts conceded an own-goal and Krankl scored twice to enable Austria to chalk up a 3-2 victory over their old rivals. In the last game in the group Holland met Italy in an ill-tempered game that decided which of the two progressed to the Final. Brandts made World Cup history by scoring for both sides, conceding an own goal in the first half and equalizing for Holland after the interval in a game which Holland, despite this setback, seemed to control throughout. Later in the second half, as Italy defended in depth, Haan broke the deadlock with a superb goal which earned Holland their second successive Final place.

Group B began in Rosario with Argentina against Poland, and the hosts still did not impress. Neither for that matter did Poland, whose defence, particularly their goalkeeper Tomaszewski, was at fault when Mario Kempes headed Argentina into a first-half lead. Kempes scored again in the 73rd minute and, with a final score of 2-0, Argentina had made the start which they needed. Brazil easily accounted for Peru in their first Group B game with two cracking long-range goals by Dirceu and a penalty by Zico, and their next tie against Argentina thus became of crucial importance. Luque returned to the Argentinian team but, still nursing a shoulder injury, did not play with much conviction. Brazil were very roughly treated from the start as the Hungarian referee failed to gain control of the game, which steadily deteriorated. Doubtless both sides were too well aware of the consequences of defeat, and with this almost paranoid approach it was inevitable that it would result in a colourless 0-0 draw.

Poland's faint hopes of reaching the Final were revived when they beat Peru 1-0 thanks to a second-half Szarmach goal and they faced Brazil in their last Group B game. Brazil took the lead via an extraordinarily good free kick by their right-back Nelinho, but Poland equalized through Lato just before half-time, having missed numerous earlier chances. In the second half Brazil raised their game and took complete control. Playing their best football of the series, Brazil besieged the Polish goal and were rewarded by two Roberto goals. So it was that Argentina went into their last game in the group knowing precisely what they needed to do to qualify for the Final – win by four clear goals! That they won by six goals to nil says less of the Argentinian performance than it does of the Peruvians' abject surrender. Little wonder that, shamed by their inept performance, Quiroga, their goalkeeper, published an open letter defending his team's efforts – an unsolicited denial of bribery! Recent evidence shows that Peru were bought off by the Argentine regime desperate to gain domestic popularity by securing a World Cup triumph. Such was Argentina's shabby progress to their first Final since 1930. Before the Final itself, of course, we had the third-place play-off. In a game which was less drab than most previous third-place ties, Italy took a first-half lead through Causio but Brazil came back after half-time and won 2-1.

Back in 1974, Holland (admittedly fielding Cruyff) had trounced Argentina 4-0, but in the Buenos Aires stadium before a fanatical capacity crowd, were aware of the problems which they faced. As in the 1930 Final, Argentina attempted to use gamesmanship to spoil Holland's chances: first they took the field late, then they complained about a bandage worn by Van Der Kerkhof. This incensed the Dutch who, from the kick-off, embarked upon a campaign of hard, if not downright violent, tackling. The referee, Mr. Gonella, appeared to be intimidated into unfair decisions by the threatening, partisan crowd and gave over 50 free kicks against Holland, many unjustified. Both defences seemed particularly shaky throughout the first half. In the 38th minute Kempes, the most dangerous forward on the field, gave Argentina the lead with a resounding left-foot shot, and just on half-time Fillol, the Argentinian goalkeeper, made a superb save from Rensenbrink. Early in the second half Fillol again saved brilliantly (this time from Neeskens) and, a quarter of an hour later, the tall Dutch substitute Nanninga was brought on in place of Rep. Smarting at some particularly bad refereeing decisions, Holland reorganized their attack and concentrating on the high ball were rewarded with a headed equalizer from Nanninga. In the final minute of the game Rensenbrink broke through the Argentinian defence and shot against the post with the keeper beaten. Thus extra-time was required and Menotti somehow raised the spirits of his weary Argentinian team who came back strongly into the match. Kempes put Argentina ahead again after 14 minutes and the Dutch threw men forward in search of an equalizer. Inevitably, five minutes from the end of extra-time, Argentina were able to exploit the gaps that this created and Bertoni sealed the victory by scoring a third goal in a thrilling climax to a somewhat uninspired match. With the final whistle the crowd erupted into ecstatic celebrations which went on throughout the night – a happy end to an ill-tempered and dreary series.

GROUP 1

	P	W	D	L	F	A	Pts
Italy	3	3	0	0	6	2	6
Argentina	3	2	0	1	4	3	4
France	3	1	0	2	5	5	2
Hungary	3	0	0	3	3	8	0

GROUP 2

	P	W	D	L	F	A	Pts
Poland	3	2	1	0	4	1	5
West Germany	3	1	2	0	6	0	4
Tunisia	3	1	1	1	3	2	3
Mexico	3	0	0	3	2	12	0

GROUP 3

	P	W	D	L	F	A	Pts
Austria	3	2	0	1	3	2	4
Brazil	3	1	2	0	2	1	4
Spain	3	1	1	1	2	2	3
Sweden	3	0	1	2	1	3	1

GROUP 4

	P	W	D	L	F	A	Pts
Peru	3	2	1	0	7	2	5
Holland	3	1	1	1	5	3	3
Scotland	3	1	1	1	5	6	3
Iran	3	0	1	2	2	8	1

QUARTER-FINALS GROUP A

	P	W	D	L	F	A	Pts
Holland	3	2	1	0	9	4	5
Italy	3	1	1	1	2	2	3
West Germany	3	0	2	1	4	5	2
Austria	3	1	0	2	4	8	2

QUARTER-FINALS GROUP B

	P	W	D	L	F	A	Pts
Argentina	3	2	1	0	8	0	5
Brazil	3	2	1	0	6	1	5
Poland	3	1	0	2	3	6	2
Peru	3	0	0	3	0	10	0

THIRD-PLACE MATCH

Brazil .... 2 Italy 0

FINAL

(After extra time)

Argentina .... (1) (1) **3** **Holland** .... (0) (1) **1**

Scorers: Kempes 2, Bertoni *Scorers: Nanninga*

Team: Fillol, Olguin, Galvan, Passarella, Taratini, Ardiles (sub. Larossa), Gallego, Kempes, Bertoni, Luque, Ortiz (sub. Houseman)

Team: Jongbloed, Krol, Poortvliet, Brandts, Jansen (sub. Suurbier), Van Der Kerkhof (W), Neeskens, Rensenbrink, Van Der Kerkhof (R)

93

TWELFTH WORLD CUP

Spain 1982

THERE WERE few objections to the selection of Spain as a venue for the 1982 series (the start of which coincided with the end of the Falklands War) but the size of the entry and the cumbersome method of groupings did cause organizational problems. Pandering to the increasing voice of Third World countries, FIFA increased the number of entrants by 50 per cent (24) necessitating a total of 52 games (14 more than in 1978). The ludicrous system of retaining second-round groups was maintained and this probably had a greater effect upon the general standard of the football than in either of the two preceding tournaments, as countries were more often content to play out draws. The competition was divided into six first-round groups of four countries, the top two of which progressed to four second-round groups of three countries. A knock-out basis then applied as each group winner went into a semi-final tie with the winners going through to the Final and the losers to the third place match.

The Home Countries were well represented as England, Scotland and Northern Ireland all qualified for the Finals. Scotland and Northern Ireland, in the same qualifying group, overcame Portugal, Sweden and Israel en route and England, somewhat fortunately, got through despite suffering defeats by Rumania, Norway and Switzerland. Wales, too, would have qualified had they not, unaccountably, failed to beat Iceland at home. Holland were also absent from the Finals, marking the end of the great series of Dutch sides of the 1970s.

In addition to the Home Countries, Europe was represented by the hosts, Spain, and Austria, Belgium, Czechoslovakia, France, Hungary, Italy, Poland, USSR, West Germany and Yugoslavia. South America was represented by Argentina, the holders, plus Brazil, Chile and Peru, and from Central and North America came El Salvador and Honduras. Algeria and Cameroon were Africa's representatives, while Kuwait and New Zealand (who played 15 qualifying games and travelled over 50,000 miles to do so) completed the truly world-wide entry to this World Cup. The countries were grouped as follows:

Group 1:   Cameroon, Italy, Peru and Poland.

Group 2:   Algeria, Austria, Chile and West Germany.

Group 3:   Argentina, Belgium, El Salvador and Hungary.

Group 4:   Czechoslovakia, England, France and Kuwait.

Group 5:   Honduras, Northern Ireland, Spain and Yugoslavia.

Group 6:   Brazil, New Zealand, Scotland and USSR.

The first game in Group 3 (before a 95,000 crowd in Barcelona) brought together the holders, Argentina, and the beaten finalists in the 1980 European Championship, Belgium. After a goalless first half in which Belgium effectively blunted the twin attacking threat of Maradona (the new hope of Argentina) and Kempes (the 1978 Final hero), the game looked set to continue the well-established trend in opening matches of 0-0 draws. However, Belgium had other ideas and, in the 62nd minute, Vandenbergh scored from a Vercauteren cross to put them in the lead. Argentina tried to come back but, in a game punctuated by numerous unnecessary free kicks, quickly ran out of ideas and became only the second defending champions to lose their opening game. The next game in the group cruelly emphasised the difference in class between the emerging soccer nations and the traditionally stronger countries, as Hungary literally took El Salvador apart. In the third minute Nyilasi headed Hungary's first goal and, thereafter, the avalanche began. At half-time the score was 3-0 and in the second half eight more goals were scored (one by El Salvador) as Hungary chalked up the highest World Cup score to date.

Hungary then faced Argentina and were brought down to earth with a thud. Maradona turned on a simply dazzling performance and lifted Argentina with goals in the 29th and 57th minutes, after Bertoni had put them ahead in the 27th minute. Ardiles (after several successful seasons with Spurs) scored a fourth as the Argentinian hopes of retaining the cup were resurrected, although Hungary themselves squeezed an undeserved 76th-minute reply.

Belgium, having begun so well, struggled against El Salvador in the next Group 3 game. El Salvador were determined not to concede another bagful of goals and packed their defence throughout the game; Coeck scored the only goal in the first half to give Belgium victory. Thus Belgium proceeded to play Hungary with four points under their belts but aware that defeat could still prevent their progression to the second round. At half-time Hungary were 1-0 up but, unspectacularly, Belgium ground their way back into the game and earned a 1-1 draw to ensure a second-round place. So it was that

Argentina began their last game in the group against El Salvador knowing that only a victory would send them through. Although they struggled against a packed defence they still managed to win 2-0, and so on they went into the second round.

Meanwhile in Group 1 Italy began with a rather lifeless 0-0 draw against Poland. The following day Peru were shocked to discover that the African 'no-hopers' Cameroon could actually play football and had a lucky escape in the 34th minute when the Cameroon striker, Milla, had a seemingly good goal disallowed for off-side. This game, too, petered out into another goalless draw, although the spirit displayed by the Africans made it an enjoyable one. Peru were unfortunate not to win their next game against Italy who, despite taking an 18th-minute lead through Bruno Conti, played without conviction or discipline. Diaz equalized in the 83rd minute and then Peru had a penalty appeal turned down when Oblitas was clearly tripped by Gentile. Bad luck indeed.

Poland had a narrow squeak against Cameroon in their next game which ended in yet another 0-0 draw. If the Cameroonian forwards had been able to shoot straight they would have been able to exploit the openings created by their enthusiastic and skilful approach work.

With four out of six games completed, only two goals had been scored and, in entertainment terms, Group 1 was becoming little more than a bad joke. Thankfully, Poland put an end to this deadlock in their game against Peru when, although the half-time score was 0-0, they found the net with a vengeance after the break. Smolarek opened the scoring ten minutes into the second half and, in the next 20 minutes, Poland scored four more goals to finish worthy 5-1 winners. The last game in the group brought together a nervous Italy against the bubbling Cameroons. Italy strove to score a goal and when at last a 60th-minute Graziani header put them ahead, to their dismay M'Bidi immediately equalized. With a 1-1 final score Italy were through to the next round only because they had scored a single goal more than Cameroon. Few people guessed what Italy would go on to achieve from these inauspicious beginnings.

Group 2 began with the biggest surprise of the tournament as Algeria beat West Germany 2-1. This result was no mere fluke as it was West Germany's second successive defeat by Algeria! Madjer scored the first goal in the 52nd minute, and when Rummenigge equalized after a further 15 minutes West Germany relaxed, allowing Belloumi to score the winner only a minute later.

In their first game, Chile were beaten 1-0 by an Austrian side ably marshalled by Prohaska in midfield, and were then faced by a determined West German side smarting from their defeat by Algeria. The wily Rummenigge gave West Germany the lead after ten minutes and went on to notch a hat trick in the second half as the Germans ran out worthy 4-1 winners.

Algeria, playing Austria in their next game, looked set to inflict on them the same sort of embarrassment as West Germany had suffered. There was no score at half-time and the Austrians were looking anything but happy. In the second half a change of tactics by the Austrian manager Schmidt quickly paid dividends and Austria were relieved to emerge 2-0 victors. Algeria learned a lesson from this encounter and in their next match with Chile threw everything into the attack. Chasing and running like men possessed they took a 3-0 half-time lead and, although inevitably they ran out of steam in the second half, they managed to hold on for a 3-2 victory.

This left Austria and West Germany knowing precisely what they needed to do in their last game to qualify for the next round. West Germany needed a win and Austria could afford a three-goal defeat, so the die was cast for a less than gripping performance. In the event the game proved to be a complete fiasco as West Germany took an early lead and then, as if by prior agreement, these traditionally stern rivals seemed bent upon maintaining the score at that. The result was 1-0, so that both Austria and West Germany qualified for the second round, but the whole episode smacked of collusion and left a very bad taste in the mouth.

In Group 4 England opened their campaign against France in the most dramatic style, when Bryan Robson scored the fastest goal in the history of the World Cup after 27 seconds. The French were caught totally unawares as Mariner's cross was smashed into the net by Robson, but they battled back into the game and equalized through Soler in the 25th minute. In the second half France's push for victory was halted in its tracks by the determined English defence, and then Robson headed a second goal in the 66th minute. Eight minutes from the end Mariner scored a third after Francis's shot had bounced off full-back Tresor's legs. England had begun their campaign in style.

After being shocked by Kuwait who deservedly held them to a 1-1 draw, Czechoslovakia lined up against England in Bilbao. At half-time the score was 0-0, but England were in complete control and with luck and better finishing could have been three or four goals up. It seemed inevitable that the constant England pressure would bear dividends and, sure enough. in the 63rd minute Trevor Francis scored from a Wilkins cross. Three minutes later Barmos deflected a Mariner cross into the Czech net and the game was all over 'bar the shouting' as England cantered to a comfortable win. The match between France and Kuwait as expected emphasized France's superiority but it is best remembered for its non-footballing aspects. Genghini gave France the lead with a superb free kick in the 31st minute and Platini scored another just before halftime. Six added a third three minutes into the second half and the Kuwait players began to lose control of themselves. The Russian referee, Stupar, had an awful game making mistake after mistake and in the 69th minute inexplicably disallowed a seemingly perfect French goal by Bossis. Kuwait scored in the 74th minute and, shortly afterwards, the fireworks began as Giresse left the Kuwait defence standing and scored a fine goal. The Kuwaitis claimed that they had stopped because someone in the crowd had blown a whistle, and the game was thrown into turmoil. After several minutes of protest, they started to leave the field and the berobed Prince Fahid went to the touchline to make them return. The ludicrous result of this extraordinary display of indiscipline was that the referee reversed his decision and disallowed the goal! Fittingly, the French scored another goal to bring the farce to a conclusion; but, after struggling to earn a 1-1 draw against Czechoslovakia in their next game, France looked to England to beat Kuwait to ensure their survival in the competition. Against Kuwait, England played dismally but scraped a 1-0 victory to progress, unbeaten, to the next round. Had the referee and linesmen not been anxious to avoid a repetition of Kuwait's histrionics against France, they might have applied the offside rule correctly, in which case England would have won by at least three goals more!

The hosts, Spain, opened Group 5 against the apparent no-hopers Honduras. To everyone's surprise, Honduras took the lead in the seventh minute and held on until midway through the second half when Ufarte equalized from the penalty spot. The game ended in a 1-1 draw, hugely disappointing for the home crowd but a fair reflection on play. Yugoslavia had to be content with a goalless draw against the admirable Northern Ireland team fielding 17-year-old Norman Whiteside, and then met Spain in their next game. Once again Spain went behind early, after only ten minutes, but this time equalized just four minutes later. Saura scored the winner for Spain in the second half and the hosts seemed set fair for the next round. Honduras showed their mettle in their next game after Northern Ireland had taken an early lead through Gerry Armstrong and threatened to take them apart. They held on, restricting the Irish to the one goal, and managed an equalizer in the 60th minute. The score remained 1-1. When Honduras lost 1-0 to Yugoslavia in their next game, Northern Ireland were really up against it, requiring at least a 1-1 draw against Spain in the last Group 5 game. In the sweltering Luis Casanova stadium in Valencia, Northern Ireland played perhaps their most outstanding World Cup game ever. They overcame all the odds – a weak referee; the heat; the hostile crowd; the cynical Spanish tackling – to hold on to a 0-0 half time score. Gerry Armstrong put them ahead two minutes into the second half but, 12 minutes later, they were staring disaster in the face when Mal Donaghy was sent off for a seemingly innocuous shove. However, the Irish (with Jennings outstanding) showed their determination by refusing to relinquish their lead and so qualified for the next round top of the group. Spain themselves squeezed through because they had scored more goals than Yugoslavia.

In the strong Group 6 Scotland soon saw what they were up against in the opening tie between Brazil and the USSR. In a free-flowing game both sides showed what formidable opponents they were. Russia took a first-half lead but Brazil stormed back late in the second half to win 2-1. Scotland began against New Zealand at a gallop with Kenny Dalglish scoring after 18 minutes and John Wark adding two more within the next quarter of an hour. However, the Scots' tendency to stumble against lowly opposition was revealed yet again as New Zealand fought back to 3-2 by the 65th minute and threatened to equalize. Scotland managed to pull themselves together and scored two further goals to win 5-2, and braced themselves for their next game – against Brazil. For the first half-hour Scotland showed that they were not overawed by playing with discipline and determination, and even snatched an 18th-minute lead through David Narey. Brazil's Zico equalized 15 minutes later and, try as they may, Scotland were then unable to contain the bubbling brilliance of the South Americans. The teams went in level at half-time but in the second half Brazil moved into overdrive and comfortably won 4-1.

With ruthless efficiency the USSR crushed New Zealand 3-0 and faced Scotland in their last Group 6 game. Once again the Scots started well, taking a first-half lead through Jordan, but in the second half were unable to maintain their momentum. Russia equalized through Chivadze and went ahead through Shengalia after a ridiculous mix-up between Hansen and Miller had given him a clear run. Although Graeme Souness scored an equalizer, the USSR never looked seriously in danger of losing the game, and Scotland as usual failed to progress beyond the first round. Finally, to wrap up Group 6, there was something of an exhibition game as Brazil turned on their skills with an untroubled 4-0 victory over New Zealand.

The second-round qualifiers were grouped as follows:

Group A: Belgium, Poland and the USSR.

Group B: England, Spain and West Germany.

Group C: Argentina, Brazil and Italy.

Group D: Austria, France and Northern Ireland.

Group A began with Zbigniew Boniek, Poland's Juventus-bound forward, scoring a hat trick against Belgium who were unable to offer any reply whatsoever. Playing Russia in their next game, Belgium reorganized their defence and held on stubbornly until, early in the second half, Oganesian scored the only goal of the match. The last game in the group brought the USSR against Poland who packed their defence in the first half before themselves going onto the offensive in the second. In the event, the final 0-0 stalemate was a just reflection on the performances of the two sides, but it ensured that Poland progressed to the semi-finals.

England met West Germany in the first Group B game and, prompted by winger Steve Coppell, seemed to have the edge over them. Striker Paul Mariner, however, was easily contained by West Germany's robust defence and the game moved inexorably towards a goalless draw as the heat rose, a fair result to a frustrating, cautious match. Spain were thus firmly in the driving seat in the group as they met West Germany in the next tie before 90,000 vociferous fans in Real Madrid's Bernabeu stadium. The Spanish midfield lacked mutual understanding and seemed incapable of supplying the necessary passes to their eager forwards, and neither side had found the net at half-time. For the first time in the series, West Germany turned on a coherent, controlled display and, with a quarter of an hour to go, were 2-0 up. Although Zamora, Spain's most outstanding player, scored in the 81st minute, the hosts had insufficient time to equalize. In the final game in the group, England met Spain requiring at least a 2-0 victory to progress to the last four. England pressed throughout the game but created few clear-cut chances and had a number of lucky escapes as the emphasis was placed on attack. As England faltered up front, Brooking and Keegan, who had been sidelined by injury, were brought on for their first appearances in the World Cup finals. Twenty minutes from the end Keegan, unbelievably, headed over an open goal and England were out of the competition.

In the first game in Group C there were fears that Italy and Argentina would clash violently (as they had in so many previous encounters) and these fears proved to be justified. Maradona was kicked out of the game and a whole string of players were booked in a torrid first half. Italy took the lead in the second half and ended worthy, but undistinguished, 2-1 victors. Brazil's spectacular challenge for the title was maintained as they took an early lead against Argentina through Zico, and then gained control of the game. Serginho and Junior added further goals in the second half and Maradona was sent off in the closing minutes when he was provoked into losing his temper. Diaz scored a late goal for Argentina but the 3-1 defeat effectively ended their challenge. Brazil were the firm favourites to beat Italy in their last game but the Italians (Paolo Rossi especially) were of a different mind. Rossi, who had recently been rehabilitated into the Italian side after a two-year exile following a bribery scandal, suddenly found his touch and scored a brilliant hat trick. Although they twice fought back to equalize, Brazil were unable to do so for the third time and Italy progressed to the last four after a really gripping battle.

In Group D France clearly demonstrated their superiority against Austria when they beat them 1-0 in the first game. The Austrians were lucky to hold on to the single-goal margin and could not have complained if the score had been 5-0. The doughty fighters of Northern Ireland held Austria to a 2-2 draw in the next game and met France requiring a victory to progress to the last four. The searing temperatures in Madrid's Calderon stadium left the Irish struggling and Platini, fit again after injury, directed a steady flow of French attacks on the wilting Irishmen. By the 70th minute France were 3-0 up, but an Armstrong goal in the 74th minute was not enough to revive the Irish who went out 4-1, so ending their wonderfully brave challenge.

In the semi-finals, Italy faced Poland in Barcelona while West Germany met France in Seville. Italy almost took the lead in the first minute against an understrength Polish side. Boniek, Poland's key attacker, was suspended and his absence proved to be the decisive factor as his country struggled to stay in the game. Rossi, again coming good for Italy, scored twice, one in each half, and Poland were unable to fight back.

The encounter between France and West Germany in the other semi-final must rank as the most thrilling match of the 1982 series. In an incident-packed game, West Germany took a 17th-minute lead through the lively Littbarski but Platini equalized from the penalty spot in the 27th minute. Platini in particular was in fine form and the skillful French midfield players were especially impressive. In the 66th minute, the German goalkeeper Schumacher earned himself everlasting notoriety for one of the most dreadful fouls (in both intent and consequence) that the World Cup has ever seen. Battiston, the French substitute, ran unmarked onto a superb Platini pass and, with only the advancing Schumacher to beat, slipped the ball past him before being hammered to the ground by the German goalkeeper. It was immediately apparent that the Frenchman was seriously injured as he lay on the ground unconcious but it was fully three minutes before he was stretchered away to hospital. How Schumacher escaped dismissal for this grotesque assault is beyond comprehension but there can be no doubt that this incident ultimately won West Germany the game. With a 1-1 scoreline at 90 minutes, the game went into extra-time and goals by Tresor and Giresse appeared to have made it safe for France. West Germany, however, brought on the half-fit, but nevertheless fresh, Rummenigge after Tresor had scored and his influence brought his country back into the game. By the end of extra-time West Germany were level and, in the first-ever World Cup penalty shootout, they went on to reach the Final by winning 5-4 on penalties.

The third-place play-off brought together France and Poland and provided a superb curtain-raiser to the Final. France continued to play the same accomplished brand of entertaining football which they had provided in the semi-final and, with Boniek and Szarmach back for Poland, the stage was set for an excellent game. The French threw away an early lead when they conceded two goals just before half-time and a third within two minutes of the restart but they refused to give up. In the 73rd minute Couriol scored for France and they went all out for an equalizer but, try as they might, they could not score again and had to be content with fourth place.

The Final began very badly for Italy when, in the seventh minute, Graziani was injured after colliding with Stielike and Altobelli came on as substitute. Nor did their luck improve when, in the 24th minute, Cabrini became the first player to miss a penalty kick in a World Cup Final. Rossi, however, once again proved to be a match-winner when he scored the first goal of the game after 56 minutes and this gave Italy the impetus which they needed. The West Germans began to cut up rough but this did not prevent Italy from going further ahead through Tardelli (in the 68th minute) and Altobelli (in the 80th minute). West Germany pulled a goal back in the 82nd minute through Breitner but could not fight their way back into the game. And so Italy became the first European country to win the World Cup three times, and this after failing to beat Cameroon in the group matches!

GROUP 1

	P	W	D	L	F	A	Pts
Poland	3	1	2	0	5	1	4
Italy	3	0	3	0	2	2	3
Cameroon	3	0	3	0	1	1	3
Peru	3	0	2	1	2	6	2

GROUP 2

	P	W	D	L	F	A	Pts
West Germany	3	2	0	1	6	3	4
Austria	3	2	0	1	3	1	4
Algeria	3	2	0	1	5	5	4
Chile	3	0	0	3	3	8	0

GROUP 3

	P	W	D	L	F	A	Pts
Belgium	3	2	1	0	3	1	5
Argentina	3	2	0	1	6	2	4
Hungary	3	1	1	1	12	6	3
El Salvador	3	0	0	3	1	13	0

GROUP 4

	P	W	D	L	F	A	Pts
England	3	0	0	6	1	6
France	3	1	1	1	6	5	3
Czechoslovakia	3	0	2	1	2	4	2
Kuwait	3	0	1	2	2	6	1

GROUP 5

	P	W	D	L	F	A	Pts
Northern Ireland	3	1	2	0	2	1	4
Spain	3	1	1	1	3	3	3
Yugoslavia	3	1	1	1	2	2	3
Honduras	3	0	2	1	2	3	2

GROUP 6

	P	W	D	L	F	A	Pts
Brazil	3	3	0	0	10	2	6
USSR	3	1	1	1	6	4	3
Scotland	3	1	1	1	8	8	3
New Zealand	3	0	0	3	2	12	0

GROUP A

	P	W	D	L	F	A	Pts
Poland	2	1	1	0	3	0	3
USSR	2	1	1	0	1	0	3
Belgium	2	0	0	2	0	4	0

GROUP B

	P	W	D	L	F	A	Pts
West Germany	2	1	1	0	2	1	3
England	2	0	2	0	0	0	2
Spain	2	0	1	1	1	2	1

GROUP C

	P	W	D	L	F	A	Pts
Italy	2	2	0	0	5	3	4
Brazil	2	1	0	1	5	4	2
Argentina	2	0	0	2	2	5	0

GROUP D

	P	W	D	L	F	A	Pts
France	2	2	0	0	5	1	4
Austria	2	0	1	1	2	3	1
Northern Ireland	2	0	1	1	3	6	1

SEMI-FINALS

(In Barcelona)
Italy .... 2 Poland 0
(In Seville)
West Germany .... 3 France 3
West Germany won 5-4 on penalties

THIRD-PLACE MATCH

(In Alicante)
Poland .... 3 France 2

FINAL

Italy .... (0) **3**   **West Germany** .... (0) **1**

Scorers: Rossi, Tardelli, Altobelli   *Scorer: Breitner*

Team: Zoff, Bergomi, Cabrini, Collavati, Scirea, Gentile, Oriali, Tardelli, Conti, Graziani (sub. Altobelli (sub. Causio)), Rossi

Team: Schumacher, Kaltz, Forster (K.H.), Stielike, Forster (B), Breitner, Dremmler (sub. Hrubesch), Briegel, Rummenigge (sub. Muller), Fischer

THIRTEENTH WORLD CUP

Mexico 1986

ALTHOUGH Colombia was the original choice of venue for the 13th World Cup, they could not raise the finance required and FIFA selected Mexico as an alternative. Severe earthquakes shook the area in 1985, but the stadiums were not affected and the possible substitute venues, Brazil, Canada and the USA were not required. Much to the dismay of many players, Mexico thus became the first country to host the World Cup twice. As in 1970, the kick-off times were arranged to coincide with peak TV viewing hours throughout the world and most games were played in extremely high temperatures.

The organization of the tournament reverted to a straight knock-out basis after the first round with the top two from each of the six first-round groups of four progressing to the second round, together with the best third-placed teams. In the event of there being a stalemate at the end of any of the knock-out games, provision was made for extra-time, followed by a penalty shoot-out as necessary.

The Home Countries were well represented as England, Scotland and Northern Ireland all qualified, as they had in 1982. England had done so in real style, winning four and drawing four of their eight games, hammering in 21 goals and conceding only two in the process. Northern Ireland were in the same qualifying group as England and earned their place by holding out for a 0-0 draw at Wembley in their last game. Scotland controversially eliminated Wales before beating Australia in a two-legged play-off for their place. Jock Stein, the Scottish manager, who was taken ill during the nail-biting game with Wales, died shortly after the final whistle, and was replaced temporarily by Alex Ferguson, boss of the highly successful Aberdeen club.

South America was represented by Argentina, Brazil, Paraguay and Uruguay and Europe by the holders, Italy, along with Belgium, Bulgaria, Denmark, England, France, Hungary, Northern Ireland, Poland, Portugal, Scotland, Spain, USSR and West Germany. The other participants were the hosts Mexico, Algeria, Canada, Iraq, Morocco and South Korea. The first-round groupings were:

Group A: Argentina, Bulgaria, Italy and South Korea.

Group B: Belgium, Iraq, Mexico and Paraguay.

Group C: Canada, France, Hungary and the USSR.

Group D: Algeria, Brazil, Northern Ireland and Spain.

Group E: Denmark, Scotland, Uruguay and West Germany.

Group F: England, Morocco, Poland and Portugal.

The competition began on 31 May 1986 in the Azteca stadium in Mexico City when the champions, Italy, met Bulgaria in the first Group A game. The opening ceremony was colourful and impressive but the manner in which the crowd drowned their President's opening address with jeers and whistles was clear proof of the Mexicans' views of their rulers. The game itself was probably the best opener for quite a number of years as Italy, who had taken the lead just before half-time through Altobelli, struggled to convert their ascendancy into further goals. Italy squandered several good chances and, with a header which Sirakov glanced past Galli (replacing the now-retired Dino Zoff in goal), Bulgaria equalized six minutes from the end.

The next game in the group enabled the Argentinians in general and Maradona in particular to display what they were capable of as they met South Korea. This Korean team was of a very different calibre (and physical size) to the one which was thrashed so soundly in 1954 and Argentina were subjected to rugged tackling by the fit and mobile Asians. Despite this, Maradona, technically and temperamentally a more mature player than in 1982, created the openings and Valdano (2) and Ruggeri scored to give Argentina a 3-1 victory.

Italy were Argentina's next opponents and Altobelli gave them an early lead with a sixth-minute penalty. The Argentinians protested loud and long but then fought their way back into the game with Maradona equalizing in the 33rd minute. In the second half both sides ran out of steam as the game degenerated into an ill-tempered kicking match and, with a 1-1 final score, Italy were left to ponder the prospect of beating South Korea in their last match in the group. The Koreans, in the meantime, earned their first World Cup point, fighting back to achieve a 1-1 draw against Bulgaria. So it was with some trepidation that Italy, still haunted by the spectre of North Korea in 1966, faced South Korea requiring a win to make the second round. Altobelli put Italy into the lead in the 18th minute but then missed a penalty in the 36th minute. Choi equalized in the first minute of the second half and the Italians became anxious until Altobelli scored a second in the 73rd minute with De Napoli adding a third three minutes from time. In the dying seconds South Korea scored again but Italy held on to their lead to qualify for the second round. Argentina, already assured of a second-round place, had little difficulty in beating Bulgaria 2-0 in the last game and so topped Group A with five points, while Bulgaria, too, had done enough to make the second round as one of the better third-placed teams.

Group B began at the Azteca stadium, with the hosts (once again hailed by the Mexican press as potential winners) against Belgium. Mexico opened the scoring and then went into a two-goal lead when the classy Hugo Sanchez scored their second in the 38th minute, although Belgium pulled one back right on half-time. Spurred on by the huge partisan crowd, Mexico pressed for further goals in the second half but, at the final whistle, the score remained 2-1. Paraguay, fielding the much-vaunted South American 'Footballer of the Year', Julio Romero, struggled to overcome the spirited Iraqis who began the match with enthusiasm and drive. The game itself was a scrappy affair and the deadlock was broken in the 35th minute when Romero scored for Paraguay. Amaiesh had the ball in the net for Iraq on the stroke of half-time but this was disallowed because, although the players had not heard it, the half-time whistle had already been blown. In the second half Paraguay should have added more goals, but the score remained 1-0.

Mexico took on Paraguay in the next match and went into a very early lead through Flores. The game then settled down into a quite dreary affair before a lively final few minutes. Paraguay equalized through Romero five minutes from the end and then Mexico won a penalty just two minutes from time. To the dismay of the 110,000 crowd, Sanchez's well-struck shot was turned onto the post by the keeper and the score remained 1-1. Iraq were unfortunate to lose 2-1 to Belgium in their next game and were therefore virtually certain of elimination before they met Mexico in their final match. Mexico had numerous chances to open the scoring and at last did so eight minutes into the second half with a fine goal from Quirarte. Thereafter Iraq came back strongly but, once more, lacked fire-power up front and, with the scoreline remaining 1-0, went out of the tournament without a point. Mexico topped the group with Paraguay second, and Belgium, too, squeezed through in third place.

Group C started with Canada facing France in their first game in any World Cup finals, and they came very close to achieving a major upset. The Canadians defended extremely well and, although the French missed a number of opportunities to score, were still in the game with a quarter of an hour to play. The European champions were becoming disconcerted until Papin, who had missed several goalscoring chances, scored the only goal of the match in the 78th minute. The next game provided one of the biggest surprises of the series as the mightily-impressive Russians gave Hungary a severe beating. Yakovenko scored in the second minute and Aleinikov a minute later as Hungary, renowned for thrashing other countries in the World Cup, themselves faced a hiding. Their manager's response was to gamble on attack by substituting an attacking midfielder for a defender but this merely served to help Russia score four more times (without reply) despite missing a penalty.

It was with some trepidation that France met the USSR in the next game in Group C but they provided a sterner test and, at half-time, the score was still 0-0. Vasily Rats opened the scoring for Russia in the 53rd mintute with one of the best goals of the series – a 30-yard drive – but Fernandez equalized eight minutes later. Despite prolonged pressure by France, the score remained 1-1 as both sides moved towards the second round. Hungary had little difficulty in beating Canada 2-0 in their next game but were easily defeated 3-0 by France in their last game in the group. Finally, USSR met Canada already assured of a secondround place and won 2-0. Canada thus ended the series without a point or a goal (but by no means disgraced) and Russia topped the group to qualify with France for the second round.

Spain were considerably disadvantaged when they met Brazil in the first game in Group D because a number of their players were incapacitated by illness. Nevertheless, the sides were pretty evenly matched and Spain were terribly unlucky not to be awarded a goal in the 52nd minute when a shot by Michel struck the underside of the bar, and then bounced down over the goal-line and out again. Nine minutes later luck deserted Spain once again, when Socrates scored the only goal of the game for Brazil despite being clearly offside. Northern Ireland's first match against Algeria was a hard, bad-tempered affair in which they failed to convert a number of chances after Norman Whiteside had scored from a free-kick in the fifth minute. In the second half Algeria equalized and were then content to play out a 1-1 draw as the Irish, wilting in the heat, dropped a vital point. Brazil, too, struggled against Algeria and in the end were quite satisfied to win 1-0, becoming the first country in the series to qualify for the second round.

Having lost to Northern Ireland in the 1982 World Cup, Spain were keen to exact revenge against them this time and took the lead through Butragueno after only one minute. Salinas scored a second after 18 minutes and, although Northern Ireland managed to pull a goal back just past half-time – after a farcical sliced clearance by Zubizarreta had been headed to Clarke – Spain deserved their 2-1 victory. Spain had few problems in beating Algeria 3-0 in their last game and thus ensured their qualification for the second round. Northern Ireland were outclassed in their last game against Brazil, who had already qualified, and despite a sterling performance by Pat Jennings (on his 41st birthday), they went down 3-0, so failing to reach the next stage.

The tough Group E was nicknamed 'the group of death' by the Mexican fans – with some justification. Denmark, in their first Finals, met Scotland in the first game and the Scots, playing with typical determination, were unlucky not to be in the lead at half-time. In the 57th minute the powerful Elkjaer scored the only goal of the game for Denmark, although the Scottish substitute, McAvennie, went close five minutes from time with a spectacular overhead kick.

West Germany played Uruguay in the next game in the group and quickly found themselves a goal down in the stifling heat. Uruguay then set about demonstrating that their method of play – a peculiar combination of skill and brutality – was a match for West Germany and so it proved until six minutes from the end when Klaus Allofs scored the equalizer. Uruguay had shown that they could not be underestimated but, in doing so, endeared themselves to no one. Scotland faced another daunting task against West Germany in the next Group E game. Gordon Strachan gave them a 17th-minute lead which they squandered, five minutes later, when Voller was allowed to score a simple equalizer. Allofs scored a second goal for the Germans five minutes into the second half and the Scots, totally lacking any bite up front, were unable to get back.

Denmark hit peak form against Uruguay. Preben Elkjaer opened the scoring in the 10th minute and Uruguay resorted to their usual violence to subdue the Danes' masterful play. The Uruguayan Bossio was sent off ten minutes later after a ghastly foul. Denmark then turned on the pressure, thrilling their growing fan-club with a superb demonstration of the skillful, attacking football which had become their hallmark, but they scored only once more before the break, via Lerby. Indeed, just on the stroke of half-time, Uruguay grabbed a goal themselves (Francescoli converting a penalty) and Denmark still had everything to do. In the second half Uruguay were, quite simply, swept aside by Denmark as Elkjaer, with lethal finishing, scored twice more to get his hat trick and, with Laudrup and Jesper Olsen also getting on to the scoresheet, the final score was 6-1.

Scotland then met Uruguay in their last game in the group, relatively confident that a win would enable them to qualify for the second round in third place. Sensationally, Uruguay were reduced to only ten men inside the first minute when Batista was ordered off for a bad foul on Strachan, but far from inspiring the Scots this seemed only to raise the morale of their opponents. Scotland gave one of their worst-ever World Cup performances, showing a total poverty of ideas against ten men. Uruguay were rarely put under pressure and, throughout the game, Uruguay's two-man attack seemed the most likely to score. The final result was 0-0 and Scotland bowed out of another World Cup in the first round, while Uruguay, cynical and unsporting though they were, deserved to progress if only through sheer determination. Denmark beat West Germany 2-0 to top the group but had the influential Frank Arnesen sent off in the last minute when he stupidly took a swipe at Matthaus.

In Group F the biggest problem with which the players had to contend, was the heat and humidity. Unlike all the other venues the altitude was not a difficulty, but, because future rounds were to be played high up, the countries in this group were at a slight disadvantage. England opened against Portugal (who were supposedly in disarray after a pay dispute) and gave a mediocre performance in which Hateley and Lineker clearly did not complement one another up front. Both missed chances to put England ahead and, after 75 minutes, a sloppy piece of defending allowed Portugal, in a rare attack, to score through Carlos Manuel. England's injury-hit captain Bryan Robson was hopelessly off form and their potential key player, Glen Hoddle, was consequently pushed into a defensive role which stifled his creative talents. Hodge replaced Robson and Beardsley came on for Waddle (who simply did not look up to this standard) and although the attack then showed signs of waking up they were unable to score the equalizer.

Facing Morocco in their next game, England retained exactly the same side that started the previous game and, frankly, they played just as badly. In the 40th minute Bryan Robson's suspect shoulder again gave way and, after Hodge had replaced him, things began to look up. Just as they did so, Wilkins, England's normally well-disciplined midfielder, was sent off when he stupidly threw the ball at the referee. This disgraceful temper-tantrum could have cost England dearly had the remaining ten men not played with increased commitment in the second half; it marked the end of the series for Wilkins. In the event England probably deserved more than the 0-0 draw but the writing was on the wall for sweeping changes for their last game against Poland.

Having themselves drawn 0-0 with Morocco, Poland had gone on to beat Portugal 1-0, much against the run of play. Bobby Robson, the England manager, at last made the team changes which were so obviously required, bringing in Reid, Trevor Steven, Hodge and Beardsley, and what a transformation this provided! In the first 35 minutes England turned on the sort of display that their fans had expected from the start as Hoddle was at last allowed to play as a creator and Lineker no longer found himself competing with Hateley for every pass. Beardsley and Hodge brought new verve and variety, as Lineker snapped up the first World Cup hat trick for England since Geoff Hurst's in the 1966 Final. Poland tried to get back into the game but the English defence were not seriously troubled by the Polish attack and the score remained 3-0 to guarantee England's qualification for the second round.

Morocco, in the meantime, completely outplayed Portugal in their last game in the group to win 3-1, and became the first African country to reach the second round of a World Cup competition. The fact that, in the process, they topped Group F without defeat put into perspective England's performance against them – reduced to ten men in the sweltering heat. Poland reached the second round as the other best-placed third team in the group. It must be said that Group F was not notable for its exciting football.

So the competition moved to the knock-out rounds and the surviving countries were matched as follows: Belgium v USSR; Brazil v Poland; Mexico v Bulgaria; Argentina v Uruguay; England v Paraguay; France v Italy; West Germany v Morocco; and Denmark v Spain.

The tie between the USSR and 'dark horses' Belgium promised little, although Russia's first-round performances had been outstanding. In the event the game proved to be not only the most electrifying of the whole series but on a par with the greatest games of earlier competitions in terms of excitement, commitment and sheer skill. Russia took the lead through Belanov in the 27th minute and the play swung from end to end throughout the remainder of the first half without further score. Ceulemans was Belgium's inspiration as they fought to equalize and, in the 54th minute, Scifo levelled the scores. Belanov scored his second goal a quarter of an hour later, but Ceulemans got Belgium back on terms in the 75th minute. The score remained 2-2 at full time and, in extra-time, Belgium took a 4-2 lead before Russia pulled a goal back, again through Belanov (who thus became the first Russian to score a World Cup hat trick). The Russians poured forward until, after a superb chip by Yevtushenko was tipped over the bar by Pfaff the Belgian goalkeeper, it was all over and Belgium were through.

The defensive Bulgarians caused Mexico few problems and barely mounted an attack before Negrete scored a spectacular goal in the 34th minute when he acrobatically volleyed a chip into the net. In the second half Servin scored a second as Mexico, to the fervent acclaim of 100,000 fans, cruised into the quarter-finals.

On 16 June Brazil had little difficulty in beating Poland 4-0 while the eyes of most of the world were turned to the potentially explosive confrontation between Uruguay and Argentina. Although the two countries had played one another frequently, this was only their second meeting in the World Cup – the first being the 1930 Final. Superb refereeing by Mr. Agnolin kept the game well under control as, once more, Maradona excelled for Argentina and he came close to scoring in the 40th minute, hitting the bar with a free kick. Two minutes later Pasculli put Argentina ahead and, in a second half best remembered for a tremendous thunderstorm, Uruguay were unable to fight their way back into the game.

After their performance against Poland, England's fans looked forward to another good display against Paraguay. Although England settled down well, after half an hour Butcher came close to giving away a goal with a stupid back-pass which went straight to Mendoza. Shilton retrieved the situation by forcing Mendoza wide before saving a close-range shot from Canete, but this escape served to motivate England who swept straight into the attack and scored through Lineker, via Hoddle and Hodge. After they had gone behind, the Paraguayans' small reserves of discipline evaporated as they harried the referee whenever any decision went against them. Worse than this was when Lineker was viciously elbowed in the windpipe early in the second half and had to be carried off on a stretcher, gasping for breath. Ironically, by this time England had the bit firmly between their teeth and Beardsley scored a second goal while Lineker was receiving attention on the touchline. The Everton striker came back onto the field and scored England's third and final goal in the 72nd minute, and England now prepared for the meeting with Argentina in the quarter-finals – the first such confrontation since the Falklands War.

The day before England's tie with Paraguay, West Germany had struggled to overcome Morocco scoring in the 89th-minute from a free kick by Matthaus. Earlier, France had met Italy in the most eagerly-awaited tie of the series. The prospect of the world champions meeting the European champions was intriguing but Italy never really got into their stride after Platini had put France ahead in only the 13th minute. France's midfield took complete control of the game and, after Stopyra had scored a second French goal in the 56th minute, the disappointing Italians faded and could find no way through.

The last second-round match, between Denmark and Spain, provided quite a surprise. After their first-round performance, Denmark were among the favourites to take the cup and, true to form, they began by attacking Spain. After the first quarter of an hour Spain began to wrest control of the midfield although Denmark took the lead through a Jesper Olsen penalty after half an hour. Olsen again featured in the second goal of the game, just before half-time, when his unnecessary back-pass across his own area was intercepted by Butragueno, who scored for Spain. In the second half Spain took the lead in the 57th minute and Denmark, piling on the pressure to equalize, missed the steadying influence of Frank Arnesen (their suspended defender) and fell apart as Spain counterattacked. The razor-sharp Butragueno completed his hat-trick and then added another for luck, as Spain ran out easy 5-1 winners after turning on their best-ever World Cup performance. The Danish dream was over, but what thrills they gave us on the way!

In the quarter-finals there were two intriguing ties, Brazil v France and Argentina v England, with Mexico v West Germany and Belgium v Spain providing the other matches. The game between Brazil and France was a real classic. Both teams played extremely well and, although Careca shot Brazil ahead after a quarter of an hour, the French never gave up as attack upon attack followed at either end. Platini scored a simple goal for France shortly before half-time to square matters but, in the second half, France began very shakily before coming back again. With 15 minutes to go, Zico (who, like Rummenigge, had been used very sparingly earlier in the tournament) was brought on as substitute for Brazil and almost immediately was given the responsibility of talking a penalty after Branco was tripped. His tame shot was saved by Bats, the French goalkeeper, and the game went into and through extra-time without further goals. Thus the French faced the prospect of a penalty shoot-out with memories of their 1982 semi-final exit fresh in their minds. Despite a miss from Platini, of all people, France won this 4-3 and once more faced the possibility of meeting West Germany in the last four.

Against Mexico, West Germany struggled in the stifling heat of Monterrey in a game which was as dreary as the previous quarter-final had been scintillating. Neither side looked capable of scoring and, although West Germany were reduced to ten men in the 65th minute when Berthold was dismissed, Mexico could not exploit their advantage. In extra-time Aquirre of Mexico was sent off, too, and the tie went into a penalty shoot-out which West Germany easily won 4-1.

All eyes were focused on the Azteca stadium the next day when England met the Argentinians. Throughout Argentina, the game was regarded as an opportunity to even up the defeat suffered at the hands of the British during the Falklands War, and it was with this in mind that the Mexican security forces turned out in force. The English fans present were greatly outnumbered by those of Argentina (Mexico City has a large Argentine community), and it is not difficult to speculate that the minor skirmishes which took place might have been considerably more serious had the result gone the other way. During the game Argentina reorganized their defence and overcame the twin threat of Lineker and Beardsley by close man-to-man marking. This effectively blunted the English attack and the game was deadlocked at 0-0 until the 50th minute. Then Maradona chased a sliced back-pass by Steve Hodge, challenged Shilton, and clearly fisted the ball into the net. Shilton's vehement protests were disregarded and the goal stood, although Maradona himself later admitted that he had used his hand! Five minutes later, as England pressed for an equalizer, Maradona picked up the ball on the halfway line and dribbled past three defenders before scoring one of the greatest goals of this or any other World Cup. England's answer, somewhat surprisingly, was to bring on Waddle – whose previous performances had been totally uninspiring – in place of Reid. This change proved ineffective and ten minutes later the English management at last realized that Argentina were playing without full-backs and brought on winger John Barnes (who had, incredibly, been omitted from the early games in Monterrey, despite his great adaptability in the heat). In the 80th minute a perfectly-timed cross from Barnes was headed by Lineker into the Argentina net but unfortunately, although Lineker almost scored three minutes from the end, England had left it too late and were out of another World Cup, their fate sealed by the hand of Maradona.

Belgium and Spain met in the last quarter-final tie and Belgium, once more, provided the surprises. The Belgian midfield struggled to get into the game although Ceulemans, who had a great World Cup, put Belgium ahead in the 34th minute. Spain mounted attack after attack but Belgium's excellent defence held firm until Senor volleyed home the equalizer five minutes from the end and the game went into extra-time. With the score still tied 1-1, a penalty shoot-out was again required and, by winning this 5-4, Belgium won through to their first World Cup semi-final, against Argentina.

The first semi-final, between France and West Germany, was a rerun of that of 1982 and provided the same result but nothing like the same excitement. Sensing that Michel Platini was France's key man, West Germany's manager Franz Beckenbauer gave Rolff the specific task of marking him out of the game and he did so with great success. In the 9th minute West Germany took the lead when the French keeper Bats fumbled a shot from full-back Brehme and allowed it to slip under his body. The French were now obliged to attack throughout but, as the game wore on, looked steadily less likely to score. In the final minute the substitute Voller scored an academic second goal to take West Germany to their second consecutive Final.

Later the same day, Diego Maradona once more demonstrated his matchwinning genius when, in an eight-minute second-half spell, he scored two goals against Belgium, the first a crafty piece of poaching and the second another breathtaking solo run. Although Argentina wasted other chances and could well have won by five or six clear goals, they were no doubt satisfied just to reach their second Final in three competitions.

In the third-place match, Belgium (who scarcely can have dreamed they would get this far) took an early lead through Ceulemans but France hit back and themselves edged ahead a little before half-time. Claesen equalized a quarter of an hour from the end and, for the third time in a fortnight, Belgium were faced with extra-time. Fatigue at last took its toll as France scored twice more to take third place.

The Final itself proved one thing above all others – that on his day Maradona ranks with the greatest names of the past. West Germany had played with little flair en route to the Final, but by dour defending and dogged persistence had won through, and an interesting contest was in prospect against the volatile South Americans. In the first half the West Germans lacked organization and did not look to be in the same class as Argentina who played with much more conviction. After 21 minutes Jose Luis Brown, the Argentinian sweeper, took advantage of a bad mistake by Schumacher, West Germany's goalkeeper, and headed his country into the lead. Maradona proved to be a real handful for the German defence and could well have scored in the first half. Five minutes after the interval Brown injured his shoulder but, after leaving the field for two minutes, returned obviously in great pain. As West Germany pressed forward, hoping to take advantage of Brown's restricted mobility, Valdano broke away on the German right and sidefooted the ball past Schumacher for Argentina's second goal. West Germany, against the run of play, pulled a goal back through Rummenigge in the 73rd minute, and were level in the 81st minute when Voller scored their second. Three minutes later, just as West Germany pressed for a winner, Maradona split their defence with a superb ball which Burrachaga ran onto and scored the winner. So it was that Argentina won their second world title and 'wonder boy' Maradona confirmed himself as the star of the best World Cup competition since 1970.

GROUP A

	P	W	D	L	F	A	Pts
Argentina	3	2	1	0	6	2	5
Italy	3	1	2	0	5	4	4
Bulgaria	3	0	2	1	2	4	2
South Korea	3	0	1	2	4	7	1

GROUP B

	P	W	D	L	F	A	Pts
Mexico	3	2	1	0	4	2	5
Paraguay	3	1	2	0	4	3	4
Belgium	3	1	1	1	5	5	3
Iraq	3	0	0	3	1	4	0

GROUP C

	P	W	D	L	F	A	Pts
USSR	3	2	1	0	9	1	5
France	3	2	1	0	5	1	5
Hungary	3	1	0	2	2	9	2
Canada	3	0	0	3	0	5	0

GROUP D

	P	W	D	L	F	A	Pts
Brazil	3	3	0	0	5	0	6
Spain	3	2	0	1	5	2	4
Northern Ireland	3	0	1	2	2	6	1
Algeria	3	0	1	2	1	5	1

GROUP E

	P	W	D	L	F	A	Pts
Denmark	3	3	0	0	9	1	6
West Germany	3	1	1	1	3	4	3
Uruguay	3	0	2	1	2	7	2
Scotland	3	0	1	2	1	3	1

GROUP F

	P	W	D	L	F	A	Pts
Morocco	3	1	2	0	3	1	4
England	3	1	1	1	3	1	3
Poland	3	1	1	1	1	3	3
Portugal	3	1	0	2	2	4	2

SECOND ROUND

Argentina	1	Uruguay	0
Paraguay	0	England	3
USSR	3	Belgium	4

(After extra time)

Spain	5	Denmark	1
Brazil	4	Poland	0
Italy	0	France	2
Morocco	0	West Germany	1
Mexico	1	Bulgaria	0

QUARTER-FINALS

Argentina	2	England	1
Belgium	1	Spain	1

After extra time – Belgium won 5-4 on penalties

Brazil	1	France	1

After extra time – France won 4-3 on penalties

West Germany	0	Mexico	0

After extra time – West Germany won 4-1 penalties

SEMI-FINALS

Argentina	2	Belgium	0
West Germany	2	France	0

THIRD-PLACE MATCH

France	4	Belgium	2

(After extra time)

FINAL

Argentina .... (1) **3**   **West Germany** .... (0) **2**

Scorers: Brown, Valdano, Burruchaga

Scorers: Rummenigge, Voller

Team: Pumpido, Ruggeri, Brown, Cuciuffo, Giusti, Enrique, Batista, Burruchaga (sub. Trobbiani), Olaricoechea, Valdano, Maradona

Team: Schumacher, Brehme, Jakobs, Forster (K.H.), Berthold, Matthaus, Magath (sub. Hoeness), Eder, Briegel, Rummenigge, Allofs (sub. Voller)

FOURTEENTH WORLD CUP

Italy 1990

ITALY'S selection as the venue for the 14th World Cup met with unanimous approval and, just as Mexico had become the first Non-European country to stage the Finals twice, Italy thus became the first European country to do so. As for the 13th series, the 24 qualifiers were divided into six groups of four with the top two from each group and the four best third-placed teams qualifying for the second round.

The hosts for the 1994 series, the USA, managed to qualify for the 14th series when Mexico (who were found guilty of deliberately fielding overaged players in FIFA youth tournaments) were penalised by being excluded from the series. Nevertheless, the USA struggled to qualify and scraped through with a 1-0 victory over Trinidad & Tobago in their last game. FIFA and US commercial interests no doubt breathed a sigh of relief!

In Brazils' qualifying group, controversy reigned. Playing at home against Chile, in front of a 141,072 crowd, Brazil were expected to cruise through to their 14th consecutive Finals series until, 66 minutes into the game, a foolish spectator threw a flare onto the pitch. Chile's goalkeeper, Roberto Rojas, crashed to the ground claiming to have been blinded by the explosion (shades of Holland v Malta from the 1988 European Championships) and the match was abandoned. Television replays of the incident proved conclusively that Rojas had been acting in an attempt to get Brazil disqualified and, as a result of the subsequent investigation, he was given a life ban for his actions. In addition, Chile was banned from international competition and members of the management team whose connivance with Rojas was seen as an attempt to qualify by cheating (which indeed it was) were also banned. Brazil were awarded the tie with a 2-0 scoreline.

The Home Countries were represented by England who responded to their ignominious exit from the 1988 European Championship by stringing together a 16-game unbeaten run and by Scotland who disposed of France en route. Irish manager, Jack Charlton (who won a World Cup medal with England in 1966) steered the Southern Irish to their first-ever World Cup Final series and, as the Irish team was made up of predominantly Football

League players, this effectively added another team for British fans to follow.

South America were represented by holders Argentina, Brazil, Columbia (whose league had been suspended as part of that country's fight against their drug barons) and Uruguay. In addition to England, Ireland and Scotland, Europe was represented by the hosts Italy and also Austria, Belgium, Czechoslovakia, Holland, Rumania, Spain, Sweden, USSR, West Germany and Yugoslavia. The African countries were Cameroon (who entered the Finals as the only country to have competed in a World Cup Finals Series undefeated) and Egypt. The other qualifiers were Costa Rica, South Korea, the United Arab Emirates (UAE) and the USA. The First-round groupings were:

Group A: Austria, Czechoslovakia, Italy, USA.

Group B: Argentina, Cameroon, Rumania, USSR.

Group C: Brazil, Costa Rica, Scotland, Sweden.

Group D: Colombia, UAE, West Germany, Yugoslavia.

Group E: Belgium, South Korea, Spain, Uruguay.

Group F: Egypt, Eire, England, Holland.

The first game of the series brought together the reigning champions, Argentina, and the African no-hopers, Cameroon. After the grand opening ceremony at the spectacularly-transformed San Siro stadium in Milan, the 73,780 crowd settled down expecting to see Maradona and his colleagues run riot against their opponents. Cameroon, however, had not read the supposed script and, just as they did in 1982 (when they drew with Italy, Poland and Peru) Cameroon showed no fear of their talented opponents. After a goalless first-half in which the Africans' delighted most of the crowd by continually stopping the Argentinians in their tracks with 'enthusiastic' tackling, particularly on Maradona, it became obvious that a major upset was on the cards. In the 62nd minute, Cameroon looked to have lost their chance of glory when referee Vautrot sent off Andre Biyick after a seemingly-innocuous challenge on the substitute Caniggia. Minutes later, the unbelievable happened when, totally unaffected by the dismissal, Cameroon stormed on to the attack and took the lead through Francois Biyick (Andre's brother) when the Argentinian goalkeeper Pumpido failed to hold his unexpected header. This goal clearly stunned the Argentinians and, even though the Cameroon side were reduced to nine men by the deserved dismissal of Massing for an awful foul on Caniggia, it was still the Africans who did all of the attacking. The final score remained 1-0 as Cameroon recorded one of the all-time shock results in the competition.

Group B continued the following day with a further surprise result when Rumania defeated the USSR 2-0 and, a few days later, all was thrown back into the melting pot, when Argentina, too, scored a 2-0 victory over the USSR. The following day the Cameroon team became the first to ensure their place in the second round as they proved that their opening victory was no mere fluke, by defeating Rumania also. Four days later the last games in the group saw Rumania and Argentina share the points, ensuring each team's progress to the second round but a decisive 4-0 Russian victory over Cameroon did not prevent the African country from winning the group.

Group A began when Italy met their old rivals, Austria, in Rome in front of a 72,303 crowd. The Italians played some delightful football, carving out opening after opening, but struggled to find the net. In the end it was not one of their millionaire superstar strikers who made the breakthrough but substitute 'Toto' Schillaci of Juventus who scored the only goal of the game. The next day, all eyes turned to the USA v Czechoslovakia game in Florence. The Americans played some neat football, but with the youngest team in the competition, struggled against the experienced and physically strong Czechs. By half-time Czechoslovakia were 2-0 ahead and the USA were showing few signs of invention up front. Soon after the break the Czechs scored a third goal and when the USA defender Wynalda was sent off somewhat harshly for pushing a Czech forward in the 51st minute, it began to look as if the Americans would be annihilated. A few minutes later, however, Caligiuri (who had scored the goal which gave the States victory over Trinidad and Tobago in their last qualifying game) pulled one back for the USA. The final score was 5-1 to the Czechs and the Italians who were to face the USA in Rome in their next game, dreamed of double-figure scores. In the event, far from a humiliating defeat, the Americans' next game probably marked their 'coming-of-age' as a soccer-playing nation. They went down 1-0 to an early Giannini goal but held out superbly against the massed attacks of the Italian forwards without once resorting to hard play and, with a little luck, might even have sneaked a draw. Czechoslovakia made sure of their second round place by beating Austria and Italy went on to record their third victory to top the group with full points.

Although Group C began with a predictable Brazilian victory over the timid Swedish team, few could have foretold the outcome of the Costa Rica v Scotland clash the next day. Qualifying for their fifth consecutive Finals series, Scotland were expected to despatch the Latin American team without difficulty but the Scots turned in the sort of lacklustre performance that their fans had grown almost to expect of them. Goalless at half-time, the game was brought to life early in the second-half when Cayasso put Costa Rica ahead. Thereafter, the Scots pressured for an equaliser but, despite creating a number of clear-cut scoring chances, were unable to find the net and, indeed, looked so shaky at the back, that they could have gone further behind. In the event, their 1-0 defeat must rank as the worst-ever Scottish World Cup performance but, almost predictably, when they faced Sweden five days later, they surprised everyone with an efficient, if not remarkable, performance. McCall gave them the lead in the tenth minute and, after dominating most of the game, they went further ahead seven minutes from time when Mo Johnston converted a penalty kick. Stromberg pulled a goal back for the Swedes a couple of minutes later but the Scots ran out deserved 2-1 winners.

Brazil, in the meantime, had already ensured their progress to the second round with an uninspired 1-0 victory over Costa Rica and Scotland went into their last game in the group against them requiring a single point to go through too. In the event the Scots played competently, although somewhat overawed by the Brazilians until, in the 82nd minute, Muller gave the South Americans the lead. Jim Leighton, the Scottish goalkeeper, was blamed by most of his countrymen for failing to hold a second shot after parrying a well-struck long-range effort but the Scottish defenders must bear the major responsibility for allowing Muller total freedom to walk the loose ball into the net. Thus the Scots failed to reach the next round as usual and the surprise second qualifier from the group became Costa Rica who had recorded a shock 2-1 victory over the hapless Swedes.

Group D began with a tie between the outsiders the United Arab Emirates and the flamboyant Colombian team. A team of the most amazing hairstyles, the Colombians' eccentric approach to the game, especially from their keeper Higuita who described himself as the Worlds' first 'sweeper-keeper', created much interest. Technically, their individual skills were superb and, although the game was goalless at half-time, they were never in danger of dropping a point after Redin had put them ahead in the 50th minute. Former South American player of the year, Valderrama, scored a second five minutes from the end. Favourites West Germany soon got into their stride and registered an easy 4-1 victory over Yugoslavia, before slamming the United Arab Emirates 6-1 in their second game to ensure their second round place.

Yugoslavia struggled to contain the lively Colombian side in their next game and were fortunate to record a 1-0 victory to set themselves on course for a second round place. In their last game they duly earned this with a comfortable 4-1 win over the United Arab Emirates. Colombia, meanwhile, faced West Germany requiring at least a point to reach the next round. In the final minute of the game (which was a particularly bruising affair with three Colombians and one West German booked) the German substitute Pierre Littbarski, put his team ahead but Rincon earned the South Americans a deserved point and second round place with an injury-time equalizer.

The first game in Group E provided few surprises as the strong Belgian team defeated South Korea 2-0 and, the following day, Spain and Uruguay played out the first goalless draw of the series. Four days later Belgium ensured their second round place with a commanding 3-1 win over Uruguay and, at the same time, Spain, too, recorded a 3-1 win over South Korea to ensure their progress also. The closing group game saw Spain hold on to a 2-1 half-time lead, to overcome Belgium and secure first-place in the group while Uruguay fought it out with South Korea. The Asians, no doubt surprised Uruguay by their intelligent play and, the game remained goalless until, with virtually the last touch of the match, Fonseca, scored to earn Uruguay a second round tie.

Group F was almost a re-run of one of the groups from the 1988 European Championship with England, Eire and Holland, once again facing one another. Widely regarded as the potentially explosive grouping in terms of crowd violence it was based way out in Sardinia and in Sicily and draconian security measures were in force from the offset. The first game brought together England and Eire and, despite being played at a tremendous pace, this could not be described as a classic. England took an early lead when Lineker beat two defenders to a Waddle cross but the Irish refused to give up and pressured the England defence whenever they could. John Barnes once again failed to make any impression upon the game at all and, playing with their usual 'flat back four', England looked far from impressive. Twenty minutes from the end Steve McMahon came on as substitute and, with almost his first touch, was robbed of possession on the edge of the England area and Ireland's Sheedy scored a deserved equaliser. The score remained 1-1 and, to everyone's surprise, Egypt managed to hold the European champions, Holland, 1-1 in the next group game.

England faced Holland in the next game and, responding to frantic press criticism, adopted a sweeper system for the first time. Derby County's Mark Wright, assumed the sweepers' role to such effect that the Dutch stars, Gullit

121

and Van Basten barely had a kick of the ball as England turned in an excellent display. Captain Bryan Robson limped off injured in the 64th minute and played no further part in the series but this did not affect the English performance at all and they were most unfortunate not to win the game. In the closing minute Stuart Pearce thundered a free-kick into the Dutch net from the edge of the penalty area but, just as the English were celebrating a 'last-gasp' victory, the referee Mr. Petrovie of Yugoslavia, ruled that it was no goal, the indirect kick having gone straight into the net.

The following day the Irish, too, drew 0-0 (with Egypt) and this left the group wide open with every team on two points. As with every group, the last two games were played at the same time and while England faced Egypt at Cagliari, Ireland met Holland in Palermo. Reverting to a 'flat back four' England struggled to overcome the Africans and they only went ahead when Gascoigne curled a 58th minute free-kick for 'man-of-the-match' Mark Wright to head his first-ever international goal. This gave England a deserved but uninspired victory and, as Holland and Eire drew 1-1, ensured their second round place as group leaders. Although both Holland and Eire qualified for the second round too, lots were drawn to decide which team were placed second and which were placed third and the Irish took the higher place.

So the competition entered the Knockout stage and the pairings for the second round were:

Spain v Yugoslavia; Brazil v Argentina; Italy v Uruguay; Eire v Rumania; West Germany v Holland; Czechoslovakia v Costa Rica; Cameroon v Colombia and England v Belgium.

The first of these games was Cameroon v Colombia and although Africans continued in the same vein as for their group matches with their own peculiar blend of enthusiasm and brutality, the score at 90 minutes remained 0-0. The match was decided in extra-time when, already 1-0 down, Colombia's flamboyant goalkeeper, Rene Higuita, tried to dribble the ball past substitute Roger Milla 30 yards out of his goal. Milla dispossessed him and raced away slotting the ball into the empty net to ensure that Cameroon became the first-ever African nation to reach the quarter-finals.

Next, the Czechs took an early lead against Costa Rica through Skuhravy but, in the second half, were pegged back to 1-1 as their opponents took the initiative. Skuhravy scored a second against the run of play in the 63rd minute and Costa Rican resistance collapsed. Skuhravy notched up his hat-trick seven minutes from the end and Czechoslovakia won the tie 4-1.

The following day Brazil met Argentina in Turin and, for a while, subjected the holders to such pressure that it seemed inevitable that they would score – but they didn't. From the offset of the competition, Argentina had played an uninspired brand of football and they were indeed fortunate to reach the second-round. They continued in the same vein against Brazil and Maradona, in particular (despite lavish praise from the World's media) played a very subdued game. However, in the 80th minute, he made amends by taking on four Brazilian defenders before passing to Caniggia who duly scored. Despite being a goal behind, Brazil failed to step up the pace of their attacks and, after having Ricardo Gomez sent off in the 83rd minute they never looked like equalising.

The first-half of the next game that day, between Holland and West Germany, is best remembered for an unsavoury incident between Holland's Rijkaard and West Germany's Voeller which resulted in both being sent off. Rijkaard behaved disgracefully after being booked when he spat in Voeller's face but Voeller was unfortunate to get his marching orders also when the two tangled shortly afterwards. The second-half of the game, however, provided quite a spectacle as both sides moved up a gear and turned on a superb display of attacking football. Klinsmann put West Germany ahead in the 50th minute and Brehme made it 2-0 five minutes from the end. Koeman pulled one back from the penalty spot three minutes later but the Germans ran out worthy winners.

The Republic of Ireland faced a Rumanian team who were without their star forward Lacatus but, despite creating the better chances, the Irish were unable to convert their superiority into goals. At the end of extra-time, the score remained goalless and the tie became the first one of the tournament to be decided on penalties. Eire progressed to the next round by converting all five penalties against Rumania's four.

Against Uruguay, Italy's first-round hero Toto Schillaci bloke the deadlock twenty minutes into the second-half when he cracked in a 22-yards shot and the hosts cruised to a 2-0 victory.

The last day of the second-round matches saw Yugoslavia triumph over Spain in extra-time in a rather poor game before England met Belgium. In a hard but sporting tie, England were pushed back on the defensive for much of the game which could have gone either way. In the final minute of extra-time, just as it began to look as if penalties would be required, substitute David Platt turned and volleyed a Paul Gascoigne free-kick, into the Belgium net to ensure Englands' quarter-final place.

The quarter-finals brought together Italy and Eire; Yugoslavia and

Argentina; England and Cameroon and West Germany and Czechoslovakia. The first of these games, the hosts against the Irish was a thrilling encounter in which Jack Charlton's team fought well but failed to penetrate Italy's magnificent defence. As this was the tenth successive game that Italy had played without conceding a goal, the Irish could be forgiven for their failure and, once again, it was that man Schillaci who scored the winner in the 38th minute.

Yugoslavia virtually threw away their chances of a semi-final place when they had Sabanadzovic needlessly sent off after 31 minutes but the lethargic Argentinians were, nevertheless, still unwilling to play attacking football. At the end of extra-time, the score in another really disappointing game, remained 0-0 and the inevitable penalty shootout followed. Argentina won this 3-2 and, once more, progressed to the next round without deserving to do so.

The following day, Cameroon, without four players who had been booked for the second time in their previous game took on England in Naples. Against the run of play, England took the lead after 26 minutes when David Platt headed home a superb Stuart Pearce cross and, for the rest of the half, they struggled to stay ahead against a lively and very physical Cameroon team. Cameroon's leading scorer, 38-years-old Roger Milla came on as a substitute after the break and immediately began to cause problems for the English defence. In the 61st minute Paul Gascoigne was adjudged to have fouled Milla in the England penalty area and Cameroon equalised from the resulting penalty. Four minutes later Milla again caught the English defence napping when he set Ekeke up to put the Africans ahead.

England, however, kept their composure and fought for the equaliser with character. Fifteen minutes from the end of ordinary time, Bobby Robson, to everyone's surprise, brought on Trevor Steven to replace Terry Butcher who had contributed little to the game. Minutes later Mark Wright suffered a badly cut eye when he clashed heads with Milla and Steven slotted comfortably into the defence as Wright, heavily bandaged, became little more than a passenger. In the 83rd minute Lineker broke loose in the penalty area and won a penalty when Massing brought him down. He converted the kick himself and, in extra-time, in almost identical circumstances, scored a second penalty to give England a deserved if somewhat fortunate win.

In the last of the quarter-final games, West Germany dominated their Czech opponents, who were nevertheless, kept in the game by a splendid goalkeeping display from Stejskal. The West German captain, Matthaus, scored the only goal of the game in the 24th minute when he converted a penalty kick but

Czechoslovakia were fortunate not to lose more heavily.

The semi-finals brought together the hosts against the holders and West Germany against England and, considering that all four had been seeded by FIFA, to that extent at least, this should have been no surprise.

First, the Italians and Argentinians fought out an interesting and at times entertaining 90 minutes in Naples in which the South Americans, for the first time in the tournament, played some quite skilful football. Schillaci put the home side ahead in the first-half but Caniggia scored the equaliser in the 67th minute when he glanced a header past keeper Zenga – the first goal conceded by Italy in 617 minutes of football (a new World record). Extra-time, however, was an abysmal sequel to a reasonable tie, littered with a succession of free kicks and marred by Argentinian Giusti's sending-off in the 105th minute, for an off-the-ball assault on Baggio. Without further score the game went to a penalty shootout and, to the bitter disappointment of the home crowd, Italy lost 4-3 and Argentina progressed to their third Final in four series.

The following day England met West Germany in Turin in the game that is generally regarded as the finest of the whole series. Playing the best football that an England side had played for years, the English rocked West Germany as they stormed onto the attack from the start. In a thrilling encounter, England dominated West Germany and were desperately unlucky to go behind on the hour when a free-kick from Brehme was deflected past Shilton in the English goal.

Ten minutes from the end of normal time Lineker beat Kohler and Augenthaler to level the scores. In extra-time England were unfortunate to have a seemingly-certain penalty appeal turned down and a Platt header disallowed and, as in the other semi-final, a penalty shootout was required. West Germany won this 4-3 and progressed to their third Final in a row and, incidentally, the first-ever 'repeat' final.

England met Italy in Bari in the Third Place Play-off and, with the pressure off, the standard of football was some of the highest in the whole competition. Italy took the lead when Peter Shilton foolishly allowed Baggio to rob him of the ball and David Platt equalised fourteen minutes later when he headed in an excellent Dorigo cross. Almost immediately Italy were awarded a penalty and Schillaci converted to become the tournament's top scorer. The after-match festivities when both teams and their supporters celebrated good-humouredly together were one of the abiding highlights of the 14th World Cup in sharp contrast to what was to follow in Rome the next day.

The atmosphere for the Final in Rome could only be described as partisan when 40,000 West Germans and almost as many Italians jeered and whistled the unpopular Argentinians from the start. The South Americans' performance during the game has been described variously as 'inept', 'cynical', 'appalling' and 'loathsome' but, objectively, can only be described as poor. Without doubt the worst game of the series, this Final was to go into the record books for all the wrong reasons. Gamesmanship by the West Germans to the point of farce was matched by a total lack of self-control within the Argentinian team – hardly the ideal blend for such a game. In the 65th minute Monzon became the first-ever player to be dismissed in a World Cup Final and, after Germany had taken the lead via a dubious penalty five minutes from the end, his Argentinian team-mate Dezotti joined him too! Finally, during the presentation of trophies at the end, the Argentinian captain, Maradona, refused to shake hands with the president of FIFA – a petulant, if rather predictable display which did him and his country no credit at all.

GROUP A

	P	W	D	L	F	A	Pts
Italy	3	3	0	0	4	0	6
Czechoslovakia	3	2	0	1	6	3	4
Austria	3	1	0	2	2	3	2
USA	3	0	0	3	2	8	0

GROUP B

	P	W	D	L	F	A	Pts
Cameroon	3	2	0	1	3	5	4
Rumania	3	1	1	1	4	3	3
Argentina	3	1	1	1	3	2	3
USSR	3	1	0	2	4	4	2

GROUP C

	P	W	D	L	F	A	Pts
Brazil	3	3	0	0	4	1	6
Costa Rica	3	2	0	1	3	2	4
Scotland	3	1	0	2	2	3	2
Sweden	3	0	0	3	3	6	0

GROUP D

	P	W	D	L	F	A	Pts
West Germany	3	2	1	0	10	3	5
Yugoslavia	3	2	0	1	6	5	4
Colombia	3	1	1	1	3	2	3
U.A.E.	3	0	0	3	2	11	0

GROUP E

	P	W	D	L	F	A	Pts
Spain	3	2	1	0	5	2	5
Belgium	3	2	0	1	6	3	4
Uruguay	3	1	1	1	2	3	3
South Korea	3	0	0	3	1	6	0

GROUP F

	P	W	D	L	F	A	Pts
England	3	1	2	0	2	1	4
Eire	3	0	3	0	2	2	3
Holland	3	0	3	0	2	2	3
Egypt	3	0	2	1	1	2	2

SECOND ROUND

Spain	1	Yugoslavia	2
Brazil	0	Argentina	1
Italy	2	Uruguay	0
Eire	0	Rumania	0

After extra time – Eire won 5-4 on penalties

West Germany	2	Holland	1
Czechoslovakia	4	Costa Rica	1
Cameroon	2	Colombia	1

(After extra time)

England	1	Belgium	0

(After extra time)

QUARTER-FINALS

Argentina	0	Yugoslavia	0

After extra time – Argentina won 3-2 on penalties

Eire	0	Italy	1
Czechoslovakia	0	West Germany	1
England	3	Cameroon	2

SEMI-FINALS

Argentina	1	Italy	1

After extra time – Argentina won 4-3 on penalties

West Germany	1	England	1

After extra time – West Germany won 4-3 on penalties

THIRD-PLACE MATCH

Italy	2	England	1

FINAL

Argentina .... (0) **0**   **West Germany** .... (0) **1**

Scorer: Brehme (pen)

Team: Goycoechea, Ruggeri (sub. Monzon), Simon, Serrizuela, Lorenzo, Basualdo, Troglio, Burruchaga (sub. Calderon), Sensini, Dezotti, Maradona (Capt.)

Team: Illgner, Berthold (sub. Reuter), Kohler, Augenthaler, Buchwald, Brehme, Littbarski, Matthaus (Capt.), Hassler, Voller, Klinsmann

The Italian team line up before their 1934 World Cup Final victory over
Czechoslovakia in Rome. The team which won that day was as follows:
Giampiero Combi (Capt.), Eraldo Monzeglio, Luigi Allemandi, Attilo Ferraris,
Luis Monti, Luigi Bertolini, Enrique Guiata, Giuseppe Meazza, Angelo Schiavio,
Giovanni Ferrari and Raimundo Orsi.

The Italian team celebrates victory after retaining the trophy by beating Hungary
4-2 in the 1938 World Cup Final.

Jules Rimet (left) and Henri Delaunay (right), the two Frenchmen who were instrumental in the formation of the FIFA World Cup.

English goalkeeper Bert Williams and the American captain Gaetjens watch the ball fall harmlessly on the outside of the net during the 1950 World Cup. Gaetjens later scored the only goal of the match to provide one of the biggest upsets in the history of the competition.

Nat Lofthouse attempts to beat the Uruguayan Andrade in the quarter-final match in Berne. Uruguay won the game 4-2 before losing to Hungary in the Semi-final.

Germany line up before the 1954 World Cup Final: Fritz Walter, Turek, Eckel, Rahn, Ottmar Walter, Leibrich, Posipal, Schaefer, Kohlmeyer, Mai and Morlock.

The West German player, Helmut Rahn, eludes a tackle by two defenders in the 1-0 quarter-final victory over Yugoslavia

Djalma Santos, Masopust, Didi and Jelinek battle for the ball in the 1962 Final.

Above: Jairzinho embraces Pele as they celebrate Brazil's opening goal in the 1970 Final.

Right: Sir Alf Ramsey, the only manager to have guided England to World Cup success.

The excellent Argentinian forward Mario Kempes attacks the Dutch defence in the 1978 World Cup Final. Kempes scored two goals in the 3-1 victory.

Gerry Armstrong puts Northern Ireland ahead in the Group match against Spain. The 1-0 victory against the host nation was against all the odds and ensured that Northern Ireland topped their Group.

Gary Lineker scores his second goal of the game (England's third) against Paraguay in the second round. Lineker scored six goals in just five games to win the 'Golden Boot' as the 1986 tournament's top scorer.

German full-back Andy Brehme scores the only goal of the dismal 1990 World Cup Final from the penalty spot.

Roberto Baggio, dejected after hitting his penalty over the crossbar, stands alone as Brazilian keeper Taffarel celebrates the 3-2 penalty shoot-out victory in the 1994 World Cup Final.

One of the sensations of the 1998 World Cup Finals, Michael Owen, attacks the Argentinian defence in England's second round defeat.

FIFTEENTH WORLD CUP

U.S.A. 1994

Four countries initially expressed a strong interest in staging the 1994 World Cup Finals – Brazil, Chile, Morocco and the U.S.A. Of these, Chile quickly dropped out and FIFA officials travelled to the three remaining countries early in 1988 to assess their suitability.

The U.S.A., having entered an unsuccessful bid to stage the 1986 tournament, were at a disadvantage because they lacked a professional football league (the NASL having collapsed in 1984). However, this did not prevent them from becoming the early favourites as the FIFA delegates were clearly impressed by the immaculate organisation, stadia and communications within the country.

Morocco, with just two stadia at Rabat and Casablanca, lacked the facilities to stage such a major event and promises to build more stadia rang hollow to the FIFA inspectors. Brazil had one enormous advantage – a footballing pedigree beyond question, backed by a population which lived and breathed the game. Unfortunately, when the inspection team travelled to Brazil, they were to find a nightmare of disorganisation with administrative chaos reigning supreme. Setting aside the economic problems of the country (372% annual inflation, and 16 murders a day in Rio alone), the country's once magnificent state-owned stadia were in dire need of renovation, the cost of which would have run into tens of millions of pounds. Add to this the fact that the finals of the 1986 domestic championship were not staged until 1987 and it is not difficult to see why the FIFA inspection team were not impresed by the Brazilian bid. In July 1988 the U.S.A. was selected as the venue with a vote of U.S.A. 10, Morocco 7 and Brazil 2.

So it was that in June 1994, 24 countries competed in the finals of the 15th World Cup competition. Organised into six groups of four, right across the country, this was to be the most widely spread tournament to date, straddling no fewer than four different time zones. The top two teams in each group automatically qualified for the sudden-death second round, together with the best four third-placed teams. Thereafter, teams progressed to single game quarter-finals, semi-finals and final with penalty shootouts to decide the winner in the event of a tie after extra-time.

The first game of the tournament was between the holders, Germany, and Bolivia and, following the razzamataz of the opening ceremony when all the glitter of American showbiz was on display, it was an uninspired performance. 63,117 packed the Soldier Field Stadium for the event which was scheduled in Group C (the best, of course, being in Group A) and the other countries in the Group were Spain and South Korea.

Bolivia had begun their World Cup qualifying competition in spectacular form, with five straight wins against their four opponents (including Brazil and Uruguay) before stumbling to two defeats and a draw in their last three games and were considered to be the dark horses of the competition. Germany quickly took control of the game with Klinsmann a constant threat, but failed to press their advantage with any degree of committment, constrained, no doubt, by FIFA's ruling that 'tackles from behind' would be punished with a red card. Despite this, Germany would have been two goals up by half-time but for poor finishing by Riedle and it was not until he was substituted (in the 59th minute) that Germany took the lead. Following the substitution, Hassler switched to the other flank to accommodate Basler the replacement and, within two minutes, Hassler deflected a ball to Klinsmann who put Germany ahead.

Bolivia continued to fight for the equaliser and came close to scoring through full-back Cristaldo but otherwise Germany retained their grip on the game with few problems. The only remaining highlight was eight minutes from the end when Bolivian substitute Etcheverry, who had only been on the field for four minutes, became the first player to be sent off in an opening Finals match when he was dismissed by referee Brizio of Mexico. The score remained 1-0 to Germany and the competition was under way with the first opening game win by the reigning champions since the holders replaced the hosts as the opening participators in 1974.

The following day, Spain met South Korea in Dallas where they received a late shock. In the first half South Korea had the better of the play (particularly after the 25th minute, when the Spanish Captain Miguel Nadal, was sent off for a foul on Ko Jeong-Woon) and could have been two goals ahead by half-time. The half-time score remained 0-0 thanks only to two excellent saves by the Spanish Keeper Canizares and, at the beginning of the second period, the Spanish brought on Guerrero and reorganised their midfield. This substitution proved to be an inspired decision as, within ten minutes, Guerrero was instrumental in the build up to two goals. Firstly, in the 51st minute, he started the move which led to Salinas opening the scoring and, just five minutes later, he set up Goikoetxea for the second goal. However, as the game progressed, the ten-man Spanish team wilted in the incredible heat (reckoned to be 43 degrees Celsius equal to 110 degrees Fahrenheit) and struggled to retain their lead. Five minutes from the end, Hong Myung-bo pulled a goal back when his free kick was deflected into the net and, in the final minute, Seo Jung-Won levelled the score.

Four days later Spain were in action again, this time against Germany and, forced to reorganise because of Nadal's suspension, brought Hierro back to sweeper and changed their midfield to accommodate this. During the opening quarter of an hour, Spain controlled the game and soon put the nervous-looking German goalkeeper, Illgner, under pressure when, in the ninth minute, Sergi forced a one-handled save when he drove a ball in from the German right flank. Five minutes later, Illgner misjudged a Goikotxea cross and could only stand and watch as it went over the line to give Spain the lead. Germany fought hard to get back into the game but were easily contained by the increasingly confident Spanish defence with first choice keeper Zubizarreta in good form behind them. The score remained 1-0 until three minutes into the second-half when Klinsmann headed a free-kick into the Spanish net. Spain fought back and should have scored again almost immediately but when Germany brought on an attacker (Voller) for midfielder Moller in the 61st minute they began to gain the upper hand. Two substitutions for Spain levelled things out and, although both sides created half-chances to score, each seemed content to settle for the resultant draw.

Over in Boston, two days later, a near capacity crowd of 53,456 saw South Korea and Bolivia play out the first goalless draw of the tournament. Despite the lack of goals, however, this was not at all a dull game and both sides fought hard to score. Bolivia was clearly surprised by the South Koreans' turn of speed and struggled throughout the game to contain their lively forward line. Unfortunately for the South Koreans (who created far more scoring opportunities), their forwards' finishing left much to be desired and it was Bolivia who came closest to breaking the deadlock when a terrific Sanchez free-kick was spectacularly saved by the Korean keeper.

On the 27th June the last two games in the group were played between Germany and South Korea in Dallas and between Bolivia and Spain in Chicago. At the Cotton Bowl Stadium in Dallas, Germany cruised to a 3-0 half-time lead. Klinsmann, in devastating form, put Germany ahead in the 11th minute with a superb swivel shot and, seven minutes later, started the move which led to Riedle scoring the second. South Korea fought hard for a goal but Klinsmann scored his second goal in the 35th minute to make the score 3-0.

South Korea made two substitutions after the break and, as Germany eased back, came into the game themselves. Seven minutes into the second half, Hwang Sun-Hong pulled a goal back with a delicate flick and nine minutes later as the Germans wilted in the heat, Hong Myung-Bo scored a terrific goal with a 30-yard drive. Sensing the danger of the situation, Berti Vogts, the German manager brought on Moller as a substitute for the injured Matthaus and changed his defensive line-up but his side still struggled to hold South Korea. For the closing 25 minutes Germany were forced to pack their defence but, even so, were saved on three occasions by the brilliance of their goalkeeper Illgner whose acrobatic performance ensured that the score remained 3-2 to the holders.

In Chicago, Bolivia and Spain played out the proverbial 'game of two halves' when a dreary first half which yielded a penalty goal for Spain and little else, was followed by a sparkling second half. Spain started the second half quietly and, for a while, seemed to be settling for a 1-0 victory until Caminero made it 2-0 in the 66th minute with a cracking low drive. Right from the kick-off Bolivia hit back with their first ever goal in the World Cup Finals – a 30 yard shot, which was deflected into the Spanish net. Thereafter, both sides went all out for another goal and, although this fell to Spain (Caminero, again, in the 71st minute), Bolivia continued to press for the remaining part of a very entertaining game. This victory confirmed Spain's progress to the next round along with Germany as the qualifiers from Group C.

Meanwhile, the hosts kicked off their tournament in Group A before a capacity crowd of 73,425 at the Detroit Pontiac Silverdome when their opponents were Switzerland who, together with Romania and Colombia made up the group.

The game was a somewhat hesitant affair. Switzerland were without striker Adrian Knup who was nursing an ankle injury and, in his absence, played with just one front man, Chapuisat, for most of the game. Nevertheless, the first real chance of the game fell to Switzerland in the 15th minute when defender Herr sent in a good header which Meola just managed to finger-tip away. Next the Swiss midfielder Sforza had a low shot well saved by Meola and, in the meantime, the American forwards caused problems for the Swiss defence who struggled to cope with their lightning breaks. In the 39th minute Dooley, the big German-born American defender, was fortunate to avoid being sent off when he brought down Sutter just outside of his penalty area but the U.S.A. were punished when Bregy scored with the resultant free-kick. On the stroke of half-time the U.S.A. equalised when Harkes was fouled 30 yards out and Wynalda crashed a tremendous free-kick shot into the top corner of the Swiss net.

The second-half was as evenly-balanced as the first and although both sides came close to scoring, it remained 1-1, a result which neither side relished.

Later that day, over the other side of the continent in Pasadena, 91,865 people were at the Rose Bowl to see Colombia and Romania in action. Colombia had been surprise qualifiers when they topped the South American Group A qualifying competition above Argentina (thanks to an amazing 5-0 victory in Argentina) and were expected to do well in the finals. Colombia began well and were allowed a great deal of possession by the Romanians who were content to defend in depth. The result was a brief spell of exhibition football by the Colombians who seemed intent upon demonstrating their superior ball play whilst, in fact, Romania's defence was not seriously challenged. As if to emphasise the point, Romania took the lead in the 16th minute with virtually their first attack of the game when Raducioiu took on three defenders before firing home a low shot. Just over a quarter of an hour later, following a further unproductive display of the Colombian's dazzling skills, Hagi made it 2-0 when he noticed Cordoba out of position and dipped a cross over his head into the net. Goalkeeper Stelea kept the Romanian lead intact with a string of excellent saves until Valencia pulled a goal back in the 43rd minute when he headed in a corner from Perez.

In the second-half Romania soaked up immense pressure from Colombia with Stelea called upon to stop goalbound attempts from Asprilla and Alvarez before Raducioiu put the result beyond doubt with his second goal in the closing minutes. In a post-match interview the Colombian manager Maturana, still confident that his side would progress further, regarded the game as a 'valuable lesson' – but realised that everything would depend on their next game against the U.S.A.

Before this game was played, Romania faced Switzerland at the Pontiac Silverdome. With Knup back from injury, Switzerland looked an altogether more balanced side and Romania, playing their usual defensive game, allowed the Swiss to dominate play almost from the offset. In the twelfth minute Sutter had a seemingly good goal disallowed for offside but was not to be denied three minutes later when he smashed a Chapuisat pass into the net from outside of the penalty area.

Romania looked to Hagi for an equaliser and, 25 minutes later, he obliged with an unstoppable 25-yard drive. The score remained 1-1 at half-time and after the break Switzerland moved up a gear and posed the Romanians real problems. They took back the lead in the 53rd minute, somewhat fortuitously, when the referee ignored appeals for a Swiss hand-ball and Chapuisat scrambled the ball into the Romanian net during a goalmouth melee. Romania were not so fortunate a few minutes later when they netted but were adjudged to have been offside and thereafter lost all of their composure. Knup made the score 3-1 in the 66th minute when the Romanians were caught with a counterattack and, six minutes later, Bregy claimed Switzerland's fourth goal which was deflected into the net via two Romanian players.

A minute later, the Romanian substitute, Vladoiu, who had come on only three minutes earlier, was sent off for a vicious foul on Ohrel and, on his way to the changing rooms, entered into a furious argument with the Romanian Coach. The hapless Romanian team struggled to score a further goal which would, at least, have improved their goal difference, but the score remained 4-1 to the dominant Swiss.

Over at Pasadena, the U.S.A. met Colombia and both sides knew that a win would be essential to be sure of progress to the next round. Colombia, bemused at their failure against Romania, seemed to be unable to accept the fact that the media hype which had ranked them amongst the favourites counted for nothing on the field and disillusionment was beginning to abound. The exclusion of Gabriel Gomez just hours before the kick-off because of 'death threats' clearly unsettled the Colombian team and, with hindsight, could have been related to the murder of another player Andres Escobar in the following month. Whatever the reason, Colombia began shakily and, in only the third minute, should have gone a goal down when Stewart missed an easy chance. Colombia attacked and came close shortly afterwards but, although they then pushed the Americans onto the defensive for a spell, no real threat was posed. In the 28th minute Wynalda saw his shot beat the Colombian keeper Cordoba only to ricochet off the post and five minutes later the U.S.A. took the lead. John Harkes fired in a hopeful cross-cum-shot and the unfortunate Escobar miskicked it into his own net. (Two weeks later Escobar was shot dead by an irate Colombian supporter – such is the price of failure in some countries).

The Colombian players reacted badly to the setback and their game plan all but evaporated as they struggled to get back on even terms. Wynalda was presented with an easy chance when Cordoba's weak clearance went straight to him, but Herrera managed to prod the ball away and, for a while, the

U.S.A. looked as if they would score a bagful of goals.

The score remained 1-0 at half-time and five minutes after the break the U.S.A. went further ahead when Stewart raced onto a through ball from Ramos and slipped the ball past the advancing keeper into the net. Lalas had a perfectly good goal disallowed and it was all the U.S.A. as the disorganised Colombians wilted. The final score was 2-1, thanks to a last-minute goal from Valencia, but the scoreline belied the total domination of the U.S.A. team in what has been hailed as 'their best-ever World Cup performance'.

The hosts were again in action at Pasadena four days later when Romania were their opponents. U.S. coach Bora Milutinovic kept the same team that had beaten Colombia but they put in a much more subdued performance this time. Playing their usual game of defence in depth with six midfielders drawn back to snuff out any U.S.A. build-up, Romania exposed the weakness of the host's attack and were rarely troubled after the opening few minutes when both Harkes and Wynalda came close. Hagi soon took control of the game and in the 16th minute, Romania counter-attacked with Dan Petrescu scoring a simple goal at the near post. Thereafter Romania easily contained everything that the U.S.A. could throw at them and should have scored more goals as, counterattacking down both wings, they came close on numerous occasions. The score remained 1-0 and, as Switzerland in the meantime had lost 0-2 to Colombia in the remaining game in the group, both Romania and the U.S.A. progressed to the next round accompanied by Switzerland.

Group B comprised the favourites, Brazil, along with Cameroon, Russia and Sweden and began on 19th June at the Rose Bowl in Pasadena when Cameroon faced Sweden. Cameroon started well and might have taken a sensational first minute lead when Ravelli was stretched to hold a shot from Embe. Six minutes later Sweden went ahead when Ljung headed home a simple free kick after the Cameroon defence had left him unmarked. The Swedish defence, however, were themselves far from perfect and 22 minutes later were badly at fault when Embe equalised for Cameroon. First Nilsson put his teammates under pressure with a weak back pass and then Patrik Andersson completely missed his tackle on Omam-Biyik leaving Embe to score a simple goal. In the first minute of the second half, Andersson was again at fault when he and keeper Ravelli misjudged a through ball and allowed Omam-Biyik to nip in and prod the ball home for Cameroon's second goal and 25 minutes later almost gave away a third. In the closing quarter, as the Cameroon players visibly tired, Sweden came back into the game and equalised when substitute Larsson's shot rebounded off the bar and Dahlin volleyed the ball in. In the final 15 minutes Sweden had two more goalbound efforts acrobatically saved by Cameroon's keeper Bell and the score remained 2-2.

Brazil faced Russia at Palo Alto the following day, enthusiastically supported by all but a handful of the 81,061 crowd. The Russian team (a number of whom had been in open conflict with their coach Sadyrin) seemed bemused by the whole thing and turned on a poor display. In the event, it was not until the 26th minute that Brazil took the lead through Romario and, thereafter, it was only a question of how many goals Russia would concede. Eight minutes into the second half Rai made it 2-0 with the first penalty of the finals when he sent Kharin the wrong way and a big score looked to be on the cards. Kharin, however, was made of sterner stuff than his teammates and he single-handedly kept out everything that the Brazilians threw at him to keep the scoreline at 0-2.

Three days later, Brazil became the first team to qualify for the next round when they beat Cameroon 3-0 at Palo Alto. Cameroon's players had initally threated to boycott the game because they had not been paid their bonuses for reaching the finals but, when they did turn out, they turned on a surprisingly good performance. Playing with enthusiasm and commitment, the Africans held the Brazilians until seven minutes before half-time when Romario finished off a superb move by Mauro Silva. In the second half Brazil took control as they switched the play to their wings and, in the 63rd minute Cameroon had a player sent off when Song hit Bebeto with a crunching late tackle. His departure (at the age of only 17) put him into the record books as the youngest player to be sent off in the World Cup Finals and, before play recommenced, another record was set when Roger Milla (at the age of 42) came on as substitute for Embe. Milla had little opportunity to shine for Cameroon as Brazil scored their second goal directly from the restart via Marcio Santos. Bebeto made it 3-0 in the 72nd minute and Brazil were in the second round.

Later that day at the Pontiac Silverdome in Detroit, Russia got off to a tremendous start against Sweden when they took a 3rd minute penalty lead through Salenko. Sweden, however, were not prepared to let this early setback trouble them and they pressured for an equaliser. Dahlin came close when he shot against the bar and, minutes later, saw the Russian keeper Kharin save a goalbound shot. Seven minutes from half-time the Russian full-back Gorlukovich (who had been booked in the first minute of the game) was lucky to remain on the pitch when he fouled Dahlin in his penalty area, but Sweden equalised from the resulting spot-kick.

Russia should have taken the lead again at the start of the second half when

Radchenko, with only the goalkeeper to beat, shot just wide and two minutes later the outcome of the game was decided. Gorlukovich, who had been involved in a running battle with Dahlin throughout the first half, was penalised for an off-the-ball offence and was given his marching orders by the French referee M. Quiniou. Sweden then took advantage of their extra man and Dahlin headed them into the lead in the 59th minute. The final half-hour of the match was controlled by Sweden and, nine minutes from the end, Dahlin made it 3-1 to ensure his country's victory.

Four days later Russia crushed the hapless Cameroon team in a game which rewrote the record books in two different ways. Firstly Oleg Salenko scored a hat-trick in the first half and then went on to become the only man to score five goals in a World Cup finals game. Secondly, Roger Milla, who came on as a second-half substitute, scored for Cameroon in the 47th minute to become the oldest person to score in the World Cup finals. These statistics apart, the game was such a one-sided afair that Russia could have reached double figures against a disorganised and dispirited Cameroon side who, in the end, should have been glad that the final score was only 6-1.

The last game in the group, between Brazil and Sweden, proved another unique World Cup finals first, in that the two sides became the first to face one another for the sixth time. Brazil had won four of their previous encounters with the other a draw and, having already qualified for the next round with two wins, were expected to coast to a third victory. Sweden, however, had other ideas and decided to take the game to the Brazilians from the kick-off. Sweden came close to scoring in the tenth minute when Ljung broke through the Brazil defence shooting just over the bar and, for the first time in the series, Brazil looked vulnerable. In the 21st minute, Kennet Andersson put Sweden ahead after Brolin had chipped a delightful ball over the heads of the Brazilian defenders and, for the remainder of the first half, the Swedes threatened to score more. Seconds before half-time Patrik Andersson should have made it 2-0 but missed an easy chance.

Brazil equalised two minutes into the second half through Romario and, thereafter, both teams seemed content to play out the draw which ensured Sweden's progress to the next round.

Group D was made up of Argentina, Bulgaria, Greece and Nigeria and began with a 4-0 pasting for Greece from former holders, Argentina. Diego Maradona had returned to the Argentinian team following his 15-month ban for failing a dope test whilst playing for Napoli and his presence raised the morale of the squad. Neither he nor his teammates could then have had an inkling of the problems which his return would cause only days later and he turned in a classic performance in his 20th appearance in the finals. Taking a lead in the very first minute through Batistuta, Argentina were never seriously tested by a Greek team who seemed to be in awe of the occasion, and looked as if they could score at will. In the event Batistuta scored a hat-trick (with the other goal from Maradona on the hour) to steer his country towards the second-round.

Nigeria, making their first appearance in the World Cup Finals, had a convincing win over Bulgaria later that day in Dallas. After a good start, Bulgaria (who had qualified unexpectedly by virtue of a late goal against France in their last game found themselves a goal down in the 21st minute when Yekini cracked in a cross from the right. Bulgaria kept their composure and soon struck back with a superb free-kick by Stoichkov which flew into the Nigerian net but, astonishingly, was disallowed. Just before half-time Amokachi put Nigeria 2-0 ahead and the scrappy second-half was notable only for a third Nigerian goal by Amunike.

The next game in the group featured Argentina and Nigeria and when Nigeria took the lead in only the eighth minute, memories of Argentina's 1990 defeat at the hands, or rather feet, of Cameroon were rekindled. This time, however, Argentina fought well and, with Maradona in good form, struck back through Caniggia in the 22nd minute, before taking the lead seven minutes later when he scored his second. The Nigerian defenders resorted to downright violent play and it was only a poor performance from Mr. Karlsson (the referee) that prevented them from finishing with only nine men. In the second half, few scoring chances arose and the 2-1 closing scoreline ensured Argentina's progress to the next round. Although the game itself was unmemorable, it's aftermath shook the sport to it's foundation when Maradona failed a post-match drug test. No fewer than five separate prohibited substances were found in Maradona's urine sample and, with the results of a second test the same, he was immediately banned by both FIFA and the Argentinian FA.

On 26th June, Bulgaria faced Greece in Chicago, unaware of the Maradona bombshell which was soon to explode and, in their 18th World Cup appearance, Bulgaria, at last, chalked up their first victory. Taking a 5th minute lead through a Stoichkov penalty, Bulgaria were never seriously troubled by a Greek team which fielded only four of the players who had started their previous game. The end result was an easy 4-0 victory for Bulgaria and this time the Greek Coach Panagoulias blamed the referee for his team's defeat!

The Maradona drug sensation actually surfaced only hours before Argentina met Bulgaria in Dallas and the effect on the Argentinian team was shattering. So much of Argentina's team spirit and strategy had been built upon the rejuvenated Maradona that, when he was suddenly gone, the team struggled. After a nervy, goalless first half, Bulgaria settled to the task after the break and took the lead through Stoichkov on the hour. Thereafter they defended in depth and somehow kept Argentina from scoring an equaliser. Indeed, in injury time, they even managed to score a second through Sirakov and this goal gave them second-place in the group above Argentina.

Meanwhile in the Foxboro Stadium in Massachusetts, Greece, already out of the competition, faced Nigeria with another greatly-changed team. This time, however, they held out until the final minute of the first half before conceding a goal. Similarly, in the second half, Greece, although posing no threat to the Nigerian goal, held out until injury-time before conceding a second goal. This was scored by Amokachi and, effectively, took Nigeria from third to first place in the group and a plum second round tie.

Group E was made up of Eire, Italy, Mexico and Norway and began with an unexpected result when Italy faced Ireland in New Jersey. In 1990 Italy had put paid to Ireland's chances of glory when they beat them 1-0 in the quarter-finals and a very determined Irish team was looking for revenge. Supported by a huge part of the 74,826 who were packed into the Giants' Stadium, Eire did not take long to show Italy that they meant business when, in only the 12th minute, they took the lead. Ray Houghton ran the ball along the edge of the Italian penalty area and, seeing Pagliuca off his line, dipped a shot just under the bar. Italy seemed to be stunned by this unexpected turn of events and failed to respond with anything approaching a cohesive attack, leaving only Roberto Baggio to take on the resolute Irish defence. Italy failed to create a single chance in the first half and were lucky not to find themselves two down after the break when John Sheridan rifled a shot against their bar. As the tempo of the game slowed in the terrific heat, Ireland retained their edge and composure and held on for a shock win.

Over in Washington, Norway, through to their first finals game since 1938, took on Mexico in the heat of the RFK Stadium and surprised everyone by adapting to the conditions better. Up front, Mexico had Hugo Sanchez and Zague who both looked the part as they displayed their great ball-skills, but Norway's resolute defence was rarely troubled by their antics. On the half-hour, Norway seemed to have taken a deserved lead only to have the 'goal' disallowed for offside and, three minutes before the interval, Mexico had a further escape when Bratseth headed wide with the keeper beaten.

And so it continued in the second half as the Mexican attack promised much but delivered nothing while all the real threats came from Norway. In the 77th minute midfielder Kjetil Rekdal replaced Erik Mykland and with only five minutes left to play, collected the ball when Fjortoft was pulled back on the edge of the Mexican area, slipping it into the net at the far post. Mexico came close to equalising bizarrely when a diving Zague header struck the Norwegian post, bounced back and hit him on the head, then was cleared by Berg as it trickled towards the net. Norway held onto the lead and faced Italy in their next game which was played in New Jersey.

Italy, with the support of most of the 74,624 crowd, were desperate for a win to avoid an early return home and they were quickly onto the attack against the Scandinavians. In the first 20 minutes the two Baggios, Roberto and Dino, (not related) both came close to giving Italy the lead but Thorstvedt in the Norwegian goal kept them out. Then, in the 21st minute, Italy's keeper, Pagliuca, entered the record books in a way that he would have wished to avoid when, following a foul on Leonhardsen, he became the first goalkeeper to be sent off in the World Cup Finals. The Italian coach, Sacchi, immediately brought on his standby goalkeeper and, to everyone's amazement, decided that Roberto Baggio should be the player to be substituted.

Norway, however, failed to grasp their advantage and, for the remainder of the first half, were unable to muster an attack worth mentioning. At half-time they replaced Rushfeldt with Jahn Ivar Jakobsen and, in the third minute of the second half, came close to scoring when Mykland headed over the bar. Almost immediately Italy had to replace Baresi who was injured but still, Norway were unable to make any headway against their depleted opponents. Indeed, it was Italy who posed the greatest threat and, in the 69th minute, Dino Baggio headed them into the lead. In the closing quarter of the game, Italy were virtually reduced to nine men when Maldini injured his ankle and became little more than a passenger and Norway, with increasing desperation, pressed for an equaliser. A few minutes from the end they thought that they had achieved this when they got the ball into the Italian net but the goal was disallowed for an infringement as Italy held on for the win.

The following day, Eire met Mexico in the steaming heat of Orlando in a game that is best remembered for the antics of the Irish manager Jack Charlton who, once again, found himself in confrontation with FIFA officials. Ireland set off at a furious rate and went all out to take the lead during the first 20 minutes but Mexico held firm. As half-time approached it was Mexico who took the lead with a thunderous 20 metre drive from Luis Garcia and this left the weary Irish chasing the game. In the 66th minute Garcia scored a second and the irate Ireland manager Jack Charlton then had his infamous confrontation with FIFA officials who seemed intent upon preventing substitute Aldridge from taking the field even through Coyne had already been withdrawn. When the managerial confrontation had ended, Ireland fought back well and were rewarded with an 84th minute consolation goal which was to prove vital in deciding their final position in the group.

On the 28th June the final two games in the group were played simultaneously, Ireland against Norway in New Jersey and Italy against Mexico in Washington and the final scorelines of each game reflected the tightness of the group.

In New Jersey, Ireland went for a win to ensure their progression to the next round while Norway played their usual defensive game in a far from memorable tie. After the dullest first half of the series, the Irish came closest to breaking the deadlock in the second half but, as the match ground to a goalless draw, both sides looked anxiously to the game in Washington to see if they had reached the next round.

Over in Washington, Italy and Mexico fought out another draw in an equally poor game which ended 1-1 and confirmed Mexico as the group winners above Ireland on goal difference. Italy finished third but were delighted to progress to the next round as one of the best third-placed teams.

Group F was made up of Belgium, Holland, Morocco and Saudi Arabia and opened with a game in the Citrus Bowl Stadium, Orlando, between Belgium and Morocco. Despite the tremendous humidity and heat, it was the Belgians who controlled the first half with an uncharacteristic display of attacking football. Degryse went close in the seventh minute then, three minutes later, headed what was to be the only goal of the game when the Moroccan defence failed to clear a Scifo cross. Belgium could have grabbed three more goals as they pounded the Moroccan defence but Chaouch came close to levelling the score twice when first the bar and then Preud'homme in the Belgium goal denied him. In the 88th minute goalkeeper Alaoui became the first person to come on as a third substitute in the World Cup finals when he replaced Azmi.

The following day Holland got off to a nervous start against Saudi Arabia in Washington. The Saudis went ahead in the 18th minute through an Amin header and, throughout the first half, looked capable of scoring more against the disorganised Dutch defence. After the break Holland went onto the attack and, in the 50th minute, equalised through Jonk. In the closing minutes, as the game seemed destined to be a draw, the Saudi goalkeeper Al Deayea handed Holland victory when he misjudged a lob and presented Taument with an open goal.

The next game in the group brought together keen rivals Belgium and Holland in one of the most thrilling games of the series. With play swinging from end to end the outcome was decided by an outstanding display from the Belgian goalkeeper Michel Preud'homme who commanded his area in a way that few other keepers ever have. Both sides created openings to score but not until the 65th minute was it that Phillipe Albert broke the deadlock when he drove the ball home for Belgium from a corner. Five minutes later Albert should have scored a second but somehow managed to miss the open goal and throught the final quarter keeper Preud'homme, virtually single-handedly, kept Holland at bay to give Belgium an historic win.

The same day, the first-ever all-Arab finals clash between Saudi Arabia and Morocco took place in New Jersey and it was the Saudis playing only their second final series game who came out on top. After taking an 8th minute lead from the penalty spot, the Saudis struggled to retain their advantage and it came as no surprise when Morocco equalised 20 minutes later. On the stroke of half-time, Saudi Arabia went ahead again when the Moroccan keeper diverted a weak shot into his own net and, in the second-half, the Saudi keeper played a 'blinder' to ensure his country's historic victory.

In the closing games of the group, Morocco v Holland and Belgium v Saudi Arabia, the greatest pressure was undeniably on Holland whose talented squad had not performed to the best of their abilities in the opening two games. Morocco, with nothing to lose, took a physical approach and, in the first half-hour, had four players booked for 'overenthusiastic' tackling. Three minutes from the interval Bergkamp put Holland ahead as the Moroccan goalkeeper and two defenders comically collided and ended up in an undignified heap.

Morocco hit back in the opening minute of the second half when Nader took advantage of a defensive lapse and it was not until the 79th minute that Roy gave the Dutch the lead again and, thanks to an unexpected result in the other game, top place in the group.

The 'unexpected' result arose in Washington where Belgium were defeated 1-0 by the Saudis thanks to an amazing 5th minute goal from Owairan. Taking the ball in his own half, Owairan took on and beat no fewer than four Belgian outfielders before cracking a terrific shot past Michael Preud'homme. Belgium were, thereafter, chasing the game and, although they attacked continually, the Saudis defended in depth and threatened to add a second on the counter-attack. In the end, Saudi Arabia leapfrogged over Belgium to take second-place on goal difference although Belgium, too, qualified as one of the best third-placed teams.

The line-ups for the straight-knockout second round were thus decided and the eight ties were as follows: – Germany v Belgium; Spain v Switzerland; Saudi Arabia v Sweden; Romania v Argentina; Holland v Eire; Brazil v USA; Nigeria v Italy and Mexico v Bulgaria.

In the first of these ties Germany faced Belgium in Chicago in the sort of playing conditions that most European teams had been praying for – cool, windy and wet – a welcome change from the stifling heat of the group games. Despite this, the game started explosively as Germany took a fifth minute lead in their first real attack of the tie. The scorer was Rudi Voller (brought back into the team because of the change in the weather) and his presence enabled the Germans to regain their championship-winning form. Belgium pulled a goal back in the eight minute but with Klinsmann able to play his preferred deeper game because of the presence of Voller, the Germans were 2-1 ahead three minutes later. Voller scored his second goal in the 40th minute and, in the second half, Klinsmann came close to adding two further goals but was thwarted by Preud'homme in the Belgium goal. With a quarter of an hour to play the German defender Helmer merited being sent off when he blatantly pulled down Weber in the area but the incident was ignored by the Swiss referee. (It was not, however, ignored by FIFA and the referee in question, Mr. Rothlisberger, was harshly sent home for missing such an obvious foul).

German substitute, Kuntz, missed a sitter in the 88th minute and, when Albert scored a second for Belgium a minute later, Belgium threw everything into attack for the remaining few minutes of injury-time in a vain effort to level the score.

Switzerland, under the guidance of Roy Hodgson, their English-born manager, had surprised many by reaching the second round and they began confidently against Spain despite the absence of the injured Sutter who had played so well in the earlier games. Chapuisat caused the Spanish defence all kinds of problems in the first ten minutes but was then involved in a peculiar incident which led to Spain taking the lead. Collecting the ball on the halfway line he was poleaxed by a crunching Nadal tackle and, as the Swiss appealed for a foul, Pascolo ran onto a through ball and put Spain ahead. As Spain dropped back to defend their lead, Switzerland pressed for an equaliser but found the Spanish keeper Zubizaretta in commanding form, making a string of saves including an incredible reflex-save in the 65th minute. Ten minutes later, Luis Enrique put Spain 2-0 up and the Swiss fightback was at an end, an 87th minute penalty bringing the final score to 3-0.

In Dallas the next day, Saudi Arabia's hopes of further progress against the Swedes were quickly and clinically crushed as Sweden went ahead in only the fifth minute through Dahlin. Throughout the rest of the first half Sweden created opening after opening and should have been four goals up by half-time. In the second half, the Swedes tired in the torrid heat but still managed to go 2-0 up through Kennet Andersson in the 50th minute. Although substitute Al Ghesheyan pulled a goal back in the 85th minute, Sweden were not seriously tested and ran out 3-1 winners.

Over in Pasadena the demoralised Argentinian team were still reeling from the after-effects of Maradona's expulsion from the tournament, and quickly found themselves 1-0 down against Romania when Dumitrescu scored in the 11th minute. Although Batistuta pulled a goal back from the penalty spot five minutes later, Argentina were no match for the Hagi-led Romanian team who went back into the lead within two minutes. Hagi himself made it 3-1 in the 56th minute and despite a relatively respectable final scoreline of 3-2, Argentina were hopelessly outplayed.

In Orlando, two slip-ups, one by full-back Phelan and another by goalkeeper Bonner, put an end to the Republic of Ireland's hopes of progressing to the quarter-finals. Despite a welcome cloud-cover, the temperature on the pitch was a sweltering 90° Fahrenheit and after only ten minutes Phelan attempted to head the ball back to a teammate but, instead, found Overmars whose pass left Bergkamp to score a simple goal. Undeterred, the Irish fought back with their usual tenacity but caused the Dutch defence few problems. Five minutes from half-time Ireland were shocked when Holland went 2-0 up as a result of keeper Bonner's misjudgement of a tame 30 metre strike from Jonk.

The second-half continued with more of the same from the Irish who surged gamely forward in numbers but, in reality, rarely troubled the Dutch defence who had little difficulty in holding their 2-0 lead.

Over at the Stanford Stadium in Palo Alto, the stage was set for the coming-of-age of American soccer as the home side faced the most consistent World Cup country, Brazil. Given that the game was played on the 4th July, American Independence day, hopes were high for a home victory but, unfortunately, Brazil forgot to read the script! The goalless first half is best remembered for the dismissal of Brazil's Leonardo for the vicious elbowing of Ramos a minute from half-time but, with Ramos having to leave the field with a fractured skull, the U.S.A.'s advantage was clearly eroded. Indeed, in the second half with the U.S.A. unable to create a single scoring opportunity, it was Brazil who seemed to have the extra man as they took the lead in the 74th minute through Bebeto. The U.S.A., too, were reduced to ten men in the 87th minute when Clavijo committed a second bookable offence, but by then it was clear that the home team would progress no further.

The following day Nigeria took a 27th minute lead over Italy and, for the next hour seemed destined for a quarter-final place. In an over-physical game, Nigeria had four players booked and were fortunate not to have two of them sent off while Italy were unfortunate to have even more players booked thanks to some curious decisions from the Mexican referee. Indeed, when the Italian substitute Zola was sent off for no apparent reason in the 76th minute, Italy looked to be on their way out of the tournament. Throwing caution to the wind Italy pressed for an equaliser and, in the 88th minute were rewarded when Roberto Baggio slipped the ball wide of the Nigerian goalkeeper into the net. In extra-time Italy gained the upper hand despite being a man down and the Nigerian defending became very ragged as the game progressed. Roberto Baggio scored a second from the penalty spot in the 102nd minute and Italy held on to their hard-earned victory.

The last second-round game between Mexico and Bulgaria will probably be remembered more for the farcical refereeing than for the game itself. Mr. Al Sharif (the Syrian official for the game) clearly lacked the experience to handle such a demanding tie and, thanks to his ineptitude, the game became something of a lottery. Bulgaria took a sixth minute lead through Stoichkov but the scores were levelled ten minutes later when Aspe converted a questionable penalty. The game degenerated as the referee's decisions became even more erratic and, while vicious fouls went unpunished, players found themselves booked and even sent off for no apparent reason. With the scores still tied 1-1 at the end of extra-time the game became the first in the series to go to penalties and Bulgaria easily won the shootout 3-1.

So it was that no fewer than seven European countries progressed to the quarter-finals – a feat unequalled since 1958 when, curiously enough, Brazil was also the only non-European qualifier. The first of the quarter-final games was played at the Foxboro Stadium and featured Italy and Spain.

Having twice come within minutes of elimination in the previous rounds, Italy again rode their luck in the quarter-final. They began brightly enough and were unruffled by the at times violent tackling of the Spanish – particularly Abelardo who collected an early booking. In the 13th minute, Roberto Baggio looked certain to score until his shot ricocheted off Ferrer for a corner and, twelve minutes later, the other Baggio, Dino, put Italy ahead with a 25 metre drive.

Spain, too, did their share of attacking and midfielder Caminero put in two good efforts in the first half-hour. On the hour, Caminero had another shot and, this time, thanks to deflection off an Italian defender, the ball found the net. This equaliser gave a tremendous boost to the Spaniards who took complete control of the game as their Italian opponents visibly wilted. In the 83rd minute, Spain looked certain to take the lead when substitute Salinas was clean through with only Pagliuca to beat but his shot struck the keeper's outstretched leg and was deflected away. Strangely, this miss seemed to give the exhausted Italians new life and, within five minutes, Roberto Baggio, Italy's lone striker, spurted clear of the Spanish defence, rounded the keeper and shot his team into the semi-finals.

Over in Dallas, Holland took on Brazil in a hard-fought encounter. After an unmemorable first-half in which neither side created a single clear-cut chance of a goal, the game came alive early in the second-half and the pressure was on Holland. Romario opened the scoring in the 52nd minute with a low drive and both he and Bebeto came close to grabbing a second within the next five minutes as Holland struggled to contain the Brazilian attack. Bebeto made it 2-0 in the 62nd minute when the linesman ignored a clear offside and this seemed to spur Holland into action. Dennis Bergkamp made it 2-1 within two minutes and, when Winter headed Holland's second just over ten minutes later, the game could have gone either way. In the event, it was Brazilian Branco who broke the deadlock when he thundered in a 30 metre free kick into the Dutch net to put Brazil into the semi-finals for the first time since 1970.

Next day, in the Giants Stadium, New Jersey, the reigning champions Germany took on Bulgaria in a game which, according to the formbook, should have been a formality. In the 11th minute Bulgaria gave Germany a brief taste of what was to come when Sirakov's goalbound shot was blocked by Illgner and Balakov clattered the rebound against the post. Throughout the first half, Bulgaria had the most possession and it was only because Germany managed to shackle Stoichkov by close man-marking that more goalscoring chances were denied them. Germany, too, had their moments and, early in the second-half Klinsmann was brought down by Penev and Matthaus scored from the resulting penalty.

Undeterred, Bulgaria counterattacked but made little headway and, in the 73rd minute Germany seemed to have gone 2-0 up when Voller netted a rebounding Moller shot. The referee, however, ruled that Voller was offside and within two minutes Bulgaria were back on level terms. The scorer, inevitably, was Stoichkov, who curled a wonderful free-kick over the defensive wall into the German net. Three minutes later, Bulgaria went ahead when Lechkov's diving header flew into the German net and, in the remaining few minutes, Germany threw everything into the attack. Bulgaria brought on a defender for Stoichkov, tightened their defence and, with Mikhailov in fine form between the posts, denied Germany the equaliser, to reach their first semi-final.

The last quarter-final between Sweden and Romania was the only one to go to extra time and, eventually, to penalties. After an early chance when Dahlin headed against the Romanian post, little was seen of either attack until the closing quarter of normal time. On 75 minutes, Ingesson had a goal disallowed for a foul on the Romanian goalkeeper and, just three minutes later, Brolin ran onto a free-kick and, from a tight angle, smacked the ball into the Romanian net. As Romania came looking for an equaliser, Sweden made the mistake of easing back and in the 88th minute Raducioiu levelled the score from close range. Ten minutes into extra-time Raducioiu scored a second and when, two minutes later, Swedish midfielder Schwarz was sent off for a foul on Dumitrescu, Sweden's hopes of reaching the semi-finals seemed to have been crushed. Sweden, however, responded by sending on Larsson for Dahlin and from the resultant pressure, Kennet Andersson headed a late equaliser. When the penalty shootout took place the score was tied 4-4 after the first five shots and substitute Larsson scored with the next kick to give Sweden the last semi-final place.

Just three days later Bulgaria faced Italy and Sweden met Brazil to decide which teams would contest the final on 17th July. The first of these in New Jersey brought Italy back to the venue where they had fared so badly against Eire but this time it was a different story. For most of the first half Italy were in complete control against a Bulgarian side that seemed content to have reached the semi-final itself, and Roberto Baggio, in particular, was in sparkling form. In the 20th minute he created an opening from nowhere when he collected a throw-in, ghosted past two players and curled a perfect shot just inside the Bulgarian post to put Italy ahead. For a brief time the Italians looked as if they would overrun Bulgaria and, after Albertini had twice shot against the bar, Baggio scored his second in the 25th minute. Bulgaria, however, were made of stern stuff and, weathering the Italian onslaught, they came back at the end of the first half when Stoichkov converted a penalty to become the tournament's joint top-scorer.

The second half proved to be something of an anticlimax with neither side creating an opening of note. Bulgaria claimed late penalties for a handball and a foul on Lechkov but these were turned down by the French referee Joel Quiniou who was aware of the Bulgarians' tendency to 'play' for free-kicks. So Italy progressed to the Final and Bulgaria to the play-off, both physically drained by the heat and the constant travelling.

Over in Pasadena, the Swedish side, who had already travelled enormous distances in their previous games, found themselves back at the Rose Bowl facing a much fresher Brazilian team. Brazil dominated whilst Sweden could only hang on and hope – such was their obvious exhaustion in the tremendous heat. The game was goalless at half-time despite a barrage of Brazilian shots at the Swedish goal and when Sweden were reduced to ten men with the dismissal of Thern in the 63rd minute, their fate was sealed. Yet it was not until the 80th minute that Brazil finally took the lead through Romario and the 1-0 closing scoreline was a testimony to the courage and determination of the Swedish side.

Three days later a revitalised Swedish side turned out again at the Rose Bowl for the 3rd Place Play-off and this time it was their Bulgarian opponents who were jet-lagged and out of touch. The result? Almost a walkover for Sweden, 4-0 up at half-time before they eased off and more of a testimony to the good fortune of the team which did not have to travel than a reflection on either side's ability.

And so to the Final in Pasadena the following day when Brazil were the lucky ones who didn't have to fly across four time zones. With both countries having already won the World Cup three times, the winner would become the first fourth-time holder of the trophy but which would it be?

Italian coach Sacchi surprised everyone by recalling Franco Baresi into the centre of his defence just three weeks after having a cartilage operation and, in a way, his gamble paid off. Italy's hero from the earlier games, Roberto Baggio, pronounced himself fit despite a hamstring injury and the game started before a crowd of 94,194.

In only the third minute Brazil showed that they meant business when Mazinho flattened Berti and was booked and nine minutes later, Romario's header was easily saved by Pagliuca. Five minutes on and the two survivors from Italy's 1982 World Championship team, (Baresi and Massaro), almost put Italy ahead when Baresi's defence-splitting pass was collected by Massaro whose goalward run was stopped by the diving Brazilian keeper. In the 25th minute a 'Branco special' free kick was scrambled away by Pagliuca and, as the game swung from end to end, neither side was able to take control. Indeed, it was not until the 75th minute that either keeper was seriously troubled and then it was Pagliuca who mishandled a Mauro Silva shot which struck the post and rebounded into his arms.

With the score still 0-0 at the end of 90 minutes, extra-time brought rather more chances. In the third minute of extra-time Brazil had the best opening yet when Pagliuca totally missed a Cafu cross presenting Bebeto with an open goal which, wrongfooted, he missed. Three minutes later, Roberto Baggio's 25 metre volley almost caught Taffarel but he recovered to tip the ball over the bar. At the end of the first period of extra-time the referee, Sandor Puhl, demanded an immediate turnaround but, amusingly, he was ignored by all 22 players who tracked to the touchline and the beckoning water bottles. The second period of extra-time provided few openings of note and with the first-ever 0-0 final score, the penalty shootout ensued.

Bravely but rather foolishly, Baresi, who had received treatment for cramp only minutes earlier, took the first penalty and blasted it over the bar. Brazil, however, were unable to exploit this as Marcio Santos's weak shot was easily saved by Pagliuca. Thereafter, Albertini and Evani scored for Italy and Romario and Branco scored for Brazil to leave the aggregate 2-2. However, the next Italian, Massaro, had his shot well-saved by Taffarel and, after Dunga had made it 3-2 it fell to the limping Roberto Baggio to keep Italy in the game. His shot sailed over the bar and Brazil became the champions for the fourth time.

As the exhausted players tramped off the field at the end, FIFA officials must have been asking themselves if their decision to play the tournament with venues that were such great distances apart had been a wise one.

GROUP A

	P	W	D	L	F	A	Pts
Romania	3	2	0	1	5	5	6
Switzerland	3	1	1	1	6	4	4
USA	3	1	1	1	3	3	4
Colombia	3	1	0	2	4	6	3

GROUP B

	P	W	D	L	F	A	Pts
Brazil	3	2	1	0	6	1	7
Sweden	3	1	2	0	6	4	5
Russia	3	1	0	2	7	6	3
Cameroon	3	0	1	2	3	11	1

GROUP C

	P	W	D	L	F	A	Pts
Germany	3	2	1	0	5	3	7
Spain	3	1	2	0	6	4	5
South Korea	3	0	2	1	4	5	2
Bolivia	3	0	1	2	1	4	1

GROUP D

	P	W	D	L	F	A	Pts
Nigeria	3	2	0	1	6	2	6
Bulgaria	3	2	0	1	6	3	6
Argentina	3	2	0	1	6	3	6
Greece	3	0	0	3	0	10	0

GROUP E

	P	W	D	L	F	A	Pts
Mexico	3	1	1	1	3	3	4
Eire	3	1	1	1	2	2	4
Italy	3	1	1	1	2	2	4
Norway	3	1	1	1	1	1	4

GROUP F

	P	W	D	L	F	A	Pts
Holland	3	2	0	1	4	3	6
Saudi Arabia	3	2	0	1	4	3	6
Belgium	3	2	0	1	2	1	6
Morocco	3	0	0	3	2	5	0

SECOND ROUND

Germany 3   Belgium 2
Spain 3   Switzerland 0
Saudi Arabia 1   Sweden 3
Romania 3   Argentina 2
Holland 2   Eire 0
Brazil 1   USA 0
Nigeria 1   Italy 2
(After extra time)

Mexico 1   Bulgaria 1
After extra time – Bulgaria won 3-1 on penalties

QUARTER-FINALS

Italy 2   Spain 1
Holland 2   Brazil 3
Bulgaria 2   Germany 1
Romania 2   Sweden 2
After extra time – Sweden won 5-4 on penalties

SEMI-FINALS

Bulgaria 1   Italy 2
Sweden 0   Brazil 1

THIRD-PLACE MATCH

Sweden 4   Bulgaria 0

FINAL

Brazil .... (0) (0) **0**   **Italy** .... (0) (0) **0**

After extra time – Brazil won 3-2 on penalties

Team: Taffarel, Jorginho (sub. Cafu), Aldair, Marcio Santos, Branco, Mazinho (sub. Viola), Dunga, Mauro Silva, Zinho, Romario, Bebeto

Team: Pagliuca, Mussi (sub. Apolloni), Maldini, Baresi, Benarrivo, Berti, Albertini, Baggio (D) (sub. Evani), Donadoni, Baggio (R), Massaro

SIXTEENTH WORLD CUP

France 1998

Back to Europe, France to be precise, and the 16th World Cup Final Series was contested by the biggest number of countries ever – an increase of one third from 24 to 32. Such an increase required careful organisation and the extraordinary cooperation of the French government (accompanied by great expenditure) meant that by June 1998 no fewer than ten new and refurbished stadia were available for the 64 games to be played.

With eight groups of four countries, the 48 first-round games were purposely spread throughout the ten stadia so that every team had to travel to play their games. Supported by organiser Michel Platini whose aim was to involve as many of his fellow countrymen as possible, this widescale distribution of games enabled 56 of the 64 games to be played within just three weeks (although with hindsight, it would have been better to shorten this somewhat).

Group A was made up of the reigning champions, Brazil, together with Morocco, Norway and Scotland and kicked off on 10th June after a colourful opening ceremony in the magnificent new St. Denis Stadium in Paris. Brazil's opponents were Scotland, a team renowned for their defensive prowess, but not well-endowed with strikers. Within four minutes the champions took the lead through defender Cesar Sampaio who was given a free header from a corner-kick and, for a quarter of an hour, the Scots struggled to restrict Brazil's lead to a single goal. With their 39 year-old keeper Jim Leighton (the oldest player in the tournament) looking more like a contender for the World middleweight boxing championship with eyebrows caked in petroleum jelly, the Scots managed to get back into the game and, eight minutes before the break, were awarded a penalty for a push on Gallacher. John Collins converted the spot-kick and at half-time, the score remained 1-1. In the second-half Brazil's efforts to recover the lead were frustated by the well-organised Scottish defence and it was not until the uninspired Bebeto was replaced by Denilson in the 70th minute that the Brazilian attack looked like scoring again. Even then it required a defensive mix-up to put Brazil back in the lead and this was provided when full-back Boyd, the shakiest of Scotland's defenders, put a Leighton clearance into his own net in the 73rd minute. This virtually ended the Scots' hope of a point and gave the ordinary-looking Brazilians the start for which they had hoped.

Later the same day, in Montpellier, Norway were greatly surprised by the excellence of the Moroccan attack when, after a period of initial dominance, they found themselves struggling against a forward line lead by Hadji and Hadda. Hadji in particular teased the Norwegian defence with a series of mazy runs and, in the 38th minute, opened the scoring with a splendid shot after leaving Dan Eggen standing. The Norwegian response was to revert to the long-ball game punting high crosses into the box and, on the stroke of half-time, this paid dividends when the Morrocan keeper flapped at a Rekdal free-kick and defender Chippo headed the loose-ball into his own goal. Undeterred, Morocco regained the lead in the 58th minute with the move of the match when Hadda volleyed an unstoppable shot into the Norwegian net. Norway again peppered high balls into the Moroccan area and, within minutes, the Moroccan keeper was found wanting as Eggen headed a loose clearance into the net. In the end Morocco, having played the best football, found themselves hanging on for a point and managed to do so only because their keeper, putting aside his earlier errors, brought off a series of good saves.

This result left the group wide open and, six days later, Scotland faced Norway in Bordeaux knowing that a defeat would end their hopes of progressing beyond the first round for the first time ever. In the first-half Norway swamped the midfield and left a solitary Tore Andre Flo to battle against the Scots who, in their turn, enjoyed most of the possession and attacking play without creating any clear-cut chances. Durie might have earned Scotland a penalty when he was fouled in the area but at half-time the game remained goalless. At the start of the second-half Scotland were caught napping when Harvard Flo headed Norway into the lead virtually from the kick-off and did well to reassert their grip on the game. In the 66th minute Burley equalised when he beat two defenders to a through ball and guided the ball superbly over the advancing Norwegian keeper. For the remainder of the game the Scots pressed for the winner without any success and both sides settled for a 1-1 draw.

Later that day in Nantes, Brazil routed Morocco with the kind of attacking performance for which they are renowned. With Ronaldo in sparkling form, they took an early lead and for much of the game, threatened to run amok. Ronaldo suffered a vicious 'studding' by Hadda which, amazingly, went unpunished but that did not stop him from being man of the match which

Brazil won 3-0 to ensure their progress to the second round.

A week later, on June 23rd, Brazil faced Norway in Marseille at the same time as Scotland met Morocco in St. Etienne. Attention focused on the clash between Morocco and Scotland because it was widely assumed that Brazil would trounce Norway and the Scots fancied their chances for a victory. However, it was not to be and, within minutes, Morocco came close to scoring as Scotland struggled to hold them. In fact, this was to be Scotland's most inept performance of the tournament and, after Bassir had put Morocco into the lead in the 22nd minute, they always looked likely to score more.

As it was, Scotland held out until the start of the second-half when the Scottish defence (and keeper Leighton in particular) let Hadda in for the second goal. Minutes later Burley was sent off for a reckless challenge and Scotland's fate was sealed. Bassir scored a second goal in the 85th minute and Morocco seemed to be heading for the second-round as news filtered through from Marseille that Brazil and Norway were drawing 1-1. However, heartbreaking news greeted the Moroccans as they left the field, 3-0 victors – Norway had scored an 88th minute penalty to snatch the other qualifying place!

Group B featured Austria, Cameroon, Chile and Italy and began on 11th June with a game between Italy and Chile in Bordeaux. Italy began at a tremendous pace against a nervous Chilean side and needed only 10 minutes for Vieri to put them into the lead. Vieri, who had spent much of his childhood in Australia was promised an extra reward for scoring Italy's first goal – a free bottle of wine from each of the 264 members of Italy's National Wine Cities Association. The question is, did he share this prize with Roberto Baggio whose superb pass set up his goal?

After Italy had scored, Chile began to overcome their initial nerves and, within minutes, their renowned striking duo of Salas and Zamorano got into gear to threaten the Italian goal. As it was, Chile's vociferous fans had to wait until the final minute of the first-half before Salas equalised via Zamorano from a corner. Minutes into the second-half, he headed his second to put Chile ahead and, for the next 35 minutes, Italy struggled to equalise. Five minutes from the end Roberto Baggio's attempted cross hit the hand of Fuentes and Italy were awarded a penalty. Without hesitation Baggio (whose penalty miss had lost Italy the 1994 World Cup Final) took the kick and scored the equaliser. In so doing he became the first Italian to score in three separate tournaments and Italy's nightmare start to the 1994 competition was not repeated.

Later that day, over in Toulouse, Austria turned in an inept show against Cameroon whose own performance was little better. A tedious first-half was followed by more of the same after the interval until Cameroon's Njanka broke the deadlock with a superb goal in the 78th minute. The introduction of three substitutes did nothing to improve the Austrian's game but, just when the young Cameroon side appeared to have the game won, Polster squared it with an injury-time strike.

Chile faced Austria in St. Etienne next and, despite playing neat attacking football, struggled to gain the lead against the dour Austrians. Salas eventually scored in the 70th minute and the Austrians again fluked an injury-time equaliser through Vastic. Later that day in Montpellier, Italy took an early lead against Cameroon and, with luck, could have been three or four goals up at half-time. The Cameroon team's inexperience was reflected in their appalling defending and at times suicidal tackling and they were fortunate to end the first-half with even ten players on the field (Kalla having been sent off in the 43rd minute). In the second-half Vieri scored two more goals as Italy strolled to an easy victory.

On 23rd June the final games in the group pitched Italy against Austria in the St. Denis Stadium and Chile against Cameroon in Nantes. It goes without saying that Austria (having twice already equalised in injury-time in their group matches) should score in injury-time but, against Italy their goal was of no avail and they lost 2-1. Cameroon in the meantime were at their erratic best having two players sent off for violent play, and two seemingly good 'goals' disallowed, they, nevertheless held out for a 1-1 draw. Back in Cameroon their fans went on the rampage claiming anti-African bias, but disregarding their team's awful disciplinary performance. Rigobert Song (one of their three players sent off) became, at the age of only 21, the first player to be expelled in two tournaments!

Group C featured Denmark, France, Saudi Arabia and South Africa and began with a clash between Saudi Arabia and Denmark in Lens. A contender for the most boring match of the entire tournament, the main feature of the game was that the Saudis seemed to be intent upon preventing their opponents from scoring and little else. That their efforts were in vain was due more to the farcical way in which they handed the Danes a goal than anything the under-par Danes could achieve themselves. After holding out for almost 70 minutes the Saudis tried to catch the Danes offside but left defender Rieper completely alone to score the only goal of the game.

Later that day, in Marseille, the hosts took on the African champions, South

Africa in near-gale conditions. Prompted by man-of-the-match Zidane (who was born a short distance from the stadium) the French looked to be completely in control from the start against an uninspiring South African side. After half an hour substitute Dugarry came on for the injured Guivarc'h, and within minutes had put France ahead with an excellent header. Physically strong but lacking anything creatively, the South Africans managed to hold the score at 1-0 until the 77th minute when Issa diverted a wayward Djorkaeff shot into his own net to make it 2-0. Henry scored a superb third goal in the last minute to give France the scale of victory which they deserved.

The next group game between South Africa and Denmark followed criticism of referees for failing to clamp down on dangerous tackles and inevitably, is best remembered for overzealous refereeing. The Danes started well, took the lead in the 13th minute through Nielsen and should have scored at least two others before South Africa started to play, on the half-hour. At half-time only two players, one from each side, had been booked but, after South Africa had equalised in the 52nd minute, the referee started to use his cards in earnest. In a twelve minute spell four players were booked and two were sent off, Danish sub Molnar for trampling on an opponent off-the-ball, and South Africa sub Phiri for elbowing. Later in the game to prove that this was the game of the errant substitutes, a second Danish sub, Wieghorst, only survived for a couple of minutes before he too was sent off. The game ended 1-1 and Denmark had only themselves to blame for throwing away a certain victory.

Over in the St. Denis Stadium, France found themselves playing against just ten men when Al-Khilaiwi was sent off in the 19th minute but were only able to score two goals while they held this advantage. This was because their midfield maestro, Zidane, was himself sent off for stamping in the 70th minute. His absence, however, did not effect France's performance and they ran out easy 4-0 winners to ensure their progress to the second round.

As the final games of the group started, France versus Denmark in Lyon and South Africa versus Saudi Arabia in Bordeaux, Denmark were favourites to qualify after France because South Africa had conceded four goals already. South Africa did, however, still have a mathematical chance and opened the scoring against the Saudis (who had sacked manager Parreira after their previous game) in the 19th minute. Saudi Arabia, however, with the pressure off, were now, for the first time in the tournament, prepared to attack and, on the stroke of half-time, equalised from the penalty spot.

In Lyon, meanwhile, Michael Laudrup had equalised for Denmark against France and the South Africans began to realise that their hopes of further progress were evaporating. When Al-Thyniyan put Saudi Arabia ahead with a second penalty in the 74th minute their fate was virtually sealed and, although Bartlett squared it in injury-time and Denmark lost 2-1 to France, the Danes went into the second round.

Group D was made up of Bulgaria, Nigeria, Paraguay and Spain and kicked off in Montpellier where Paraguay and Bulgaria fought off a bland goalless draw. The next game later that day, between Spain and Nigeria was anything but bland, as the game swung from end-to-end. In the opening couple of minutes, Spain came close to scoring when Raul headed against the bar and, soon after, Ikpeba had shots saved by the Spanish keeper Zubizaretta. In the 21st minute Spain took the lead via Hierro's free-kick but Nigeria equalised four minutes later from a corner kick.

Two minutes into the second-half Raul put Spain ahead again with a superb volley and the Spaniards looked set to take the points as their forwards controlled the game. However, when Alfonso was substituted in the 57th minute, things started to slip for Spain and they yielded their advantage, letting Nigeria back into the game. In the 73rd minute Spanish keeper Zubizaretta, playing his 124th International game, committed the goalkeeping blunder of the tournament when he fumbled a weak shot from Lawal into his net. This error demoralised the Spaniards whose composure went and it was no surprise five minutes later when Oliseh scored the winner for Nigeria with a 30 yard strike.

Nigeria, boosted by their win were never troubled by the ageing and quarrelsome Bulgarians in their next game which they won 1-0 but should have won by six or seven goals. Spain, on the other hand, faced a Paraguay side captained by the magnificent Chilavert, a towering goalkeeper who had actually scored four goals in his 38 previous International games. An inspiration at the back, Chilavert, ably supported by a solid defence centred around Celso Ayala, easily handled the best that Spain could offer and the game ended 0-0.

So it was that, when the final pair of games in the group were played, Nigeria were already through but any one of the other three could have qualified in second-place. Theory apart, on the performances in the first two games, it was apparent that the Bulgarians would achieve nothing and their inept showing continued against Spain. After going 1-0 down on six minutes, they were simply not interested in going for victory and Spain had a field day running in a further five goals. Over in Toulouse, however, Paraguay took a first-minute lead over a much-changed Nigerian side and were good value for the ultimate 3-1 victory which they achieved to pip Spain for the second qualifying place.

Group E was made up of Belgium, Holland, Mexico and South Korea and started with a game at Lyon between South Korea and Mexico. Against the run of play South Korea took the lead after 28 minutes with a goal which was credited to Ha Seok-Ju but flicked off the head of a Mexican defender en route. Two minutes later, Ha slid in for a reckless challenge and was shown the red card, leaving his team to struggle with ten men. They held out until six minutes into the second-half when Mexican substitute Pelaez levelled the score. Mexico then took complete control and finished comfortable 3-1 winners. The next game in the group brought together neighbours Holland and Belgium for their 120th game against one another. Belgium were intent upon stopping the Dutch from scoring and, try as they would, Holland could not break down the Belgian defence. Both sides created and missed half-chances and the overall performance is best summed up by the fact that the highlight of the game occurred in the 81st minute when the Dutch forward Kluivert was dismissed for an assault on Staelens. The assault itself was a weak elbowing effort but Staelens' theatrical dive made it seem more sinister.

Against Mexico, in their next game, the Belgians committed themselves to attack – but only after the Mexican Pardo had been sent off in the 26th minute. Wilmots put them two up with goals either side of half-time and that should have been enough for them to win the game. However, in the 54th minute Verheyen was sent off for a foul on Ramirez and, from the resulting penalty, Mexico pulled one back. Seven minutes later Blanco levelled the score as Mexico proved once again that they could fight back.

Later that day Holland easily disposed of South Korea in a game which they dominated from the kick-off. That South Korea managed to keep it goalless until the 38th minute says much for their determination but, in truth, they were much inferior and went on to lose the game 5-0. The final games in the group were both close-fought encounters and as Holland took an early lead against Mexico and Belgium did the same against South Korea it began to look as if they would be the qualifiers. Both Mexico and South Korea, however, had other ideas and, after South Korea had clawed back to 1-1 in the 71st minute Mexico, too, came back to 2-2 to snatch the second place from Belgium.

Group F promised some interesting encounters featuring as it did Germany, Iran, USA and Yugoslavia and began with a clash between Yugoslavia and Iran in St. Etienne. Yugoslavia started as the favourites on the day but Iran proved an unexpectedly tough nut to crack. In a game dominated by defences, neither attack really got going and the match bore the hallmark of a goalless draw until Mihajlovic curled a free-kick round the Iranian defensive wall, in the 72nd minute. The following day Germany faced the USA at the Parc des Princes in Paris and were little-troubled by the uninspired American team. Ahead through an Andy Moller header after only eight minutes, the Germans never looked like yielding their early lead. Indeed, it seemed only to be a question of when they would score a second goal and it was something of a surprise that it was not until the 64th minute (courtesy of Jurgen Klinsmann). The USA brought on attacking substitutes but for all of their effort, were unable to pull back a goal.

Germany's next game against Yugoslavia reminded everyone that however badly Germany may play, they nearly always possess the determination to come back. For over 70 minutes Yugoslavia absolutely dominated the game, running up a two goal lead and threatening to score at will but then the Germans fought their way back into it. In the 74th minute Mihajlovic turned an off-target shot by Tarnat into his own net and suddenly the Germans were back in the game. Four minutes later Bierhoff came close to equalising when he had a header tipped onto the cross-bar and two minutes after that, he scored the equaliser. In the end it was the Yugoslavs who were hanging on as the final score remained 2-2.

Later that day Lyon witnessed the first-ever encounter between Iran and the USA – a tie awaited more eagerly in Iran than the largely disinterested USA. Inevitably, politics reared its ugly head and despite tight security, many protest banners were smuggled into the ground to prove one point or another. The game itself was quite a treat with a rejuvenated attack-minded USA side up against an impressively well-organised Iranian side. That is not to say that Iran played defensively and they were a continual danger on the break, as the game flowed from end-to-end. Robbed of a certain penalty in the 20th minute when Keller clearly brought down Azizi, the Iranians plugged away until they took the lead in the 40th minute through Estili.

The second-half continued even more frantically with the Americans attacking in considerable strength and the Iranians counter-attacking in reply. It seemed inevitable that the USA would be caught out again and, sure enough, in the 84th minute Mahdavikia made it 2-0. Three minutes later the USA pulled one back but Iran held out to win a thrilling tie.

This result meant that everything hinged on the final two games with only the USA definitely out of the running for a second-round place. As Germany faced Iran in Montpellier, the USA were up against Yugoslavia in Nantes.

In Nantes the USA almost shocked Yugoslavia when they hit the inside of the post within seconds of the start but, just four minutes later found themselves chasing the game when Komljenovic put the Slavs ahead. The Yugoslav coach Santrac had promised a hat full of goals but this failed to materialise. Over in Montpellier, Germany were little troubled by Iran and, after a goalless first-half took a two-goal lead within a few minutes of the restart. With news of this filtering through to the Yugoslavs they seemed to settle for second-place and no further goals were scored in either game.

Group G was made up of Colombia, England, Romania and Tunisia. It began in the wake of the usual outbreak of violence by England's hard core of drunken-lout followers when England met Tunisia in Marseille. Manager Hoddle seemed to have mastered the commercial aspects of the World Cup – fronting books and videos of all kinds – but had much to learn about team selection and tactics with a seemingly-unbalanced squad. Nevertheless, England began comfortably enough against a very ordinary Tunisian side and took the lead just before half-time through Alan Shearer. Sheringham, whose inclusion in the squad must have surprised him as much as it did the supporters, was anonymous except for one shot and Scholes managed to squander two easy chances before making it safe with England's second goal in the 89th minute. Later that day, in Lyon, a squabbling Colombian side faced a competent but uninspired Romanian team. Once again the South Americans failed to take on Romania with any real commitment and played more as eleven individuals than as a team. Asprilla in a lone striking role looked totally disinterested and, after coming close a number of times, it was inevitably the Romanians who took the lead on the stroke of half-time through Ilie. In the second-half heat Romania seemed content to settle for a 1-0 win and Colombia did little to prevent this.

More controversy followed in the wake of this game, as Asprilla virtually walked out on the Colombian squad following a stormy news conference and, regardless, a disjointed Colombian side took on and beat Tunisia in their next game. This game followed the Romania versus England game in Toulouse when Hoddle reluctantly rang the changes after Ince was injured early in the game. With the English keeper, Seaman looking decidedly out of sorts, the English defence (with the exception of Sol Campbell) turned in a lacklustre display and it was no surprise when Romania took the lead two minutes into the second-half. Up front Hoddle persisted with the hopeless Sheringham until, in the 73rd minute he brought on 'wonder-kid' Owen in his place. Within minutes Owen had scored the equaliser and, for once, England appeared to have an attack. Unfortunately, the defensive problems were still there and in the final minute an atrocious piece of defending by Le Saux and anonymous goalkeeping by Seaman let Dan Petrescu in to score the winner.

The final games in the group featured Romania who were already assured of a second-round place and Tunisia (whose coach Kasperczak had just been sacked) in the St. Denis Stadium while Colombia met England in Lens. The Romanians caused great hilarity when they all took the field sporting bleached-blonde hairstyles – but this added nothing to their play as they struggled against the rejuvenated Tunisians. Tunisia scored first with a 10th minute penalty and, after England had strolled into a 2-0 lead against the shakey Colombians, it looked for a while as if England would finish ahead of Romania. Romania, however, pulled themselves together and, bolstered by two second-half substitutes, pulled back to 1-1 to regain first place in the group.

The last group, H, featured Argentina, Croatia, Jamaica and Japan and began with Japan's first-ever Finals game, against Argentina and Jamaica's first-ever Finals game against Croatia. In Toulouse Argentina were surprised by the skillful and imaginative approach of their opponents almost as much as the enormous level of their support in the Stadium. Given that 12,000 Japanese fans were forced to abandon their plans to go to France after their promised match tickets failed to arrive, the Japanese support was incredible. Support apart, what the Japanese lacked were strikers and for all their neat play they created virtually no openings up front. Thus it was only a matter of time before Argentina scored and Batistuta duly did so in the 28th minute to win the game 1-0.

Against Jamaica, Croatia experienced few problems and took the lead in the 27th minute through Stanic. Earle equalised on the stroke of half-time and the large contingent of Jamaican supporters were, briefly, in raptures. In the second-half Croatia soon reasserted their domination and Prosinecki gave them back the lead in the 53rd minute. Thereafter, it was all Croatia and merely a question of how many they would score – the final result was 3-1.

The next game brought Croatia up against Japan who, again, turned in a lively and cultured performance without seriously threatening to score. In midfield Nakata, the Asian footballer of the Year, dominated play but, in the final quarter, Japan lacked the ability or confidence to score. Suker, having come close to scoring a number of times, eventually got the winner with 13 minutes remaining and Croatia were assured of a second-round place.

The following day Argentina joined them by demolishing Jamaica 5-0 and the two final games merely sorted out which team would finish first and which second. Jamaica managed to beat Japan 2-1 to secure third-place and Croatia seemed content to let Argentina coast to a 1-0 victory – thus avoiding a second-round tie with England.

The second-round promised some interesting ties with the clash between Argentina and England the most eagerly awaited. The other games brought Brazil against Chile, Italy against Norway, France against Paraguay, Nigeria against Denmark, Holland against Yugoslavia, Germany against Mexico and Romania against Croatia.

First of all Italy faced Norway in Marseille and found themselves up against the lofted long-ball tactics so favoured by Norwegian coach Egil Olsen. Unlike in 1994 when the Irish used this method to beat them, Norway made absolutely no headway this time and struggled to stay in the game. Were it not for the ineptitude of Del Piero, Italy would, undoubtedly have run away with the tie but he alone managed to squander four good chances. Once again, however, Vieri was on target and, ironically, it was a long-ball from Di Biagio which enabled him to score in the 18th minute. For the rest of the game it was only a question of how many Italy would score but a sparkling performance from the Norwegian keeper Grodas kept it down to 1-0.

Later that day Brazil cruised into the quarter-finals with a comprehensive 4-1 victory over Chile. Both Sampaio and Ronaldo scored two goals as the Chileans crumbled with their worst performance of the tournament against an on-form Brazil.

If Brazil had cruised to victory, in the next tie between France and Paraguay, France did anything but cruise. Facing the outstanding goalkeeper of the tournament, Chilavert, fronted by a simply magnificent defence centred around Ayala, the hosts struggled. Half-time came and went, full-time came and went but no goals were scored. Still the French plugged away until the 23rd minute of extra-time when, with the spectre of penalties beginning to loom, Blanc made World Cup history by scoring the first-ever golden goal. As the French went wild in relief, the magnificent Chilavert capped a wonderful display by lifting his downhearted team mates, physically, and taking them off to the deserved applause of the crowd.

Later that day the Danes had a surprise in store for the confident Nigerians, when they turned in one of the finest performances of the entire tournament. Deservedly one up after only three minutes, through Moller, they scored a second nine minutes later and totally dominated play. Nigeria, of course,

161

fought back but the cool Danish defence had no trouble in holding them. On the hour, Sand (who had come on as substitute only seconds earlier) headed a third goal and, when Helveg scored 15 minutes later, it was all over for the Nigerians although Babangida scored a consolation goal.

Next came Germany and Mexico in Montpellier. Mexico, having proved their credentials in group E and, if not justifying their absurdly high FIFA ranking, at least demonstrating that they were nobody's fools, gave Germany quite a fright. After absorbing quite a bit of first-half pressure, the Mexicans seemed to be planning to outrun the ageing German defence by bringing on speedy substitutes Carmona and Arellano after the break. Carmona came on first and, within a minute, Mexico took the lead through Hernandez. Arellano came on a few minutes later and, for a while the German defence struggled to cope with the oppositions' pace. Soon afterwards Arellano struck the post and, had Hernandez not missed the resulting open goal. Mexico would probably have taken the tie. As it was, minutes later Klinsmann squared matters with an opportunist goal and, four minutes from the end, Bierhoff headed Germany's winner.

Later that day, in Toulouse, Holland met Yugoslavia in a close fought encounter. After almost half and hour of fairly nondescript football Holland took control and came close with three goal attempts within a few minutes. Their continued pressure paid dividends as Bergkamp ran onto a Frank de Boer through-ball to score in the 38th minute. Soon after the start of the second-half Komljenovic levelled the score from a corner and, shortly after, Mijatovic missed a penalty for Yugoslavia. The action hotted up and Bergkamp was fortunate to remain on the field when he brought down Mihajlovic before trampling all over him – right under the assistant referee's nose. As the game progressed, the Yugoslavian players seemed to be running out of steam and pacing themselves for a period of extra-time as Edgar Davids scored an injury-time winner from a corner-kick.

The following day the still-blonde Romanians faced Croatia in Bordeaux in a stupendously boring game. Romania seemed to totally lose the plot and Croatia were little better. The deadlock was broken by Suker when he scored a first-half injury-time penalty and that was about it. In the second-half, Croatia should have scored more but missed and Romania seemed to give up when Hagi was substituted in the 56th minute.

And so to the tie that everyone had been waiting for – Argentina versus England. The last time that the two countries had met in the World Cup, the famous Maradona 'Hand of God' incident had robbed England of a result and, as play kicked-off in St. Etienne, little did the watching millions know that another controversy lay ahead. England made a poor start when, in only the 5th minute, Seaman, going for a ball which he should have left, brought down Simeone for a penalty. Batistuta converted the spot-kick and England were a goal down. Undaunted, the English attack, spearheaded by young Michael Owen threatened Argentina's defence and, within four minutes, England were awarded a penalty, too, when Owen's charge on goal was stopped by Ayala. Shearer duly scored and England were back in the game. The blistering pace of Owen was unsettling the Argentinians and a buzz of excitement went round the crowd whenever he was in possession. They did not have to wait long for another thrill when, six minutes later, Owen picked up a Beckham pass on the halfway line and made a surging run on goal. His sheer pace left the Argentina defence standing and, when his stinging shot from the right whipped into the net, the crowd acclaimed one of the goals of the tournament. As the half progressed England continued to attack and should have gone further ahead when half-chances were missed by both Ince and Owen. Scholes, who had not had a good tournament, spurned the simplest of chances and how England were to regret that miss!

Just on half-time Argentina were awarded a free-kick on the edge of the area when Campbell had needlessly pulled back Lopez and a well-rehearsed move saw Zanetti net the equaliser.

With all to play for, England started the second-half in the same attacking vein as the first, but within minutes came the incident which changed the course of the game. Floored by a bad tackle from behind which collected a booking for Simeone, Beckham, laying prostrate on the ground stupidly retaliated right under the nose of the referee and was immediately sent off. The resultant reorganisation meant that England were unable to exert the same amount of attacking pressure on Argentina and were forced to defend in depth, relying on breakaways and set-pieces for attack. These tactics proved successful in denying Argentina the barest of chances to score the winner but, effectively, took their own chief threat, Michael Owen, out of the game. At one stage, Sol Campbell even managed to get the ball into the Argentinian net from a free-kick and England appeared to be ahead. However, as he and his team-mates celebrated the 'goal' it dawned on them that the referee had disallowed it and a dreadful piece of refereeing had enabled Argentina to take the resultant free kick 20 yards upfield – giving them a free run on goal. The English defence by then bolstered by substitutes Merson and Southgate cleared the problem and extra-time came. Seven minutes into extra-time Batty came on to further tighten the defence but, as the penalty shootout loomed the question of who should take them must have been on Hoddle's mind as three of his nominated penalty-takers were off the field. And so it was that England, once more, went into a penalty shootout unprepared with a goalkeeper clearly off his form and players uncertain who would take the kicks. In the end, with the score 4-3 in Argentina's favour, it fell to David Batty (a player who had never taken a penalty at any level) to keep England in it. That he failed was, once again, an indictment of the manager who should have drilled his players in penalty-kick taking but did not.

After a brief break (the first for an overlong three weeks) Italy and France met at the St. Denis Stadium in the first of the quarter-finals. France had the edge in a game dominated by defences with full-back Thuram once again magnificent, as were Petit and Desailly. In attack both sides were lacking, the French because they relied more on their midfield for goals and Italy, because Del Piero was, once again, abysmal. Goalless at 90 minutes, substitute Roberto Baggio came close to scoring the golden goal for Italy and Djorkaeff (who had had another poor game) should have done the same for France. To the enormous relief of the home crowd, the penalty shootout went France's way as Italy lost out on penalties for the third consecutive time.

The next game later that day in Nantes was an altogether more exciting affair as Brazil took on Denmark. In only the second minute the Danes exposed the weaknesses at the centre of the Brazilian defence, when, following a quickly taken free-kick, Brian Laudrup pulled the ball back for Jorgensen to put Denmark ahead. Brazil came back well and, nine minutes later, levelled through Bebeto who out-ran Helveg before slipping a perfect shot past Schmeichel. Helveg was again at fault fifteen minutes later when he was robbed by Roberto Carlos whose pass to Ronaldo resulted in a goal for Rivaldo.

Five minutes into the second-half it was Roberto Carlos's turn to take the blame for a goal as his mishit overhead kick was collected by Brian Laudrup and despatched into the Brazilian net. On equal terms again the Danes were not content to sit back and defend and it was this that was their undoing when, on the hour, Rivaldo scored Brazil's third. Denmark piled forward looking for the equaliser but the closest they came was a minute from full-time when Rieper's header hit the bar.

The following day Holland faced Argentina in Marseille and benefitted from the South Americans' marathon second-round tie against England – which had taken a lot out of their opponents. Holland started well and should have taken the lead after only five minutes when Jonk hit the post. A few minutes later Kluivert, back from suspension, put Holland ahead (at the second attempt) when Bergkamp headed down a Ronald de Boer cross. Five minutes later Argentina caught Holland napping and Lopez had plenty of time to beat Van der Sar to level the score. Holland fought hard to regain the lead but, although they came close on a number of occasions the score remained 1-1 at half-time. Midway throught the second-half Holland were reduced to ten men when Numan committed a second bookable offence but the disappointing Argentinian side were unable to capitalise on their superiority of numbers. With just three minutes remaining, Ortega was dismissed for butting the Dutch goalkeeper and, as the game seemed to be heading for extra-time, Bergkamp sealed it for Holland. Frank de Boer picked out Bergkamp with a superb long pass which he controlled nonchalently before wrong footing Ayala and beating the Argentinian goalkeeper with an immaculate volley.

Later that day, in Lyon, Germany met Croatia in a re-run of the 1996 European Championship quarter-final. In the bad-tempered 1996 match, Croatia had promised much but, following the dismissal of Stimac, had collapsed and this game began in precisely the same aggressive and over-physical way. The difference this time, however, was that a German was sent off (Worns to be precise) for a blatant body check on Suker. He departed in the 40th minute, admitting later that he deserved the red card, and Germany reorganised to overcome their handicap. On the stroke of half-time Jarni put Croatia ahead and for the next half-hour Germany contained the Croats without seriously threatening to score an equaliser. Realising that Germany would need to press for a goal, the Croats took their time and, in the 80th minute, went further ahead through Vlaovic. Forced to attack, Germany needed to take chances at the back and Suker punished them, with a third goal in the 85th minute putting Croatia into the semi-finals just eight years after their emergence as an independent state.

In the first of the semi-finals, Brazil met Holland in Marseille in a thrilling game which could have gone either way. The first-half was goalless with both sides playing well below their best but, after the break, it was a different story. Within seconds of the restart, Ronaldo, (who had shown flashes of brilliance earlier in the game) put Brazil ahead when he sped onto a superb Rivaldo pass before easily beating Van der Sar, as Holland were caught napping. This brought the game to life as the Dutch were forced onto the attack. Ronaldo, meanwhile, had started to fire on all cylinders and, as the game swung from end-to-end, he constantly threatened to score again. That he did not do so was the result of brave goalkeeping and a superb last-ditch tackle by Davids when he was clear on goal. Holland, with Kluivert always a threat, continued to attack but were hampered by the anonymity of Dennis Bergkamp who seemed unable to settle into the game. In the 70th minute Denilson replaced Bebeto for Brazil and his first cross came close to sealing it for Brazil but it was still anybody's game. Minutes later, Van Hooijdonk replaced Zenden for Holland and he, too, was soon in the action as he created a good chance for Kluivert. With just three minutes of normal time remaining, Holland equalised through a Kluivert header and extra-time duly arrived.

Given that they had equalised just minutes from the end, Holland could have been expected to make the running for the 'golden goal' which would win them the match, but it was Brazil who took that initiative. With Ronaldo leading the way, Brazil swept onto the attack and came close to scoring as, first, Frank de Boer cleared off the line, then Van der Sar brought off a tremendous save. Still Brazil pressed and only an incredible last-ditch tackle by Frank de Boer saved Holland again. Up front Holland, too, had their chances and Kluivert was only a shade wide with a volley from a Frank de Boer pass but, as the game went to a penalty shootout, Brazil knew that they should have already won.

Brazilian, Taffarel had confounded his critics by having an excellent tournament to date and he appeared to be the most composed of the two goalkeepers despite having to face penalties in front of a sea of orange-shirted Dutch fans. After both sides had scored their first two kicks, Emerson put Brazil 3-2 ahead and Taffarel won the war of nerves as he saved, first from Cocu and then from Ronald de Boer to give Brazil a place in the Final.

The next day at the St. Denis Stadium in Paris, the hosts took on Croatia before an expectant crowd. Right from the kick-off France swept onto the attack and, Zidane, in sparkling from, worked tirelessly to give them the lead. Within minutes he forced Ladic the Croat goalkeeper into making two fine saves and also went close with a header. Once into their stride, however, Croatia always posed a threat and Suker (who was to become the tournament's top scorer) looked particularly dangerous. Indeed, after a goalless first-half he needed just 30 seconds to get his name onto the scoreboard. Asanovic split the French defence with a superb ball through the middle and Suker swept in from the right to beat Barthez.

Croatia had barely stopped celebrating before France were back on level terms a minute later. The French right-back, Lilian Thuram, always outstanding in defence, robbed Boban outside the Croatian area and, looking more like a striker than a defender, ran on to a reverse pass from Djorkaeff to slam in the equaliser. This goal seemed to knock the stuffing out of Croatia who were forced onto the defensive by an onslaught of French attacks and it became merely a matter of time before France would take the lead. This they duly did in the 69th minute and it was that man Thuram again. Hurtling in from the left, he robbed Jarni on the edge of the area before curling a wonderful low shot round the keeper inside Croatia's right-hand post.

Five minutes later, with France pressing Croatia for a third goal, the home crowd were shocked into silence by the dismissal of their star central defender, Blanc. His misdirected push on Bilic, caught him in the face and Mr Aranda, the referee, did not hesitate to send him off. Bilic, later vilified for overreacting to the push continued the game to a chorus of whistles. Immediately Aime Jacquet, the French coach, brought on substitute Frank Leboeuf to replace Blanc in the centre of France's defence as France defended their lead. Croatia were unable to take advantage of their superiority of numbers and it was not until the fourth minute of injury-time that Barthez was seriously troubled when he tipped a deflection over the bar as France moved to their first-ever Final.

The Third-Place Play-off was at the Parc des Princes and, whilst not a classic encounter was, none-the-less, enjoyable and competitive with Croatia just edging it. Croatia's Bilic paid the price for his theatrical reaction to Blanc's push in the semi-final, and was whistled whenever he touched the ball throughout the whole game. Holland enjoyed most of the possession but Croatia always threatened on breakaways and it was they who took the lead with their first attack in the 13th minute. Prosinecki was the Croatian scorer and Zenden equalised with a fine goal for the Dutch eight minutes later. A quarter of an hour later Suker scored Croatia's second goal to grab the Golden Boot award and the Croats decided to settle for a 2-1 win as they defended in depth. Holland attacked, but without much conviction, and Croatia easily held on for third-place.

The following day hosts, France faced champions Brazil in the first-ever Final of its kind. Great confusion reigned in the Brazilian camp as their star striker Ronaldo was omitted from the first team-sheet handed in to FIFA. As the World's media pondered his exclusion, a fresh team-sheet with his name included was hastily submitted, but it soon became apparent that panic had hit the Brazilian camp. The story behind the panic began to emerge as news filtered through to the world's press that Ronaldo had earlier been rushed to hospital suffering from a seizure. He was discharged despite being clearly shaken by this, and Zagallo seemed to have been pressured to include him, regardless. What really happened? We can only speculate about the causes of Ronaldo's seizure but, the disarray which the Brazilian camp was thrown into should have been avoided and, when Brazil failed to appear for their usual pre-match warm-up, the writing was on the wall.

You might assume from the foregoing comments about Ronaldo's problems, that France's battle to win on the day was made easier (and it probably was) but, even with Ronaldo in top form, it is doubtful that Brazil could have held the home team. Right from the kick-off France grasped the game by the scruff of the neck and quickly began to expose the shaky Brazilian defence. After just three minutes Zidane and Djorkaeff combined to set up Guivarc'h who should have opened the scoring with the easiest of chances, but did not. Minutes later Djorkaeff headed wide from a free-kick and, as France continued to attack, Brazil, forced into an unfamiliar defending role, simply did not know how to get into the game. Up front Ronaldo barely touched the ball but, in truth, was badly supported by his struggling team mates. It seemed to be just a question of time before France would take the lead and it fell to their best player, Zidane, in the 27th minute. Roberto Carlos, the Brazilian left-back renowned for his powerful attacking play, was found wanting in defensive ability and conceded an unnecessary corner, which Zidane headed home. France continued to press and Djorkaeff, Petit and Guivarc'h all had good chances as, time and again, Brazil's shaky defence was breached. France were hardly troubled by the Brazilian attack who barely mustered a first-half shot and, on the stroke of half-time went further ahead, again from a corner and again via Zidane.

After the break Denilson came on as substitute for the anonymous Leonardo as Brazil threw everything into the attack and, for a few minutes, the champions called all of the shots as France defended with vigour. First Desailly then Karembeu were booked as France drew everything back into defence and, after Ronaldo's only decent chance of the game was well saved by Barthez, the Brazilian attacks seemed to run out of steam. In the 60th minute Bebeto's shot was cleared off the line after Barthez had been beaten but it was still France who controlled the game. Guivarc'h missed the simplest of chances to put France 3-0 up and was replaced by Dugarry shortly afterwards. Two minutes later France were reduced to ten men when Desailly committed a second bookable offence but Brazil could not exploit their advantage. Drawing all of their midfield back into defence with Dugarry left as a lone striker, France easily contained Brazil and soon realised that they had little to fear from the Brazilian attackers. Indeed, it was France who created the better chances on the break and Dugarry should have scored ten minutes from the end as the Brazilian defence were exposed yet again. As it was, France's third goal was scored in injury-time when Vieira put Petit through, to give France the winning margin they so richly deserved. In the words of the English song 'Football Came Home' that night as the country which had given birth to the World Cup finally won it themselves!

GROUP A

	P	W	D	L	F	A	Pts
Brazil	3	2	0	1	6	3	6
Norway	3	1	2	0	5	4	5
Morocco	3	1	1	1	5	5	4
Scotland	3	0	1	2	2	6	1

GROUP B

	P	W	D	L	F	A	Pts
Italy	3	2	1	0	7	3	7
Chile	3	0	3	0	4	4	3
Austria	3	0	2	1	3	4	2
Cameroon	3	0	2	1	2	5	2

GROUP C

	P	W	D	L	F	A	Pts
France	3	3	0	0	9	1	9
Denmark	3	1	1	1	3	3	4
South Africa	3	0	2	1	3	6	2
Saudi Arabia	3	0	1	2	2	7	1

GROUP D

	P	W	D	L	F	A	Pts
Nigeria	3	2	0	1	5	5	6
Paraguay	3	1	2	0	3	1	5
Spain	3	1	1	1	8	4	4
Bulgaria	3	0	1	2	1	7	1

GROUP E

	P	W	D	L	F	A	Pts
Holland	3	1	2	0	7	2	5
Mexico	3	1	2	0	7	5	5
Belgium	3	0	3	0	3	3	3
South Korea	3	0	1	2	2	9	1

GROUP F

	P	W	D	L	F	A	Pts
Germany	3	2	1	0	6	2	7
Yugoslavia	3	2	1	0	4	2	7
Iran	3	1	0	2	2	4	3
USA	3	0	0	3	1	5	0

GROUP G

	P	W	D	L	F	A	Pts
Romania	3	2	1	0	4	2	7
England	3	2	0	1	5	2	6
Colombia	3	1	0	2	1	3	3
Tunisia	3	0	1	2	1	4	1

GROUP H

	P	W	D	L	F	A	Pts
Argentina	3	3	0	0	7	0	9
Croatia	3	2	0	1	4	2	6
Jamaica	3	1	0	2	3	9	3
Japan	3	0	0	3	1	4	0

SECOND ROUND

Italy 1   Norway 0
Brazil 4   Chile 1
France 1   Paraguay 0
(After extra time)
Nigeria 1   Denmark 4
Germany 2   Mexico 1
Holland 2   Yugoslavia 1
Romania 0   Croatia 1
Argentina 2   England 2
After extra time – Argentina won 4-3 on penalties

QUARTER-FINALS

Italy 0   France 0
After extra time – France won 4-3 on penalties
Brazil 3   Denmark 2
Holland 2   Argentina 1
Germany 0   Croatia 3

SEMI-FINALS

Brazil 1   Holland 1
After extra time – Brazil won 4-2 on penalties
France 2   Croatia 1

THIRD-PLACE MATCH

Holland 1   Croatia 2

FINAL

Brazil .... (0) **0**   **France** .... (2) **3**

Scorers: Zidane 2, Petit

Team: Taffarel, Cafu, Junior Baiano, Aldair, Roberto Carlos, Leonardo (sub. Denilson), Cesar Sampaio (sub. Edmundo), Dunga, Rivaldo, Ronaldo, Bebeto

Team: Barthez, Thuram, Desailly, Leboeuf, Lizarazu, Karembeu (sub. Boghossian), Deschamps, Petit, Zidane, Djorkaeff (sub Vieira), Guivarc'h (sub. Dugarry)

QUALIFYING COMPETITION RESULTS 1934-1998

1930 – NO QUALIFYING COMPETITION

1934 – QUALIFYING COMPETITION

(32 Entries)

Turkey and Chile withdrew without participating

GROUP 1

ROUND 1

| 28 Jan 1934 | Haiti vs Cuba | 1-3 |
| 4 Feb 1934 | Cuba vs Haiti | 6-0 |

Cuba qualified for 2nd Round

ROUND 2

4 Mar 1934	Mexico vs Cuba	3-2
11 Mar 1934	Mexico vs Cuba	5-0
18 Mar 1934	Mexico vs Cuba	4-1

Mexico qualified for Group Final

GROUP FINAL (In Italy)

| 24 Mar 1934 | USA vs Mexico | 4-2 |

USA qualified for Finals

GROUP 2

Brazil & Peru
Peru withdrew
Brazil qualified for Finals

GROUP 3

Argentina
Argentina qualified for Finals

GROUP 4

| 10 Mar 1934 | Egypt vs Palestine | 7-1 |
| 6 Mar 1934 | Palestine vs Egypt | 1-4 |

Egypt qualified for Finals

GROUP 5

| 11 Jun 1933 | Sweden vs Estonia | 6-2 |
| 29 Jun 1933 | Lithuania vs Sweden | 0-2 |

Estonia vs Lithuania not played

	P	W	D	L	F	A	Pts
Sweden	2	2	0	0	8	2	4
Lithuania	1	0	0	1	0	2	0
Estonia	1	0	0	1	2	6	0

Sweden qualified for Finals

GROUP 6

| 11 Mar 1934 | Spain vs Portugal | 9-0 |
| 18 Mar 1934 | Portugal vs Spain | 1-2 |

Spain qualified for Finals

GROUP 7

| 25 Mar 1934 | Italy vs Greece | 4-0 |

Italy qualified for Finals

GROUP 8

25 Mar 1934	Bulgaria vs Hungary	1-4
25 Apr 1934	Austria vs Bulgaria	6-1
29 Apr 1934	Hungary vs Bulgaria	4-1
	(in Austria)	

	P	W	D	L	F	A	Pts
Hungary	2	2	0	0	8	2	4
Austria	1	1	0	0	6	1	2
Bulgaria	3	0	0	3	3	14	0

Hungary & Austria qualified for Finals

GROUP 9

| 15 Oct 1934 | Poland vs Czechoslovakia | 1-2 |

Czechoslovakia qualified for Finals

GROUP 10

24 Sep 1933	Yugoslavia vs Switzerland	2-2
29 Oct 1933	Switzerland vs Romania	2-2
29 Apr 1934	Romania vs Yugoslavia	2-1

	P	W	D	L	F	A	Pts
Romania	2	1	1	0	4	3	3
Switzerland	2	0	2	0	4	4	2
Yugoslavia	2	0	1	1	3	4	1

Romania & Switzerland qualified for Finals

GROUP 11

25 Feb 1934	Eire vs Belgium	4-4
8 Apr 1934	Holland vs Eire	5-2
29 Apr 1934	Belgium vs Holland	2-4

	P	W	D	L	F	A	Pts
Holland	2	2	0	0	9	4	4
Belgium	2	0	1	1	6	8	1
Eire	2	0	1	1	6	9	1

Holland & Belgium qualified for Finals

GROUP 12

| 11 Mar 1934 | Luxembourg vs Germany | 1-9 |
| 15 Apr 1934 | Luxembourg vs France | 1-6 |

	P	W	D	L	F	A	Pts
Germany	1	1	0	0	9	1	2
France	1	1	0	0	3	1	2
Luxembourg	2	0	0	2	2	15	0

Germany & France qualified for Finals

1938 – QUALIFYING COMPETITION

(36 Entries)

Colombia, Costa Rica, Dutch Guiana, El Salvador, Japan, Mexico, Spain & U.S.A. all withdrew without participating.

GROUP 1

16 Jun 1937	Sweden vs Finland	4-0
20 Jun 1937	Sweden vs Estonia	7-2
29 Jun 1937	Finland vs Germany	0-2
19 Aug 1937	Estonia vs Finland	1-0
29 Aug 1937	Germany vs Estonia	4-1

	P	W	D	L	F	A	Pts
Sweden	2	2	0	0	11	2	4
Germany	2	2	0	0	6	1	4
Estonia	3	1	0	2	4	11	2
Finland	3	0	0	3	0	7	0

Germany & Sweden qualified for Finals

GROUP 2

10 Oct 1937	Norway vs Eire	3-2
10 Oct 1937	Poland vs Yugoslavia	4-0
7 Nov 1937	Eire vs Norway	3-3
3 Apr 1938	Yugoslavia vs Poland	1-0

	P	W	D	L	F	A	Pts
Norway	2	1	1	0	6	5	3
Poland	2	1	0	1	4	1	2
Yugoslavia	2	1	0	1	1	4	2
Eire	2	0	1	1	5	6	1

Norway & Poland qualified for Finals

GROUP 3

Egypt vs Romania
(Egypt withdrew)
Romania qualified for Finals

GROUP 4

1 May 1938	Switzerland vs Portugal	2-1
	(in Italy)	

Switzerland qualified for Finals

GROUP 5

ROUND 1

22 Jan 1938	Palestine vs Greece	1-3
20 Feb 1938	Greece vs Palestine	1-0

Greece qualified for 2nd Round

ROUND 2

25 Mar 1938	Hungary vs Greece	11-1

Hungary qualified for Finals

GROUP 6

7 Nov 1937	Bulgaria vs Czechoslovakia	1-1
24 Apr 1938	Czechoslovakia vs Bulgaria	6-0

Czechoslovakia qualified for Finals

GROUP 7

ROUND 1

29 Jul 1937	Lithuania vs Latvia	2-4
3 Sep 1937	Latvia vs Lithuania	5-1

Latvia qualified for 2nd Round

ROUND 2

5 Oct 1937	Austria vs Latvia	2-1

Austria qualified for Finals but withdrew

GROUP 8

28 Nov 1937	Holland vs Luxembourg	4-0
13 Mar 1938	Luxembourg vs Belgium	2-3

3 Apr 1938	Belgium vs Holland	1-1

	P	W	D	L	F	A	Pts
Holland	2	1	1	0	5	1	3
Belgium	2	1	1	0	4	3	3
Luxembourg	2	0	0	2	2	7	0

Holland & Belgium qualified for Finals

GROUP 9

Cuba & Brazil
Cuba & Brazil qualified for Finals

GROUP 10

Dutch East Indies
Dutch East Indies qualified for Finals

France (hosts) and Italy (holders) were exempt from the qualifying rounds.

1950 – QUALIFYING COMPETITION

(34 Entries)

Austria, Belgium, Indonesia & the Phillipines withdrew without participating.

GROUP 1

1 Oct 1949	Northern Ireland vs Scotland	2-8
15 Oct 1949	Wales vs England	1-4
9 Nov 1949	Scotland vs Wales	2-0
16 Nov 1949	England vs Northern Ireland	9-2
8 Mar 1950	Wales vs Northern Ireland	0-0
15 Apr 1950	Scotland vs England	0-1

	P	W	D	L	F	A	Pts
England	3	3	0	0	14	3	6
Scotland	3	2	0	1	10	3	4
Wales	3	0	1	2	1	6	1
N.Ireland	3	0	1	2	4	17	1

England & Scotland qualified for Finals

Scotland withdrew

GROUP 2

20 Nov 1949	Turkey vs Syria	7-0

Turkey qualified for Finals but withdrew

GROUP 3

ROUND 1

21 Aug 1949	Yugoslavia vs Israel	6-0
18 Aug 1949	Israel vs Yugoslavia	2-5

Yugoslavia qualified for 2nd Round

ROUND 2

9 Oct 1949	Yugoslavia vs France	1-1
30 Oct 1949	France vs Yugoslavia	1-1

Play-off (In Italy)
11 Dec 1949	Yugoslavia vs France	3-2

Yugoslavia qualified for Finals

GROUP 4

| 26 Jun 1949 | Switzerland vs Luxembourg | 5-2 |
| 18 Sep 1949 | Luxembourg vs Switzerland | 2-3 |

Switzerland qualified for Finals

GROUP 5

25 Jun 1949	Sweden vs Eire	3-1
8 Sep 1949	Eire vs Finland	3-0
9 Oct 1949	Finland vs Eire	1-1
13 Nov 1949	Eire vs Sweden	1-3

	P	W	D	L	F	A	Pts
Sweden	2	2	0	0	6	2	4
Eire	4	1	1	2	6	7	3
Finland	2	0	0	1	1	4	1

Sweden qualified for Finals

GROUP 6

| 2 Apr 1950 | Spain vs Portugal | 5-1 |
| 9 Apr 1950 | Portugal vs Spain | 2-2 |

Spain qualified for Finals

GROUP 7

Bolivia, Chile & Argentina
(Argentina withdrew)

Bolivia & Chile qualified for Finals

GROUP 8

Uruguay, Paraguay, Ecuador & Peru
(Ecuador & Peru withdrew)

Uruguay & Paraguay qualified for Finals

GROUP 9

Following matches played in Mexico

4 Sep 1949	Mexico vs USA	6-0
11 Sep 1949	Mexico vs Cuba	2-0
14 Sep 1949	USA vs Cuba	1-1
18 Sep 1949	Mexico vs USA	6-2
21 Sep 1949	USA vs Cuba	5-2
25 Sep 1949	Mexico vs Cuba	3-0

	P	W	D	L	F	A	Pts
Mexico	4	4	0	0	17	2	8
USA	4	1	1	2	8	15	3
Cuba	4	0	1	3	3	11	1

Mexico & USA qualified for Finals

GROUP 10

Burma & India
(Both withdrew)

Brazil (hosts) and Italy (holders) were exempt from the qualifying competition.

1954 – QUALIFYING COMPETITION

(38 Entries)

Chile withdrew without participating

GROUP 1

24 Jun 1953	Norway vs Saar	2-3
19 Aug 1953	Norway vs West Germany	1-1
11 Oct 1953	West Germany vs Saar	3-0
8 Nov 1953	Sarr vs Norway	0-0
22 Nov 1953	West Germany vs Norway	5-1
28 Mar 1954	Saar vs West Germany	1-3

	P	W	D	L	F	A	Pts
West Germany	4	3	1	0	12	3	5
Saar	4	1	1	2	4	8	3
Norway	4	0	2	2	4	9	2

West Germany qualified for Finals

GROUP 2

25 May 1953	Finland vs Belgium	2-4
28 May 1953	Sweden vs Belgium	2-3
5 Aug 1953	Finland vs Sweden	3-3
16 Aug 1953	Sweden vs Finland	4-0
23 Sep 1953	Belgium vs Finland	2-2
8 Oct 1953	Belgium vs Sweden	2-0

	P	W	D	L	F	A	Pts
Belgium	4	3	1	0	11	6	7
Sweden	4	1	1	2	9	8	3
Finland	4	0	2	2	7	13	2

Belgium qualified for Finals

GROUP 3

3 Oct 1953	Northern Ireland vs Scotland	1-3
10 Oct 1953	Wales vs England	1-4
4 Nov 1953	Scotland vs Wales	3-3
11 Nov 1953	England vs Northern Ireland	3-1
31 Mar 1954	Wales vs Northern Ireland	1-2
3 Apr 1954	Scotland vs England	2-4

	P	W	D	L	F	A	Pts
England	3	3	0	0	11	4	6
Scotland	3	1	1	1	8	8	3
N.Ireland	3	1	0	2	4	7	2
Wales	3	0	1	2	5	9	1

England & Scotland qualified for Finals

GROUP 4

20 Sep 1953	Luxembourg vs France	1-6
4 Oct 1953	Eire vs France	3-5
28 Oct 1953	Eire vs Luxembourg	4-1
25 Nov 1953	France vs Eire	1-0
17 Dec 1953	France vs Luxembourg	8-0
7 Mar 1954	Luxembourg vs Eire	0-1

	P	W	D	L	F	A	Pts
France	4	4	0	0	20	4	8
Eire	4	2	0	2	8	7	4
Luxembourg	4	0	0	4	2	19	0

France qualified for Finals

GROUP 5

| 27 Sep 1953 | Austria vs Portugal | 9-1 |
| 29 Nov 1953 | Portugal vs Austria | 0-0 |

Austria qualified for Finals

GROUP 6

6 Jan 1954	Spain vs Turkey	4-1
14 Mar 1954	Turkey vs Spain	1-0

Play-off (in Italy)

17 Mar 1954	Turkey vs Spain	2-2

Turkey qualified for Finals

GROUP 7

Hungary and Poland
(Poland withdrew)
Hungary qualified for Finals

GROUP 8

14 Jun 1953	Czechoslovakia vs Romania	2-0
28 Jun 1953	Romania vs Bulgaria	3-1
6 Sep 1953	Bulgaria vs Czechoslovakia	1-2
11 Oct 1953	Bulgaria vs Romania	1-2
25 Oct 1953	Romania vs Czechoslovakia	0-1
8 Nov 1953	Czechoslovakia vs Bulgaria	0-0

	P	W	D	L	F	A	Pts
Czechoslovakia	4	3	1	0	5	1	7
Romania	4	2	0	2	5	5	4
Bulgaria	4	0	1	3	3	7	1

Czechoslovakia qualified for Finals

GROUP 9

13 Nov 1953	Egypt vs Italy	1-2
24 Jan 1954	Italy vs Egypt	5-1

Italy qualified for Finals

GROUP 10

9 May 1953	Yugoslavia vs Greece	1-0
1 Nov 1953	Greece vs Israel	1-0
8 Nov 1953	Yugoslavia vs Israel	1-0
8 Mar 1954	Israel vs Greece	0-2
21 Mar 1954	Israel vs Yugoslavia	0-1
28 Mar 1954	Greece vs Yugoslavia	0-1

	P	W	D	L	F	A	Pts
Yugoslavia	4	4	0	0	4	0	8
Greece	4	2	0	2	3	2	4
Israel	4	0	0	4	0	5	0

Yugoslavia qualified for Finals

GROUP 11

19 Jul 1953	Mexico vs Haiti	8-0
27 Dec 1953	Haiti vs Mexcio	0-4
14 Jan 1954	Mexico vs USA	3-1
3 Apr 1954	USA vs Haiti	3-2
4 Apr 1954	Haiti vs USA	0-3

	P	W	D	L	F	A	Pts
Mexico	3	3	0	0	15	1	6
USA	3	2	0	1	7	5	4
Haiti	4	0	0	4	2	18	0

Mexico qualified for Finals

GROUP 12

14 Feb 1954	Paraguay vs Chile	4-0
21 Feb 1954	Chile vs Paraguay	1-3
28 Feb 1954	Chile vs Brazil	0-2
7 Mar 1954	Paraguay vs Brazil	0-1
14 Mar 1954	Brazil vs Chile	1-0
21 Mar 1954	Brazil vs Paraguay	4-1

	P	W	D	L	F	A	Pts
Brazil	4	4	0	0	8	1	8
Paraguay	4	2	0	2	8	6	4
Chile	4	0	0	4	1	10	0

Brazil qualified for Finals

GROUP 13

7 Mar 1954	Japan vs South Korea	1-5
14 Mar 1954	South Korea vs Japan	2-2

South Korea qualified for Finals

Switzerland (hosts) and Uruguay (Holders) were
exempt from the qualifying rounds.

1958 – QUALIFYING COMPETITION

(51 Entries)

EUROPE

GROUP 1

3 Oct 1956	Eire vs Denmark	2-1
5 Dec 1956	England vs Denmark	5-2
8 May 1957	England vs Eire	5-1
15 May 1957	Denmark vs England	1-4
19 May 1957	Eire vs England	1-1
2 Oct 1957	Denmark vs Eire	0-2

	P	W	D	L	F	A	Pts
England	4	3	1	0	15	5	7
Eire	4	2	1	1	6	7	5
Denmark	4	0	0	4	4	13	0

England qualified for Finals

GROUP 2

11 Nov 1956	France vs Belgium	6-3
2 Jun 1957	France vs Iceland	8-0
5 Jun 1957	Belgium vs Iceland	8-3
1 Sep 1957	Iceland vs France	1-5
4 Sep 1957	Iceland vs Belgium	2-5
27 Oct 1957	Belgium vs France	0-0

	P	W	D	L	F	A	Pts
France	4	3	1	0	19	4	7
Belgium	4	2	1	1	16	11	5
Iceland	4	0	0	4	6	26	0

France qualified for Finals

GROUP 3

22 May 1957	Norway vs Bulgaria	1-2
12 Jun 1957	Norway vs Hungary	2-1
23 Jun 1957	Hungary vs Bulgaria	4-1

15 Sep 1957	Bulgaria vs Hungary	1-2
3 Nov 1957	Bulgaria vs Norway	7-0
10 Nov 1957	Hungary vs Norway	5-0

	P	W	D	L	F	A	Pts
Hungary	4	3	0	1	12	4	6
Bulgaria	4	2	0	2	11	7	4
Norway	4	1	0	3	3	15	2

Hungary qualified for Finals

GROUP 4

1 May 1957	Czechoslovakia vs Wales	2-0
19 May 1957	East Germany vs Wales	2-1
26 May 1957	Wales vs Czechoslovakia	1-0
16 Jun 1957	Czechoslovakia vs East Germany	3-1
25 Sep 1957	Wales vs East Germany	4-1
27 Oct 1957	East Germany vs Czechoslovakia	1-4

	P	W	D	L	F	A	Pts
Czechoslovakia	4	3	0	1	9	3	6
Wales	4	2	0	2	6	5	4
East Germany	4	1	0	3	5	12	2

Czechoslovakia qualified for Finals

Wales elected to play in Afro-Asian Final

GROUP 5

30 Sep 1956	Austria vs Luxembourg	7-0
30 Mar 1957	Holland vs Luxembourg	4-1
26 May 1957	Austria vs Holland	3-2
25 Sep 1957	Holland vs Austria	1-1
29 Sep 1957	Luxembourg vs Austria	0-3
11 Sep 1957	Holland vs Luxembourg	5-2

	P	W	D	L	F	A	Pts
Austria	4	3	1	0	14	3	7
Holland	4	2	1	1	12	7	5
Luxembourg	4	0	0	4	3	19	0

Austria qualified for Finals

GROUP 6

23 June 1957	USSR vs Poland	3-0
5 Jul 1957	Finland vs Poland	1-3
27 Jul 1957	USSR vs Finland	2-1
15 Aug 1957	Finland vs USSR	0-10
20 Oct 1957	Poland vs USSR	2-1
3 Nov 1957	Poland vs Finland	4-0

	P	W	D	L	F	A	Pts
USSR	4	3	0	1	16	3	6
Poland	4	3	0	1	9	5	6
Finland	4	0	0	4	2	19	0

Play-off
| 24 Nov 1957 | USSR vs Poland | 3-1 |

USSR qualified for Finals

GROUP 7

5 May 1957	Greece vs Yugoslavia	0-0
16 May 1957	Greece vs Romania	1-2
29 Sep 1957	Romania vs Yugoslavia	1-1
3 Nov 1957	Romania vs Greece	3-0

| 10 Nov 1957 | Yugoslavia vs Greece | 4-1 |
| 17 Nov 1957 | Yugoslavia vs Romania | 2-0 |

	P	W	D	L	F	A	Pts
Yugoslavia	4	2	2	0	7	2	6
Romania	4	2	1	1	6	4	5
Greece	4	0	1	3	2	9	1

Yugoslavia qualified for Finals

GROUP 8

16 Jan 1957	Portugal vs Northern Ireland	1-1
25 Apr 1957	Italy vs Northern Ireland	1-0
1 May 1957	Northern Ireland vs Portugal	3-0
26 May 1957	Portugal vs Italy	3-0
22 Dec 1957	Italy vs Portugal	3-0
15 Jan 1958	Northern Ireland vs Italy	2-1

	P	W	D	L	F	A	Pts
Northern Ireland	4	2	1	1	6	3	5
Italy	4	2	0	2	5	5	4
Portugal	4	1	1	2	4	7	3

Northern Ireland qualified for Finals

GROUP 9

10 Mar 1957	Spain vs Switzerland	2-2
8 May 1957	Scotland vs Spain	4-2
19 May 1957	Switzerland vs Scotland	1-2
26 May 1957	Spain vs Scotland	4-1
6 Nov 1957	Scotland vs Switzerland	3-2
24 Nov 1957	Switzerland vs Spain	1-4

	P	W	D	L	F	A	Pts
Scotland	4	3	0	1	10	9	6
Spain	4	2	1	1	12	8	5
Switzerland	4	0	1	3	6	11	1

Scotland qualified for Finals

SOUTH AMERICA

GROUP 1

| 14 Apr 1957 | Peru vs Brazil | 1-1 |
| 22 Apr 1957 | Brazil vs Peru | 1-0 |

Brazil qualified for Finals

GROUP 2

22 Sep 1957	Chile vs Bolivia	2-1
29 Sep 1957	Bolivia vs Chile	3-0
6 Oct 1957	Bolivia vs Argentina	2-0
13 Oct 1957	Chile vs Argentina	0-2
20 Oct 1957	Argentina vs Chile	4-0
27 Oct 1957	Argentina vs Bolivia	4-0

	P	W	D	L	F	A	Pts
Argentina	4	3	0	1	10	2	6
Bolivia	4	2	0	2	6	6	4
Chile	4	1	0	3	2	10	2

Argentina qualified for Finals

GROUP 3

| 16 Jun 1957 | Colombia vs Uruguay | 1-1 |
| 20 Jun 1957 | Colombia vs Paraguay | 2-3 |

30 Jun 1957	Uruguay vs Colombia						1-0
7 Jul 1957	Paraguay vs Colombia						3-0
14 Jul 1957	Paraguay vs Uruguay						5-0
28 Jul 1957	Uruguay vs Paraguay						2-0

	P	W	D	L	F	A	Pts
Paraguay	4	3	0	1	11	4	6
Uruguay	4	2	1	1	4	6	5
Colombia	4	0	1	3	3	8	4

Paraguay qualified for Finals

CENTRAL & NORTH AMERICAN GROUP

SUB-GROUP 1

10 Feb 1957	Guatemala vs Costa Rica	2-6
17 Feb 1957	Costa Rica vs Guatemala	3-1
3 Mar 1957	Costa Rica vs Curacao	4-0
10 Mar 1957	Guatemala vs Curacao	1-3
1 Aug 1957	Curacao vs Costa Rica	1-2
8 Aug 1957	Curacao vs Guatemala	3-1

	P	W	D	L	F	A	Pts
Costa Rica	4	4	0	0	15	4	8
Curacao	4	2	0	2	7	8	4
Guatemala	4	0	0	4	5	15	0

Costa Rica qualified for Group Final

SUB-GROUP 2

7 Apr 1957	Mexico vs USA	6-0
28 Apr 1957	USA vs Mexico	2-7
22 Jun 1957	Canada vs USA	5-1
30 Jun 1957	Mexico vs Canada	3-0
4 Jul 1957	Mexico vs Canada	2-0
6 Jul 1957	USA vs Canada	2-3

	P	W	D	L	F	A	Pts
Mexico	4	4	0	0	18	2	8
Canada	4	2	0	2	8	8	4
USA	4	0	0	4	5	21	0

Mexico qualified for Group Final

GROUP FINAL

20 Oct 1957	Mexico vs Costa-Rica	2-0
27 Oct 1957	Costa Rica vs Mexico	1-1

Mexico qualified for Finals

AFRO-ASIAN GROUP

SUB-GROUP 1

12 May 1957	Indonesia vs Nationalist China	2-0
27 Jun 1957	Nationalist China vs Indonesia	4-3

Play-off
23 Jun 1957	Indonesia vs Nationalist China	0-0

Indonesia qualified for Group Final but withdrew

SUB-GROUP 2

Israel qualified for Group Final (Turkey withdrew)

SUB-GROUP 3

Egypt qualified for Group Final

Cyprus withdrew – but Egypt also withdrew

SUB-GROUP 4

8 Mar 1957	Sudan vs Syria	1-0
24 May 1957	Syria vs Sudan	1-1

Sudan qualified for Group Final but withdrew

GROUP FINAL

After the withdrawal of all qualifiers for the Group Final except Israel, Wales were nominated to play Israel in Group Final for a place in the Finals.

15 Jan 1958	Israel vs Wales	0-2
5 Feb 1958	Wales vs Israel	2-0

Wales qualified for Finals

Sweden (hosts) and West Germany (Holders) were exempt from the qualifying rounds.

1962 – QUALIFYING COMPETITION

(56 Entries)

Austria, Canada & Indonesia withdrew without participating.

GROUP 1

19 Oct 1960	Sweden vs Belgium	2-0
20 Nov 1960	Belgium vs Switzerland	2-4
20 May 1961	Switzerland vs Belgium	2-1
28 May 1961	Sweden vs Switzerland	4-0
4 Oct 1961	Belgium vs Sweden	0-2
29 Oct 1961	Switzerland vs Sweden	3-2

	P	W	D	L	F	A	Pts
Switzerland	4	3	0	1	9	9	6
Sweden	4	3	0	1	10	3	6
Belgium	4	0	0	4	3	10	0

Play-off (In West Germany)
12 Nov 1961	Switzerland vs Sweden	2-1

Switzerland qualified for Finals

GROUP 2

25 Sep 1960	Finland vs France	1-2
11 Dec 1960	France vs Bulgaria	3-0
16 Jun 1961	Finland vs Bulgaria	0-2
28 Sep 1961	France vs Finland	5-1
29 Oct 1961	Bulgaria vs Finland	3-1
12 Nov 1961	Bulgaria vs France	1-0

	P	W	D	L	F	A	Pts
Bulgaria	4	3	0	1	6	4	6
France	4	3	0	1	10	3	6
Finland	4	0	0	4	3	12	0

Play-off (in Italy)
16 Dec 1961	Bulgaria vs France	1-0

Bulgaria qualified for Finals

GROUP 3

26 Oct 1960	Northern Ireland vs West Germany 3-4
20 Nov 1960	Greece vs West Germany 0-3
3 May 1961	Greece vs Northern Ireland 2-1
10 May 1961	W. Germany vs Northern Ireland 2-1
17 Oct 1961	Northern Ireland vs Greece 2-0
22 Oct 1961	West Germany vs Greece 2-1

	P	W	D	L	F	A	Pts
West Germany	4	4	0	0	11	5	8
Northern Ireland	4	1	0	3	7	8	2
Greece	4	1	0	3	3	8	2

West Germany qualified for Finals

GROUP 4

16 Apr 1961	Hungary vs East Germany 2-0
30 Apr 1961	Holland vs Hungary 0-3
14 May 1961	East Germany vs Holland 1-1
10 Sep 1961	East Germany vs Hungary 2-3
22 Oct 1961	Hungary vs Holland 3-3

Holland vs East Germany was not played

	P	W	D	L	F	A	Pts
Hungary	4	3	1	0	11	5	7
Holland	3	0	2	1	4	7	2
East Germany	3	0	1	2	3	6	1

Hungary qualified for Finals

GROUP 5

1 Jun 1961	Norway vs Turkey 0-1
18 Jun 1961	USSR vs Turkey 1-0
1 Jul 1961	USSR vs Norway 5-2
23 Aug 1961	Norway vs USSR 0-3
29 Oct 1961	Turkey vs Norway 2-1
12 Nov 1961	Turkey vs USSR 1-2

	P	W	D	L	F	A	Pts
USSR	4	4	0	0	11	3	8
Turkey	4	2	0	2	4	4	4
Norway	4	0	0	4	3	11	0

USSR qualified for Finals

GROUP 6

19 Oct 1960	Luxembourg vs England 0-9
19 Mar 1961	Portugal vs Luxembourg 6-0
21 May 1961	Portugal vs England 1-1
28 Sep 1961	England vs Luxembourg 4-1
8 Oct 1961	Luxembourg vs Portugal 4-2
25 Oct 1961	England vs Portugal 2-0

	P	W	D	L	F	A	Pts
England	4	3	1	0	16	2	7
Portugal	4	1	1	2	9	7	3
Luxembourg	4	1	0	3	5	21	2

England qualified for Finals

GROUP 7

ROUND ONE

23 Nov 1960	Cyprus vs Israel 1-1
27 Nov 1960	Israel vs Cyprus 6-1

Israel qualified for Round Two

ROUND TWO

14 Mar 1961	Israel vs Ethiopia 1-0
19 Mar 1961	Ethiopia vs Israel 2-3

Romania vs Italy (Romania withdrew)

Israel qualified for Group Final

Italy qualified for Group Final

GROUP FINAL

15 Oct 1961	Israel vs Italy 2-4
4 Nov 1961	Italy vs Israel 6-0

Italy qualified for Finals

GROUP 8

3 May 1961	Scotland vs Eire 4-1
7 May 1961	Eire vs Scotland 0-3
14 May 1961	Czechoslovakia vs Scotland 4-0
26 Sep 1961	Scotland vs Czechoslovakia 3-2
8 Oct 1961	Eire vs Czechoslovakia 1-3
29 Oct 1961	Czechoslovakia vs Eire 7-1

	P	W	D	L	F	A	Pts
Czechoslovakia	4	3	0	1	16	5	6
Scotland	4	3	0	1	10	7	6
Eire	4	0	0	4	3	17	0

Play-off (in Belgium)

29 Nov 1961	Czechoslovakia vs Scotland 4-2

Czechoslovakia qualified for Finals

GROUP 9

ROUND 1

30 Oct 1960	Morocco vs Tunisia 2-1
13 Nov 1960	Tunisia vs Morocco 2-1

Play-off

22 Jan 1961	Morocco vs Tunisia 1-1

Morocco qualified for Round Two on the toss of a coin

28 Aug 1960	Ghana vs Nigeria 4-1
10 Sep 1960	Nigera vs Ghana 2-2

Ghana qualified for Round Two

Sudan vs Egypt (both withdrew)

ROUND 2

2 Apr 1961	Ghana vs Morocco 0-0
28 May 1961	Morocco vs Ghana 1-0

Morocco qualified for Group Final

19 Apr 1961	Wales vs Spain 1-2
18 May 1961	Spain vs Wales 1-1

Spain qualified for Group Final

GROUP FINAL

12 Nov 1961	Morocco vs Spain 0-1
23 Nov 1961	Spain vs Morocco 3-2

Spain qualified for Finals

GROUP 10

ROUND 1

6 Nov 1960	South Korea vs Japan 2-1

11 Jun 1961   Japan vs South Korea 0-2
South Korea qualified for Group Final
4 Jun 1961   Yugoslavia vs Poland 2-1
25 Jun 1961   Poland vs Yugoslavia 1-1
Yugoslavia qualified for Group Final

GROUP FINAL

8 Oct 1961   Yugoslavia vs South Korea 5-1
26 Nov 1961   South Korea vs Yugoslavia 1-3
Yugoslavia qualified for Finals

CENTRAL AMERICA & NORTH AMERICA

SUB-GROUP 1

6 Nov 1960   USA vs Mexico 3-3
13 Nov 1960   Mexico vs USA 3-0
Mexico qualified for Group Final Pool

SUB-GROUP 2

21 Aug 1960   Costa Rica vs Guatemala 3-2
28 Aug 1960   Guatemala vs Costa Rica 4-4
4 Sep 1960   Honduras vs Costa Rica 2-1
11 Sep 1960   Costa Rica vs Honduras 5-0
25 Sep 1960   Honduras vs Guatemala 1-1

	P	W	D	L	F	A	Pts
Costa Rica	4	2	1	1	13	8	5
Honduras	3	1	1	1	3	7	3
Guatemala	3	0	2	1	7	8	2

Play-off (In Guatemala)
14 Jan 1961   Costa Rica vs Honduras 1-0
Costa Rica qualified for Group Final Pool

SUB-GROUP 3

2 Oct 1960   Surinam vs Netherlands Antilles 1-2
27 Nov 1960   Netherlands Antilles vs Surinam 0-0
Netherlands Antilles qualified for Group Final Pool

GROUP FINAL POOL

22 Mar 1961   Costa Rica vs Mexico 1-0
29 Mar 1961   Costa Rica vs Netherlands Antilles 6-0
5 Apr 1961   Mexico vs Netherlands Antilles 7-0
12 Apr 1961   Mexico vs Costa Rica 4-1
23 Apr 1961   Netherlands Antilles vs Costa Rica 2-0
21 May 1961   Netherlands Antilles vs Mexico 0-0

	P	W	D	L	F	A	Pts
Mexico	4	2	1	1	11	2	5
Costa Rica	4	2	0	2	8	6	4
Netherlands Antilles	4	1	1	2	2	13	3

Mexico qualified for Group Final play-off

GROUP FINAL PLAY-OFF

29 Oct 1961   Mexico vs Paraguay 1-0
5 Nov 1961   Paraguay vs Mexico 0-0
Mexico qualified for Finals

SOUTH AMERICA

GROUP 1

4 Dec 1960   Ecuador vs Argentina 3-6
17 Dec 1960   Argentina vs Ecuador 5-0
Argentina qualified for Finals

GROUP 2

15 Jul 1961   Bolivia vs Uruguay 1-1
30 Jul 1961   Uruguay vs Bolivia 2-1
Uruguay qualified for Finals

GROUP 3

30 Apr 1961   Colombia v Peru 1-0
7 May 1961   Peru v Colombia 1-1
Colombia qualified for Finals

Chile (hosts) and Brazil (holders) were exempt from the qualifying rounds.

1966 – QUALIFYING COMPETITION

(70 Entries)

GROUP 1

9 May 1965   Belgium vs Israel 1-0
13 Jun 1965   Bulgaria vs Israel 4-0
26 Sep 1965   Bulgaria vs Belgium 3-0
27 Oct 1965   Belgium vs Bulgaria 5-0
10 Nov 1965   Israel vs Belgium 0-5
21 Nov 1965   Israel vs Bulgaria 1-2

	P	W	D	L	F	A	Pts
Bulgaria	4	3	0	1	9	6	6
Belgium	4	3	0	1	11	3	6
Israel	4	0	0	4	1	12	0

Play-off (in Italy)
29 Dec 1965   Bulgaria vs Belgium 2-1
Bulgaria qualified for Finals

GROUP 2

4 Nov 1964   West Germany vs Sweden 1-1
24 Apr 1965   West Germany vs Cyprus 5-0
5 May 1965   Sweden vs Cyprus 3-0
26 Sep 1965   Sweden vs West Germany 1-2
7 Nov 1965   Cyprus vs Sweden 0-5
14 Nov 1965   Cyprus vs West Germany 0-6

	P	W	D	L	F	A	Pts
West Germany	4	3	1	0	14	2	7
Sweden	4	2	1	1	10	3	5
Cyprus	4	0	0	4	0	19	0

West Germany qualified for Finals

GROUP 3

20 Sep 1964   Yugoslavia vs Luxembourg 3-1
4 Oct 1964   Luxembourg vs France 0-2
8 Nov 1964   Luxembourg vs Norway 0-2

11 Nov 1964	France vs Norway	1-0
18 Apr 1965	Yugoslavia vs France	1-0
27 May 1965	Norway vs Luxembourg	4-2
16 Jun 1965	Norway vs Yugoslavia	3-0
13 Sep 1965	Norway vs France	0-1
19 Sep 1965	Luxembourg vs Yugoslavia	2-5
9 Oct 1965	France vs Yugoslavia	1-0
6 Nov 1965	France vs Luxembourg	4-1
7 Nov 1965	Yugoslavia vs Norway	1-1

	P	W	D	L	F	A	Pts
France	6	5	0	1	9	2	10
Norway	6	3	1	2	10	5	7
Yugoslavia	6	3	1	2	10	8	7
Luxembourg	6	0	0	6	6	20	0

France qualified for Finals

GROUP 4

24 Jan 1965	Portugal vs Turkey	5-1
19 Apr 1965	Turkey vs Portugal	0-1
25 Apr 1965	Czechoslovakia vs Portugal	0-1
2 May 1965	Romania vs Turkey	3-0
30 May 1965	Romania vs Czechoslovakia	1-0
13 Jun 1965	Portugal vs Romania	2-1
19 Sep 1965	Czechoslovakia vs Romania	3-1
9 Oct 1965	Turkey vs Czechoslovakia	0-6
23 Oct 1965	Turkey vs Romania	2-1
31 Oct 1965	Portugal vs Czechoslovakia	0-0
21 Nov 1965	Czechoslovakia vs Turkey	3-1
21 Nov 1965	Romania vs Portugal	2-0

	P	W	D	L	F	A	Pts
Portugal	6	4	1	1	9	4	9
Czechoslovakia	6	3	1	2	12	4	7
Romania	6	3	0	3	9	7	6
Turkey	6	1	0	5	4	19	2

Portugal qualified for Finals

GROUP 5

24 May 1964	Holland vs Albania	2-0
14 Oct 1964	Northern Ireland vs Switzerland	1-0
25 Oct 1964	Albania vs Holland	0-2
14 Nov 1964	Switzerland vs Northern Ireland	2-1
17 Mar 1965	Northern Ireland vs Holland	2-1
7 Apr 1965	Holland vs Northern Irelland	0-0
11 Apr 1965	Albania vs Switzerland	0-2
2 May 1965	Switzerland vs Albania	1-0
7 May 1965	Northern Ireland vs Albania	4-1
17 Oct 1965	Holland vs Switzerland	0-0
14 Nov 1965	Switzerland vs Holland	2-1
24 Nov 1965	Albania vs Northern Ireland	1-1

	P	W	D	L	F	A	Pts
Switzerland	6	4	1	1	7	3	9
Northern Ireland	6	3	2	1	9	5	8
Holland	6	2	2	2	6	4	6
Albania	6	0	1	5	2	12	1

Switzerland qualified for Finals

GROUP 6

25 Apr 1965	Austria vs East Germany	1-1
23 May 1965	East Germany vs Hungary	1-1
13 Jun 1965	Austria vs Hungary	0-1
5 Sep 1965	Hungary vs Austria	3-0
9 Oct 1965	Hungary vs East Germany	3-2
31 Oct 1965	East Germany vs Austria	1-0

	P	W	D	L	F	A	Pts
Hungary	4	3	1	0	8	5	7
East Germany	4	1	2	1	5	5	4
Austria	4	0	1	3	3	6	1

Hungary qualified for Finals

GROUP 7

21 Oct 1964	Denmark vs Wales	1-0
29 Nov 1964	Greece vs Denmark	4-2
9 Dec 1964	Greece vs Wales	2-0
17 Mar 1965	Wales vs Greece	4-1
23 May 1965	USSR vs Greece	3-1
30 May 1965	USSR vs Wales	2-1
27 Jun 1965	USSR vs Denmark	6-0
3 Oct 1965	Greece vs USSR	1-4
17 Oct 1965	Denmark vs USSR	1-3
27 Oct 1965	Denmark vs Greece	1-1
27 Oct 1965	Wales vs USSR	2-1
1 Dec 1965	Wales vs Denmark	4-2

	P	W	D	L	F	A	Pts
USSR	6	5	0	1	19	6	10
Wales	6	3	0	3	11	9	6
Greece	6	2	1	3	10	14	5
Denmark	6	1	1	4	7	18	3

USSR qualified for Finals

GROUP 8

21 Oct 1964	Scotland vs Finland	3-1
4 Nov 1964	Italy vs Finland	6-1
18 Apr 1965	Poland vs Italy	0-0
23 May 1965	Poland vs Scotland	1-1
27 May 1965	Finland vs Scotland	1-2
23 Jun 1965	Finland vs Italy	0-2
26 Sep 1965	Finland vs Poland	2-0
13 Oct 1965	Scotland vs Poland	1-2
24 Oct 1965	Poland vs Finland	7-0
1 Nov 1965	Italy vs Poland	6-1
9 Nov 1965	Scotland vs Italy	1-0
8 Dec 1965	Italy vs Scotland	3-0

	P	W	D	L	F	A	Pts
Italy	6	4	1	1	17	3	9
Scotland	6	3	1	2	8	8	7
Poland	6	2	2	2	11	10	6
Finland	6	1	0	5	5	20	2

Italy qualified for Finals

GROUP 9

5 May 1965	Eire vs Spain	1-0
27 Oct 1965	Spain vs Eire	4-1

Syria withdrew

Play-off (in France)

10 Nov 1965	Spain vs Eire	1-0

Spain qualified for Finals

GROUP 10

England (hosts) exempt from the qualifying competition

GROUP 11

16 May 1965	Peru vs Venezuela	1-0
23 May 1965	Uruguay vs Venezuela	5-0
30 May 1965	Venezuela vs Uruguay	1-3
2 Jun 1965	Venezuela vs Peru	3-6
6 Jun 1965	Peru vs Uruguay	0-1
13 Jun 1965	Uruguay vs Peru	2-1

	P	W	D	L	F	A	Pts
Uruguay	4	4	0	0	11	2	8
Peru	4	2	0	2	8	6	4
Venezuela	4	0	0	4	4	15	0

Uruguay qualified for Finals

GROUP 12

20 Jul 1965	Colombia vs Ecuador	0-1
25 Jul 1965	Ecuador vs Colombia	2-0
1 Aug 1965	Chile vs Colombia	7-2
7 Aug 1965	Colombia vs Chile	2-0
15 Aug 1965	Ecuador vs Chile	2-2
22 Aug 1965	Chile vs Ecuador	3-1

	P	W	D	L	F	A	Pts
Chile	4	2	1	1	12	7	5
Ecuador	4	2	1	1	6	5	5
Colombia	4	1	0	3	4	10	2

Play-off (in Peru)

| 12 Oct 1965 | Chile vs Ecuador | 2-1 |

Chile qualified for Finals

GROUP 13

25 July 1965	Paraguay vs Bolivia	2-0
1 Aug 1965	Argentina vs Paraguay	3-0
8 Aug 1965	Paraguay vs Argentina	0-0
17 Aug 1965	Argentina vs Bolivia	4-1
22 Aug 1965	Bolivia vs Paraguay	2-1
29 Aug 1965	Bolivia vs Argentina	1-2

	P	W	D	L	F	A	Pts
Argentina	4	3	1	0	9	2	7
Paraguay	4	1	1	2	3	5	3
Bolivia	4	1	0	3	4	9	2

Argentina qualified for Finals

GROUP 14

Brazil (holders) exempt from the qualifying competition

GROUP 15

SUB-GROUP 1

16 Jan 1965	Jamaica vs Cuba	2-0
20 Jan 1965	Netherlands Antilles vs Cuba	1-1
23 Jan 1965	Jamaica vs Netherlands Antilles	2-0
30 Jan 1965	Cuba vs Netherlands Antilles	0-1
3 Feb 1965	Netherlands Antilles vs Jamaica	0-0
8 Feb 1965	Cuba vs Jamaica	2-1

	P	W	D	L	F	A	Pts
Jamaica	4	2	1	1	4	2	5
Cuba	4	2	0	2	3	3	4
Netherlands Antilles	4	1	1	2	1	3	3

Jamaica qualified for Group Finals

SUB-GROUP 2

7 Feb 1965	Trinidad vs Surinam	4-1
12 Feb 1965	Costa Rica vs Surinam	1-0
21 Feb 1965	Costa Rica vs Trinidad	4-0
28 Feb 1965	Surinam vs Costa Rica	1-3
7 Mar 1965	Trinidad vs Costa Rica	0-1
14 Mar 1965	Surinam vs Trinidad	6-1

	P	W	D	L	F	A	Pts
Costa Rica	4	4	0	0	9	1	8
Surinam	4	1	0	3	8	9	2
Trinidad	4	1	0	3	5	12	2

Costa Rica qualified for Group Finals

SUB-GROUP 3

28 Feb 1965	Honduras vs Mexico	0-1
4 Mar 1965	Mexico vs Honduras	3-0
7 Mar 1965	USA vs Mexico	2-2
12 Mar 1965	Mexico vs USA	2-0
17 Mar 1965	Honduras vs USA	0-1
21 Mar 1965	USA vs Honduras	1-1

	P	W	D	L	F	A	Pts
Mexico	4	3	1	0	8	2	7
USA	4	1	2	1	4	5	4
Honduras	4	0	1	3	1	6	1

Mexico qualified for Group Finals

GROUP FINALS

25 Apr 1965	Costa Rica vs Mexico	0-0
3 May 1965	Jamaica vs Mexico	2-3
7 May 1965	Mexico vs Jamaica	8-0
11 May 1965	Costa Rica vs Jamaica	7-0
16 May 1965	Mexico vs Costa Rica	1-0
22 May 1965	Jamaica vs Costa Rica	1-1

	P	W	D	L	F	A	Pts
Mexico	4	3	1	0	12	2	7
Costa Rica	4	1	2	1	8	2	4
Jamaica	4	0	1	3	3	19	1

Mexico qualified for Finals

GROUP 16

South Korea, South Africa, Ghana, Guinea, Sudan, Cameroons, Tunisia, Algeria, Liberia, Morocco, Senegal, Ethiopia, Gabon, United Arab Republic, Libya and Nigeria all withdrew from this group.

| 21 Nov 1965 | North Korea vs Australia | 6-1 |
| 24 Nov 1965 | North Korea vs Australia | 3-1 |

North Korea qualified for Finals

1970 – QUALIFYING COMPETITION

(71 Entries)

GROUP 1

12 Oct 1968	Switzerland vs Greece	1-0
27 Oct 1968	Portugal vs Romania	3-0
23 Nov 1968	Romania vs Switzerland	2-0
11 Dec 1968	Greece vs Portugal	4-2
16 Apr 1969	Portugal vs Switzerland	0-2
16 Apr 1969	Greece vs Romania	2-2
4 May 1969	Portugal vs Greece	2-2
14 May 1969	Switzerland vs Romania	0-1
12 Oct 1969	Romania vs Portugal	1-0
15 Oct 1969	Greece vs Switzerland	4-1
2 Nov 1969	Switzerland vs Portugal	1-1
16 Nov 1969	Romania vs Greece	1-1

	P	W	D	L	F	A	Pts
Romania	6	3	2	1	7	6	8
Greece	6	2	3	1	13	9	7
Switzerland	6	2	1	3	5	8	5
Portugal	6	1	2	3	8	10	4

Romania qualified for Finals

GROUP 2

25 Sep 1968	Denmark vs Czechoslovakia	0-3
20 Oct 1968	Czechoslovakia vs Denmark	1-0
4 May 1969	Eire vs Czechoslovakia	1-2
25 May 1969	Hungary vs Czechslovakia	2-0
27 May 1969	Denmark vs Eire	2-0
8 Jun 1969	Eire vs Hungary	1-2
15 Jun 1969	Denmark vs Hungary	3-2
14 Sep 1969	Czechoslovakia vs Hungary	3-3
7 Oct 1969	Czechoslovakia vs Eire	3-0
15 Oct 1969	Eire vs Denmark	1-1
22 Oct 1969	Hungary vs Denmark	3-0
5 Nov 1969	Hungary vs Eire	4-0

	P	W	D	L	F	A	Pts
Czechoslovakia	6	4	1	1	12	6	9
Hungary	6	4	1	1	16	7	9
Denmark	6	2	1	3	6	10	5
Eire	6	0	1	5	3	14	1

Play-off (in France)

3 Dec 1969	Czechoslovakia vs Hungary	4-1

Czechoslovakia qualified for Finals

GROUP 3

23 Oct 1968	Wales vs Italy	0-1
29 Mar 1969	East Germany vs Italy	2-2
16 Apr 1969	East Germany vs Wales	2-1
22 Oct 1969	Wales vs East Germany	1-3
4 Nov 1969	Italy vs Wales	4-1
22 Nov 1969	Italy vs East Germany	3-0

	P	W	D	L	F	A	Pts
Italy	4	3	1	0	10	3	7
East Germany	4	2	1	1	7	7	5
Wales	4	0	0	4	3	10	0

Italy qualified for Finals

GROUP 4

23 Oct 1968	Northern Ireland vs Turkey	4-1
11 Dec 1968	Turkey vs Nothern Ireland	0-3
10 Sep 1969	Northern Ireland vs USSR	0-0
15 Oct 1969	USSR vs Turkey	3-0
22 Oct 1969	USSR vs Northern Ireland	2-0
16 Nov 1969	Turkey vs USSR	1-3

	P	W	D	L	F	A	Pts
USSR	4	3	1	0	8	1	7
Northern Ireland	4	2	1	1	7	3	5
Turkey	4	0	0	4	2	13	0

USSR qualified for Finals

GROUP 5

9 Oct 1968	Sweden vs Norway	5-0
6 Dec 1968	France vs Norway	0-1
19 Jun 1969	Norway vs Sweden	2-5
10 Sep 1969	Norway vs France	1-3
15 Oct 1969	Sweden vs France	2-0
2 Nov 1969	France vs Sweden	3-0

	P	W	D	L	F	A	Pts
Sweden	4	3	0	1	12	5	6
France	4	2	0	2	6	4	4
Norway	4	1	0	3	4	13	2

Sweden qualified for Finals

GROUP 6

16 Jun 1968	Finland vs Belgium	1-2
25 Sep 1968	Yugoslavia vs Finland	9-1
9 Oct 1968	Belgium vs Finland	6-1
16 Oct 1968	Belgium vs Yugoslavia	3-0
27 Oct 1968	Yugoslavia vs Spain	0-0
11 Nov 1968	Spain vs Belgium	1-1
23 Feb 1969	Belgium vs Spain	2-1
30 Apr 1969	Spain vs Yugoslavia	2-1
4 Jun 1969	Finland vs Yugoslavia	1-5
25 Jun 1969	Finland vs Spain	2-0
15 Oct 1969	Spain vs Finland	6-0
19 Oct 1969	Yugoslavia vs Belgium	4-0

	P	W	D	L	F	A	Pts
Belgium	6	4	1	1	14	8	9
Yugoslavia	6	3	1	2	19	7	7
Spain	6	2	2	2	10	6	6
Finland	6	1	0	5	6	28	2

Belgium qualified for Finals

GROUP 7

19 May 1968	Austria vs Cyprus	7-1
13 Oct 1968	Austria vs West Germany	0-2
6 Nov 1968	Scotland vs Austria	2-1
23 Nov 1968	Cyprus vs West Germany	0-1
11 Dec 1968	Cyprus vs Scotland	0-5
16 Apr 1969	Scotland vs West Germany	1-1
19 Apr 1969	Cyprus vs Austria	1-2
10 May 1969	West Germany vs Austria	1-0
17 May 1969	Scotland vs Cyprus	8-0
21 May 1969	West Germany vs Cyprus	12-0
22 Oct 1969	West Germany vs Scotland	3-2
5 Nov 1969	Austria vs Scotland	2-0

	P	W	D	L	F	A	Pts
West Germany	6	5	1	0	20	3	11
Scotland	6	3	1	2	18	7	7
Austria	6	3	0	3	12	7	6
Cyprus	6	0	0	6	2	35	0

West Germany qualified for Finals

GROUP 8

4 Sep 1968	Luxembourg vs Holland	0-2
27 Oct 1968	Bulgaria vs Holland	2-0
26 Mar 1969	Holland vs Luxembourg	4-0
20 Apr 1969	Poland vs Luxembourg	8-1
23 Mar 1969	Bulgaria vs Luxembourg	2-1
7 May 1969	Holland vs Poland	1-0
15 Jun 1969	Bulgaria vs Poland	4-1
7 Sep 1969	Poland vs Holland	2-1
12 Oct 1969	Luxembourg vs Poland	1-5
22 Oct 1969	Holland vs Bulgaria	1-1
9 Nov 1969	Poland vs Bulgaria	3-0
7 Dec 1969	Luxembourg vs Bulgaria	1-3

	P	W	D	L	F	A	Pts
Bulgaria	6	4	1	1	12	7	9
Poland	6	4	0	2	19	8	8
Holland	6	3	1	2	9	5	7
Luxembourg	6	0	0	6	4	24	0

Bulgaria qualified for Finals

GROUP 9

England (holders) exempt from qualifying competition

GROUP 10

27 Jul 1969	Bolivia vs Argentina	3-1
3 Aug 1969	Peru vs Argentina	1-0
10 Aug 1969	Bolivia vs Peru	2-1
17 Aug 1969	Peru vs Bolivia	3-0
24 Aug 1969	Argentina vs Bolivia	1-0
31 Aug 1969	Argentina vs Peru	2-2

	P	W	D	L	F	A	Pts
Peru	4	2	1	1	7	4	5
Bolivia	4	2	0	2	5	6	4
Argentina	4	1	1	2	4	6	3

Peru qualified for Finals

GROUP 11

27 Jul 1969	Colombia vs Venezuela	3-0
2 Aug 1969	Venezuela vs Colombia	1-1
6 Aug 1969	Colombia vs Brazil	0-2
7 Aug 1969	Venezuela vs Paraguay	0-2
10 Aug 1969	Colombia vs Paraguay	0-1
10 Aug 1969	Venezuela vs Brazil	0-5
17 Aug 1969	Paraguay vs Brazil	0-3
21 Aug 1969	Brazil vs Colombia	6-2
21 Aug 1969	Paraguay vs Venezuela	1-0
24 Aug 1969	Brazil vs Venezuela	6-0
24 Aug 1969	Paraguay vs Colombia	2-1
31 Aug 1969	Brazil vs Paraguay	1-0

	P	W	D	L	F	A	Pts
Brazil	6	6	0	0	23	2	12
Paraguay	6	4	0	2	6	5	8
Colombia	6	1	1	4	7	12	3
Venezuela	6	0	1	5	1	18	1

Brazil qualified for Finals

GROUP 12

6 July 1969	Ecuador vs Uruguay	0-2
13 July 1969	Chile vs Uruguay	0-0
20 July 1969	Uruguay vs Ecuador	1-0
27 July 1969	Chile vs Ecuador	4-1
3 Aug 1969	Ecuador vs Chile	1-1
10 Aug 1969	Uruguay vs Chile	2-0

	P	W	D	L	F	A	Pts
Uruguay	4	3	1	0	5	0	7
Chile	4	1	2	1	5	4	4
Ecuador	4	0	1	3	2	8	1

Uruguay qualified for Finals

GROUP 13

SUB-GROUP A

27 Nov 1968	Costa Rica vs Jamaica	3-0
1 Dec 1968	Jamaica vs Costa Rica	1-3
5 Dec 1968	Honduras vs Jamaica	3-1
8 Dec 1968	Jamaica vs Honduras	0-2
22 Dec 1968	Honduras vs Costa Rica	1-0
29 Dec 1968	Costa Rica vs Honduras	1-1

	P	W	D	L	F	A	Pts
Honduras	4	3	1	0	7	2	7
Costa Rica	4	2	1	1	7	3	5
Jamaica	4	0	0	4	2	11	0

Honduras qualified for 2nd Round

SUB-GROUP B

17 Nov 1968	Guatemala vs Trinidad	4-0
20 Nov 1968	Trinidad vs Guatemala	0-0
	(in Guatemala)	
23 Nov 1968	Trinidad vs Haiti	0-4
25 Nov 1968	Haiti vs Trinidad	2-4
8 Dec 1968	Haiti vs Guatemala	2-0
23 Feb 1969	Guatemala vs Haiti	1-1

	P	W	D	L	F	A	Pts
Haiti	4	2	1	1	8	4	5
Guatemala	4	1	2	1	4	2	4
Trinidad	4	1	1	2	4	10	3

Haiti qualified for 2nd Round

SUB-GROUP C

24 Nov 1968	Surinam vs Netherlands Antilles	6-0
1 Dec 1968	El Salvador vs Surinam	6-0
5 Dec 1968	Netherlands Antilles vs Surinam	2-0
12 Dec 1968	El Salvador vs Netherlands Antilles	1-0
15 Dec 1968	Netherlands Antilles vs El Salvador	1-2
22 Dec 1968	Surinam vs El Salvador	4-1

	P	W	D	L	F	A	Pts
El Salvador	4	3	0	1	10	5	6
Surinam	4	2	0	2	10	9	4
Netherlands Antilles	4	1	0	3	3	9	2

El Salvador qualified for 2nd Round

SUB-GROUP D

6 Oct 1968	Canada vs Bermuda	4-0
13 Oct 1968	Canada vs USA	4-2
20 Oct 1968	Bermuda vs Canada	0-0
26 Oct 1968	USA vs Canada	1-0
3 Nov 1968	USA vs Bermuda	6-2
11 Nov 1968	Bermuda vs USA	0-2

	P	W	D	L	F	A	Pts
USA	4	3	0	1	11	6	6
Canada	4	2	1	1	8	3	5
Bermuda	4	0	1	3	2	12	1

USA qualified for 2nd Round

ROUND TWO

20 Apr 1969	Haiti vs USA	2-0
11 May 1969	USA vs Haiti	0-1
8 Jun 1969	Honduras vs El Salvador	1-0
15 Jun 1969	El Salvador vs Honduras	3-0

Haiti qualified for Group Final

Play-off (in Mexico)

| 28 Jun 1969 | El Salvador vs Honduras , | 3-2 |

El Salvador qualified for Group Final

GROUP FINAL

| 21 Sep 1969 | Haiti vs El Salvador | 1-2 |
| 28 Sep 1969 | El Salvador vs Haiti | 0-3 |

Play-off (in Jamaica)

| 8 Oct 1969 | El Salvador vs Haiti | 1-0 |

El Salvador qualified for Finals

GROUP 14

Mexico (hosts) exempt from qualifying competition

GROUP 15

SUB-GROUP A

10 Oct 1969	Australia vs Japan	3-1
12 Oct 1969	South Korea vs Japan	2-2
14 Oct 1969	Australia vs South Korea	2-1
16 Oct 1969	Japan vs Australia	1-1
18 Oct 1969	South Korea vs Japan	2-0
20 Oct 1969	South Korea vs Australia	1-1

	P	W	D	L	F	A	Pts
Australia	4	2	2	0	7	4	6
South Korea	4	1	2	1	6	5	4
Japan	4	0	2	2	4	8	2

Australia qualified for 2nd Round

SUB-GROUP B

| 28 Sep 1969 | Israel vs New Zealand | 4-0 |
| 1 Oct 1969 | New Zealand vs Israel | 0-2 |

North Korea withdrew from this group

Israel qualified for Group Final

ROUND TWO

| 23 Nov 1969 | Australia vs Rhodesia | 1-1 |
| 27 Nov 1969 | Rhodesia vs Australia | 0-0 |

Play-off

| 1 Dec 1969 | Australia vs Rhodesia | 3-1 |

Australia qualified for Group Final

GROUP FINAL

| 4 Dec 1969 | Israel vs Australia | 1-0 |
| 14 Dec 1969 | Australia vs Israel | 1-1 |

Israel qualified for Finals

GROUP 16

ROUND 1

| 17 Nov 1968 | Algeria vs Tunisia | 1-2 |
| 29 Dec 1968 | Tunisia vs Algeria | 0-0 |

Tunisia qualified for 2nd Round

| 3 Nov 1968 | Morocco vs Senegal | 1-0 |
| 1 Jan 1969 | Senegal vs Morocco | 2-1 |

Play-off (in Las Palmas)

| 13 Feb 1969 | Morocco vs Senegal | 2-0 |

Morocco qualified for 2nd Round

| 26 Jan 1969 | Libya vs Ethiopia | 2-0 |
| 9 Feb 1969 | Ethiopia vs Libya | 5-1 |

Ethiopia qualified for 2nd Round

| 27 Oct 1968 | Zambia vs Sudan | 4-2 |
| 8 Nov 1968 | Sudan vs Zambia | 4-2 |

Sudan qualified for 2nd Round due to scoring most goals in the second game

| 7 Dec 1968 | Nigeria vs Cameroons | 1-1 |
| 22 Dec 1968 | Cameroons vs Nigeria | 2-3 |

Nigeria qualified for 2nd Round

Ghana received a bye

ROUND 2

| 27 Apr 1969 | Tunisia vs Morocco | 0-0 |
| 18 May 1969 | Morocco vs Tunisia | 0-0 |

Play-off (in France)

| 13 Jun 1969 | Morocco vs Tunisia | 2-2 |

Morocco qualified for Group Finals on toss of coin

| 4 May 1969 | Ethiopia vs Sudan | 1-1 |
| 11 May 1969 | Sudan vs Ethiopia | 3-1 |

Sudan qualified for Group Finals

| 10 May 1969 | Nigeria vs Ghana | 2-1 |
| 18 May 1969 | Ghana vs Nigeria | 1-1 |

Nigeria qualified for Group Finals

GROUP FINALS

13 Sep 1969	Nigeria vs Sudan	2-2
21 Sep 1969	Morocco vs Nigeria	2-1
3 Oct 1969	Sudan vs Nigeria	3-3
10 Oct 1969	Sudan vs Morocco	0-0
26 Oct 1969	Morocco vs Sudan	3-0
8 Nov 1969	Nigeria vs Morocco	1-0

	P	W	D	L	F	A	Pts
Morocco	4	2	1	1	5	2	5
Nigeria	4	1	2	1	7	7	4
Sudan	4	0	3	1	5	8	3

Morocco qualified for Finals

1974 – QUALIFYING COMPETITION

(95 Entries)

EUROPE

GROUP 1

14 Nov 1971	Malta vs Hungary	0-2
30 Apr 1972	Austria vs Malta	4-0
6 May 1972	Hungary vs Malta	3-0
25 May 1972	Sweden vs Hungary	0-0
10 Jun 1972	Austria vs Sweden	2-0
15 Oct 1972	Sweden vs Malta	7-0
15 Oct 1972	Austria vs Hungary	2-2
25 Nov 1972	Malta vs Austria	0-2
29 Apr 1973	Hungary vs Austria	2-2
24 May 1972	Sweden vs Austria	3-2
13 Jun 1973	Hungary vs Sweden	3-3
11 Nov 1973	Malta vs Sweden	1-2

	P	W	D	L	F	A	Pts
Sweden	6	3	2	1	14	7	8
Austria	6	3	2	1	15	8	8
Hungary	6	2	4	0	12	7	8
Malta	6	0	0	6	1	20	0

Play-off (in West Germany)

27 Nov 1973	Sweden vs Austria	2-1

Sweden qualified for Finals

GROUP 2

8 Oct 1972	Luxembourg vs Italy	0-4
21 Oct 1972	Switzerland vs Italy	0-0
22 Oct 1972	Luxembourg vs Turkey	2-0
10 Dec 1972	Turkey vs Luxembourg	3-0
13 Jan 1973	Italy vs Turkey	0-0
25 Feb 1973	Turkey vs Italy	0-1
31 Mar 1973	Italy vs Luxembourg	5-0
8 Apr 1973	Luxembourg vs Switzerland	0-1
9 May 1973	Switzerland vs Turkey	0-0
26 Sep 1973	Switzerland vs Luxembourg	1-0
20 Oct 1973	Italy vs Switzerland	2-0
18 Nov 1973	Turkey vs Switzerland	2-0

	P	W	D	L	F	A	Pts
Italy	6	4	2	0	12	0	10
Turkey	6	2	2	2	5	3	6
Switzerland	6	2	2	2	2	4	6
Luxembourg	6	1	0	5	2	14	2

Italy qualified for Finals

GROUP 3

18 May 1972	Belgium vs Iceland	4-0
23 May 1972	Iceland vs Belgium	0-4
2 Aug 1972	Norway vs Iceland	4-1
4 Oct 1972	Norway vs Belgium	0-2
1 Nov 1972	Holland vs Norway	9-0
19 Nov 1972	Belgium vs Holland	0-0
2 Aug 1973	Iceland vs Norway	0-4
22 Aug 1973	Holland vs Iceland	5-0
29 Aug 1973	Iceland vs Holland	1-8
	(in Holland)	
12 Sep 1973	Norway vs Holland	1-2
31 Oct 1973	Belgium vs Norway	2-0
18 Nov 1973	Holland vs Belgium	0-0

	P	W	D	L	F	A	Pts
Holland	6	4	2	0	24	2	10
Belgium	6	4	2	0	12	0	10
Norway	6	2	0	4	9	16	4
Iceland	6	0	0	6	2	29	0

Holland qualified for Finals

GROUP 4

21 Jun 1972	Finland vs Albania	1-0
20 Sep 1972	Finland vs Romania	1-1
7 Oct 1972	East Germany vs Finland	5-0
22 Oct 1972	Romania vs Albania	2-0
8 Apr 1973	East Germany vs Albania	2-0
6 May 1973	Albania vs Romania	1-4
27 May 1973	Romania vs East Germany	1-0
6 Jun 1973	Finland vs East Germany	1-5
26 Sep 1973	East Germany vs Romania	2-0
10 Oct 1973	Albania vs Finland	1-0
14 Oct 1973	Romania vs Finland	9-0
3 Nov 1973	Albania vs East Germany	1-4

	P	W	D	L	F	A	Pts
East Germany	6	5	0	1	18	3	10
Romania	6	4	1	1	17	4	9
Finland	6	1	1	4	3	21	3
Albania	6	1	0	5	3	13	2

East Germany qualified for Finals

GROUP 5

15 Nov 1972	Wales vs England	0-1
24 Jan 1973	England vs Wales	1-1
28 Mar 1973	Wales vs Poland	2-0
6 Jun 1973	Poland vs England	2-0
26 Sep 1973	Poland vs Wales	3-0
17 Oct 1973	England vs Poland	1-1

	P	W	D	L	F	A	Pts
Poland	4	2	1	1	6	3	5
England	4	1	2	1	3	4	4
Wales	4	1	1	2	3	5	3

Poland qualified for Finals

GROUP 6

29 Mar 1972	Portugal vs Cyprus	4-0
10 May 1972	Cyprus vs Portugal	0-1
18 Oct 1972	Bulgaria vs Northern Ireland	3-0
19 Nov 1972	Cyprus vs Bulgaria	0-4
14 Feb 1973	Cyprus vs Northern Ireland	1-0
28 Mar 1973	Northern Ireland vs Portugal	1-1
2 May 1973	Bulgaria vs Portugal	2-1
8 May 1973	Northern Ireland vs Cyprus	3-0
26 Sep 1973	Northern Ireland vs Bulgaria	0-0
13 Oct 1973	Portugal vs Bulgaria	2-2
14 Nov 1973	Portugal vs Northern Ireland	1-1
18 Nov 1973	Bulgaria vs Cyprus	2-0

	P	W	D	L	F	A	Pts
Bulgaria	6	4	2	0	13	3	10
Portugal	6	2	3	1	10	6	7
Northern Ireland	6	1	3	2	5	6	5
Cyprus	6	1	0	5	1	14	2

Bulgaria qualified for Finals

GROUP 7

19 Oct 1972	Spain vs Yugoslavia	2-2
19 Nov 1972	Yugoslavia vs Greece	1-0
17 Jan 1973	Greece vs Spain	2-3
21 Feb 1973	Spain vs Greece	3-1
21 Oct 1973	Yugoslavia vs Spain	0-0
12 Dec 1973	Greece vs Yugoslavia	2-4

	P	W	D	L	F	A	Pts
Yugoslavia	4	2	2	0	7	4	6
Spain	4	2	2	0	8	5	6
Greece	4	0	0	4	5	11	0

Play-off (in West Germany)
13 Feb 1974	Spain vs Yugoslavia	0-1

Yugoslavia qualified for Finals

GROUP 8

18 Oct 1972	Denmark vs Scotland	1-4
15 Nov 1972	Scotland vs Denmark	2-0
2 May 1973	Denmark vs Czechoslovakia	1-1
6 Jun 1973	Czechoslovakia vs Denmark	6-0
26 Sep 1973	Scotland vs Czechoslovakia	2-1
17 Oct 1973	Czechoslovakia vs Denmark	1-0

	P	W	D	L	F	A	Pts
Scotland	4	3	0	1	8	3	6
Czechoslovakia	4	2	1	1	9	3	5
Denmark	4	0	1	3	2	13	1

Scotland qualified for Finals

GROUP 9

13 Oct 1972	France vs USSR	1-0
18 Oct 1972	Eire vs USSR	1-2
15 Nov 1972	Eire vs France	2-1
13 May 1973	USSR vs Eire	1-0
19 May 1973	France vs Eire	1-1
26 May 1973	USSR vs France	2-0

	P	W	D	L	F	A	Pts
USSR	4	3	0	1	5	2	6
Eire	4	1	1	2	4	5	3
France	4	1	1	2	3	5	3

USSR qualified for play-off with winners of South American Group Three

GROUP 10

West Germany (hosts) exempt from qualifying rounds

SOUTH AMERICA

GROUP 1

21 Jun 1973	Colombia vs Ecuador	1-1
24 Jun 1973	Colombia vs Uruguay	0-0
28 Jun 1973	Ecuador vs Colombia	1-1
1 Jul 1973	Ecuador vs Uruguay	1-2
5 Jul 1973	Uruguay vs Colombia	0-1
8 Jul 1973	Uruguay vs Ecuador	4-0

	P	W	D	L	F	A	Pts
Uruguay	4	2	1	1	6	2	5
Colombia	4	1	3	0	3	2	5
Ecuador	4	0	2	2	3	8	2

Uruguay qualified for Finals

GROUP 2

2 Sep 1973	Bolivia vs Paraguay	1-2
9 Sep 1973	Argentina vs Bolivia	4-0
16 Sep 1973	Paraguay vs Argentina	1-1
23 Sep 1973	Bolivia vs Argentina	0-1
30 Sep 1973	Paraguay vs Bolivia	4-0
7 Oct 1973	Argentina vs Paraguay	3-1

	P	W	D	L	F	A	Pts
Argentina	4	3	1	0	9	2	7
Paraguay	4	2	1	1	8	5	5
Bolivia	4	0	0	4	1	11	0

Argentina qualified for Finals

GROUP 3

29 May 1973	Peru vs Chile	2-0
13 Jun 1973	Chile vs Peru	2-0

Play-off
15 Aug 1973	Chile vs Peru	2-1

Chile qualified for play-off with winners of European Group Three

PLAY-OFF between winners of Group 9 (Europe) and Group 3 (South America)
29 Sep 1973	USSR vs Chile	0-0

USSR withdrew before playing second leg

Chile qualified for Finals

GROUP 4

Brazil (holders) exempt from qualifying competition

CENTRAL & NORTH AMERICAN GROUP

ROUND 1

SUB-GROUP 1

24 Aug 1972	Canada vs Mexico	0-1
20 Aug 1972	Canada vs USA	3-2
29 Aug 1972	USA vs Canada	2-2
3 Oct 1972	Mexico vs USA	3-1
6 Oct 1972	Mexico vs Canada	2-1
10 Oct 1972	USA vs Mexico	1-1

	P	W	D	L	F	A	Pts
Mexico	4	4	0	0	8	3	8
Canada	4	1	1	2	6	7	3
USA	4	0	1	3	6	10	1

Mexico qualified for Group Finals

SUB-GROUP 2

3 Oct 1972   Guatemala vs El Salvador 1-0
10 Oct 1972   El Salvador vs Guatemala 0-1

Guatemala qualified for Group Finals

SUB-GROUP 3

3 Dec 1972   Honduras vs Costa Rica 2-1
10 Dec 1972   Costa Rica vs Honduras 3-3

Honduras qualified for Group Finals

SUB-GROUP 4

Jamaica vs Netherlands Antilles
Jamaica withdrew

Netherlands Antilles qualified for Group Finals

SUB-GROUP 5

15 Apr 1972   Haiti vs Puerto Rico 7-0
26 Sep 1972   Puerto Rico vs Haiti 0-5

Haiti qualified for Group Finals

SUB-GROUP 6

26 Nov 1972   Surinam vs Trinidad 1-2
30 Nov 1972   Trinidad vs Surinam 1-1
10 Dec 1972   Surinam vs Antigua 3-1
3 Dec 1972   Antigua vs Surinam 0-6
10 Nov 1972   Trinidad vs Antigua 11-1
19 Nov 1972   Antigua vs Trinidad 1-2

	P	W	D	L	F	A	Pts
Trinidad	4	3	1	0	16	4	7
Surinam	4	2	1	1	11	4	5
Antigua	4	0	0	4	3	22	0

Trinidad qualified for Group Finals

GROUP FINALS

Following matches played in Haiti

29 Nov 1973   Honduras vs Trinidad 2-1
30 Nov 1973   Mexico vs Guatemala 0-0
1 Dec 1973   Haiti vs Netherlands Antilles 3-0
3 Dec 1973   Honduras vs Mexico 1-1
5 Dec 1973   Netherlands Antilles vs Guatemala 2-2
7 Dec 1973   Haiti vs Honduras 1-0
8 Dec 1973   Mexico vs Netherlands Antilles 8-0
10 Dec 1973   Trinidad vs Guatemala 1-0
12 Dec 1973   Honduras vs Netherlands Antilles 2-2
13 Dec 1973   Haiti vs Guatemala 2-1
14 Dec 1973   Trinidad vs Mexico 4-0
15 Dec 1973   Honduras vs Guatemala 1-1
16 Dec 1973   Haiti vs Trinidad 2-1
17 Dec 1973   Trinidad vs Netherlands Antilles 4-0
18 Dec 1973   Mexico vs Haiti 1-0

	P	W	D	L	F	A	Pts
Haiti	5	4	0	1	8	3	8
Trinidad	5	3	0	2	11	4	6
Mexico	5	2	2	1	10	5	6
Honduras	5	1	3	1	6	6	5
Guatemala	5	0	3	2	4	6	3
Netherlands Antilles	5	0	2	3	4	19	2

Haiti qualified for Finals

ASIAN GROUP

SUB-GROUP A1

24 May 1973   Hong Kong vs South Vietnam 1-0
20 May 1973   Japan vs South Vietnam 4-0
22 May 1973   Japan vs Hong Kong 0-1

	P	W	D	L	F	A	Pts
Hong Kong	2	2	0	0	2	0	4
Japan	2	1	0	1	4	1	2
South Vietnam	2	0	0	2	0	5	0

Hong Kong & Japan qualified for 2nd Round

SUB-GROUP A2

19 May 1973   South Korea vs Thailand 4-0
21 May 1973   Israel vs Thailand 6-0
23 May 1973   Malaysia vs Thailand 2-0
23 May 1973   South Korea vs Israel 0-0
21 May 1973   South Korea vs Malaysia 0-0
19 May 1973   Israel vs Malaysia 3-0

	P	W	D	L	F	A	Pts
Israel	3	2	1	0	9	0	5
South Korea	3	1	2	0	4	0	4
Malaysia	3	1	1	1	2	3	3
Thailand	3	0	0	3	0	12	0

Israel & South Korea qualified for 2nd Round

SUB-GROUP B1

4 Mar 1973   Australia vs New Zealand 1-1
11 Mar 1973   Australia vs Iraq 3-1
11 Mar 1973   Indonesia vs New Zealand 1-1
13 Mar 1973   Iraq vs New Zealand 2-0
13 Mar 1973   Australia vs Indonesia 2-1
16 Mar 1973   Iraq vs Indonesia 1-1
16 Mar 1973   Australia vs New Zealand 3-3
18 Mar 1973   Indonesia vs New Zealand 1-0
18 Mar 1973   Australia vs Iraq 0-0
21 Mar 1973   Iraq vs Indonesia 3-2
24 Mar 1973   Iraq vs New Zealand 4-0
24 Mar 1973   Australia vs Indonesia 6-0

	P	W	D	L	F	A	Pts
Australia	6	3	3	0	15	6	9
Iraq	6	3	2	1	11	6	8
Indonesia	6	1	2	3	6	13	4
New Zealand	6	0	3	3	5	12	3

Australia qualified for 3rd Round

SUB-GROUP B2

4 May 1973   North Korea vs Iran 0-0
4 May 1973   Syria vs Kuwait 2-1
6 May 1973   Iran vs Kuwait 2-1
6 May 1973   North Korea vs Syria 1-1
8 May 1973   Iran vs Syria 1-0
8 May 1973   Kuwait vs North Korea 0-0
11 May 1973   North Korea vs Iran 1-2
11 May 1973   Syria vs Kuwait 2-0
13 May 1973   Iran vs Kuwait 2-0
13 May 1973   North Korea vs Syria 3-0
15 May 1973   Syria vs Iran 1-0
15 May 1973   Kuwait vs North Korea 2-0

	P	W	D	L	F	A	Pts
Iran	6	4	1	1	7	3	8
Syria	6	3	1	2	6	6	7
North Korea	6	1	3	2	5	5	5
Kuwait	6	1	1	4	4	8	3

Iran qualified for 3rd Round

ROUND TWO

26 May 1973   South Korea vs Hong Kong 3-1
South Korea qualified for 3rd Round
26 May 1973   Israel vs Japan 1-0
Israel qualified for 3rd Round

ROUND THREE

27 May 1973   South Korea vs Israel 1-0
South Korea qualified for Group Final
18 Aug 1973   Australia vs Iran 3-0
24 Aug 1973   Iran vs Australia 2-0
Australia qualified for Group Final

GROUP FINAL

28 Oct 1973   Australia vs South Korea 0-0
10 Nov 1973   South Korea vs Australia 2-2

Play-off

17 Nov 1973   Australia vs South Korea 1-0
Australia qualified for Finals

AFRICAN GROUP

ROUND ONE

19 Nov 1972   Morocco vs Senegal 0-0
3 Dec 1972   Senegal vs Morocco 1-2
Morocco qualified for 2nd Round
2 Mar 1972   Algeria vs Guinea 1-0
12 Mar 1972   Guinea vs Algeria 5-1
Guinea qualified for 2nd Round
8 Dec 1972   Egypt vs Tunisia 2-1
17 Dec 1972   Tunisia vs Egypt 2-0
Tunisia qualified for 2nd Round
15 Oct 1972   Sierra Leone vs Ivory Coast 0-1
29 Oct 1972   Ivory Coast vs Sierra Leone 2-0
Ivory Coast qualified for 2nd Round
Mauritius Walk Over
Madagascar withdrew
Mauritius qualified for 2nd Round
25 Nov 1972   Ethiopia vs Tanzania 0-0
3 Dec 1972   Tanzania vs Ethiopia 1-1

Play-off

                    Ethiopia vs Tanzania 3-0
Ethiopia qualified for 2nd Round
5 Aug 1972   Nigeria vs Congo Brazzaville 2-1
15 Aug 1972   Congo Brazzaville vs Nigeria 1-1
Nigeria qualified for 2nd Round
18 Jun 1972   Dahomey vs Ghana 0-5
2 Jul 1972   Ghana vs Dahomey 5-1
Ghana qualified for 2nd Round

6 Jun 1972   Togo vs Zaire 0-0
20 Jun 1972   Zaire vs Togo 4-0
Zaire qualified for 2nd Round
Cameroons and Gabon
Gabon withdrew
Cameroons qualified for 2nd Round
30 Apr 1972   Lesotho vs Zambia 0-0
4 Jun 1972   Zambia vs Lesotho 6-1
Zambia qualified for 2nd Round

ROUND TWO

11 Feb 1973   Guinea vs Morocco 1-1
25 Feb 1973   Morocco vs Guinea 2-0
Morocco qualified for 3rd Round
11 Feb 1973   Tunisia vs Ivory Coast 1-1
25 Feb 1973   Ivory Coast vs Tunisia 2-1
Ivory Coast qualified for 3rd Round
10 Dec 1972   Mauritius vs Kenya 1-3
17 Dec 1972   Kenya vs Mauritius 2-2
Kenya qualified for 3rd Round
29 April 1973   Ethiopia vs Zambia 0-0
8 April 1973   Zambia vs Ethiopia 4-2
Zambia qualified for 3rd Round
10 Feb 1973   Nigeria vs Ghana 2-3
25 Feb 1973   Ghana vs Nigeria 1-1
Ghana qualified for 3rd Round
4 Feb 1973   Cameroons vs Zaire 0-1
25 Feb 1973   Zaire vs Cameroons 1-1
Play-off
27 Feb 1973   Zaire vs Cameroons 2-0
Zaire qualified for 3rd Round

ROUND THREE

20 May 1973   Ivory Coast vs Morocco 1-1
3 Jun 1973   Morocco vs Ivory Coast 4-1
Morocco qualified for Group Finals
12 Dec 1973   Zambia vs Kenya 2-0
19 Dec 1973   Kenya vs Zambia 2-2
Zambia qualified for Group Finals
5 Aug 1973   Ghana vs Zaire 1-0
19 Aug 1973   Zaire vs Ghana 4-1
Zaire qualified for Group Finals

GROUP FINALS

21 Oct 1973   Zambia vs Morocco 4-0
4 Nov 1973   Zambia vs Zaire 0-2
18 Nov 1973   Zaire vs Zambia 2-1
25 Nov 1973   Morocco vs Zambia 2-0
9 Dec 1973   Zaire vs Morocco 3-0
Morocco vs Zaire not Played

	P	W	D	L	F	A	Pts
Zaire	3	3	0	0	7	1	6
Zambia	4	1	0	3	5	6	2
Morocco	3	1	0	2	2	7	2

Zaire qualified for Finals

1978 – QUALIFYING COMPETITION

(103 Entries)

EUROPE

GROUP 1

23 May 1976	Cyprus vs Denmark	1-5
16 Oct 1976	Portugal vs Poland	0-2
27 Oct 1976	Denmark vs Cyprus	5-0
31 Oct 1976	Poland vs Cyprus	5-0
17 Nov 1976	Portugal vs Denmark	1-0
5 Dec 1976	Cyprus vs Portugal	1-2
1 May 1977	Denmark vs Poland	1-2
15 May 1977	Cyprus vs Poland	1-3
21 Sep 1977	Poland vs Denmark	4-1
9 Oct 1977	Denmark vs Portugal	2-4
29 Oct 1977	Poland vs Portugal	1-1
16 Nov 1977	Portugal vs Cyprus	4-0

	P	W	D	L	F	A	Pts
Poland	6	5	1	0	17	4	11
Portugal	6	4	1	1	12	6	9
Denmark	6	2	0	4	14	12	4
Cyprus	6	0	0	6	3	24	0

Poland qualified for Finals

GROUP 2

13 Jun 1976	Finland vs England	1-4
22 Sep 1976	Finland vs Luxembourg	7-1
13 Oct 1976	England vs Finland	2-1
16 Oct 1976	Luxembourg vs Italy	1-4
17 Nov 1976	Italy vs England	2-0
30 Mar 1977	England vs Luxembourg	5-0
26 May 1977	Luxembourg vs Finland	0-1
8 Jun 1977	Finland vs Italy	0-3
12 Oct 1977	Luxembourg vs England	0-2
15 Oct 1977	Italy vs Finland	6-1
16 Nov 1977	England vs Italy	2-0
3 Dec 1977	Italy vs Luxembourg	3-0

	P	W	D	L	F	A	Pts
Italy	6	5	0	1	18	4	10
England	6	5	0	1	15	4	10
Finland	6	2	0	4	11	16	4
Luxembourg	6	0	0	6	2	22	0

Italy qualified for Finals

GROUP 3

31 Oct 1976	Turkey vs Malta	4-0
17 Nov 1976	East Germany vs Turkey	1-1
5 Dec 1976	Malta vs Austria	0-1
2 Apr 1977	Malta vs East Germany	0-1
17 Apr 1977	Austria vs Turkey	1-0
30 Apr 1977	Austria vs Malta	9-0
24 Sep 1977	Austria vs East Germany	1-1
12 Oct 1977	East Germany vs Austria	1-1
29 Oct 1977	East Germany vs Malta	9-0
30 Oct 1977	Turkey vs Austria	0-1
16 Nov 1977	Turkey vs East Germany	1-2
27 Nov 1977	Malta vs Turkey	0-3

	P	W	D	L	F	A	Pts
Austria	6	4	2	0	14	2	10
East Germany	6	3	3	0	15	4	9
Turkey	6	2	1	3	9	5	5
Malta	6	0	0	6	0	27	0

Austria qualified for Finals

GROUP 4

5 Sep 1976	Iceland vs Belgium	0-1
8 Sep 1976	Iceland vs Holland	0-1
13 Oct 1976	Holland vs Northern Ireland	2-2
10 Nov 1976	Belgium vs Northern Ireland	2-0
26 Mar 1976	Belgium vs Holland	0-2
11 Jun 1977	Iceland vs Northern Ireland	1-0
31 Aug 1977	Holland vs Iceland	4-1
4 Sep 1977	Belgium vs Iceland	4-0
21 Sep 1977	Northern Ireland vs Iceland	2-0
12 Oct 1977	Northern Ireland vs Holland	0-1
26 Oct 1977	Holland vs Belgium	1-0
16 Nov 1977	Northern Ireland vs Belgium	3-0

	P	W	D	L	F	A	Pts
Holland	6	5	1	0	11	3	11
Belgium	6	3	0	3	7	6	6
Northern Ireland	6	2	1	3	7	6	5
Iceland	6	1	0	5	2	12	2

Holland qualified for Finals

GROUP 5

9 Oct 1976	Bulgaria vs France	2-2
17 Nov 1976	France vs Eire	2-0
30 Mar 1977	Eire vs France	1-0
1 Jun 1977	Bulgaria vs Eire	2-1
12 Oct 1977	Eire vs Bulgaria	0-0
16 Nov 1977	France vs Bulgaria	3-1

	P	W	D	L	F	A	Pts
France	4	2	1	1	7	4	5
Bulgaria	4	1	2	1	5	6	4
Eire	4	1	1	2	4	3	3

France qualified for Finals

GROUP 6

16 Jun 1976	Sweden vs Norway	2-0
8 Sep 1976	Norway vs Switzerland	1-0
9 Oct 1976	Switzerland vs Sweden	1-2
8 Jun 1977	Sweden vs Switzerland	2-1
7 Sep 1977	Norway vs Sweden	2-1
30 Oct 1977	Switzerland vs Norway	1-0

	P	W	D	L	F	A	Pts
Sweden	4	3	0	1	7	4	6
Norway	4	2	0	2	3	4	4
Switzerland	4	1	0	3	3	5	2

Sweden qualified for Finals

GROUP 7

13 Oct 1976	Czechoslovakia vs Scotland	2-0
17 Nov 1976	Scotland vs Wales	1-0
30 Oct 1977	Wales vs Czechoslovakia	3-0
21 Sep 1977	Scotland vs Czechoslovakia	3-1

189

12 Oct 1977　　Wales vs Scotland 0-2
16 Nov 1977　　Czechoslovakia vs Wales 1-0

	P	W	D	L	F	A	Pts
Scotland	4	3	0	1	6	3	6
Czechoslovakia	4	2	0	2	4	6	4
Wales	4	1	0	3	3	4	2

Scotland qualified for Finals

GROUP 8

10 Oct 1976　　Spain vs Yugoslavia 1-0
6 Apr 1977　　Romania vs Spain 1-0
8 May 1977　　Yugoslavia vs Romania 0-2
26 Oct 1977　　Spain vs Romania 2-0
13 Nov 1977　　Romania vs Yugoslavia 4-6
30 Nov 1977　　Yugoslavia vs Spain 0-1

	P	W	D	L	F	A	Pts
Spain	4	3	0	1	4	1	6
Romania	4	2	0	2	7	8	4
Yugoslavia	4	1	0	3	6	8	2

Spain qualified for Finals

GROUP 9

9 Oct 1976　　Greece vs Hungary 1-1
24 Apr 1977　　USSR vs Greece 2-0
30 Apr 1977　　Hungary vs USSR 2-1
10 May 1977　　Greece vs USSR 1-0
18 May 1977　　USSR vs Hungary 2-0
25 May 1977　　Hungary vs Greece 3-0

	P	W	D	L	F	A	Pts
Hungary	4	2	1	1	6	4	5
USSR	4	2	0	2	5	3	4
Greece	4	1	1	2	2	6	3

*Hungary qualified for play-off with winners of Group Two
(South America)*

SOUTH AMERICA

GROUP 1

20 Feb 1977　　Colombia vs Brazil 0-0
24 Feb 1977　　Colombia vs Paraguay 0-1
6 Mar 1977　　Paraguay vs Colombia 1-1
9 Mar 1977　　Brazil vs Colombia 6-0
13 Mar 1977　　Paraguay vs Brazil 0-1
20 Mar 1977　　Brazil vs Paraguay 1-1

	P	W	D	L	F	A	Pts
Brazil	4	2	2	0	8	1	6
Paraguay	4	1	2	1	3	3	4
Colombia	4	0	2	2	1	8	2

Brazil qualified for Final Play-off Group

GROUP 2

9 Feb 1977　　Venezuela vs Uruguay 1-1
27 Feb 1977　　Bolivia vs Uruguay 1-0
6 Mar 1977　　Venezuela vs Bolivia 1-3
13 Mar 1977　　Bolivia vs Venezuela 2-0
17 Mar 1977　　Uruguay vs Venezuela 2-0
27 Mar 1977　　Uruguay vs Bolivia 2-2

	P	W	D	L	F	A	Pts
Bolivia	4	3	1	0	8	3	7
Uruguay	4	1	2	1	5	4	4
Venezuela	4	0	1	3	2	8	1

Bolivia qualified for Final Play-off Group

GROUP 3

20 Feb 1977　　Ecuador vs Peru 1-1
27 Feb 1977　　Ecuador vs Chile 0-1
6 Mar 1977　　Chile vs Peru 1-1
12 Mar 1977　　Peru vs Ecuador 4-0
20 Mar 1977　　Chile vs Ecuador 3-0
26 Mar 1977　　Peru vs Chile 2-0

	P	W	D	L	F	A	Pts
Peru	4	2	2	0	8	2	6
Chile	4	2	1	1	5	3	5
Ecuador	4	0	1	3	1	9	1

Peru qualified for Final Play-off Group

PLAY-OFF GROUP

10 Jul 1977　　Brazil vs Peru 1-0
14 Jul 1977　　Brazil vs Bolivia 8-0
17 Jul 1977　　Peru vs Bolivia 5-0

	P	W	D	L	F	A	Pts
Brazil	2	2	0	0	9	0	4
Peru	2	1	0	1	5	1	2
Bolivia	2	0	0	2	0	13	0

Brazil & Peru qualified for Finals

Bolivia qualified for play-off with winners of Group 9 (Europe)

PLAY-OFF

Winners Group 9 (Europe) and third place Play-off
Group (South America)

29 Oct 1977　　Hungary vs Bolivia 6-0
30 Nov 1977　　Bolivia vs Hungary 2-3

Hungary qualified for Finals

CENTRAL & NORTH AMERICA

SUB-GROUP 1

24 Sep 1976　　Canada vs USA 1-1
3 Oct 1976　　USA vs Mexico 0-0
10 Oct 1976　　Canada vs Mexico 1-0
15 Oct 1976　　Mexico vs USA 3-0
20 Oct 1976　　USA vs Canada 2-0
27 Oct 1976　　Mexico vs Canada 0-0

	P	W	D	L	F	A	Pts
Mexico	4	1	2	1	3	1	4
USA	4	1	2	1	3	4	4
Canada	4	1	2	1	2	3	4

Mexico qualified for Group Finals

Play-off for 2nd place

22 Dec 1976　　Canada vs USA 3-0
　　　　　　　　　(in Haiti)

Canada qualified for Group Finals

SUB-GROUP 2

4 Apr 1976	Panama vs Costa Rica	3-2
2 May 1976	Panama vs El Salvador	1-1
11 July 1976	Costa Rica vs Panama	3-0
1 Aug 1976	El Salvador vs Panama	4-1
17 Sep 1976	Panama vs Guatemala	2-4
26 Sep 1976	Guatemala vs Panama	7-0
1 Dec 1976	El Salvador vs Costa Rica	1-1
5 Dec 1976	Costa Rica vs Guatemala	0-0
8 Dec 1976	Guatemala vs El Salvador	3-1
12 Dec 1976	Guatemala vs Costa Rica	1-1
17 Dec 1976	Costa Rica vs El Salvador	1-1
19 Dec 1976	El Salvador vs Guatemala	2-0

	P	W	D	L	F	A	Pts
Guatemala	6	3	2	1	15	6	8
El Salvador	6	2	3	1	10	7	7
Costa Rica	6	1	4	1	8	6	6
Panama	6	1	1	4	7	21	3

Guatemala & El Salvador qualified for Group Finals

SUB-GROUP 3

PRELIMINARY ROUND

2 Apr 1976	Dominican Republic vs Haiti	0-3
17 Apr 1976	Haiti vs Dominican Republic	3-0

Haiti qualified for 1st Round

ROUND ONE

4 Jul 1976	Guyana vs Surinam	2-0
29 Jul 1976	Surinam vs Guyana	3-0

Surinam qualified for 2nd Round

31 Jul 1976	Netherlands Antilles vs Haiti	1-2
14 Aug 1976	Haiti vs Netherlands Antilles	7-0

Haiti qualified for 2nd Round

15 Aug 1976	Jamaica vs Cuba	1-3
29 Aug 1976	Cuba vs Jamaica	2-0

Cuba qualified for 2nd Round

15 Aug 1976	Barbados vs Trinidad & Tobago	2-1
31 Aug 1976	Trinidad & Tobago vs Barbados	1-0

Play-off

14 Sep 1976	Barbados vs Trinidad & Tobago	1-3

Trinidad & Tobago qualified for 2nd Round

ROUND TWO

14 Nov 1976	Surinam vs Trinidad & Tobago	1-1
28 Nov 1976	Trinidad & Tobago vs Surinam	2-2

Play-off

18 Dec 1976	Surinam vs Trinidad & Tobago (in French Guyana)	3-2

Surinam qualified for Group Finals

28 Nov 1976	Cuba vs Haiti	1-1
11 Dec 1976	Haiti vs Cuba	1-1

Play-off

29 Dec 1976	Cuba vs Haiti (in Panama)	0-2

Haiti qualified for Group Finals

GROUP FINALS

8 Sep 1977	Guatemala vs Surinam	3-2
8 Sep 1977	El Salvador vs Canada	2-1
9 Sep 1977	Mexico vs Haiti	4-1
12 Sep 1977	Canada vs Surinam	2-1
12 Sep 1977	Haiti vs Guatemala	2-1
12 Sep 1977	Mexico vs El Salvador	3-1
15 Sep 1977	Mexico vs Surinam	8-1
16 Sep 1977	Canada vs Guatemala	2-1
16 Sep 1977	Haiti vs El Salvador	1-0
19 Sep 1977	Mexico vs Guatemala	2-1
20 Sep 1977	Canada vs Haiti	1-1
20 Sep 1977	El Salvador vs Surinam	3-2
22 Sep 1977	Mexico vs Canada	3-1
23 Sep 1977	Haiti vs Surinam	1-0
23 Sep 1977	Guatemala vs El Salvador	2-2

	P	W	D	L	F	A	Pts
Mexico	5	5	0	0	20	5	10
Haiti	5	3	1	1	6	6	7
Canada	5	2	1	2	7	8	5
El Salvador	5	2	1	2	8	9	5
Guatemala	5	1	1	3	8	10	3
Surinam	5	0	0	5	6	17	0

Mexico qualified for Finals

AFRICA

PRELIMINARY ROUND

7 Mar 1976	Sierra Leone vs Niger	5-1
21 Mar 1976	Niger vs Sierra Leone	2-1

Sierra Leone qualified for 1st Round

13 Mar 1976	Upper Volta vs Mauritania	1-1
28 Mar 1976	Mauritania vs Upper Volta	0-2

Upper Volta qualified for 1st Round

ROUND ONE

1 Apr 1976	Algeria vs Libya	1-0
16 Apr 1976	Libya vs Algeria	0-0

Algeria qualified for 2nd Round

12 Dec 1976	Morocco vs Tunisia	1-1
9 Jan 1977	Tunisia vs Morocco	1-1

Tunisia qualified for 2nd Round (4-2 on penalties)

17 Oct 1976	Togo vs Senegal	1-0
31 Oct 1976	Senegal vs Togo	1-1

Togo qualified for 2nd Round

10 Oct 1976	Ghana vs Guinea	2-1
24 Oct 1976	Guinea vs Ghana	2-1

Play-off

16 Jan 1977	Guinea vs Ghana (in Togo)	2-0

Guinea qualified for 2nd Round

Zaire vs Central African Republic
Central African Republic withdrew

Zaire qualified for 2nd Round

16 Oct 1976	Sierra Leone vs Nigeria	0-0
30 Oct 1976	Nigeria vs Sierra Leone	6-2

Nigeria qualified for 2nd Round

17 Oct 1976	Congo vs Cameroon	2-2
31 Oct 1976	Cameroon vs Congo	1-2

Congo qualified for 2nd Round

4 Sep 1976	Upper Volta vs Ivory Coast	1-1
25 Sep 1976	Ivory Coast vs Upper Volta	2-0

Ivory Coast qualified for 2nd Round

29 Oct 1976	Egypt vs Ethiopia	3-0
14 Nov 1976	Ethiopia vs Egypt	1-2

Egypt qualified for 2nd Round

Kenya vs Sudan
Sudan withdrew

Kenya qualified for 2nd Round

Uganda vs Tanzania
Tanzania withdrew

Uganda qualified for 2nd Round

9 May 1976	Zambia vs Malawi	4-1
30 May 1976	Malawi vs Zambia	0-1

Zambia qualified for 2nd Round

ROUND TWO

6 Feb 1977	Tunisia vs Algeria	2-0
28 Feb 1977	Algeria vs Tunisia	1-1

Tunisia qualified for 3rd Round

13 Feb 1977	Togo vs Guinea	0-2
27 Feb 1977	Guinea vs Togo	2-1

Guinea qualified for 3rd Round

13 Feb 1977	Ivory Coast vs Congo	3-2
27 Feb 1977	Congo vs Ivory Coast	1-3

Ivory Coast qualified for 3rd Round

6 Feb 1977	Kenya vs Egypt	0-0
27 Feb 1977	Egypt vs Kenya	1-0

Egypt qualified for 3rd Round

13 Feb 1977	Uganda vs Zambia	1-0
27 Feb 1977	Zambia vs Uganada	4-2

Zambia qualified for 3rd Round

Nigeria vs Zaire
Zaire withdrew

Nigeria qualified for 3rd Round

ROUND THREE

5 Jun 1977	Guinea vs Tunisia	1-0
19 Jun 1977	Tunisia vs Guinea	3-1

Tunisia qualified for Group Finals

10 Jul 1977	Nigeria vs Ivory Coast	4-0
24 Jul 1977	Ivory Coast vs Nigeria	2-2

Nigeria qualified for Group Finals

15 Jul 1977	Egypt vs Zambia	2-0
31 Jul 1977	Zambia vs Egypt	0-0

Egypt qualified for Group Finals

GROUP FINALS

25 Sep 1977	Tunisia vs Nigeria	0-0
8 Oct 1977	Nigeria vs Egypt	4-0
21 Oct 1977	Egypt vs Nigeria	3-1
12 Nov 1977	Nigeria vs Tunisia	0-1
25 Nov 1977	Egypt vs Tunisia	3-2

11 Dec 1977	Tunisia vs Egypt	4-1

	P	W	D	L	F	A	Pts
Tunisia	4	2	1	1	7	4	5
Egypt	4	2	0	2	7	11	4
Nigeria	4	1	1	2	5	4	3

Tunisia qualified for Finals

ASIA/OCEANIA

OCEANIA SUB-GROUP

13 Mar 1977	Australia vs Taiwan (in Fiji)	3-0
16 Mar 1977	Taiwan vs Australia (in Fiji)	1-2
20 Mar 1977	New Zealand vs Taiwan	6-0
23 Mar 1977	Taiwan vs New Zealand (in New Zealand)	0-6
27 Mar 1977	Australia vs New Zealand	3-1
30 Mar 1977	New Zealand vs Australia	1-1

	P	W	D	L	F	A	Pts
Australia	4	3	1	0	9	3	7
New Zealand	4	2	1	1	14	4	5
Taiwan	4	0	0	4	1	17	0

Australia qualified for Group Finals

ASIAN SUB-GROUP

Following matches in Singapore

27 Feb 1977	Singapore vs Thailand	2-0
28 Feb 1977	Hong Kong vs Indonesia	4-1
1 Mar 1977	Malaysia vs Thailand	6-4
2 Mar 1977	Hong Kong vs Singapore	2-2
3 Mar 1977	Indonesia vs Malaysia	0-0
5 Mar 1977	Thailand vs Hong Kong	1-2
6 Mar 1977	Singapore vs Malaysia	1-0
7 Mar 1977	Thailand vs Indonesia	3-2
8 Mar 1977	Malaysia vs Hong Kong	1-1
9 Mar 1977	Indonesia vs Singapore	4-0

	P	W	D	L	F	A	Pts
Hong Kong	4	2	2	0	9	5	6
Singapore	4	2	1	1	5	6	5
Malaysia	4	1	2	1	7	6	4
Indonesia	4	1	1	2	7	7	3
Thailand	4	1	0	3	8	12	2

Hong Kong & Singapore qualified for Sub-Group Final

SUB-GROUP FINAL

12 Mar 1977	Singapore vs Hong Kong	0-1

Hong Kong qualified for Group Finals

ASIAN SUB-GROUP 2

27 Feb 1977	Israel vs South Korea	0-0
6 Mar 1977	Israel vs Japan	2-0
10 Mar 1977	Japan vs Israel (in Israel)	0-2
20 Mar 1977	South Korea vs Israel	3-1
26 Mar 1977	Japan vs South Korea	0-0
3 Apr 1977	South Korea vs Japan	1-0

North Korea withdrew

	P	W	D	L	F	A	Pts
South Korea	4	2	2	0	4	1	6
Israel	4	2	1	1	5	3	5
Japan	4	0	1	3	0	5	1
North Korea	0	0	0	0	0	0	0

South Korea qualified for Group Finals

ASIAN SUB-GROUP 3

12 Nov 1976	Saudi Arabia vs Syria	2-0
26 Nov 1976	Syria vs Saudi Arabia	2-1
7 Jan 1977	Saudi Arabia vs Iran	0-3
28 Jan 1977	Syria vs Iran	0-1
8 Apr 1977	Iran vs Syria	

Syria withdrew. Game was awarded to Iran 2-0

22 Apr 1977	Iran vs Saudi Arabia	2-0

	P	W	D	L	F	A	Pts
Iran	4	4	0	0	8	0	8
Saudi Arabia	4	1	0	3	3	7	2
Syria	4	1	0	3	2	6	2

Iran qualified for Group Finals

SUB-GROUP 4

Following matches in Qatar

11 Mar 1977	Bahrain vs Kuwait	0-2
13 Mar 1977	Bahrain vs Qatar	0-2
15 Mar 1977	Qatar vs Kuwait	0-2
17 Mar 1977	Bahrain vs Kuwait	1-2
19 Mar 1977	Qatar vs Bahrain	0-3
21 Mar 1977	Qatar vs Kuwait	1-4

United Arab Emirates withdrew

	P	W	D	L	F	A	Pts
Kuwait	4	4	0	0	10	2	8
Qatar	4	1	0	3	3	9	2
Bahrain	4	1	0	3	4	6	2

Kuwait qualified for Group Finals

GROUP FINALS

19 Jun 1977	Hong Kong vs Iran	0-2
26 Jun 1977	Hong Kong vs South Korea	0-1
3 Jul 1977	South Korea vs Iran	0-0
10 Jul 1977	Australia vs Hong Kong	3-0
14 Aug 1977	Australia vs Iran	0-1
27 Aug 1977	Australia vs South Korea	2-1
2 Oct 1977	Hong Kong vs Kuwait	1-3
9 Oct 1977	South Korea vs Kuwait	1-0
23 Oct 1977	Australia vs Kuwait	1-2
23 Oct 1977	South Korea vs Australia	0-0
28 Oct 1977	Iran vs Kuwait	1-0
30 Oct 1977	Hong Kong vs Australia	2-5
5 Nov 1977	Kuwait vs South Korea	2-2
11 Nov 1977	Iran vs South Korea	2-2
12 Nov 1977	Kuwait vs Hong Kong	4-0
18 Nov 1977	Iran vs Hong Kong	3-0
19 Nov 1977	Kuwait vs Australia	1-0
25 Nov 1977	Iran vs Australia	1-0
3 Dec 1977	Kuwait vs Iran	1-2
4 Dec 1977	South Korea vs Hong Kong	5-2

	P	W	D	L	F	A	Pts
Iran	8	6	2	0	12	3	14
South Korea	8	3	4	1	12	8	10
Kuwait	8	4	1	3	13	8	9
Australia	8	3	1	4	11	8	7
Hong Kong	8	0	0	8	5	26	0

Iran qualified for Finals

Argentina (hosts) and West Germany (holders) were exempt from the qualifying rounds.

1982 – QUALIFYING COMPETITION

(109 Entries)

EUROPE

GROUP 1

4 Jun 1980	Finland vs Bulgaria	0-2
3 Sep 1980	Albania vs Finland	2-0
24 Sep 1980	Finland vs Austria	0-2
19 Oct 1980	Bulgaria vs Albania	2-1
15 Nov 1980	Austria vs Albania	5-0
3 Dec 1980	Bulgaria vs West Germany	1-3
6 Dec 1980	Albania vs Austria	0-1
1 Apr 1981	Albania vs West Germany	0-2
29 Apr 1981	West Germany vs Austria	2-0
13 May 1981	Bulgaria vs Finland	4-0
24 May 1981	Finland vs West Germany	0-4
28 May 1981	Austria vs Bulgaria	2-0
17 May 1981	Austria vs Finland	5-1
2 Sep 1981	Finland vs Albania	2-1
23 Sep 1981	West Germany vs Finland	7-1
14 Oct 1981	Austria vs West Germany	1-3
14 Oct 1981	Albania vs Bulgaria	0-2
11 Nov 1981	Bulgaria vs Austria	0-0
18 Nov 1981	West Germany vs Albania	8-0
22 Nov 1981	West Germany vs Bulgaria	4-0

	P	W	D	L	F	A	Pts
West Germany	8	8	0	0	33	3	16
Austria	8	5	1	2	16	6	11
Bulgaria	8	4	1	3	11	10	9
Albania	8	1	0	7	4	22	2
Finland	8	1	0	7	4	27	2

West Germany & Austria qualified for Finals

GROUP 2

26 Mar 1980	Cyprus vs Eire	2-3
10 Sep 1980	Eire vs Holland	2-1
11 Oct 1980	Cyprus vs France	0-7
15 Oct 1980	Eire vs Belgium	1-1
28 Oct 1980	France vs Eire	2-0
19 Nov 1980	Belgium vs Holland	1-0
19 Nov 1980	Eire vs Cyprus	6-0
21 Dec 1980	Cyprus vs Belgium	0-2
18 Feb 1981	Belgium vs Cyprus	3-2
22 Feb 1981	Holland vs Cyprus	3-0
25 Mar 1981	Holland vs France	1-0
25 Mar 1981	Belgium vs Eire	1-0

29 Apr 1981	France vs Belgium						3-2
29 Apr 1981	Cyprus vs Holland						0-1
9 Sep 1981	Holland vs Eire						2-2
9 Sep 1981	Belgium vs France						2-0
14 Oct 1981	Holland vs Belgium						3-0
14 Oct 1981	Eire vs France						3-2
18 Nov 1981	France vs Holland						2-0
5 Dec 1981	France vs Cyprus						4-0

	P	W	D	L	F	A	Pts
Belgium	8	5	1	2	12	9	11
France	8	5	0	3	20	8	10
Eire	8	4	2	2	17	11	10
Holland	8	4	1	3	11	7	9
Cyprus	8	0	0	8	4	29	0

Belgium & France qualified for Finals

GROUP 3

2 Jun 1980	Iceland vs Wales	0-4
3 Sep 1980	Iceland vs USSR	1-2
24 Sep 1980	Turkey vs Iceland	1-3
15 Oct 1980	Wales vs Turkey	4-0
15 Oct 1980	USSR vs Iceland	5-0
19 Nov 1980	Wales vs Czechoslovakia	1-0
3 Dec 1980	Czechoslovakia vs Turkey	2-0
25 Mar 1981	Turkey vs Wales	0-1
15 Apr 1981	Turkey vs Czechoslovakia	0-3
27 May 1981	Czechoslovakia vs Iceland	6-1
30 May 1981	Wales vs USSR	0-0
9 Sep 1981	Iceland vs Turkey	2-0
9 Sep 1981	Czechoslovakia vs Wales	2-0
23 Sep 1981	Iceland vs Czechoslovakia	1-1
23 Sep 1981	USSR vs Turkey	4-0
7 Oct 1981	Turkey vs USSR	0-3
14 Oct 1981	Wales vs Iceland	2-2
28 Oct 1981	USSR vs Czechoslovakia	2-0
18 Nov 1981	USSR vs Wales	3-0
29 Nov 1981	Czechoslovakia vs USSR	1-1

	P	W	D	L	F	A	Pts
USSR	8	6	2	0	20	2	14
Czechoslovakia	8	4	2	2	15	6	10
Wales	8	4	2	2	12	7	10
Iceland	8	2	2	4	10	21	6
Turkey	8	0	0	8	1	22	0

USSR & Czechoslovakia qualified for Finals

GROUP 4

10 Sep 1980	England vs Norway	4-0
24 Sep 1980	Norway vs Romania	1-1
15 Oct 1980	Romania vs England	2-1
29 Oct 1980	Switzerland vs Norway	1-2
19 Nov 1980	England vs Switzerland	2-1
28 Apr 1981	Switzerland vs Hungary	2-2
29 Apr 1981	England vs Romania	0-0
13 May 1981	Hungary vs Romania	1-0
20 May 1981	Norway vs Hungary	1-2
30 May 1981	Switzerland vs England	2-1
3 Jun 1981	Romania vs Norway	1-0
6 Jun 1981	Hungary vs England	1-3
17 Jun 1981	Norway vs Switzerland	1-1
9 Sep 1981	Norway vs England	2-1

23 Sep 1981	Romania vs Hungary	0-0
10 Oct 1981	Romania vs Switzerland	1-2
14 Oct 1981	Hungary vs Switzerland	3-0
31 Oct 1981	Hungary vs Norway	4-1
11 Nov 1981	Switzerland vs Romania	0-0
18 Nov 1981	England vs Hungary	1-0

	P	W	D	L	F	A	Pts
Hungary	8	4	2	2	13	8	10
England	8	4	1	3	13	8	9
Romania	8	2	4	5	5	8	8
Switzerland	8	2	3	3	9	12	7
Norway	8	2	2	4	8	15	6

Hungary & England qualified for Finals

GROUP 5

10 Sep 1980	Luxembourg vs Yugoslavia	0-5
27 Sep 1980	Yugoslavia vs Denmark	2-1
11 Oct 1980	Luxembourg vs Italy	0-2
15 Oct 1980	Denmark vs Greece	0-1
1 Nov 1980	Italy vs Denmark	2-0
15 Nov 1980	Italy vs Yugoslavia	2-0
19 Nov 1980	Denmark vs Luxembourg	4-0
6 Dec 1980	Greece vs Italy	0-2
28 Jan 1981	Greece vs Luxembourg	2-0
11 Mar 1981	Luxembourg vs Greece	0-2
29 Apr 1981	Yugoslavia vs Greece	5-1
1 May 1981	Luxembourg vs Denmark	1-2
3 Jun 1981	Denmark vs Italy	3-1
9 Sep 1981	Denmark vs Yugoslavia	1-2
14 Oct 1981	Greece vs Denmark	2-3
17 Oct 1981	Yugoslavia vs Italy	1-1
14 Nov 1981	Italy vs Greece	1-1
21 Nov 1981	Yugoslavia vs Luxembourg	5-0
29 Nov 1981	Greece vs Yugoslavia	1-2
5 Dec 1981	Italy vs Luxembourg	1-0

	P	W	D	L	F	A	Pts
Yugoslavia	8	6	1	1	22	7	13
Italy	8	5	2	1	12	5	12
Denmark	8	4	0	4	14	11	8
Greece	8	3	1	4	10	13	7
Luxembourg	8	0	0	8	1	23	0

Yugoslavia & Italy qualified for Finals

GROUP 6

26 Mar 1980	Israel vs Northern Ireland	0-0
18 Jun 1980	Sweden vs Israel	1-1
10 Sep 1980	Sweden vs Scotland	0-1
15 Oct 1980	Northern Ireland vs Sweden	3-0
15 Oct 1980	Scotland vs Portugal	0-0
12 Nov 1980	Israel vs Sweden	0-0
19 Nov 1980	Portugal vs Northern Ireland	1-0
17 Dec 1980	Portugal vs Israel	3-0
25 Feb 1981	Israel vs Scotland	0-1
25 Mar 1981	Scotland vs Northern Ireland	1-1
28 Apr 1981	Scotland vs Israel	3-1
29 Apr 1981	Northern Ireland vs Portugal	1-0
3 Jun 1981	Sweden vs Northern Ireland	1-0
24 Jun 1981	Sweden vs Portugal	3-0
9 Sep 1981	Scotland vs Sweden	2-0
14 Oct 1981	Portugal vs Sweden	1-2

| | | 14 Oct 1981 | Northern Ireland vs Scotland .... 0-0 |
| | | 28 Oct 1981 | Israel vs Portugal .... 4-1 |

14 Oct 1981 Northern Ireland vs Scotland 0-0
28 Oct 1981 Israel vs Portugal 4-1
18 Nov 1981 Northern Ireland vs Israel 1-0
18 Nov 1981 Portugal vs Scotland 2-1

	P	W	D	L	F	A	Pts
Scotland	8	4	3	1	9	4	11
Northern Ireland	8	3	3	2	6	3	9
Sweden	8	3	2	3	7	8	8
Portugal	8	3	1	4	8	11	7
Israel	8	1	3	4	6	10	5

Scotland & Northern Ireland qualified for Finals

GROUP 7

7 Dec 1980 Malta vs Poland 0-2
4 Apr 1981 Malta vs East Germany 1-2
2 May 1981 Poland vs East Germany 1-0
10 Oct 1981 East Germany vs Poland 2-3
11 Nov 1981 East Germany vs Malta 5-1
15 Nov 1981 Poland vs Malta 6-0

	P	W	D	L	F	A	Pts
Poland	4	4	0	0	12	2	8
East Germany	4	2	0	2	9	6	4
Malta	4	0	0	4	2	15	0

Poland qualified for Finals

SOUTH AMERICA

GROUP 1

8 Feb 1981 Venezuela vs Brazil 0-1
15 Feb 1981 Bolivia vs Venezuela 3-0
22 Feb 1981 Bolivia vs Brazil 1-2
15 Mar 1981 Venezuela vs Bolivia 1-0
22 Mar 1981 Brazil vs Bolivia 3-1
29 Mar 1981 Brazil vs Venezuela 5-0

	P	W	D	L	F	A	Pts
Brazil	4	4	0	0	11	2	8
Bolivia	4	1	0	3	5	6	2
Venezuela	4	1	0	3	1	9	2

Brazil qualified for Finals

GROUP 2

26 Jul 1981 Colombia vs Peru 1-1
9 Aug 1981 Uruguay vs Colombia 3-2
16 Aug 1981 Peru vs Colombia 2-0
23 Aug 1981 Uruguay vs Peru 1-2
6 Sep 1981 Peru vs Uruguay 0-0
13 Sep 1981 Colombia vs Uruguay 1-1

	P	W	D	L	F	A	Pts
Peru	4	2	2	0	5	2	6
Uruguay	4	1	2	1	5	5	4
Colombia	4	0	2	2	4	7	2

Peru qualified for Finals

GROUP 3

17 May 1981 Ecuador vs Paraguay 1-0
24 May 1981 Ecuador vs Chile 0-0
31 May 1981 Paraguay vs Ecuador 3-1

7 Jun 1981 Paraguay vs Chile 0-1
14 Jun 1981 Chile vs Ecuador 2-0
21 Jun 1981 Chile vs Paraguay 3-0

	P	W	D	L	F	A	Pts
Chile	4	3	1	0	6	0	7
Ecuador	4	1	1	2	2	5	3
Paraguay	4	1	0	3	3	6	2

Chile qualified for Finals

AFRICA

ROUND ONE

22 Jun 1980 Senegal vs Morocco 0-1
6 Jul 1980 Morocco vs Senegal 0-0
Morocco qualified for 2nd Round

13 Jul 1980 Zaire vs Mozambique 5-2
27 Jul 1980 Mozambique vs Zaire 1-2
Zaire qualified for 2nd Round

29 Jun 1980 Cameroon vs Malawi 3-0
20 Jul 1980 Malawi vs Cameroon 1-1
Cameroon qualified for 2nd Round

22 Jun 1980 Guinea vs Lesotho 3-1
6 Jun 1980 Lesotho vs Guinea 1-1
Guinea qualified for 2nd Round

29 Jun 1980 Tunisia vs Nigeria 2-0
12 Jul 1980 Nigeria vs Tunisia 2-0
Nigeria qualified for 2nd Round (4-3 on penalties)

8 May 1980 Libya vs Gambia 2-1
6 Jul 1980 Gambia vs Libya 0-0
Libya qualified for 2nd Round

18 May 1980 Ethiopia vs Zambia 0-0
1 Jun 1980 Zambia vs Ethiopia 4-0
Zambia qualified for 2nd Round

16 Jul 1980 Niger vs Somalia 0-0
27 Jul 1980 Somalia vs Niger 1-1
Niger qualified for 2nd Round

31 May 1980 Sierra Leone vs Algeria 2-2
13 Jun 1980 Algeria vs Sierra Leone 3-1
Algeria qualified for 2nd Round

5 Jul 1980 Kenya vs Tanzania 3-1
19 Jul 1980 Tanzania vs Kenya 5-0
Tanzania qualified for 2nd Round

Ghana vs Egypt
Ghana withdrew
Egypt qualified for 2nd Round

Uganda vs Madagascar
Uganda withdrew
Madagascar qualified for 2nd Round

Zimbabwe received a bye
Sudan received a bye
Liberia received a bye
Togo received a bye

ROUND TWO

12 Dec 1980 Algeria vs Sudan 2-0
28 Dec 1980 Sudan vs Algeria 1-1
Algeria qualified for 3rd Round

| 14 Dec 1980 | Niger vs Togo | 0-1 |
| 28 Dec 1980 | Togo vs Niger | 1-2 |

Niger qualified for 3rd Round

| 7 Dec 1980 | Liberia vs Guinea | 0-0 |
| 21 Dec 1980 | Guinea vs Liberia | 1-0 |

Guinea qualified for 3rd Round

| 12 Oct 1980 | Cameroon vs Zimbabwe | 2-0 |
| 16 Nov 1980 | Zimbabwe vs Cameroon | 1-0 |

Cameroon qualified for 3rd Round

| 16 Nov 1980 | Morocco vs Zambia | 2-0 |
| 30 Nov 1980 | Zambia vs Morocco | 2-0 |

Morocco qualified for 3rd Round (5-4 on penalties)

| 6 Dec 1980 | Nigeria vs Tanzania | 1-1 |
| 20 Dec 1980 | Tanzania vs Nigeria | 0-2 |

Nigeria qualified for 3rd Round

| 16 Nov 1980 | Madagascar vs Zaire | 1-1 |
| 21 Dec 1980 | Zaire vs Madagascar | 3-2 |

Zaire qualified for 3rd Round

Libya vs Egypt
Libya withdrew

Egypt qualified for 3rd Round

ROUND THREE

| 1 May 1981 | Algeria vs Niger | 4-0 |
| 31 May 1981 | Niger vs Algeria | 1-0 |

Algeria qualified for Group Finals

| 12 Apr 1981 | Guinea vs Nigeria | 1-1 |
| 25 Apr 1981 | Nigeria vs Guinea | 1-0 |

Nigeria qualified for Group Finals

| 26 Apr 1981 | Morocco vs Egypt | 1-0 |
| 8 May 1981 | Egypt vs Morocco | 0-0 |

Morocco qualified for Group Finals

| 12 Apr 1981 | Zaire vs Cameroon | 1-0 |
| 26 Apr 1981 | Cameroon vs Zaire | 6-1 |

Cameroon qualified for Group Finals

GROUP FINALS

| 10 Oct 1981 | Nigeria vs Algeria | 0-2 |
| 30 Oct 1981 | Algeria vs Nigeria | 2-1 |

Algeria qualified for Finals

| 15 Nov 1981 | Morocco vs Cameroon | 0-2 |
| 29 Nov 1981 | Cameroon vs Morocco | 2-1 |

Cameroon qualified for Finals

CENTRAL & NORTH AMERICA

NORTHERN ZONE

18 Oct 1980	Canada vs Mexico	1-1
25 Oct 1980	USA vs Canada	0-0
1 Nov 1980	Canada vs USA	2-1
9 Nov 1980	Mexico vs USA	5-1
16 Nov 1980	Mexico vs Canada	1-1
23 Nov 1980	USA vs Mexico	2-1

	P	W	D	L	F	A	Pts
Canada	4	1	3	0	4	3	5
Mexico	4	1	2	1	8	5	4
USA	4	1	1	2	4	8	3

Canada & Mexico qualified for Group Finals

CENTRAL ZONE

2 Jul 1980	Panama vs Guatemala	0-2
30 Jul 1980	Panama vs Honduras	0-2
10 Aug 1980	Panama vs Costa Rica	1-1
24 Aug 1980	Panama vs El Salvador	1-3
1 Oct 1980	Costa Rica vs Honduras	2-3
5 Oct 1980	El Salvador vs Panama	4-1
12 Oct 1980	Guatemala vs Costa Rica	0-0
26 Oct 1980	Honduras vs Guatemala	0-0
26 Oct 1980	El Salvador vs Costa Rica	

Costa Rica forfeited match, awarded 2-0 to El Salvador

5 Nov 1980	Costa Rica vs Panama	2-0
9 Nov 1980	Guatemala vs El Salvador	0-0
16 Nov 1980	Guatemala vs Panama	5-0
16 Nov 1980	Honduras vs Costa Rica	1-1
23 Nov 1980	El Salvador vs Honduras	2-1
26 Nov 1980	Costa Rica vs Guatemala	0-3
30 Nov 1980	Honduras vs El Salvador	2-0
7 Dec 1980	Guatemala vs Honduras	0-1
10 Dec 1980	Costa Rica vs El Salvador	0-0
14 Dec 1980	Honduras vs Panama	5-0
21 Dec 1980	El Salvador vs Guatemala	1-0

Honduras & El Salvador qualified for Group Finals

CARIBBEAN ZONE

PRELIMINARY ROUND

| 30 Mar 1980 | Guyana vs Grenada | 5-2 |
| 13 Apr 1980 | Grenada vs Guyana | 2-3 |

Guyana qualified for Zone Group

ZONE GROUP A

17 Aug 1980	Cuba vs Surinam	3-0
7 Sep 1980	Surinam vs Cuba	0-0
28 Sep 1980	Guyana vs Surinam	0-1
12 Oct 1980	Surinam vs Guyana	4-0
9 Nov 1980	Cuba vs Guyana	1-0
30 Nov 1980	Guyana vs Cuba	0-3

	P	W	D	L	F	A	Pts
Cuba	4	3	1	0	7	0	7
Surinam	4	2	1	1	5	3	5
Guyana	4	0	0	4	0	9	0

Cuba qualified for Group Finals

ZONE GROUP B

1 Aug 1980	Haiti vs Trinidad & Tobago	2-0
17 Aug 1980	Trinidad & Tobago vs Haiti	1-0
12 Sep 1980	Haiti vs Netherlands Antilles	1-0
9 Nov 1980	Trinidad & Tobago vs Neth. Antilles	0-0
29 Nov 1980	Netherlands Antilles vs Trin. & Tobago	0-0
12 Dec 1980	Netherlands Antilles vs Haiti	1-1

	P	W	D	L	F	A	Pts
Haiti	4	2	1	1	4	2	5
Trinidad & Tobago	4	1	2	1	1	2	4
Netherlands Antilles	4	0	3	1	1	2	3

Haiti qualified for Group Finals

GROUP FINALS

Following matches in Honduras

1 Nov 1981	Mexico vs Cuba	4-0
2 Nov 1981	Canada vs El Salvador	1-0
3 Nov 1981	Honduras vs Haiti	4-0
6 Nov 1981	Haiti vs Canada	1-1
6 Nov 1981	Mexico vs El Salvador	0-1
8 Nov 1981	Honduras vs Cuba	2-0
11 Nov 1981	El Salvador vs Cuba	0-0
11 Nov 1981	Mexico vs Haiti	1-1
12 Nov 1981	Honduras vs Canada	2-1
15 Nov 1981	Haiti vs Cuba	0-2
15 Nov 1981	Mexico vs Canada	1-1
16 Nov 1981	Honduras vs El Salvador	0-0
19 Nov 1981	Haiti vs El Salvador	0-1
22 Nov 1981	Cuba vs Canada	2-2
22 Nov 1981	Honduras vs Mexico	0-0

	P	W	D	L	F	A	Pts
Honduras	5	3	2	0	8	1	8
El Salvador	5	2	2	1	2	1	6
Mexico	5	1	3	1	6	3	5
Canada	5	1	3	1	6	6	5
Cuba	5	1	2	2	4	8	4
Haiti	5	0	2	3	2	9	2

Honduras & El Salvador qualified for Finals

ASIA/OCEANIA

SUB-GROUP 1

25 Apr 1981	New Zealand vs Australia	3-3
3 May 1981	Fiji vs New Zealand	0-4
7 May 1981	Taiwan vs New Zealand	0-0
11 May 1981	Indonesia vs New Zealand	0-2
16 May 1981	Australia vs New Zealand	0-2
20 May 1981	Australia vs Indonesia	2-0
23 May 1981	New Zealand vs Indonesia	5-0
30 May 1981	New Zealand vs Taiwan	2-0
31 May 1981	Fiji vs Indonesia	0-0
6 Jun 1981	Fiji vs Taiwan	2-1
10 Jun 1981	Australia vs Taiwan	3-2
15 Jun 1981	Indonesia vs Taiwan	1-0
28 Jun 1981	Taiwan vs Indonesia	2-0
26 Jul 1981	Fiji vs Australia	1-4
4 Aug 1981	Taiwan vs Fiji	0-0
10 Aug 1981	Indonesia vs Fiji	3-3
14 Aug 1981	Australia vs Fiji	10-0
16 Aug 1981	New Zealand vs Fiji	13-0
30 Aug 1981	Indonesia vs Australia	1-0
6 Sep 1981	Taiwan vs Australia	0-0

	P	W	D	L	F	A	Pts
New Zealand	8	6	2	0	31	3	14
Australia	8	4	2	2	22	9	10
Indonesia	8	2	2	4	5	14	6
Taiwan	8	1	3	4	5	8	5
Fiji	8	1	3	4	6	35	5

New Zealand qualified for Group Finals

SUB-GROUP 2

Following matches in Saudi Arabia

18 Mar 1981	Qatar vs Iraq	0-1
19 Mar 1981	Syria vs Bahrain	0-1
21 Mar 1981	Iraq vs Saudi Arabia	0-1
22 Mar 1981	Qatar vs Bahrain	3-0
24 Mar 1981	Syria vs Saudi Arabia	0-2
25 Mar 1981	Iraq vs Bahrain	2-0
27 Mar 1981	Qatar vs Syria	2-1
28 Mar 1981	Bahrain vs Saudi Arabia	0-1
30 Mar 1981	Iraq vs Syria	2-1
31 Mar 1981	Qatar vs Saudi Arabia	0-1

	P	W	D	L	F	A	Pts
Saudi Arabia	4	4	0	0	5	0	8
Iraq	4	3	0	1	5	2	6
Qatar	4	2	0	2	5	3	4
Bahrain	4	1	0	3	1	6	2
Syria	4	0	0	4	2	7	0

Saudi Arabia qualified for Group Finals

SUB-GROUP 3

Following matches in Kuwait

21 Apr 1981	Malaysia vs South Korea	1-2
22 Apr 1981	Kuwait vs Thailand	6-0
24 Apr 1981	South Korea vs Thailand	5-1
25 Apr 1981	Kuwait vs Malaysia	4-0
27 Apr 1981	Malaysia vs Thailand	2-2
29 Apr 1981	Kuwait vs South Korea	2-0

	P	W	D	L	F	A	Pts
Kuwait	3	3	0	0	12	0	6
South Korea	3	2	0	1	7	4	4
Malaysia	3	0	1	2	3	8	1
Thailand	3	0	1	2	3	13	1

Kuwait qualified for Group Finals

SUB-GROUP 4

Following matches in Hong Kong

21 Dec 1980	Hong Kong vs China	0-1
22 Dec 1980	North Korea vs Macao	3-0
22 Dec 1980	Singapore vs Japan	0-1
24 Dec 1980	China vs Macao	3-0
24 Dec 1980	Hong Kong vs Singapore	1-1
26 Dec 1980	China vs Japan	1-0
26 Dec 1980	Singapore vs North Korea	0-1
28 Dec 1980	Japan vs Macao	3-0
28 Dec 1980	Hong Kong vs North Korea	2-2

	P	W	D	L	F	A	Pts
China	3	3	0	0	5	0	6
North Korea	3	2	1	0	6	2	5
Japan	3	2	0	1	4	1	4
Hong Kong	3	0	2	1	3	4	2
Singapore	3	0	1	2	1	3	1
Macao	3	0	0	3	0	9	0

China, North Korea, Japan and Hong Kong qualified for Sub-Group Semi-Finals

SUB-GROUP SEMI-FINALS

30 Dec 1980   North Korea vs Japan 1-0
              (in Hong Kong)

North Korea qualified for Sub-Group Final

31 Dec 1980   China vs Hong Kong 0-0
              (in Hong Kong)

China qualified for Sub-Group Final (5-4 on Penalties)

SUB-GROUP FINAL

4 Jan 1981   China vs North Korea 4-2
              (in Hong Kong)

China qualified for Group Finals

GROUP FINALS

24 Sep 1981	China vs New Zealand	0-0
3 Oct 1981	New Zealand vs China	1-0
10 Oct 1981	New Zeland vs Kuwait	1-2
18 Oct 1981	China vs Kuwait	3-0
4 Nov 1981	Saudi Arabia vs Kuwait	0-1
12 Nov 1981	Saudi Arabia vs China	2-4
	(in Malaysia)	
19 Nov 1981	China vs Saudi Arabia	2-0
	(in Malaysia)	
28 Nov 1981	New Zealand vs Saudi Arabia	2-2
30 Nov 1981	Kuwait vs China	1-0
7 Dec 1981	Kuwait vs Saudi Arabia	2-0
14 Dec 1981	Kuwait vs New Zealand	2-2
19 Dec 1981	Saudi Arabia vs New Zealand	0-5

	P	W	D	L	F	A	Pts
Kuwait	6	4	1	1	8	6	9
New Zealand	6	2	3	1	11	6	7
China	6	3	1	2	9	4	7
Saudi Arabia	6	0	1	5	4	16	1

Kuwait qualified for Finals

New Zealand & China tied and qualified for play-off for 2nd place

Play-off

10 Jan 1982   New Zealand vs China 2-1
              (in Singapore)

New Zealand qualified for Finals

Spain (hosts) and Argentina (holders) were exempt from the qualifying rounds.

1986 – QUALIFYING COMPETITION

(108 Entries)

EUROPE

GROUP 1

17 Oct 1984	Belgium vs Albania	3-1
17 Oct 1984	Poland vs Greece	3-1
31 Oct 1984	Poland vs Albania	2-2
19 Dec 1984	Greece vs Belgium	0-0

22 Dec 1984	Albania vs Belgium	2-(
27 Feb 1985	Greece vs Albania	2-(
27 Mar 1985	Belgium vs Greece	2-(
1 May 1985	Belgium vs Poland	2-(
19 May 1985	Greece vs Poland	1-(
30 May 1985	Albania vs Poland	0-1
11 Sep 1985	Poland vs Belgium	0-(
30 Oct 1985	Albania vs Greece	1-1

	P	W	D	L	F	A	Pts
Poland	6	3	2	1	10	6	8
Belgium	6	3	2	1	7	3	8
Albania	6	1	2	3	6	9	4
Greece	6	1	2	3	5	10	4

Poland qualified for Finals

Belgium qualified for Play-offs

GROUP 2

23 May 1984	Sweden vs Malta	4-(
12 Sep 1984	Sweden vs Portugal	0-(
14 Oct 1984	Portugal vs Czechoslovakia	2-1
17 Oct 1984	West Germany vs Sweden	2-(
31 Oct 1984	Czechoslovakia vs Malta	4-(
14 Nov 1984	Portugal vs Sweden	1-1
16 Dec 1984	Malta vs West Germany	2-:
10 Feb 1985	Malta vs Portugal	1-1
24 Feb 1985	Portugal vs West Germany	1-2
27 Mar 1985	West Germany vs Malta	6-(
21 Apr 1985	Malta vs Czechoslovakia	0-(
1 May 1985	Czechoslovakia vs West Germany	1-1
5 Jun 1985	Sweden vs Czechoslovakia	2-1
25 Sep 1985	Sweden vs West Germany	2-:
25 Sep 1985	Czechoslovakia vs Portugal	1-(
12 Oct 1985	Portugal vs Malta	3-:
16 Oct 1985	Czechoslovakia vs Sweden	2-1
16 Oct 1985	West Germany vs Portugal	0-1
17 Nov 1985	West Germany vs Czechoslovakia	2-:
17 Nov 1985	Malta vs Sweden	1-:

	P	W	D	L	F	A	Pts
West Germany	8	5	2	1	22	9	12
Portugal	8	5	0	3	12	10	10
Sweden	8	4	1	3	14	9	9
Czechoslovakia	8	3	2	3	11	12	8
Malta	8	0	1	7	6	25	1

West Germany qualified for Finals

GROUP 3

27 May 1984	Finland vs Northern Ireland	1-(
12 Sep 1984	Northern Ireland vs Romania	3-:
17 Oct 1984	England vs Finland	5-(
31 Oct 1984	Turkey vs Finland	1-:
14 Nov 1984	Northern Ireland vs Finland	2-1
14 Nov 1984	Turkey vs England	0-{
27 Feb 1985	Northern Ireland vs England	0-1
3 Apr 1985	Romania vs Turkey	3-(
1 May 1985	Northern Ireland vs Turkey	2-(
1 May 1985	Romania vs England	0-(
22 May 1985	Finland vs England	1-1
6 Jun 1985	Finland vs Romania	1-1
28 Aug 1985	Romania vs Finland	2-(
11 Sep 1985	Turkey vs Northern Ireland	0-(

11 Sep 1985	England vs Romania	....	1-1
25 Sep 1985	Finland vs Turkey	....	1-0
16 Oct 1985	Romania vs Northern Ireland	....	0-1
16 Oct 1985	England vs Turkey	....	5-0
13 Nov 1985	England vs Northern Ireland	....	0-0
13 Nov 1985	Turkey vs Romania	....	1-3

	P	W	D	L	F	A	Pts
England	8	4	4	0	21	2	12
Northern Ireland	8	4	2	2	8	5	10
Romania	8	3	3	2	12	7	9
Finland	8	3	2	3	7	12	8
Turkey	8	0	1	7	2	24	1

England & Northern Ireland qualified for Finals

GROUP 4

29 Sep 1984	Yugoslavia vs Bulgaria	....	0-0
13 Oct 1984	Luxembourg vs France	....	0-4
20 Oct 1984	East Germany vs Yugoslavia	....	2-3
17 Nov 1984	Luxembourg vs East Germany	....	0-5
21 Nov 1984	France vs Bulgaria	....	1-0
5 Dec 1984	Bulgaria vs Luxembourg	....	4-0
8 Dec 1984	France vs East Germany	....	2-0
27 Mar 1985	Yugoslavia vs Luxembourg	....	1-0
3 Apr 1985	Yugoslavia vs France	....	0-0
6 Apr 1985	Bulgaria vs East Germany	....	1-0
1 May 1985	Luxembourg vs Yugoslavia	....	0-1
2 May 1985	Bulgaria vs France	....	2-0
18 May 1985	East Germany vs Luxembourg	....	3-1
1 Jun 1985	Bulgaria vs Yugoslavia	....	2-1
11 Sep 1985	East Germany vs France	....	2-0
25 Sep 1985	Luxembourg vs Bulgaria	....	1-3
28 Sep 1985	Yugoslavia vs East Germany	....	1-2
30 Oct 1985	France vs Luxembourg	....	6-0
16 Nov 1985	France vs Yugoslavia	....	2-0
16 Nov 1985	East Germany vs Bulgaria	....	2-1

	P	W	D	L	F	A	Pts
France	8	5	1	2	15	4	11
Bulgaria	8	5	1	2	13	5	11
East Germany	8	5	0	3	16	9	10
Yugoslavia	8	3	2	3	7	8	8
Luxembourg	8	0	0	8	2	27	0

France & Bulgaria qualified for Finals

GROUP 5

2 May 1984	Cyprus vs Austria	....	1-2
26 Sep 1984	Hungary vs Austria	....	3-1
17 Oct 1984	Holland vs Hungary	....	1-2
14 Nov 1984	Austria vs Holland	....	1-0
17 Nov 1984	Cyprus vs Hungary	....	1-2
23 Dec 1984	Cyprus vs Holland	....	0-1
27 Feb 1985	Holland vs Cyprus	....	7-1
3 Apr 1985	Hungary vs Cyprus	....	2-0
17 Apr 1985	Austria vs Hungary	....	0-3
1 May 1985	Holland vs Austria	....	1-1
14 May 1985	Austria vs Cyprus	....	4-0
14 May 1985	Hungary vs Holland	....	0-1

	P	W	D	L	F	A	Pts
Hungary	6	5	0	1	12	4	10
Holland	6	3	1	2	11	5	7

	P	W	D	L	F	A	Pts
Austria	6	3	1	2	9	8	7
Cyprus	6	0	0	6	3	18	0

Hungary qualified for Finals

Holland qualified for Play-offs

GROUP 6

12 Sep 1984	Eire vs USSR	....	1-0
12 Sep 1984	Norway vs Switzerland	....	0-1
26 Sep 1984	Denmark vs Norway	....	1-0
10 Oct 1984	Norway vs USSR	....	1-1
17 Oct 1984	Switzerland vs Denmark	....	1-0
17 Oct 1984	Norway vs Eire	....	1-0
14 Nov 1984	Denmark vs Eire	....	3-0
17 Apr 1985	Switzerland vs USSR	....	2-2
1 May 1985	Eire vs Norway	....	0-0
2 May 1985	USSR vs Switzerland	....	4-0
2 Jun 1985	Eire vs Switzerland	....	3-0
5 Jun 1985	Denmark vs USSR	....	4-2
11 Sep 1985	Switzerland vs Eire	....	0-0
25 Sep 1985	USSR vs Denmark	....	1-0
9 Oct 1985	Denmark vs Switzerland	....	0-0
16 Oct 1985	Norway vs Denmark	....	1-5
16 Oct 1985	USSR vs Eire	....	2-0
30 Oct 1985	USSR vs Norway	....	1-0
13 Nov 1985	Switzerland vs Norway	....	1-1
13 Nov 1985	Eire vs Denmark	....	1-4

	P	W	D	L	F	A	Pts
Denmark	8	5	1	2	17	6	11
USSR	8	4	2	2	13	8	10
Switzerland	8	2	4	2	5	10	8
Eire	8	2	2	4	5	10	6
Norway	8	1	3	4	4	10	5

Denmark & USSR qualified for Finals

GROUP 7

12 Sep 1984	Iceland vs Wales	....	1-0
17 Oct 1984	Spain vs Wales	....	3-0
17 Oct 1984	Scotland vs Iceland	....	3-0
14 Nov 1984	Scotland vs Spain	....	3-1
14 Nov 1984	Wales vs Iceland	....	2-1
27 Feb 1985	Spain vs Scotland	....	1-0
27 Mar 1985	Scotland vs Wales	....	0-1
30 Apr 1985	Wales vs Spain	....	3-0
28 May 1985	Iceland vs Scotland	....	0-1
12 Jun 1985	Iceland vs Spain	....	1-2
10 Sep 1985	Wales vs Scotland	....	1-1
25 Sep 1985	Spain vs Iceland	....	2-1

	P	W	D	L	F	A	Pts
Spain	6	4	0	2	9	8	8
Scotland	6	3	1	2	8	4	7
Wales	6	3	1	2	7	6	7
Iceland	6	1	0	5	4	10	2

Spain qualified for Finals

Scotland qualified for Play-offs

GROUPS 1 & 5 PLAY-OFF

16 Oct 1985	Belgium vs Holland	....	1-0
20 Nov 1985	Holland vs Belgium	....	2-0

Belgium qualified for Finals on away goals (2-2 aggregate)

PLAY-OFF

| 20 Nov 1985 | Scotland vs Australia | 2-0 |
| 4 Dec 1985 | Australia vs Scotland | 0-0 |

Scotland qualified for Finals 2-0 on aggregate

NORTH & CENTRAL AMERICA

ROUND ONE

GROUP 1

| 29 Jul 1984 | El Salvador vs Puerto Rico | 5-0 |
| 5 Aug 1984 | Puerto Rico vs El Salvador | 0-3 |

El Salvador qualified for 2nd Round

| 29 Sep 1984 | Netherlands Antilles vs USA | 0-0 |
| 6 Oct 1984 | USA vs Netherlands Antilles | 4-0 |

USA qualified for 2nd Round

Canada vs Jamaica
Jamaica withdrew

Canada qualified for 2nd Round

GROUP 2

| 15 Jun 1984 | Panama vs Honduras | 0-3 |
| 24 Jun 1984 | Honduras vs Panama | 1-0 |

Honduras qualified for 2nd Round

Costa Rica vs Barbados
Barbados withdrew

Costa Rica qualified for 2nd Round

GROUP 3

| 4 Aug 1984 | Antigua vs Haiti | 0-4 |
| 17 Aug 1984 | Haiti vs Antigua | 1-2 |

Haiti qualified for 2nd Round

| 15 Aug 1984 | Surinam vs Guyana | 1-0 |
| 29 Aug 1984 | Guyana vs Surinam | 1-1 |

Surinam qualified for 2nd Round

Grenada vs Trinidad & Tobago
Grenada withdrew

Trinidad & Tobago qualified for 2nd Round

ROUND TWO

GROUP 1

24 Feb 1985	Surinam vs El Salvador	0-3
27 Feb 1985	El Salvador vs Surinam	3-0
3 Mar 1985	Surinam vs Honduras	1-1
6 Mar 1985	Honduras vs Surinam	2-1
10 Mar 1985	El Salvador vs Honduras	1-2
14 Mar 1985	Honduras vs El Salvador	0-0

	P	W	D	L	F	A	Pts
Honduras	4	2	2	0	5	3	6
El Salvador	4	2	1	1	7	2	5
Surinam	4	0	1	3	2	9	1

Honduras qualified for 3rd Round

GROUP 2

13 Apr 1985	Canada vs Haiti	2-0
20 Apr 1985	Canada vs Guatemala	2-1
26 Apr 1985	Haiti vs Guatemala	0-1
5 May 1985	Guatemala vs Canada	1-1
8 May 1985	Haiti vs Canada	0-2
15 May 1985	Guatemala vs Haiti	4-0

	P	W	D	L	F	A	Pts
Canada	4	3	1	0	7	2	7
Guatemala	4	2	1	1	7	3	5
Haiti	4	0	0	4	0	9	0

Canada qualified for 3rd Round

GROUP 3

24 Apr 1985	Trinidad & Tobago vs Costa Rica	0-3
28 Apr 1985	Costa Rica vs Trinidad & Tobago	1-1
15 May 1985	USA vs Trinidad & Tobago	2-1
19 May 1985	Trinidad & Tobago vs USA	0-1
26 May 1985	Costa Rica vs USA	1-1
31 May 1985	USA vs Costa Rica	0-1

	P	W	D	L	F	A	Pts
Costa Rica	4	2	2	0	6	2	6
USA	4	2	1	1	4	3	5
Trinidad & Tobago	4	0	1	3	2	7	1

Costa Rica qualified for 3rd Round

ROUND THREE

11 Aug 1985	Costa Rica vs Honduras	2-2
17 Aug 1985	Canada vs Costa Rica	1-1
25 Aug 1985	Honduras vs Canada	0-1
1 Sep 1985	Costa Rica vs Canada	0-0
8 Sep 1985	Honduras vs Costa Rica	3-1
14 Sep 1985	Canada vs Honduras	2-1

	P	W	D	L	F	A	Pts
Canada	4	2	2	0	4	2	6
Honduras	4	1	1	2	6	6	3
Costa Rica	4	0	3	1	4	6	3

Canada qualified for Finals

SOUTH AMERICA

GROUP 1

26 May 1985	Colombia vs Peru	1-0
26 May 1985	Venezuela vs Argentina	2-3
2 Jun 1985	Colombia vs Argentina	1-3
2 Jun 1985	Venezuela vs Peru	0-1
9 Jun 1985	Peru vs Colombia	0-0
9 Jun 1985	Argentina vs Venezuela	3-0
16 Jun 1985	Peru vs Venezuela	4-1
16 Jun 1985	Argentina vs Colombia	1-0
23 Jun 1985	Venezuela vs Colombia	2-2
23 Jun 1985	Peru vs Argentina	1-0
30 Jun 1985	Colombia vs Venezuela	2-0
30 Jun 1985	Argentina vs Peru	2-2

	P	W	D	L	F	A	Pts
Argentina	6	4	1	1	12	6	9
Peru	6	3	2	1	8	4	8
Colombia	6	2	2	2	6	6	4
Venezuela	6	0	1	5	5	15	1

Argentina qualified for Finals

Peru & Colombia qualified for Play-off Group

GROUP 2

3 Mar 1985	Ecuador vs Chile	1-1
10 Mar 1985	Uruguay vs Ecuador	2-1
17 Mar 1985	Chile vs Ecuador	6-2
24 Mar 1985	Chile vs Uruguay	2-0
31 Mar 1985	Ecuador vs Uruguay	0-2
7 Apr 1985	Uruguay vs Chile	2-1

	P	W	D	L	F	A	Pts
Uruguay	4	3	0	1	6	4	6
Chile	4	2	1	1	10	5	5
Ecuador	4	0	1	3	4	11	1

Uruguay qualified for Finals

Chile qualified for Play-off Group

GROUP 3

26 May 1985	Bolivia vs Paraguay	1-1
2 Jun 1985	Bolivia vs Brazil	0-2
9 Jun 1985	Paraguay vs Bolivia	3-0
16 Jun 1985	Paraguay vs Brazil	0-2
23 Jun 1985	Brazil vs Paraguay	1-1
30 Jun 1985	Brazil vs Bolivia	1-1

	P	W	D	L	F	A	Pts
Brazil	4	2	2	0	6	2	6
Paraguay	4	1	2	1	5	4	4
Bolivia	4	0	2	2	2	7	2

Brazil qualified for Finals

Paraguay qualified for Play-off Group

PLAY-OFF GROUP

| 27 Oct 1985 | Paraguay vs Colombia | 3-0 |
| 3 Nov 1985 | Colombia vs Paraguay | 2-1 |

Paraguay qualified for play-off decider

| 27 Oct 1985 | Chile vs Peru | 4-2 |
| 3 Nov 1985 | Peru vs Chile | 0-1 |

Chile qualified for play-off decider

PLAY-OFF DECIDER

| 10 Nov 1985 | Paraguay vs Chile | 3-0 |
| 17 Nov 1985 | Chile vs Paraguay | 2-2 |

Paraguay qualified for Finals

AFRICA

ROUND ONE

| 28 Aug 1984 | Egypt vs Zimbabwe | 1-0 |
| 30 Sep 1984 | Zimbabwe vs Egypt | 1-1 |

Egypt qualified for 2nd Round

| 13 Oct 1984 | Kenya vs Ethiopia | 2-1 |
| 28 Oct 1984 | Ethiopia vs Kenya | 3-3 |

Kenya qualified for 2nd Round

| 15 Jul 1984 | Mauritius vs Malawi | 0-1 |
| 28 Jul 1984 | Malawi vs Mauritius | 4-0 |

Malawi qualified for 2nd Round

| 29 Jul 1984 | Zambia vs Uganda | 3-0 |
| 25 Aug 1984 | Uganda vs Zambia | 1-0 |

Zambia qualified for 2nd Round

| 13 Oct 1984 | Tanzania vs Sudan | 1-1 |
| 25 Oct 1984 | Sudan vs Tanzania | 0-0 |

Sudan qualified for 2nd Round on away goals

| 30 Jun 1984 | Sierra Leone vs Morocco | 0-1 |
| 15 Jul 1984 | Morocco vs Sierra Leone | 4-0 |

Morocco qualified for 2nd Round

| 28 Oct 1984 | Benin vs Tunisia | 0-2 |
| 11 Nov 1984 | Tunisia vs Benin | 4-0 |

Tunisia qualified for 2nd Round

| 21 Oct 1984 | Ivory Coast vs Gambia | 4-0 |
| 4 Nov 1984 | Gambia vs Ivory Coast | 3-2 |

Ivory Coast qualified for 2nd Round

| 20 Oct 1984 | Nigeria vs Liberia | 3-0 |
| 3 Nov 1984 | Liberia vs Nigeria | 0-1 |

Nigeria qualified for 2nd Round

| 1 Jul 1984 | Angola vs Senegal | 1-0 |
| 15 Jul 1984 | Senegal vs Angola | 1-0 |

Angola qualified for 2nd Round (4-3 on penalties)

ROUND TWO

| 7 Apr 1985 | Zambia vs Cameroon | 4-1 |
| 21 Apr 1985 | Cameroon vs Zambia | 1-1 |

Zambia qualified for 3rd Round

| 10 Feb 1985 | Guinea vs Tunisia | 1-0 |
| 24 Feb 1985 | Tunisia vs Guinea | 2-0 |

Tunisia qualified for 3rd Round

| 22 Feb 1985 | Sudan vs Libya | 0-0 |
| 8 Mar 1985 | Libya vs Sudan | 4-0 |

Libya qualified for 3rd Round

| 5 Apr 1985 | Egypt vs Madagascar | 1-0 |
| 21 Apr 1985 | Madagascar vs Egypt | 1-0 |

Egypt qualified for 3rd Round (3-2 on penalties)

| 7 Apr 1985 | Morocco vs Malawi | 2-0 |
| 21 Apr 1985 | Malawi vs Morocco | 0-0 |

Morocco qualified for 3rd Round

| 31 Mar 1985 | Angola vs Algeria | 0-0 |
| 19 Apr 1985 | Algeria vs Angola | 3-2 |

Algeria qualified for 3rd Round

| 6 Apr 1985 | Kenya vs Nigeria | 0-3 |
| 20 Apr 1985 | Nigeria vs Kenya | 3-1 |

Nigeria qualified for 3rd Round

| 7 Apr 1985 | Ivory Coast vs Ghana | 0-0 |
| 21 Apr 1985 | Ghana vs Ivory Coast | 2-0 |

Ghana qualified for 3rd Round

ROUND THREE

| 13 Jul 1985 | Algeria vs Zambia | 2-0 |
| 28 Jul 1985 | Zambia vs Algeria | 0-1 |

Algeria qualified for Group Finals

| 14 Jul 1985 | Ghana vs Libya | 0-0 |
| 26 Jul 1985 | Libya vs Ghana | 2-0 |

Libya qualified for Group Finals

| 6 Jul 1985 | Nigeria vs Tunisia | 1-0 |
| 20 Jul 1985 | Tunisia vs Nigeria | 2-0 |

Tunisia qualified for Group Finals

| 12 Jul 1985 | Egypt vs Morocco | 0-0 |
| 28 Jul 1985 | Morocco vs Egypt | 2-0 |

Morocco qualified for Group Finals

GROUP FINALS

| 6 Oct 1985 | Morocco vs Libya | 3-0 |
| 18 Oct 1985 | Libya vs Morocco | 1-0 |

Morocco qualified for Finals

| 6 Oct 1985 | Tunisia vs Algeria | 1-4 |
| 18 Oct 1985 | Algeria vs Tunisia | 3-0 |

Algeria qualified for Finals

OCEANIA

3 Sep 1985	Israel vs Taiwan	6-0
8 Sep 1985	Taiwan vs Israel	0-5
21 Sep 1985	New Zealand vs Australia	0-0
5 Oct 1985	New Zealand vs Taiwan	5-1
8 Oct 1985	Israel vs Australia	1-2
12 Oct 1985	Taiwan vs New Zealand	0-5
	(in New Zealand)	
20 Oct 1985	Australia vs Israel	1-1
23 Oct 1985	Australia vs Taiwan	7-0
26 Oct 1985	New Zealand vs Israel	3-1
27 Oct 1985	Taiwan vs Australia	0-8
	(in Australia)	
3 Nov 1985	Australia vs New Zealand	2-0
10 Nov 1985	Israel vs New Zealand	3-0

	P	W	D	L	F	A	Pts
Australia	6	4	2	0	20	2	10
Israel	6	3	1	2	17	6	7
New Zealand	6	3	1	2	13	7	7
Taiwan	6	0	0	6	1	36	0

Australia qualified for a Play-off against Scotland

ASIA

GROUP 1

SUB-GROUP A

| 12 Apr 1985 | Saudi Arabia vs United Arab Emirates | 0-0 |
| 19 Apr 1985 | United Arab Emirates vs Saudi Arabia | 1-0 |

Oman withdrew

United Arab Emirates qualified for 2nd Round

SUB-GROUP B

15 Mar 1985	Jordan vs Qatar	1-0
29 Mar 1985	Jordan vs Iraq	2-3
5 Apr 1985	Qatar vs Iraq	3-0
12 Apr 1985	Qatar vs Jordan	2-0
19 Apr 1985	Iraq vs Jordan	2-0
5 May 1985	Iraq vs Qatar	2-1

Lebanon withdrew

	P	W	D	L	F	A	Pts
Iraq	4	3	0	1	7	6	6
Qatar	4	2	0	2	6	3	4
Jordan	4	1	0	3	3	7	2

Iraq qualified for 2nd Round

GROUP 2

SUB-GROUP A

22 Mar 1985	Syria vs Kuwait	1-?
29 Mar 1985	Yemen AR vs Syria	0-?
5 Apr 1985	Kuwait vs Yemen AR	5-?
12 Apr 1985	Kuwait vs Syria	0-?
19 Apr 1985	Syria vs Yemen AR	3-?
26 Apr 1985	Yemen AR vs Kuwait	1-?

	P	W	D	L	F	A	Pts
Syria	4	3	1	0	5	0	7
Kuwait	4	2	1	1	8	2	5
Yemen AR	4	0	0	4	1	12	0

Syria qualified for 2nd Round

SUB-GROUP B

| 29 Mar 1985 | Yemen PDR vs Bahrain | 1-? |
| 14 Apr 1985 | Bahrain vs Yemen PDR | 3-? |

Iran withdrew

Bahrain qualified for 2nd Round

GROUP 3

SUB-GROUP A

2 Mar 1985	Nepal vs South Korea	0-?
10 Mar 1985	Malaysia vs South Korea	1-?
16 Mar 1985	Nepal vs Malaysia	0-0
31 Mar 1985	Malaysia vs Nepal	5-?
6 Apr 1985	South Korea vs Nepal	4-0
19 May 1985	South Korea vs Malaysia	2-?

	P	W	D	L	F	A	Pts
South Korea	4	3	0	1	8	1	6
Malaysia	4	2	1	1	6	2	5
Nepal	4	0	1	3	0	11	1

South Korea qualified for 2nd Round

SUB-GROUP B

15 Mar 1985	Indonesia vs Thailand	1-?
18 Mar 1985	Indonesia vs Bangladesh	2-?
21 Mar 1985	Indonesia vs India	2-1
23 Mar 1985	Thailand vs Bangladesh	3-?
26 Mar 1985	Thailand vs India	0-0
29 Mar 1985	Thailand vs Indonesia	0-1
30 Mar 1985	Bangladesh vs India	1-2
2 Apr 1985	Bangladesh vs Indonesia	2-1
5 Apr 1985	Bangladesh vs Thailand	1-?
6 Apr 1985	India vs Indonesia	1-1
9 Apr 1985	India vs Thailand	1-1
12 Apr 1985	India vs Bangladesh	2-1

	P	W	D	L	F	A	Pts
Indonesia	6	4	1	1	8	4	9
India	6	2	3	1	7	6	7
Thailand	6	1	2	3	4	4	4
Bangladesh	6	2	0	4	5	10	4

Indonesia qualified for 2nd Round

GROUP 4

SUB-GROUP A

| 17 Feb 1985 | Macau vs Brunei | 2-0 |

17 Feb 1985	Hong Kong vs China						0-0
20 Feb 1985	Macau vs China						0-4
23 Feb 1985	Hong Kong vs Brunei						8-0
26 Feb 1985	China vs Brunei						8-0
1 Mar 1985	Brunei vs China						0-4
6 Apr 1985	Brunei vs Hong Kong						1-5
13 Apr 1985	Brunei vs Macau						1-2
28 Apr 1985	Macau vs Hong Kong						0-2
4 May 1985	Hong Kong vs Macau						2-0
12 May 1985	China vs Macau						6-0
19 May 1985	China vs Hong Kong						1-2

	P	W	D	L	F	A	Pts
Hong Kong	6	5	1	0	19	2	11
China	6	4	1	1	23	2	9
Macau	6	2	0	4	4	15	4
Brunei	6	0	0	6	2	29	0

Hong Kong qualified for 2nd Round

SUB-GROUP B

19 Jan 1985	Singapore vs North Korea	1-1
23 Feb 1985	Singapore vs Japan	1-3
21 Mar 1985	Japan vs North Korea	1-0
30 Apr 1985	North Korea vs Japan	0-0
18 May 1985	Japan vs Singapore	5-0
25 May 1985	North Korea vs Singapore	2-0

	P	W	D	L	F	A	Pts
Japan	4	3	1	0	9	1	7
North Korea	4	1	2	1	3	2	4
Singapore	4	0	1	3	2	11	1

Japan qualified for 2nd Round

ROUND TWO

21 Jul 1985	South Korea vs Indonesia	2-0
30 Jul 1985	Indonesia vs South Korea	1-4

South Korea qualified for Play-offs

20 Sep 1985	United Arab Emirates vs Iraq	2-3
27 Sep 1985	Iraq vs United Arab Emirates	1-2

Iraq qualified for Play-offs on away goals

6 Sep 1985	Bahrain vs Syria	1-1
20 Sep 1985	Syria vs Bahrain	1-0

Syria qualified for Play-offs

11 Aug 1985	Japan vs Hong Kong	3-0
22 Sep 1985	Hong Kong vs Japan	1-2

Japan qualified for Play-offs

ASIAN PLAY-OFF FINALS

26 Oct 1985	Japan vs South Korea	1-2
3 Nov 1985	South Korea vs Japan	1-0

South Korea qualified for Finals

15 Nov 1985	Syria vs Iraq	0-0
29 Nov 1985	Iraq vs Syria	3-1

Iraq qualified for Finals

1990 – QUALIFYING COMPETITION

(110 Entries)

EUROPE

GROUP 1

9 Oct 1988	Greece vs Denmark	1-1
19 Oct 1988	Bulgaria vs Romania	1-3
2 Nov 1988	Romania vs Greece	3-0
2 Nov 1988	Denmark vs Bulgaria	1-1
26 Apr 1989	Greece vs Romania	0-0
26 Apr 1989	Bulgaria vs Denmark	0-2
17 May 1989	Romania vs Bulgaria	1-0
17 May 1989	Denmark vs Greece	7-1
11 Oct 1989	Bulgaria vs Greece	4-0
11 Oct 1989	Denmark vs Romania	3-0
15 Nov 1989	Greece vs Bulgaria	1-0
15 Nov 1989	Romania vs Denmark	3-1

	P	W	D	L	F	A	Pts
Romania	6	4	1	1	10	5	9
Denmark	6	3	2	1	15	6	8
Greece	6	1	2	3	3	15	4
Bulgaria	6	1	1	4	6	8	3

Romania qualified for Finals

GROUP 2

19 Oct 1988	England vs Sweden	0-0
19 Oct 1988	Poland vs Albania	1-0
5 Nov 1988	Albania vs Sweden	1-2
8 Mar 1989	Albania vs England	0-2
26 Apr 1989	England vs Albania	5-0
7 May 1989	Sweden vs Poland	2-1
3 Jun 1989	England vs Poland	3-0
6 Sep 1989	Sweden vs England	0-0
8 Oct 1989	Sweden vs Albania	3-1
11 Oct 1989	Poland vs England	0-0
25 Oct 1989	Poland vs Sweden	0-2
15 Nov 1989	Albania vs Poland	1-2

	P	W	D	L	F	A	Pts
Sweden	6	4	2	0	9	3	10
England	6	3	3	0	10	0	9
Poland	6	2	1	3	4	8	5
Albania	6	0	0	6	3	15	0

Sweden & England qualified for Finals

GROUP 3

31 Aug 1988	Iceland vs USSR	1-1
12 Oct 1988	Turkey vs Iceland	1-1
19 Oct 1988	USSR vs Austria	2-0
19 Oct 1988	East Germany vs Iceland	2-0
2 Nov 1988	Austria vs Turkey	3-2
30 Nov 1988	Turkey vs East Germany	3-1
12 Apr 1989	East Germany vs Turkey	0-2
26 Apr 1989	USSR vs East Germany	3-0
10 May 1989	Turkey vs USSR	0-1
20 May 1989	East Germany vs Austria	1-1
31 May 1989	USSR vs Iceland	1-1
14 Jun 1989	Iceland vs Austria	0-0
23 Aug 1989	Austria vs Iceland	2-1

6 Sep 1989	Austria vs USSR	0-0
6 Sep 1989	Iceland vs East Germany	0-3
20 Sep 1989	Iceland vs Turkey	2-1
8 Oct 1989	East Germany vs USSR	2-1
25 Oct 1989	Turkey vs Austria	3-0
15 Nov 1989	USSR vs Turkey	2-0
15 Nov 1989	Austria vs East Germany	3-0

	P	W	D	L	F	A	Pts
USSR	8	4	3	1	11	4	11
Austria	8	3	3	2	9	9	9
Turkey	8	3	1	4	12	10	7
East Germany	8	3	1	4	9	13	7
Iceland	8	1	4	3	6	11	6

USSR & Austria qualified for Finals

GROUP 4

31 Aug 1988	Finland vs West Germany	0-4
14 Sep 1988	Holland vs Wales	1-0
19 Oct 1988	Wales vs Finland	2-2
19 Oct 1988	West Germany vs Holland	0-0
24 Apr 1989	Holland vs West Germany	1-1
31 May 1989	Wales vs West Germany	0-0
31 May 1989	Finland vs Holland	0-1
6 Sep 1989	Finland vs Wales	1-0
4 Oct 1989	West Germany vs Finland	6-1
11 Oct 1989	Wales vs Holland	1-2
15 Nov 1989	West Germany vs Wales	2-1
15 Nov 1989	Holland vs Finland	3-0

	P	W	D	L	F	A	Pts
Holland	6	4	2	0	8	2	10
West Germany	6	3	3	0	13	3	9
Finland	6	1	1	4	4	16	3
Wales	6	0	2	4	4	8	2

Holland & West Germany qualified for Finals

GROUP 5

14 Sep 1988	Norway vs Scotland	1-2
28 Sep 1988	France vs Norway	1-0
19 Oct 1988	Scotland vs Yugoslavia	1-1
22 Oct 1988	Cyprus vs France	1-1
2 Nov 1988	Cyprus vs Norway	0-3
19 Nov 1988	Yugoslavia vs France	3-2
11 Dec 1988	Yugoslavia vs Cyprus	4-0
8 Feb 1989	Cyprus vs Scotland	2-3
8 Mar 1989	Scotland vs France	2-0
26 Apr 1989	Scotland vs Cyprus	2-1
29 Apr 1989	France vs Yugoslavia	0-0
21 May 1989	Norway vs Cyprus	3-1
14 Jun 1989	Norway vs Yugoslavia	1-2
5 Sep 1989	Norway vs France	1-1
6 Sep 1989	Yugoslavia vs Scotland	3-1
11 Oct 1989	Yugoslavia vs Norway	1-0
11 Oct 1989	France vs Scotland	3-0
28 Oct 1989	Cyprus vs Yugoslavia	1-2
15 Nov 1989	Scotland vs Norway	1-1
18 Nov 1989	France vs Cyprus	2-0

	P	W	D	L	F	A	Pts
Yugoslavia	8	6	2	0	16	6	14
Scotland	8	4	2	2	12	12	10

	P	W	D	L	F	A	Pts
France	8	3	3	2	10	7	9
Norway	8	2	2	4	10	9	6
Cyprus	8	0	1	7	6	20	1

Yugoslavia & Scotland qualified for Finals

GROUP 6

21 May 1988	Northern Ireland vs Malta	3-0
14 Sep 1988	Northern Ireland vs Eire	0-0
19 Oct 1988	Hungary vs Northern Ireland	1-0
16 Nov 1988	Spain vs Eire	2-0
11 Dec 1988	Malta vs Hungary	2-2
21 Dec 1988	Spain vs Northern Ireland	4-0
22 Jan 1989	Malta vs Spain	0-2
8 Feb 1989	Northern Ireland vs Spain	0-2
8 Mar 1989	Hungary vs Eire	0-0
22 Mar 1989	Spain vs Malta	4-0
12 Apr 1989	Hungary vs Malta	1-1
26 Apr 1989	Malta vs Northern Ireland	0-2
26 Apr 1989	Eire vs Spain	1-0
28 May 1989	Eire vs Malta	2-0
4 Jun 1989	Eire vs Hungary	2-0
6 Sep 1989	Northern Ireland vs Hungary	1-2
11 Oct 1989	Hungary vs Spain	2-2
11 Oct 1989	Eire vs Northern Ireland	3-0
15 Nov 1989	Spain vs Hungary	4-0
15 Nov 1989	Malta vs Eire	0-2

	P	W	D	L	F	A	Pts
Spain	8	6	1	1	20	3	13
Eire	8	5	2	1	10	2	12
Hungary	8	2	4	2	8	12	8
Northern Ireland	8	2	1	5	6	12	5
Malta	8	0	2	6	3	18	2

Spain & Eire qualified for Finals

GROUP 7

1 Sep 1988	Luxembourg vs Switzerland	1-4
19 Oct 1988	Luxembourg vs Czechoslovakia	0-2
19 Oct 1988	Belgium vs Switzerland	1-0
16 Nov 1988	Czechoslovakia vs Belgium	0-0
16 Nov 1988	Portugal vs Luxembourg	1-0
15 Feb 1989	Portugal vs Belgium	1-1
26 Apr 1989	Portugal vs Switzerland	3-1
30 Apr 1989	Belgium vs Czechoslovakia	2-1
19 May 1989	Czechoslovakia vs Luxembourg	4-0
1 Jun 1989	Luxembourg vs Belgium	0-5
7 Jun 1989	Switzerland vs Czechoslovakia	0-1
6 Sep 1989	Belgium vs Portugal	3-0
20 Sep 1989	Switzerland vs Portugal	1-2
6 Oct 1989	Czechoslovakia vs Portugal	2-1
11 Oct 1989	Luxembourg vs Portugal	0-3
11 Oct 1989	Switzerland vs Belgium	2-2
25 Oct 1989	Czechoslovakia vs Switzerland	3-0
25 Oct 1989	Belgium vs Luxembourg	1-1
15 Nov 1989	Portugal vs Czechoslovakia	0-0
15 Nov 1989	Switzerland vs Luxembourg	2-1

	P	W	D	L	F	A	Pts
Belgium	8	4	4	0	15	5	12
Czechoslovakia	8	5	2	1	13	3	12
Portugal	8	4	2	2	11	8	10
Switzerland	8	2	1	5	10	14	5

| Luxembourg | 8 | 0 | 1 | 7 | 3 | 22 | 1 |

Belgium & Czechoslovakia qualified for Finals

Winners and runner-ups from Group 3, 5, 6 and 7 qualified for the Finals along with the winners of Groups 1, 2 and 4 plus the two runners-up from Groups 1, 2 and 4 with the best comparative records.

AFRICA

ROUND ONE

| 7 Aug 1988 | Angola vs Sudan | 0-0 |
| 11 Nov 1988 | Sudan vs Angola | 1-2 |

Angola qualified for 2nd Round

Zimbabwe walk over vs Lesotho

Zimbabwe qualified for 2nd Round

Zambia walk over vs Rwanda (withdrew)

Zambia qualified for 2nd Round

| 16 Jul 1988 | Uganda vs Malawi | 1-0 |
| 30 Jul 1988 | Malawi vs Uganda | 3-1 |

Malawi qualified for 2nd Round

| 3 Jun 1989 | Libya vs Burkino Faso | 3-0 |
| 3 July 1989 | Burkino Faso vs Libya | 2-0 |

Libya qualified for 2nd Round

| 7 Aug 1988 | Ghana vs Liberia | 0-0 |
| 21 Aug 1988 | Liberia vs Ghana | 2-0 |

Liberia qualified for 2nd Round

| 5 Aug 1988 | Tunisia vs Guinea | 5-0 |
| 21 Aug 1988 | Guinea vs Tunisia | 3-0 |

Tunisia qualified for 2nd Round

Gabon walk over vs Togo

Gabon qualified for 2nd Round

ROUND TWO

GROUP A

6 Jan 1989	Algeria vs Zimbabwe	3-0
22 Jan 1989	Zimbabwe vs Ivory Coast	0-0
11 Jun 1989	Ivory Coast vs Algeria	0-0
25 Jun 1989	Zimbabwe vs Algeria	1-2
13 Aug 1989	Ivory Coast vs Zimbabwe	5-0
25 Aug 1989	Algeria vs Ivory Coast	1-0

	P	W	D	L	F	A	Pts
Algeria	4	3	1	0	6	1	7
Ivory Coast	4	1	2	1	5	1	4
Zimbabwe	4	0	1	3	1	10	1

Algeria qualified for 3rd Round

GROUP B

6 Jan 1989	Egypt vs Liberia	2-0
7 Jan 1989	Kenya vs Malawi	1-1
21 Jan 1989	Malawi vs Egypt	1-1
22 Jan 1989	Liberia vs Kenya	0-0
10 Jun 1989	Kenya vs Egypt	0-0
11 Jun 1989	Liberia vs Malawi	1-0
24 Jun 1989	Malawi vs Kenya	1-0
25 Jun 1989	Liberia vs Egypt	1-0
11 Aug 1989	Egypt vs Malawi	1-0

12 Aug 1989	Kenya vs Liberia	1-0
25 Aug 1989	Egypt vs Kenya	2-0
26 Aug 1989	Malawi vs Liberia	0-0

	P	W	D	L	F	A	Pts
Egypt	6	3	2	1	6	2	8
Liberia	6	2	2	2	2	3	6
Malawi	6	1	3	2	3	4	5
Kenya	6	1	3	2	2	4	5

Egypt qualified for 3rd Round

GROUP C

7 Jan 1989	Nigeria vs Gabon	1-0
8 Jan 1989	Cameroon vs Angola	1-1
22 Jan 1989	Gabon vs Cameroon	1-3
22 Jan 1989	Angola vs Nigeria	2-2
10 Jun 1989	Nigeria vs Cameroon	2-0
10 Jun 1989	Angola vs Gabon	2-0
25 Jun 1989	Angola vs Cameroon	1-2
25 Jun 1989	Gabon vs Nigeria	2-1
12 Aug 1989	Nigeria vs Angola	1-0
13 Aug 1989	Cameroon vs Gabon	2-1
27 Aug 1989	Cameroon vs Nigeria	1-0
27 Aug 1989	Gabon vs Angola	1-0

	P	W	D	L	F	A	Pts
Cameroon	6	4	1	1	9	6	9
Nigeria	6	3	1	2	7	5	7
Angola	6	1	2	3	6	7	4
Gabon	6	2	0	4	5	9	4

Cameroon qualified for 3rd Round

GROUP D

8 Jan 1989	Morocco vs Zambia	1-0
8 Jan 1989	Zaire vs Tunisia	3-1
22 Jan 1989	Tunisia vs Morocco	2-1
22 Jan 1989	Zambia vs Zaire	4-2
11 Jun 1989	Zaire vs Morocco	0-0
11 Jun 1989	Zambia vs Tunisia	1-0
25 Jun 1989	Zambia vs Morocco	2-1
25 Jun 1989	Tunisia vs Zaire	1-0
13 Aug 1989	Morocco vs Tunisia	0-0
13 Aug 1989	Zaire vs Zambia	1-0
27 Aug 1989	Tunisia vs Zambia	1-0
27 Aug 1989	Morocco vs Zaire	1-1

	P	W	D	L	F	A	Pts
Tunisia	6	3	1	2	5	5	7
Zambia	6	3	0	3	7	6	6
Zaire	6	2	2	2	7	7	6
Morocco	6	1	3	2	4	5	5

Tunisia qualified for 3rd Round

ROUND THREE

| 8 Oct 1989 | Algeria vs Egypt | 0-0 |
| 22 Oct 1989 | Egypt vs Algeria | 1-0 |

Egypt qualified for Finals

| 8 Oct 1989 | Cameroon vs Tunisia | 2-0 |
| 19 Nov 1989 | Tunisia vs Cameroon | 0-1 |

Cameroon qualified for Finals

ASIA

WEST ASIA

GROUP 1

6 Jan 1989	Qatar vs Jordan	1-0
6 Jan 1989	Oman vs Iraq	1-1
13 Jan 1989	Oman vs Qatar	0-0
13 Jan 1989	Jordan vs Iraq	0-1
20 Jan 1989	Jordan vs Oman	2-0
20 Jan 1989	Qatar vs Iraq	1-0
27 Jan 1989	Jordan vs Qatar	1-1
27 Jan 1989	Iraq vs Oman	3-1
3 Feb 1989	Qatar vs Oman	3-0
3 Feb 1989	Iraq vs Jordan	4-0
10 Feb 1989	Oman vs Jordan	0-2
10 Feb 1989	Iraq vs Qatar	2-2

	P	W	D	L	F	A	Pts
Qatar	6	3	3	0	8	3	9
Iraq	6	3	2	1	11	5	8
Jordan	6	2	1	3	5	7	5
Oman	6	0	2	4	2	11	2

Qatar qualified for 2nd Round

GROUP 2

10 Mar 1989	Yemen AR vs Syria	0-1
15 Mar 1989	Saudi Arabia vs Syria	5-4
20 Mar 1989	Yemen AR vs Saudi Arabia	0-1
25 Mar 1989	Syria vs Yemen AR	2-0
30 Mar 1989	Syria vs Saudi Arabia	0-0
5 Apr 1989	Saudi Arabia vs Yemen AR	1-0

Bahrain withdrew

	P	W	D	L	F	A	Pts
Saudi Arabia	4	3	1	0	7	4	7
Syria	4	2	1	1	7	5	5
Yemen AR	4	0	0	4	0	5	0

Saudi Arabia qualified for 2nd Round

GROUP 3

6 Jan 1989	Pakistan vs Kuwait	0-1
13 Jan 1989	Kuwait vs United Arab Emirates	3-2
20 Jan 1989	United Arab Emirates vs Pakistan	5-0
27 Jan 1989	Kuwait vs Pakistan	2-0
3 Feb 1989	United Arab Emirates vs Kuwait	1-0
10 Feb 1989	Pakistan vs United Arab Emirates	1-4

Yemen withdrew

	P	W	D	L	F	A	Pts
United Arab Emirates	4	3	0	1	12	4	6
Kuwait	4	3	0	1	6	3	6
Pakistan	4	0	0	4	1	2	0

United Arab Emirates qualified for 2nd Round

GROUP 4

India withdrew so Nepal switched from Group 5

Following matches all in South Korea

23 May 1989	Malaysia vs Nepal	2-0
23 May 1989	Singapore vs South Korea	0-3
25 May 1989	Malaysia vs Singapore	1-0
25 May 1989	Nepal vs South Korea	0-9
27 May 1989	Singapore vs Nepal	3-0
27 May 1989	South Korea vs Malaysia	3-0

Following matches all in Singapore

3 Jun 1989	Singapore vs Malaysia	2-2
3 Jun 1989	South Korea vs Nepal	4-0
5 Jun 1989	Malaysia vs South Korea	0-3
5 Jun 1989	Nepal vs Singapore	0-7
7 Jun 1989	Singapore vs South Korea	0-3
7 Jun 1989	Malaysia vs Nepal	3-0

	P	W	D	L	F	A	Pts
South Korea	6	6	0	0	25	0	12
Malaysia	6	3	1	2	8	8	7
Singapore	6	2	1	3	12	9	5
Nepal	6	0	0	6	0	28	0

South Korea qualified for 2nd Round

GROUP 5

20 Feb 1989	Thailand vs Bangladesh	1-0
23 Feb 1989	China vs Bangladesh	2-0
23 Feb 1989	Thailand vs Iran	0-3
27 Feb 1989	Bangladesh vs Iran	1-2
28 Feb 1989	Thailand vs China	0-3
4 Mar 1989	Bangladesh vs China	0-2
8 Mar 1989	Bangladesh vs Thailand	3-1
17 Mar 1989	Iran vs Bangladesh	1-0
30 May 1989	Iran vs Thailand	3-0
15 Jul 1989	China vs Iran	2-0
22 Jul 1989	Iran vs China	3-2
29 Jul 1989	China vs Thailand	2-0

	P	W	D	L	F	A	Pts
China	6	5	0	1	13	3	10
Iran	6	5	0	1	12	7	10
Bangladesh	6	1	0	5	4	9	2
Thailand	6	1	0	5	2	14	2

China qualified for 2nd Round

GROUP 6

21 May 1989	Indonesia vs North Korea	0-0
21 May 1989	Hong Kong vs Japan	0-0
27 May 1989	Hong Kong vs North Korea	1-2
28 May 1989	Indonesia vs Japan	0-0
4 Jun 1989	Hong Kong vs Indonesia	1-1
4 Jun 1989	Japan vs North Korea	2-1
11 Jun 1989	Japan vs Indonesia	5-0
18 Jun 1989	Japan vs Hong Kong	0-0
25 Jun 1989	North Korea vs Japan	2-0
25 Jun 1989	Indonesia vs Hong Kong	3-2
2 Jul 1989	North Korea vs Hong Kong	4-1
9 Jul 1989	North Korea vs Indonesia	2-1

	P	W	D	L	F	A	Pts
North Korea	6	4	1	1	11	5	9
Japan	6	2	3	1	7	3	7
Indonesia	6	1	3	2	5	10	5
Hong Kong	6	0	3	3	5	10	3

North Korea qualified for 2nd Round

ROUND TWO

Play-off section in Singapore, except for United Arab Emirates vs South Korea in Kuala Lumpur and Saudia Arabia vs North Korea in Kuanton.

12 Oct 1989	United Arab Emirates vs North Korea	 0-0
12 Oct 1989	China vs Saudi Arabia	2-1
13 Oct 1989	South Korea vs Qatar	0-0
16 Oct 1989	Qatar vs Saudi Arabia	1-1
16 Oct 1989	South Korea v North Korea	1-0
17 Oct 1989	China vs United Arab Emirates	1-2
20 Oct 1989	China vs South Korea	0-1
20 Oct 1989	North Korea vs Qatar	2-0
21 Oct 1989	Saudia Arabia vs United Arab Emirates	..0-0
24 Oct 1989	United Arab Emirates vs Qatar	1-1
24 Oct 1989	North Korea vs China	0-1
25 Oct 1989	Saudia Arabia vs South Korea	0-2
28 Oct 1989	United Arab Emirates vs South Korea	 1-1
28 Oct 1989	Saudia Arabia vs North Korea	2-0
28 Oct 1989	Qatar vs China	2-1

	P	W	D	L	F	A	Pts
South Korea	5	3	2	0	5	1	8
UAE	5	1	4	0	4	3	6
Qatar	5	1	3	1	4	5	5
China	5	2	0	3	5	6	4
Saudi Arabia	5	1	2	2	4	5	4
North Korea	5	1	1	3	2	4	3

South Korea & United Arab Emirates qualified for Finals

NORTH/CENTRAL AMERICA

ROUND ONE

19 Jun 1988	Antigua vs Netherlands Antilles	 0-1
29 Jul 1988	Netherlands Antilles vs Antigua	 3-1

Netherlands Antilles qualified for 2nd Round

12 May 1988	Jamaica vs Puerto Rico	1-0
29 May 1988	Puerto Rico vs Jamaica	1-2

Jamaica qualified for 2nd Round

17 Apr 1988	Guyana vs Trinidad & Tobago	0-4
8 May 1988	Trinidad & Tobago vs Guyana	1-0

Trinidad & Tobago qualified for 2nd Round

17 Jul 1988	Costa Rica vs Panama	1-1
31 Jul 1988	Panama vs Costa Rica	0-2

Costa Rica qualified for 2nd Round

30 Apr 1988	Cuba vs Guatemala	0-1
15 May 1988	Guatemala vs Cuba	1-1

Guatemala qualified for 2nd Round

ROUND TWO

1 Oct 1988	Netherlands Antilles vs El Salvador	 0-1
16 Oct 1988	El Salvador vs Netherlands Antilles	 5-0

El Salvador qualified for 3rd Round

30 Oct 1988	Trinidad & Tobago vs Honduras	0-0
13 Nov 1988	Honduras vs Trinidad & Tobago	1-1

Trinidad & Tobago qualified for 3rd Round on away goals

24 Jul 1988	Jamaica vs USA	0-0
13 Aug 1988	USA vs Jamaica	5-1

USA qualified for 3rd Round

9 Oct 1988	Guatemala vs Canada	1-0
15 Oct 1988	Canada vs Guatemala	3-2

Guatemala qualified for 3rd Round on away goals

Costa Rica walk over vs Mexico

Costa Rica qualified for 3rd Round

ROUND THREE

19 Mar 1989	Guatemala vs Costa Rica	1-0
2 Apr 1989	Costa Rica vs Guatemala	2-1
16 Apr 1989	Costa Rica vs USA	1-0
30 Apr 1989	USA vs Costa Rica	1-0
13 May 1989	USA vs Trinidad & Tobago	1-1
28 May 1989	Trindad & Tobago vs Costa Rica	1-1
11 Jun 1989	Costa Rica vs Trinidad & Tobago	1-0
17 Jun 1989	USA vs Guatemala	2-1
25 Jun 1989	El Salvador vs Costa Rica	2-4
16 Jul 1989	Costa Rica vs El Salvador	1-0
30 Jul 1989	Trinidad & Tobago vs El Salvador	2-0
13 Aug 1989	El Salvador vs Trinidad & Tobago	0-0
20 Aug 1989	Guatemala vs Trinidad &Tobago	0-1
3 Sep 1989	Trinidad & Tobago vs Guatemala	2-1
17 Sep 1989	El Salvador vs USA	0-1
8 Oct 1989	Guatemala vs USA	0-0
5 Nov 1989	USA vs El Salvador	0-1
18 Nov 1989	Trinidad & Tobago vs USA	0-1

The two games between Guatemala and El Salvador were not played due to the domestic situation in El Salvador

	P	W	D	L	F	A	Pts
Costa Rica	8	5	1	2	10	6	11
USA	8	4	3	1	6	3	10
Trinidad & Tobago	8	3	3	2	7	5	9
Guatemala	6	1	1	4	4	7	3
El Salvador	6	0	2	4	2	8	2

Costa Rica & USA qualified for Finals

OCEANIA

ROUND ONE

11 Dec 1988	Taiwan vs New Zealand	0-4
18 Dec 1988	New Zealand vs Taiwan	4-1

New Zealand qualified for 2nd Round

26 Nov 1988	Fiji vs Australia	1-0
3 Dec 1988	Australia vs Fiji	5-1

Australia qualified for 2nd Round

ROUND TWO

5 Mar 1989	Israel vs New Zealand	1-0
12 Mar 1989	Australia vs New Zealand	4-1
19 Mar 1989	Israel vs Australia	1-1
2 Apr 1989	New Zealand vs Australia	2-0
9 Apr 1989	New Zealand vs Israel	2-2
16 Apr 1989	Australia vs Israel	1-1

	P	W	D	L	F	A	Pts
Israel	4	1	3	0	5	4	5
Australia	4	1	2	1	6	5	4
New Zealand	4	1	1	2	5	7	3

Israel qualified to play Colombia for a place in the Finals

SOUTH AMERICA

GROUP 1

20 Aug 1989	Bolivia vs Peru	2-1
27 Aug 1989	Peru vs Uruguay	0-2
3 Sep 1989	Bolivia vs Uruguay	2-1
10 Sep 1989	Peru vs Bolivia	1-2
17 Sep 1989	Uruguay vs Bolivia	2-0
24 Sep 1989	Uruguay vs Peru	2-0

	P	W	D	L	F	A	Pts
Uruguay	4	3	0	1	7	2	6
Bolivia	4	3	0	1	6	5	6
Peru	4	0	0	4	2	8	0

Uruguay qualified for Finals

GROUP 2

20 Aug 1989	Colombia vs Ecuador	2-0
27 Aug 1989	Paraguay vs Colombia	2-1
3 Sep 1989	Ecuador vs Colombia	0-0
10 Sep 1989	Paraguay vs Ecuador	2-1
24 Sep 1989	Colombia vs Paraguay	2-1
1 Oct 1989	Ecuador vs Paraguay	3-1

	P	W	D	L	F	A	Pts
Colombia	4	2	1	1	4	3	5
Paraguay	4	2	0	2	5	6	4
Ecuador	4	1	1	2	3	3	3

Colombia qualified to play Israel for a place in the Finals

GROUP 3

30 Jul 1989	Venezuela vs Brazil	1-3
6 Aug 1989	Venezuela vs Chile	1-3
13 Aug 1989	Chile vs Brazil	1-1
20 Aug 1989	Brazil vs Venezuela	6-0
27 Aug 1989	Chile vs Venezuela	5-0
3 Sep 1989	Brazil vs Chile	2-0

	P	W	D	L	F	A	Pts
Brazil	4	3	1	0	12	2	7
Chile	4	2	1	1	9	4	5
Venezuela	4	0	0	4	2	17	0

Brazil qualified for Finals

SOUTH AMERICA/OCEANIA PLAY-OFF

| 15 Oct 1989 | Colombia vs Israel | 1-0 |
| 30 Oct 1989 | Israel vs Colombia | 0-0 |

Colombia qualified for Finals

1994 – QUALIFYING COMPETITION

(143 Entries)

EUROPE

GROUP 1

16 Aug 1992	Estonia vs Switzerland	0-6
9 Sep 1992	Switzerland vs Scotland	3-1
14 Oct 1992	Italy vs Switzerland	2-2
14 Oct 1992	Scotland vs Portugal	0-0
25 Oct 1992	Malta vs Estonia	0-0
18 Nov 1992	Scotland vs Italy	0-0
18 Nov 1992	Switzerland vs Malta	3-0
19 Dec 1992	Malta vs Italy	1-2
24 Jan 1993	Malta vs Portugal	0-1
17 Feb 1993	Scotland vs Malta	3-0
24 Feb 1993	Portugal vs Italy	1-3
24 Mar 1993	Italy vs Malta	6-1
31 Mar 1993	Switzerland vs Portugal	1-1
14 Apr 1993	Italy vs Estonia	2-0
17 Apr 1993	Malta vs Switzerland	0-2
28 Apr 1993	Portugal vs Scotland	5-0
1 May 1993	Switzerland vs Italy	1-0
12 May 1993	Estonia vs Malta	0-1
19 May 1993	Estonia vs Scotland	0-3
2 Jun 1993	Scotland vs Estonia	3-1
19 Jun 1993	Portugal vs Malta	4-0
5 Sep 1993	Estonia vs Portugal	0-2
8 Sep 1993	Scotland vs Switzerland	1-1
22 Sep 1993	Estonia vs Italy	0-3
13 Oct 1993	Portugal vs Switzerland	1-0
13 Oct 1993	Italy vs Scotland	3-1
10 Nov 1993	Portugal vs Estonia	3-0
17 Nov 1993	Italy vs Portugal	1-0
17 Nov 1993	Malta vs Scotland	0-2
17 Nov 1993	Switzerland vs Estonia	4-0

	P	W	D	L	F	A	Pts
Italy	10	7	2	1	22	7	16
Switzerland	10	6	3	1	23	6	15
Portugal	10	6	2	2	18	5	14
Scotland	10	4	3	3	14	13	11
Malta	10	1	1	8	3	23	3
Estonia	10	0	1	9	1	27	1

Italy & Switzerland qualified for Finals

GROUP 2

9 Sep 1992	Norway vs San Marino	10-0
23 Sep 1992	Norway vs Holland	2-1
23 Sep 1992	Poland vs Turkey	1-0
7 Oct 1992	San Marino vs Norway	0-2
14 Oct 1992	England vs Norway	1-1
14 Oct 1992	Holland vs Poland	2-2
28 Oct 1992	Turkey vs San Marino	4-1
18 Nov 1992	England vs Turkey	4-0
16 Dec 1992	Turkey vs Holland	1-3
17 Feb 1993	England vs San Marino	6-0
24 Feb 1993	Holland vs Turkey	3-1
10 Oct 1993	San Marino vs Turkey	0-0
24 Mar 1993	Holland vs San Marino	6-0
31 Mar 1993	Turkey vs England	0-2
28 Apr 1993	England vs Holland	2-2
28 Apr 1993	Norway vs Turkey	3-1
28 Apr 1993	Poland vs San Marino	1-0
19 May 1993	San Marino vs Poland	0-3
29 May 1993	Poland vs England	1-1
2 Jun 1993	Norway vs England	2-0
9 Jun 1993	Holland vs Norway	0-0
8 Sep 1993	England vs Poland	3-0
22 Sep 1993	Norway vs Poland	1-0
22 Sep 1993	San Marino vs Holland	0-7
13 Oct 1993	Holland vs England	2-0

13 Oct 1993	Poland vs Norway	....				0-3
27 Oct 1993	Turkey vs Poland	....				2-1
10 Nov 1993	Turkey vs Norway	....				2-1
17 Nov 1993	San Marino vs England	....				1-7
17 Nov 1993	Poland vs Holland	....				1-3

	P	W	D	L	F	A	Pts
Norway	10	7	2	1	25	5	16
Holland	10	6	3	1	29	9	15
England	10	5	3	2	26	9	13
Poland	10	3	2	5	10	15	8
Turkey	10	3	1	6	11	19	7
San Marino	10	0	1	9	2	46	1

Norway & Holland qualified for Finals

GROUP 3

22 Apr 1992	Spain vs Albania	3-0
28 Apr 1992	Northern Ireland vs Lithuania	2-2
26 May 1992	Eire vs Albania	2-0
3 Jun 1992	Albania vs Lithuania	1-0
12 Aug 1992	Latvia vs Lithuania	1-2
26 Aug 1992	Latvia vs Denmark	0-0
9 Sep 1992	Eire vs Latvia	4-0
9 Sep 1992	Northern Ireland vs Albania	3-0
23 Sep 1992	Latvia vs Spain	0-0
23 Sep 1992	Lithuania vs Denmark	0-0
14 Oct 1992	Denmark vs Eire	0-0
14 Oct 1992	Northern Ireland vs Spain	0-0
28 Oct 1992	Lithuania vs Latvia	1-1
11 Nov 1992	Albania vs Latvia	1-1
18 Nov 1992	Northern Ireland vs Denmark	0-1
18 Nov 1992	Spain vs Eire	0-0
16 Dec 1992	Spain vs Latvia	5-0
17 Feb 1993	Albania vs Northern Ireland	1-2
24 Feb 1993	Spain vs Lithuania	5-0
31 Mar 1993	Denmark vs Spain	1-0
31 Mar 1993	Eire vs Northern Ireland	3-0
14 Apr 1993	Denmark vs Latvia	2-0
14 Apr 1993	Lithuania vs Albania	3-1
28 Apr 1993	Eire vs Denmark	1-1
28 Apr 1993	Spain vs Northern Ireland	3-1
15 May 1993	Latvia vs Albania	0-0
25 May 1993	Lithuania vs Northern Ireland	0-1
26 May 1993	Albania vs Eire	1-2
2 Jun 1993	Denmark vs Albania	4-0
2 Jun 1993	Latvia vs Northern Ireland	1-2
2 Jun 1993	Lithuania vs Spain	0-2
9 Jun 1993	Latvia vs Eire	0-2
16 Jun 1993	Lithuania vs Eire	0-1
25 Aug 1993	Denmark vs Lithuania	4-0
8 Sep 1993	Albania vs Denmark	0-1
8 Sep 1993	Eire vs Lithuania	2-0
8 Sep 1993	Northern Ireland vs Latvia	2-0
22 Sep 1993	Albania vs Spain	1-5
13 Oct 1993	Denmark vs Northern Ireland	1-0
13 Oct 1993	Eire vs Spain	1-3
17 Nov 1993	Northern Ireland vs Eire	1-1
17 Nov 1993	Spain vs Denmark	1-0

	P	W	D	L	F	A	Pts
Spain	12	8	3	1	27	4	19
Eire	12	7	4	1	19	6	18

	P	W	D	L	F	A	Pts
Denmark	12	7	4	1	15	2	18
Northern Ireland	12	5	3	4	14	13	13
Lithuania	12	2	3	7	8	21	7
Latvia	12	0	5	7	4	21	5
Albania	12	1	2	9	6	26	4

Spain & Eire qualified for Finals

GROUP 4

22 Apr 1992	Belgium vs Cyprus	1-0
6 May 1992	Romania vs Faroe Islands	7-0
20 May 1992	Romania vs Wales	5-1
3 Jun 1992	Faroe Islands vs Belgium	0-3
18 Jun 1992	Faroe Islands vs Cyprus	0-2
2 Sep 1992	Czechoslovakia vs Belgium	1-2
9 Sep 1992	Wales vs Faroe Islands	6-0
23 Sep 1992	Czechoslovakia vs Faroe Islands	4-0
14 Oct 1992	Belgium vs Romania	1-0
14 Oct 1992	Cyprus vs Wales	0-1
14 Nov 1992	Romania vs Czechoslovakia	1-1
18 Nov 1992	Belgium vs Wales	2-0
29 Nov 1992	Cyprus vs Romania	1-4
13 Feb 1993	Cyprus vs Belgium	0-3
24 Mar 1993	Cyprus vs Czechoslovakia	1-1
31 Mar 1993	Wales vs Belgium	2-0
14 Apr 1993	Romania vs Cyprus	2-1
25 Apr 1993	Cyprus vs Faroe Islands	3-1
28 Apr 1993	Czechoslovakia vs Wales	1-1
22 May 1993	Belgium vs Faroe Islands	3-0
2 Jun 1993	Czechoslovakia vs Romania	5-2
6 Jun 1993	Faroe Islands vs Wales	0-3
16 Jun 1993	Faroe Islands vs Czechoslovakia	0-3
8 Sep 1993	Wales vs Czechoslovakia	2-2
8 Sep 1993	Faroe Islands vs Romania	0-4
13 Oct 1993	Romania vs Belgium	2-1
13 Oct 1993	Wales vs Cyprus	2-0
27 Oct 1993	Czechoslovakia vs Cyprus	3-0
17 Nov 1993	Wales vs Romania	1-2
17 Nov 1993	Belgium vs Czechoslovakia	0-0

	P	W	D	L	F	A	Pts
Romania	10	7	1	2	29	12	15
Belgium	10	7	1	2	16	5	15
Czechoslovakia	10	4	5	1	21	9	13
Wales	10	5	2	3	19	12	12
Cyprus	10	2	1	7	8	18	5
Faroe Islands	10	0	0	10	1	38	0

Romania & Belgium qualified for Finals

GROUP 5

13 May 1992	Greece vs Iceland	1-0
3 Jun 1992	Hungary vs Iceland	1-2
9 Sep 1992	Luxembourg vs Hungary	0-3
7 Oct 1992	Iceland vs Greece	0-1
14 Oct 1992	Russia vs Iceland	1-0
28 Oct 1992	Russia vs Luxembourg	2-0
11 Nov 1992	Greece vs Hungary	0-0
17 Feb 1993	Greece vs Luxembourg	2-0
31 Mar 1993	Hungary vs Greece	0-1
14 Apr 1993	Luxembourg vs Russia	0-4
28 Apr 1993	Russia vs Hungary	3-0
20 May 1993	Luxembourg vs Iceland	1-1
23 May 1993	Russia vs Greece	1-1

209

2 Jun 1993	Iceland vs Russia	1-1
16 Jun 1993	Iceland vs Hungary	2-0
8 Sep 1993	Hungary vs Russia	1-3
8 Sep 1993	Iceland vs Luxembourg	1-0
12 Oct 1993	Luxembourg vs Greece	1-3
27 Oct 1993	Hungary vs Luxembourg	1-0
17 Nov 1993	Greece vs Russia	1-0

Yugoslavia were excluded due to UN sanctions

	P	W	D	L	F	A	Pts
Greece	8	6	2	0	10	2	14
Russia	8	5	2	1	15	4	12
Iceland	8	3	2	3	7	6	8
Hungary	8	2	1	5	6	11	5
Luxembourg	8	0	1	7	2	17	1

Russia & Greece qualified for Finals

GROUP 6

14 May 1992	Finland vs Bulgaria	0-3
9 Sep 1992	Bulgaria vs France	2-0
9 Sep 1992	Finland vs Sweden	0-1
7 Oct 1992	Sweden vs Bulgaria	2-0
14 Oct 1992	France vs Austria	2-0
28 Oct 1992	Austria vs Israel	5-2
11 Nov 1992	Israel vs Sweden	1-3
14 Nov 1992	France vs Finland	2-1
2 Dec 1992	Israel vs Bulgaria	0-2
17 Feb 1993	Israel vs France	0-4
27 Mar 1993	Austria vs France	0-1
14 Apr 1993	Austria vs Bulgaria	3-1
28 Apr 1993	France vs Sweden	2-1
28 Apr 1993	Bulgaria vs Finland	2-0
12 May 1993	Bulgaria vs Israel	2-2
13 May 1993	Finland vs Austria	3-1
19 May 1993	Sweden vs Austria	1-0
2 Jun 1993	Sweden vs Israel	5-0
16 Jun 1993	Finland vs Israel	0-0
22 Aug 1993	Sweden vs France	1-1
25 Aug 1993	Austria vs Finland	3-0
8 Sep 1993	Finland vs France	0-2
8 Sep 1993	Bulgaria vs Sweden	1-1
13 Oct 1993	France vs Israel	2-3
13 Oct 1993	Bulgaria vs Austria	4-1
13 Oct 1993	Sweden vs Finland	3-2
27 Oct 1993	Israel vs Austria	1-1
10 Nov 1993	Austria vs Sweden	1-1
10 Nov 1993	Israel vs Finland	1-3
17 Nov 1993	France vs Bulgaria	1-2

	P	W	D	L	F	A	Pts
Sweden	10	6	3	1	19	8	15
Bulgaria	10	6	2	2	19	10	14
France	10	6	1	3	17	10	13
Austria	10	3	2	5	15	16	8
Finland	10	2	1	7	9	18	5
Israel	10	1	3	6	10	27	5

Sweden & Bulgaria qualified for Finals

AFRICA

ROUND ONE
GROUP A

9 Oct 1992	Algeria vs Burundi	3-1
25 Oct 1992	Burundi vs Ghana	1-0
20 Dec 1992	Ghana vs Algeria	2-0
17 Jan 1993	Burundi vs Algeria	0-0
31 Jan 1993	Ghana vs Burundi	1-0
26 Feb 1993	Algeria vs Ghana	2-1

Uganda withdrew

	P	W	D	L	F	A	Pts
Algeria	4	2	1	1	5	4	5
Ghana	4	2	0	2	4	3	4
Burundi	4	1	1	2	2	4	3

Algeria qualified for 2nd Round

GROUP B

18 Oct 1992	Cameroon vs Swaziland	5-0
25 Oct 1992	Swaziland vs Zaire	1-0
10 Jan 1993	Zaire vs Cameroon	1-2
17 Jan 1993	Swaziland vs Cameroon	0-0
29 Feb 1993	Cameroon vs Zaire	0-0

Zaire vs Swaziland was not played
Liberia withdrew

	P	W	D	L	F	A	Pts
Cameroon	4	2	2	0	7	1	6
Swaziland	3	1	1	1	1	5	3
Zaire	3	0	1	2	1	3	1

Cameroon qualified for 2nd Round

GROUP C

11 Oct 1992	Egypt vs Angola	1-0
11 Oct 1992	Zimbabwe vs Togo	1-0
25 Oct 1992	Togo vs Egypt	1-4
20 Dec 1992	Zimbabwe vs Egypt	2-1
10 Jan 1993	Angola vs Zimbabwe	1-1
17 Jan 1993	Togo vs Zimbabwe	1-2
18 Jan 1993	Angola vs Egypt	0-0
31 Jan 1993	Egypt vs Togo	3-0
31 Jan 1993	Zimbabwe vs Angola	2-1
28 Feb 1993	Egypt vs Zimbabwe	2-1

Result declared void after a protest

Replay (in Lyons)

15 Apr 1993	Egypt vs Zimbabwe	0-0
28 Feb 1993	Togo vs Angola	0-1

Angola vs Togo was not played
Sierra Leone withdrew and were replaced by Togo

	P	W	D	L	F	A	Pts
Zimbabwe	6	4	2	0	8	4	10
Egypt	6	3	2	1	9	3	8
Angola	5	1	2	2	3	4	4
Togo	5	0	0	5	2	11	0

Zimbabwe qualified for 2nd Round

GROUP D

10 Oct 1992	Nigeria vs South Africa	4-0
25 Oct 1992	South Africa vs Congo	1-0

20 Dec 1992	Congo vs Nigeria	0-1
17 Jan 1993	South Africa vs Nigeria	0-0
31 Jan 1993	Congo vs South Africa	0-1
27 Feb 1993	Nigeria vs Congo	2-0

Sao Tome e Principe withdrew
Libya withdrew

	P	W	D	L	F	A	Pts
Nigeria	4	3	1	0	7	0	7
South Africa	4	2	1	1	2	4	5
Congo	4	0	0	4	0	5	0

Nigeria qualified for 2nd Round

GROUP E

11 Oct 1992	Ivory Coast vs Botswana	6-0
11 Oct 1992	Niger vs Ivory Coast	0-0
20 Dec 1992	Botswana vs Niger	0-1
17 Jan 1993	Botswana vs Ivory Coast	0-0
31 Jan 1993	Ivory Coast vs Niger	1-0
28 Feb 1993	Niger vs Botswana	2-1

Sudan withdrew

	P	W	D	L	F	A	Pts
Ivory Coast	4	2	2	0	7	0	6
Niger	4	2	1	1	3	2	5
Botswana	4	0	1	3	1	9	1

Ivory Coast qualified for 2nd Round

GROUP F

11 Oct 1992	Morocco vs Ethiopia	5-0
11 Oct 1992	Tunisia vs Benin	5-1
25 Oct 1992	Ethiopia vs Tunisia	0-0
25 Oct 1992	Benin vs Morocco	0-1
20 Dec 1992	Tunisia vs Morocco	1-1
20 Dec 1992	Ethiopia vs Benin	3-1
17 Jan 1993	Ethiopia vs Morocco	0-1
17 Jan 1993	Benin vs Tunisia	0-5
31 Jan 1993	Tunisia vs Ethiopia	3-0
31 Jan 1993	Morocco vs Benin	5-0
28 Feb 1993	Benin vs Ethiopia	1-0
28 Feb 1993	Morocco vs Tunisia	0-0

Malawi withdrew and were replaced by Benin

	P	W	D	L	F	A	Pts
Morocco	6	4	2	0	13	1	10
Tunisia	6	3	3	0	14	2	9
Ethiopia	6	1	1	4	3	11	3
Benin	6	1	0	5	3	19	2

Morocco qualified for 2nd Round

GROUP G

11 Oct 1992	Gabon vs Mozambique	3-1
25 Oct 1992	Mozambique vs Senegal	0-1
19 Dec 1992	Gabon vs Senegal	3-2
17 Feb 1993	Mozambique vs Gabon	1-1
30 Jan 1993	Senegal vs Mozambique	6-1
27 Feb 1993	Senegal vs Gabon	1-0

Mauritania withdrew

	P	W	D	L	F	A	Pts
Senegal	4	3	0	1	10	4	6
Gabon	4	2	1	1	7	5	5
Mozambique	4	0	1	3	3	11	1

Senegal qualified for 2nd Round

GROUP H

11 Jan 1992	Madagascar vs Namibia	3-0
25 Oct 1992	Namibia vs Zambia	0-4
20 Dec 1992	Madagascar vs Zambia	2-0
17 Jan 1993	Namibia vs Madagascar	0-1
30 Jan 1993	Zambia vs Namibia	4-0
27 Feb 1993	Zambia vs Madagascar	3-1

Burkina Faso withdrew and were replaced by Namibia
Tanzania also withdrew

	P	W	D	L	F	A	Pts
Zambia	4	3	0	1	11	3	6
Madagascar	4	3	0	1	7	3	6
Namibia	4	0	0	4	0	12	0

Zambia qualified for 2nd Round

GROUP I

20 Dec 1992	Guinea vs Kenya	4-0
27 Feb 1993	Kenya vs Guinea	2-0

Gambia withdrew
Mali withdrew

	P	W	D	L	F	A	Pts
Guinea	2	1	0	1	4	2	2
Kenya	2	1	0	1	2	4	2

Guinea qualified for 2nd Round

ROUND TWO

GROUP A

16 Apr 1993	Algeria vs Ivory Coast	1-1
2 May 1993	Ivory Coast vs Nigeria	2-1
3 Jul 1993	Nigeria vs Algeria	4-1
18 Jul 1993	Ivory Coast vs Algeria	1-0
25 Sep 1993	Nigeria vs Ivory Coast	4-1
8 Oct 1993	Algeria vs Nigeria	1-1

	P	W	D	L	F	A	Pts
Nigeria	4	2	1	1	10	5	5
Ivory Coast	4	2	1	1	5	6	5
Algeria	4	0	2	2	3	7	2

Nigeria qualified for Finals

GROUP B

18 Apr 1993	Morocco vs Senegal	1-0
4 Jul 1993	Zambia vs Morocco	2-1
17 Jul 1993	Senegal vs Morocco	1-3
7 Aug 1993	Senegal vs Zambia	0-0
26 Sep 1993	Zambia vs Senegal	4-0
10 Oct 1993	Morocco vs Zambia	1-0

	P	W	D	L	F	A	Pts
Morocco	4	3	0	1	6	3	6
Zambia	4	2	1	1	6	2	5
Senegal	4	0	1	3	1	8	1

Morocco qualified for Finals

GROUP C

18 Apr 1993	Cameroon vs Guinea	3-1
2 May 1993	Guinea vs Zimbabwe	3-0
4 Jul 1993	Zimbabwe vs Cameroon	1-0
18 Jul 1993	Guinea vs Cameroon	0-1
26 Sep 1993	Zimbabwe vs Guniea	1-0
10 Oct 1993	Cameroon vs Zimbabwe	3-1

	P	W	D	L	F	A	Pts
Cameroon	4	3	0	1	7	3	6
Zimbabwe	4	2	0	2	3	6	4
Guinea	4	1	0	3	4	5	2

Cameroon qualified for Finals

CONCACAF

PRE-PRELIMINARY ROUND

CARIBBEAN REGION – NORTH

| 21 Mar 1992 | Dominican Republic vs Puerto Rico | 1-2 |
| 29 Mar 1992 | Puerto Rico vs Dominican Republic | 1-1 |

Puerto Rico qualified for Preliminary Round

| 22 Mar 1992 | St. Lucia vs St. Vincent | 1-0 |
| 29 Mar 1992 | St. Vincent vs St. Lucia | 3-1 |

St. Vincent qualified for Preliminary Round

PRELIMINARY ROUND

CARIBBEAN REGION – NORTH

| 26 Apr 1992 | Bermuda vs Haiti | 1-0 |
| 25 May 1992 | Haiti vs Bermuda | 2-1 |

Bermuda qualified for 1st Round

| 25 May 1992 | Jamaica vs Puerto Rico | 2-1 |
| 30 May 1992 | Puerto Rico vs Jamaica | 0-1 |

Jamaica qualified for 1st Round

Cuba vs St. Vincent – Cuba withdrew

St. Vincent qualified for 1st Round

CARIBBEAN REGION – SOUTH

| 19 Apr 1992 | Netherlands Antilles vs Antigua | 1-1 |
| 26 Apr 1992 | Antigua vs Netherlands Antilles | 3-0 |

Antigua qualified for 1st Round

| 26 Apr 1992 | Guyana vs Surinam | 1-2 |
| 25 May 1992 | Surinam vs Guyana | 1-1 |

Surinam qualified for 1st Round

| 24 May 1992 | Barbados vs Trinidad & Tobago | 1-2 |
| 31 May 1992 | Trinidad & Tobago vs Barbados | 3-0 |

Trinidad & Tobago qualified for 1st Round

ROUND ONE

CENTRAL REGION

| 19 Jul 1992 | Guatemala vs Honduras | 0-0 |
| 26 Jul 1992 | Honduras vs Guatemala | 2-0 |

Honduras qualified for 2nd Round

| 19 Jul 1992 | Nicaragua vs El Salvador | 0-5 |
| 23 Jul 1992 | El Salvador vs Nicaragua | 5-1 |

El Salvador qualified for 2nd Round

| 16 Aug 1992 | Panama vs Costa Rica | 1-0 |
| 23 Aug 1992 | Costa Rica vs Panama | 5-1 |

Costa Rica qualified for 2nd Round

CARIBBEAN REGION

| 14 Jun 1992 | Antigua vs Bermuda | 0-3 |
| 4 Jul 1992 | Bermuda vs Antigua | 2-1 |

Bermuda qualified for 2nd Round

| 5 Jul 1992 | Trinidad & Tobago vs Jamaica | 1-2 |
| 16 Aug 1992 | Jamaica vs Trinidad & Tobago | 1-1 |

Jamaica qualified for 2nd Round

| 2 Aug 1992 | Surinam vs St. Vincent | 0-0 |
| 30 Aug 1992 | St. Vincent vs Surinam | 2-1 |

St. Vincent qualified for 2nd Round

ROUND TWO

GROUP A

8 Nov 1992	Costa Rica vs Honduras	2-3
8 Nov 1992	St. Vincent vs Mexico	0-4
15 Nov 1992	Mexico vs Honduras	2-0
15 Nov 1992	St. Vincent vs Costa Rica	0-1
22 Nov 1992	Mexico vs Costa Rica	4-0
22 Nov 1992	St. Vincent vs Honduras	0-4
28 Nov 1992	Honduras vs St. Vincent	4-0
29 Nov 1992	Costa Rica vs Mexico	2-0
5 Dec 1992	Honduras vs Costa Rica	2-1
6 Dec 1992	Mexico vs St. Vincent	11-0
13 Dec 1992	Costa Rica vs St. Vincent	5-0
13 Dec 1992	Honduras vs Mexico	1-1

	P	W	D	L	F	A	Pts
Mexico	6	4	1	1	22	3	9
Honduras	6	4	1	1	14	6	9
Costa Rica	6	3	0	3	11	9	6
St. Vincent	6	0	0	6	0	29	0

Mexico & Honduras qualified for Final Round

GROUP B

18 Oct 1992	Jamaica vs Canada	1-1
18 Oct 1992	Bermuda vs El Salvador	1-0
25 Oct 1992	El Salvador vs Canada	1-1
25 Oct 1992	Bermuda vs Jamaica	1-1
1 Nov 1992	Canada vs Jamaica	1-0
1 Nov 1992	El Salvador vs Bermuda	4-1
8 Nov 1992	Canada vs El Salvador	2-3
8 Nov 1992	Jamaica vs Bermuda	3-2
15 Nov 1992	Canada vs Bermuda	4-2
22 Nov 1992	Jamaica vs El Salvador	0-2
6 Dec 1992	Bermuda vs Canada	0-0
6 Dec 1992	El Salvador vs Jamaica	2-1

	P	W	D	L	F	A	Pts
El Salvador	6	4	1	1	12	6	9
Canada	6	2	3	1	9	7	7
Jamaica	6	1	2	3	6	9	4
Bermuda	6	1	2	3	7	12	4

El Salvador & Canada qualified for Final Round

FINAL ROUND

4 Apr 1993	El Salvador vs Mexico	2-1
4 Apr 1993	Honduras vs Canada	2-2
11 Apr 1993	Mexico vs Honduras	3-0
11 Apr 1993	Canada vs El Salvador	2-0
18 Apr 1993	Canada vs Honduras	3-1
18 Apr 1993	Mexico vs El Salvador	3-1
25 Apr 1993	Mexico vs Canada	4-0
25 Apr 1993	Honduras vs El Salvador	2-0
2 May 1993	Honduras vs Mexico	1-4
2 May 1993	El Salvador vs Canada	1-2
9 May 1993	Canada vs Mexico	1-2
9 May 1993	El Salvador vs Honduras	2-1

	P	W	D	L	F	A	Pts
Mexico	6	5	0	1	17	5	10
Canada	6	3	1	2	10	10	7
El Salvador	6	2	0	4	6	11	4
Honduras	6	1	1	4	7	14	3

Mexico qualified for Finals

Canada qualified for Play-off with Australia

Play-off

31 Jul 1993	Canada vs Australia	2-1
15 Aug 1993	Australia vs Canada	2-1

Australia won 4-1 on penalties & qualified for Play-off with Argentina.

SOUTH AMERICA

GROUP A

1 Aug 1993	Colombia vs Paraguay	0-0
1 Aug 1993	Peru vs Argentina	0-1
8 Aug 1993	Paraguay vs Argentina	1-3
8 Aug 1993	Peru vs Colombia	0-1
15 Aug 1993	Colombia vs Argentina	2-1
15 Aug 1993	Paraguay vs Peru	2-1
22 Aug 1993	Argentina vs Peru	2-1
22 Aug 1993	Paraguay vs Colombia	1-1
29 Aug 1993	Argentina vs Paraguay	0-0
29 Aug 1993	Colombia vs Peru	4-0
5 Sep 1993	Argentina vs Colombia	0-5
5 Sep 1993	Peru vs Paraguay	2-2

	P	W	D	L	F	A	Pts
Colombia	6	4	2	0	13	2	10
Argentina	6	3	1	2	7	9	7
Paraguay	6	1	4	1	6	7	6
Peru	6	0	1	5	4	12	1

Colombia qualified for Finals

Argentina qualified for Play-off with Australia

GROUP B

18 Jul 1993	Ecuador vs Brazil	0-0
18 Jul 1993	Venezuela vs Bolivia	1-7
25 Jul 1993	Bolivia vs Brazil	2-0
25 Jul 1993	Venezuela vs Uruguay	0-1
1 Aug 1993	Uruguay vs Ecuador	0-0
1 Aug 1993	Venezuela vs Brazil	1-5
8 Aug 1993	Bolivia vs Uruguay	3-1

8 Aug 1993	Ecuador vs Venezuela	5-0
15 Aug 1993	Bolivia vs Ecuador	1-0
15 Aug 1993	Uruguay vs Brazil	1-1
22 Aug 1993	Bolivia vs Venezuela	7-0
22 Aug 1993	Brazil vs Ecuador	2-0
29 Aug 1993	Brazil vs Bolivia	6-0
29 Aug 1993	Uruguay vs Venezuela	4-0
5 Sep 1993	Brazil vs Venezuela	4-0
5 Sep 1993	Ecuador vs Uruguay	0-1
12 Sep 1993	Uruguay vs Bolivia	2-1
12 Sep 1993	Venezuela vs Ecuador	2-1
19 Sep 1993	Brazil vs Uruguay	2-0
19 Sep 1993	Ecuador vs Bolivia	1-1

	P	W	D	L	F	A	Pts
Brazil	8	5	2	1	20	4	12
Bolivia	8	5	1	2	22	11	11
Uruguay	8	4	2	2	10	7	10
Ecuador	8	1	3	4	7	7	5
Venezuela	8	1	0	7	4	34	2

Brazil and Bolivia qualified for Finals

Play-off

31 Oct 1993	Australia vs Argentina	1-1
17 Nov 1993	Argentina vs Australia	1-0

Argentina won 2-1 on aggregate & qualified for Finals

OCEANIA

GROUP 1

11 Jul 1992	Solomon Islands vs Tahiti	1-1
4 Sep 1992	Solomon Islands vs Australia	1-2
11 Sep 1992	Tahiti vs Australia	0-3
20 Sep 1992	Australia vs Tahiti	2-0
25 Sep 1992	Australia vs Solomon Islands	6-1
9 Oct 1992	Tahiti vs Solomon Islands	4-2

	P	W	D	L	F	A	Pts
Australia	4	4	0	0	13	2	8
Tahiti	4	1	1	2	5	8	3
Solomon Islands	4	0	1	3	5	13	1

Australia qualified for Final play-off

GROUP 2

7 Jun 1992	New Zealand vs Fiji	3-0
27 Jun 1992	Vanuatu vs New Zealand	1-4
1 Jul 1992	New Zealand vs Vanuatu	8-0
12 Sep 1992	Fiji vs Vanuatu	3-0
19 Sep 1992	Fiji vs New Zealand	0-0
26 Sep 1992	Vanuatu vs Fiji	0-3

	P	W	D	L	F	A	Pts
New Zealand	4	3	1	0	15	1	7
Fiji	4	2	1	1	6	3	5
Vanuatu	4	0	0	4	1	18	0

New Zealand qualified for Final play-off

Play-off

30 May 1993	New Zealand vs Australia	0-1
6 Jun 1993	Australia vs New Zealand	3-0

Australia won 4-0 on aggregate and met Canada in a play-off

ASIA

ROUND ONE

GROUP A

Following matches all played in Amman, Jordan

22 May 1993	Jordan vs Yemen	1-1
22 May 1993	Pakistan vs China	0-5
24 May 1993	Jordan vs Iraq	1-1
24 May 1993	Yemen vs Pakistan	5-1
26 May 1993	Jordan vs China	0-3
26 May 1993	Yemen vs Iraq	1-6
28 May 1993	Pakistan vs Iraq	0-8
28 May 1993	Yemen vs China	1-0
30 May 1993	Jordan vs Pakistan	3-1
30 May 1993	Iraq vs China	1-0

Following matches all played in Beijing, China

12 Jun 1993	Yemen vs Jordan	1-1
12 Jun 1993	China vs Pakistan	3-0
14 Jun 1993	Iraq vs Jordan	4-0
14 Jun 1993	Pakistan vs Yemen	0-3
16 Jun 1993	China vs Jordan	4-1
16 Jun 1993	Iraq vs Yemen	3-0
18 Jun 1993	Iraq vs Pakistan	4-0
18 Jun 1993	China vs Yemen	1-0
20 Jun 1993	Pakistan vs Jordan	0-5
20 Jun 1993	China vs Iraq	2-1

	P	W	D	L	F	A	Pts
Iraq	8	6	1	1	28	4	13
China	8	6	0	2	18	4	12
Yemen	8	3	2	3	12	13	8
Jordan	8	2	3	3	12	15	7
Pakistan	8	0	0	8	2	36	0

Iraq qualified for 2nd Round

GROUP B

Following matches all played in Tehran, Iran

23 Jun 1993	Iran vs Oman	0-0
23 Jun 1993	Taiwan vs Syria	0-2
25 Jun 1993	Oman vs Syria	0-0
25 Jun 1993	Iran vs Taiwan	6-0
27 Jun 1993	Oman vs Taiwan	2-1
27 Jun 1993	Iran vs Syria	1-1

Following matches all played in Damascus, Syria

2 Jul 1993	Oman vs Iran	0-1
2 Jul 1993	Syria vs Taiwan	8-1
4 Jul 1993	Syria vs Oman	2-1
4 Jul 1993	Taiwan vs Iran	0-6
6 Jul 1993	Taiwan vs Oman	1-7
6 Jul 1993	Syria vs Iran	1-1

Myanmar (formerly Burma) withdrew

	P	W	D	L	F	A	Pts
Iran	6	3	3	0	15	2	9
Syria	6	3	3	0	14	4	9
Oman	6	2	2	2	10	5	6
Taiwan	6	0	0	6	3	31	0

Iran qualified for 2nd Round

GROUP C

Following matches all played in Doha, Qatar

9 Apr 1993	Qatar vs Indonesia	3-1
9 Apr 1993	North Korea vs Vietnam	3-0
11 Apr 1993	North Korea vs Singapore	2-1
11 Apr 1993	Qatar vs Vietnam	4-0
13 Apr 1993	North Korea vs Indonesia	4-0
13 Apr 1993	Vietnam vs Singapore	2-3
16 Apr 1993	Qatar vs Singapore	4-1
16 Apr 1993	Vietnam vs Indonesia	1-0
18 Apr 1993	Indonesia vs Singapore	0-2
18 Apr 1993	Qatar vs North Korea	1-2

Following matches all played in Singapore

24 Apr 1993	Indonesia vs Qatar	1-4
24 Apr 1993	Vietnam vs North Korea	0-1
26 Apr 1993	Singapore vs North Korea	1-3
26 Apr 1993	Vietnam vs Qatar	0-4
28 Apr 1993	Indonesia vs North Korea	1-2
28 Apr 1993	Singapore vs Vietnam	1-0
30 Apr 1993	Singapore vs Qatar	1-0
30 Apr 1993	Indonesia vs Vietnam	2-1
2 May 1993	Singapore vs Indonesia	2-1
2 May 1993	North Korea vs Qatar	2-2

	P	W	D	L	F	A	Pts
North Korea	8	7	1	0	19	6	15
Qatar	8	5	1	2	22	8	11
Singapore	8	5	0	3	12	12	10
Indonesia	8	1	0	7	6	19	2
Vietnam	8	1	0	7	4	18	2

North Korea qualified for 2nd Round

GROUP D

Following matches all played in Beirut, Lebanon

7 May 1993	Lebanon vs India	2-2
7 May 1993	Hong Kong vs Bahrain	2-1
9 May 1993	Bahrain vs South Korea	0-0
9 May 1993	Lebanon vs Hong Kong	2-2
11 May 1993	India vs Hong Kong	1-2
11 May 1993	Lebanon vs South Korea	0-1
13 May 1993	Lebanon vs Bahrain	0-0
13 May 1993	India vs South Korea	0-3
15 May 1993	Hong Kong vs South Korea	0-3
15 May 1993	Bahrain vs India	2-1

Following matches all played in Seoul, South Korea

5 Jun 1993	South Korea vs Hong Kong	3-0
5 Jun 1993	Bahrain vs Lebanon	0-0
7 Jun 1993	India vs Bahrain	0-3
7 Jun 1993	South Korea vs Lebanon	2-0
9 Jun 1993	Hong Kong vs Lebanon	1-2
9 Jun 1993	South Korea vs India	7-0
11 Jun 1993	India vs Lebanon	1-2
11 Jun 1993	Bahrain vs Hong Kong	3-0
13 Jun 1993	South Korea vs Bahrain	3-0
13 Jun 1993	Hong Kong vs India	1-3

	P	W	D	L	F	A	Pts
South Korea	8	7	1	0	22	6	15
Bahrain	8	3	3	2	9	6	9
Lebanon	8	2	4	2	8	9	8
Hong Kong	8	2	1	5	8	18	5

India	8	1	1	6	8	22	3

South Korea qualified for 2nd Round

GROUP E

Following matches all played in Kuala Lumpur, Malaysia

1 May 1993	Saudi Arabia vs Macao 6-0
1 May 1993	Malaysia vs Kuwait 1-1
3 May 1993	Kuwait vs Macao 10-1
3 May 1993	Malaysia vs Saudi Arabia 1-1
5 May 1993	Saudi Arabia vs Kuwait 0-0
5 May 1993	Malaysia vs Macao 9-0

Following matches all played in Riyadh, Saudi Arabia

14 May 1993	Malaysia vs Kuwait 0-2
14 May 1993	Saudi Arabia vs Macao 8-0
16 May 1993	Macao vs Kuwait 0-8
16 May 1993	Saudi Arabia vs Malaysia 3-0
18 May 1993	Malaysia vs Macao 5-0
18 May 1993	Saudi Arabia vs Kuwait 2-0

	P	W	D	L	F	A	Pts
Saudi Arabia	6	4	2	0	20	1	10
Kuwait	6	3	2	1	21	4	8
Malaysia	6	2	2	2	16	7	6
Macao	6	0	0	6	1	46	0

Saudi Arabia qualified for 2nd Round

GROUP F

Following matches all played in Tokyo, Japan

8 Apr 1993	Japan vs Thailand 1-0
8 Apr 1993	Sri Lanka vs United Arab Emirates 0-4
11 Apr 1993	Japan vs Bangladesh 8-0
11 Apr 1993	Thailand vs Sri Lanka 1-0
13 Apr 1993	Sri Lanka vs Bangladesh 0-1
13 Apr 1993	United Arab Emirates vs Thailand 1-0
15 Apr 1993	Japan vs Sri Lanka 5-0
15 Apr 1993	United Arab Emirates vs Bangladesh 1-0
18 Apr 1993	Japan vs United Arab Emirates 2-0
18 Apr 1993	Thailand vs Bangladesh 4-1

Following matches all played in Dubai, United Arab Emirates

28 Apr 1993	Thailand vs Japan 0-1
28 Apr 1993	United Arab Emirates vs Sri Lanka 3-0
30 Apr 1993	Bangladesh vs Japan 1-4
30 Apr 1993	Thailand vs United Arab Emirates 1-2
3 May 1993	Bangladesh vs United Arab Emirates 0-7
3 May 1993	Sri Lanka vs Thailand 0-3
5 May 1993	Bangladesh vs Thailand 1-4
5 May 1993	Sri Lanka vs Japan 0-6
7 May 1993	Bangladesh vs Sri Lanka 3-0
7 May 1993	United Arab Emirates vs Japan 1-1

	P	W	D	L	F	A	Pts
Japan	8	7	1	0	28	2	15
United Arab Emirates	8	6	1	1	19	4	13
Thailand	8	4	0	4	13	7	8
Bangladesh	8	2	0	6	7	28	4
Sri Lanka	8	0	0	8	0	26	0

Japan qualified for 2nd Round

ROUND TWO

Following matches all played in Doha, Qatar

15 Oct 1993	North Korea vs Iraq 3-2
15 Oct 1993	Saudi Arabia vs Japan 0-0
16 Oct 1993	Iran vs South Korea 0-3
18 Oct 1993	North Korea vs Saudi Arabia 1-2
18 Oct 1993	Japan vs Iran 1-2
19 Oct 1993	Iraq vs South Korea 2-2
21 Oct 1993	North Korea vs Japan 0-3
22 Oct 1993	Iran vs Iraq 1-2
22 Oct 1993	South Korea vs Saudi Arabia 1-1
24 Oct 1993	Iraq vs Saudi Arabia 1-1
25 Oct 1993	Japan vs South Korea 1-0
25 Oct 1993	Iran vs North Korea 2-1
28 Oct 1993	South Korea vs North Korea 3-0
28 Oct 1993	Saudi Arabia vs Iran 4-3
28 Oct 1993	Iraq vs Japan 2-2

	P	W	D	L	F	A	Pts
Saudi Arabia	5	2	3	0	8	6	7
South Korea	5	2	2	1	9	4	6
Japan	5	2	2	1	7	4	6
Iraq	5	1	3	1	9	9	5
Iran	5	2	0	3	8	11	4
North Korea	5	1	0	4	5	12	2

Saudi Arabia & South Korea qualified for Finals

1998 – QUALIFYING COMPETITION

EUROPE

GROUP 1

24 Apr 1996	Greece vs Slovenia 2-0
1 Sep 1996	Greece vs Bosnia 3-0
1 Sep 1996	Slovenia vs Denmark 0-2
8 Oct 1996	Bosnia vs Croatia 1-4
9 Oct 1996	Denmark vs Greece 2-1
10 Nov 1996	Slovenia vs Bosnia 1-2
10 Nov 1996	Croatia vs Greece 1-1
29 Mar 1997	Croatia vs Denmark 1-1
2 Apr 1997	Croatia vs Slovenia 3-3
2 Apr 1997	Bosnia vs Greece 0-1
30 Apr 1997	Denmark vs Slovenia 4-0
30 Apr 1997	Greece vs Croatia 0-1
8 Jun 1997	Denmark vs Bosnia 2-0
20 Aug 1997	Bosnia vs Denmark 3-0
6 Sep 1997	Croatia vs Bosnia 3-2
6 Sep 1997	Slovenia vs Greece 0-3
10 Sep 1997	Denmark vs Croatia 3-1
10 Sep 1997	Bosnia vs Slovenia 1-0
11 Oct 1997	Greece vs Denmark 0-0
11 Oct 1997	Slovenia vs Croatia 1-3

	P	W	D	L	F	A	Pts
Denmark	8	5	2	1	14	6	17
Croatia	8	4	3	1	17	12	15
Greece	8	4	2	2	11	4	14
Bosnia-Herzegovina	8	3	0	5	9	14	9
Slovenia	8	0	1	7	5	20	1

Denmark qualified for Finals

Croatia qualified for Play-offs

215

GROUP 2

1 Sep 1996	Moldova vs England	0-3
5 Oct 1996	Moldova vs Italy	1-3
9 Oct 1996	England vs Poland	2-1
9 Oct 1996	Italy vs Georgia	1-0
9 Nov 1996	Georgia vs England	0-2
10 Nov 1996	Poland vs Moldova	2-1
12 Feb 1997	England vs Italy	0-1
29 Mar 1997	Italy vs Moldova	3-0
2 Apr 1997	Poland vs Italy	0-0
30 Apr 1997	England vs Georgia	2-0
30 Apr 1997	Italy vs Poland	3-0
31 May 1997	Poland vs England	0-2
7 Jun 1997	Georgia vs Moldova	2-0
14 Jun 1997	Poland vs Georgia	4-1
10 Sep 1997	England vs Moldova	4-0
10 Sep 1997	Georgia vs Italy	0-0
29 Sep 1997	Moldova vs Georgia	0-1
7 Oct 1997	Moldova vs Poland	0-3
11 Oct 1997	Italy vs England	0-0
11 Oct 1997	Georgia vs Poland	3-0

	P	W	D	L	F	A	Pts
England	8	6	1	1	15	2	19
Italy	8	5	3	0	11	1	18
Poland	8	3	1	4	10	12	10
Georgia	8	3	1	4	7	9	10
Moldova	8	0	0	8	2	21	0

England qualified for Finals

Italy qualified for Play-offs

GROUP 3

2 Jun 1996	Norway vs Azerbaijan	5-0
31 Aug 1996	Azerbaijan vs Switzerland	1-0
1 Sep 1996	Hungary vs Finland	1-0
6 Oct 1996	Finland vs Switzerland	2-3
9 Oct 1996	Norway vs Hungary	3-0
10 Nov 1996	Switzerland vs Norway	0-1
10 Nov 1996	Azerbaijan vs Hungary	0-3
2 Apr 1997	Azerbaijan vs Finland	1-2
30 Apr 1997	Norway vs Finland	1-1
30 Apr 1997	Switzerland vs Hungary	1-0
8 Jun 1997	Finland vs Azerbaijan	3-0
8 Jun 1997	Hungary vs Norway	1-1
20 Aug 1997	Finland vs Norway	0-4
20 Aug 1997	Hungary vs Switzerland	1-1
6 Sep 1997	Switzerland vs Finland	1-2
6 Sep 1997	Azerbaijan vs Norway	0-1
10 Sep 1997	Hungary vs Azerbaijan	3-1
10 Sep 1997	Norway vs Switzerland	5-0
11 Oct 1997	Finland vs Hungary	1-1
11 Oct 1997	Switzerland vs Azerbaijan	5-0

	P	W	D	L	F	A	Pts
Norway	8	6	2	0	21	2	20
Hungary	8	3	3	2	10	8	12
Finland	8	3	2	3	11	12	11
Switzerland	8	3	1	4	11	12	10
Azerbaijan	8	1	0	7	3	22	3

Norway qualified for Finals

Hungary qualified for Play-offs

GROUP 4

1 Jun 1996	Sweden vs Belarus	5-1
31 Aug 1996	Austria vs Scotland	0-0
31 Aug 1996	Belarus vs Estonia	1-0
1 Sep 1996	Latvia vs Sweden	1-2
5 Oct 1996	Estonia vs Belarus	1-0
5 Oct 1996	Latvia vs Scotland	0-2
9 Oct 1996	Sweden vs Austria	0-1
9 Oct 1996	Estonia vs Scotland	Postponed
9 Oct 1996	Belarus vs Latvia	1-1
9 Nov 1996	Austria vs Latvia	2-1
10 Nov 1996	Scotland vs Sweden	1-0
11 Feb 1997	Estonia vs Scotland	0-0
29 Mar 1997	Scotland vs Estonia	2-0
2 Apr 1997	Scotland vs Austria	2-0
30 Apr 1997	Austria vs Estonia	2-0
30 Apr 1997	Sweden vs Scotland	2-1
30 Apr 1997	Latvia vs Belarus	2-0
18 May 1997	Estonia vs Latvia	1-3
8 Jun 1997	Estonia vs Sweden	2-3
8 Jun 1997	Latvia vs Austria	1-3
8 Jun 1997	Belarus vs Scotland	0-1
20 Aug 1997	Estonia vs Austria	0-3
20 Aug 1997	Belarus vs Sweden	1-2
6 Sep 1997	Austria vs Sweden	1-0
6 Sep 1997	Latvia vs Estonia	1-0
7 Sep 1997	Scotland vs Belarus	4-1
10 Sep 1997	Sweden vs Latvia	1-0
10 Sep 1997	Belarus vs Austria	0-1
11 Oct 1997	Austria vs Belarus	4-0
11 Oct 1997	Scotland vs Latvia	2-0
11 Oct 1997	Sweden vs Estonia	1-0

	P	W	D	L	F	A	Pts
Austria	10	8	1	1	17	4	25
Scotland	10	7	2	1	15	3	23
Sweden	10	7	0	3	16	9	21
Latvia	10	3	1	6	10	14	10
Estonia	10	1	1	8	4	16	4
Belarus	10	1	1	8	5	21	4

Austria qualified for Finals

Scotland qualified for Finals as Best runner-up

GROUP 5

1 Sep 1996	Israel vs Bulgaria	2-1
1 Sep 1996	Russia vs Cyprus	4-0
8 Oct 1996	Luxembourg vs Bulgaria	1-2
9 Oct 1996	Israel vs Russia	1-1
10 Nov 1996	Cyprus vs Israel	2-0
10 Nov 1996	Luxembourg vs Russia	0-4
14 Dec 1996	Cyprus vs Bulgaria	1-3
15 Dec 1996	Israel vs Luxembourg	1-0
29 Mar 1997	Cyprus vs Russia	1-1
30 Mar 1997	Luxembourg vs Israel	0-3
2 Apr 1997	Bulgaria vs Cyprus	4-1
30 Apr 1997	Israel vs Cyprus	2-0
30 Apr 1997	Russia vs Luxembourg	3-0
8 Jun 1997	Bulgaria vs Luxembourg	4-0
8 Jun 1997	Russia vs Israel	2-0
20 Aug 1997	Bulgaria vs Israel	1-0
7 Sep 1997	Luxembourg vs Cyprus	1-3
10 Sep 1997	Bulgaria vs Russia	1-0

| 11 Oct 1997 | Cyprus vs Luxembourg | 2-0 |
| 11 Oct 1997 | Russia vs Bulgaria | 4-2 |

	P	W	D	L	F	A	Pts
Bulgaria	8	6	0	2	18	9	18
Russia	8	5	2	1	19	5	17
Israel	8	4	1	3	9	7	13
Cyprus	8	3	1	4	10	15	10
Luxembourg	8	0	0	8	2	22	0

Bulgaria qualified for Finals
Russia qualified for Play-offs

GROUP 6

24 Apr 1996	Yugoslavia vs Faroe Islands	3-1
2 Jun 1996	Yugoslavia vs Malta	6-0
31 Aug 1996	Faroe Islands vs Slovakia	1-2
4 Sep 1996	Faroe Islands vs Spain	2-6
18 Sep 1996	Czech Republic vs Malta	6-0
22 Sep 1996	Slovakia vs Malta	6-0
6 Oct 1996	Faroe Islands vs Yugoslavia	1-8
9 Oct 1996	Czech Republic vs Spain	0-0
23 Oct 1996	Slovakia vs Faroe Islands	3-0
10 Nov 1996	Yugoslavia vs Czech Republic	1-0
13 Nov 1996	Spain vs Slovakia	4-1
14 Dec 1996	Spain vs Yugoslavia	2-0
18 Dec 1996	Malta vs Spain	0-3
12 Feb 1997	Spain vs Malta	4-0
31 Mar 1997	Malta vs Slovakia	0-2
2 Apr 1997	Czech Republic vs Yugoslavia	1-2
30 Apr 1997	Malta vs Faroe Islands	1-2
30 Apr 1997	Yugoslavia vs Spain	1-1
8 Jun 1997	Spain vs Czech Republic	1-0
8 Jun 1997	Yugoslavia vs Slovakia	2-0
8 Jun 1997	Faroe Islands vs Malta	2-1
20 Aug 1997	Czech Republic vs Faroe Islands	2-0
24 Aug 1997	Slovakia vs Czech Republic	2-1
6 Sep 1997	Faroe Islands vs Czech Republic	0-2
10 Sep 1997	Slovakia vs Yugoslavia	1-1
24 Sep 1997	Malta vs Czech Republic	0-1
24 Sep 1997	Slovakia vs Spain	1-2
11 Oct 1997	Malta vs Yugoslavia	0-5
11 Oct 1997	Spain vs Faroe Islands	3-1
11 Oct 1997	Czech Republic vs Slovakia	3-0

	P	W	D	L	F	A	Pts
Spain	10	8	2	0	26	6	26
Yugoslavia	10	7	2	1	29	7	23
Czech Republic	10	5	1	4	16	6	16
Slovakia	10	5	1	4	18	14	16
Faroe Islands	10	2	0	8	10	31	6
Malta	10	0	0	10	2	37	0

Spain qualified for Finals
Yugoslavia qualified for Play-offs

GROUP 7

2 Jun 1996	San Marino vs Wales	0-5
31 Aug 1996	Belgium vs Turkey	2-1
31 Aug 1996	Wales vs San Marino	6-0
5 Oct 1996	Wales vs Holland	1-3
9 Oct 1996	San Marino vs Belgium	0-3
9 Nov 1996	Holland vs Wales	7-1
10 Nov 1996	Turkey vs San Marino	7-0
14 Dec 1996	Belgium vs Holland	0-3

14 Dec 1996	Wales vs Turkey	0-0
29 Mar 1997	Holland vs San Marino	4-0
29 Mar 1997	Wales vs Belgium	1-2
2 Apr 1997	Turkey vs Holland	1-0
30 Apr 1997	Turkey vs Belgium	1-3
30 Apr 1997	San Marino vs Holland	0-6
7 Jun 1997	Belgium vs San Marino	6-0
20 Aug 1997	Turkey vs Wales	6-4
6 Sep 1997	Holland vs Belgium	3-1
10 Sep 1997	San Marino vs Turkey	0-5
11 Oct 1997	Belgium vs Wales	3-2
11 Oct 1997	Holland vs Turkey	0-0

	P	W	D	L	F	A	Pts
Holland	8	6	1	1	26	4	19
Belgium	8	6	0	2	20	11	18
Turkey	8	4	2	2	21	9	14
Wales	8	2	1	5	20	21	7
San Marino	8	0	0	8	0	42	0

Holland qualified for Finals
Belgium qualified for Play-offs

GROUP 8

24 Apr 1996	Macedonia vs Liechtenstein	3-0
1 Jun 1996	Iceland vs Macedonia	1-1
31 Aug 1996	Liechtenstein vs Eire	0-5
31 Aug 1996	Romania vs Lithuania	3-0
5 Oct 1996	Lithuania vs Iceland	2-0
9 Oct 1996	Iceland vs Romania	0-4
9 Oct 1996	Eire vs Macedonia	3-0
9 Oct 1996	Lithuania vs Liechtenstein	2-1
9 Nov 1996	Liechtenstein vs Macedonia	1-11
10 Nov 1996	Eire vs Iceland	0-0
14 Dec 1996	Macedonia vs Romania	0-3
29 Mar 1997	Romania vs Liechtenstein	8-0
2 Apr 1997	Lithuania vs Romania	0-1
2 Apr 1997	Macedonia vs Eire	3-2
30 Apr 1997	Liechtenstein vs Lithuania	0-2
30 Apr 1997	Romania vs Eire	1-0
21 May 1997	Eire vs Liechtenstein	5-0
7 Jun 1997	Macedonia vs Iceland	1-0
11 Jun 1997	Iceland vs Lithuania	0-0
20 Aug 1997	Liechtenstein vs Iceland	0-4
20 Aug 1997	Eire vs Lithuania	0-0
20 Aug 1997	Romania vs Macedonia	4-2
6 Sep 1997	Iceland vs Eire	2-4
6 Sep 1997	Liechtenstein vs Romania	1-8
6 Sep 1997	Lithuania vs Macedonia	2-0
10 Sep 1997	Romania vs Iceland	4-0
10 Sep 1997	Lithuania vs Eire	1-2
11 Oct 1997	Iceland vs Liechtenstein	4-0
11 Oct 1997	Eire vs Romania	1-1
11 Oct 1997	Macedonia vs Lithuania	1-2

	P	W	D	L	F	A	Pts
Romania	10	9	1	0	37	4	28
Eire	10	5	3	2	22	8	18
Lithuania	10	5	2	3	11	8	17
FYR Macedonia	10	4	1	5	22	18	13
Iceland	10	2	3	5	11	16	9
Liechtenstein	10	0	0	10	3	52	0

Romania qualified for Finals
Eire qualified for Play-offs

GROUP 9

31 Aug 1996	Northern Ireland vs Ukraine	0-1
31 Aug 1996	Armenia vs Portugal	0-0
5 Oct 1996	Northern Ireland vs Armenia	1-1
5 Oct 1996	Ukraine vs Portugal	2-1
9 Oct 1996	Albania vs Portugal	0-3
9 Oct 1996	Armenia vs Germany	1-5
9 Nov 1996	Albania vs Armenia	1-1
9 Nov 1996	Germany vs Northern Ireland	1-1
9 Nov 1996	Portugal vs Ukraine	1-0
14 Dec 1996	Northern Ireland vs Albania	2-0
14 Dec 1996	Portugal vs Germany	0-0
29 Mar 1997	Albania vs Ukraine	0-1
29 Mar 1997	Northern Ireland vs Portugal	0-0
2 Apr 1997	Albania vs Germany	2-3
2 Apr 1997	Ukraine vs Northern Ireland	2-1
30 Apr 1997	Germany vs Ukraine	2-0
30 Apr 1997	Armenia vs Northern Ireland	0-0
7 May 1997	Ukraine vs Armenia	1-1
7 Jun 1997	Portugal vs Albania	2-0
7 Jun 1997	Ukraine vs Germany	0-0
20 Aug 1997	Northern Ireland vs Germany	1-3
20 Aug 1997	Portugal vs Armenia	3-1
20 Aug 1997	Ukraine vs Albania	1-0
6 Sep 1997	Germany vs Portugal	1-1
6 Sep 1997	Armenia vs Albania	3-0
10 Sep 1997	Albania vs Northern Ireland	1-0
10 Sep 1997	Germany vs Armenia	4-0
11 Oct 1997	Germany vs Albania	4-3
11 Oct 1997	Portugal vs Northern Ireland	1-0
11 Oct 1997	Armenia vs Ukraine	0-2

	P	W	D	L	F	A	Pts
Germany	10	6	4	0	23	9	22
Ukraine	10	6	2	2	10	6	20
Portugal	10	5	4	1	12	4	19
Armenia	10	1	5	4	8	17	8
Northern Ireland	10	1	4	5	6	10	7
Albania	10	1	1	8	7	20	4

Germany qualified for Finals

Ukraine qualified for Play-offs

PLAY-OFFS

29 Oct 1997	Russia vs Italy	1-1
29 Oct 1997	Hungary vs Yugoslavia	1-7
29 Oct 1997	Croatia vs Ukraine	2-0
29 Oct 1997	Eire vs Belgium	1-1
15 Nov 1997	Italy vs Russia	1-0

Italy won 2-1 on aggregate

15 Nov 1997	Yugoslavia vs Hungary	5-0

Yugoslavia won 12-1 on aggregate

15 Nov 1997	Ukraine vs Croatia	1-1

Croatia won 3-1 on aggregate

15 Nov 1997	Belgium vs Eire	2-1

Belgium won 3-2 on aggregate

Italy, Yugoslavia, Croatia and Belgium qualified for Finals

OCEANIA

ROUND ONE

MELANESIAN GROUP

16 Sep 1996	Papua New Guinea vs Solomon Islands	1-1
18 Sep 1996	Solomon Islands vs Vanuatu	1-1
20 Sep 1996	Papua New Guinea vs Vanuatu	2-1

	P	W	D	L	F	A	Pts
Papua New Guinea	2	1	1	0	3	2	4
Solomon Islands	2	0	2	0	2	2	2
Vanuatu	2	0	1	1	2	3	1

Papua New Guinea qualified for Round Two

Solomon Islands qualified for Round One Play-off

POLYNESIAN GROUP

11 Nov 1996	Tonga vs Cook Islands	2-0
13 Nov 1996	Western Samoa vs Cook Islands	2-1
15 Nov 1996	Tonga vs Western Samoa	1-0

	P	W	D	L	F	A	Pts
Tonga	2	2	0	0	3	0	6
Western Samoa	2	1	0	1	2	2	3
Cook Islands	2	0	0	2	1	4	0

Tonga qualified for Round One Play-off

ROUND ONE PLAY-OFF

15 Feb 1997	Tonga vs Solomon Islands	0-4
1 Mar 1997	Solomon Islands vs Tonga	9-0

Solomon Islands won 13-0 on aggregate and qualified for Round Two

ROUND TWO

GROUP 1

11 Jun 1997	Australia vs Solomon Islands	13-0
13 Jun 1997	Australia vs Tahiti	5-0
15 Jun 1997	Solomon Islands vs Tahiti	4-1
17 Jun 1997	Solomon Islands vs Australia	2-6
19 Jun 1997	Tahiti vs Australia	0-2
21 Jun 1997	Tahiti vs Solomon Islands	1-1

	P	W	D	L	F	A	Pts
Australia	4	4	0	0	26	2	12
Solomon Islands	4	1	1	2	7	21	4
Tahiti	4	0	1	3	2	12	1

Australia qualified for Round Three Play-off

GROUP 2

31 May 1997	Papua New Guinea vs New Zealand	1-0
7 Jun 1997	Fiji vs New Zealand	0-1
11 Jun 1997	New Zealand vs Papua New Guinea	7-0
15 Jun 1997	Fiji vs Papua New Guinea	3-1
18 Jun 1997	New Zealand vs Fiji	5-0
21 Jun 1997	Papua New Guinea vs Fiji	0-1

	P	W	D	L	F	A	Pts
New Zealand	4	3	0	1	13	1	9
Fiji	4	2	0	2	4	7	6

Papua New Guinea   4 1 0 3 2 11 3
New Zealand qualified for Round Three Play-off

ROUND THREE PLAY-OFF

28 Jun 1997   New Zealand vs Australia 0-3
21 Jun 1997   Australia vs New Zealand 2-0

Australia won 5-0 on aggregate

Australia qualified for Asia-Oceania Play-off

SOUTH AMERICA

ROUND ROBIN GROUP

24 Apr 1996   Argentina vs Bolivia 3-1
24 Apr 1996   Colombia vs Paraguay 1-0
24 Apr 1996   Ecuador vs Peru 4-1
24 Apr 1996   Venezuela vs Uruguay 0-2
2 Jun 1996   Ecuador vs Argentina 2-0
2 Jun 1996   Peru vs Colombia 1-1
2 Jun 1996   Uruguay vs Paraguay 0-2
2 Jun 1996   Venezuela vs Chile 1-1
7 Jul 1996   Bolivia vs Venezuela 6-1
7 Jul 1996   Chile vs Ecuador 4-1
7 Jul 1996   Colombia vs Uruguay 3-1
7 Jul 1996   Peru vs Argentina 0-0
1 Sep 1996   Argentina vs Paraguay 1-1
1 Sep 1996   Bolivia vs Peru 0-0
1 Sep 1996   Colombia vs Chile 4-1
1 Sep 1996   Ecuador vs Venezuela 1-0
8 Oct 1996   Uruguay vs Bolivia 1-0
9 Oct 1996   Ecuador vs Colombia 0-1
9 Oct 1996   Paraguay vs Chile 2-1
9 Oct 1996   Venezuela vs Argentina 2-5
10 Nov 1996   Bolivia vs Colombia 2-2
10 Nov 1996   Paraguay vs Ecuador 1-0
10 Nov 1996   Peru vs Venezuela 4-1
12 Nov 1996   Chile vs Uruguay 1-0
15 Dec 1996   Argentina vs Chile 1-1
15 Dec 1996   Bolivia vs Paraguay 0-0
15 Dec 1996   Uruguay vs Peru 2-0
15 Dec 1996   Venezuela vs Colombia 0-2
12 Jan 1997   Bolivia vs Ecuador 2-0
12 Jan 1997   Peru vs Chile 2-1
12 Jan 1997   Uruguay vs Argentina 0-0
12 Jan 1997   Venezuela vs Paraguay 0-2
12 Feb 1997   Bolivia vs Chile 1-1
12 Feb 1997   Colombia vs Argentina 0-1
12 Feb 1997   Ecuador vs Uruguay 4-0
12 Feb 1997   Paraguay vs Peru 2-1
2 Apr 1997   Bolivia vs Argentina 2-1
2 Apr 1997   Paraguay vs Colombia 2-1
2 Apr 1997   Peru vs Ecuador 1-1
2 Apr 1997   Uruguay vs Venezuela 3-1
30 Apr 1997   Argentina vs Ecuador 2-1
30 Apr 1997   Chile vs Venezuela 6-0
30 Apr 1997   Colombia vs Peru 0-1
30 Apr 1997   Paraguay vs Uruguay 3-1
8 Jun 1997   Argentina vs Peru 2-0
8 Jun 1997   Ecuador vs Chile 1-1
8 Jun 1997   Uruguay vs Colombia 1-1
8 Jun 1997   Venezuela vs Bolivia 1-1
6 Jul 1997   Chile vs Colombia 4-1

6 Jul 1997   Paraguay vs Argentina 1-2
6 Jul 1997   Peru vs Bolivia 2-1
6 Jul 1997   Venezuela vs Ecuador 1-1
20 Jul 1997   Argentina vs Venezuela 2-0
20 Jul 1997   Bolivia vs Uruguay 1-0
20 Jul 1997   Chile vs Paraguay 2-1
20 Jul 1997   Colombia vs Ecuador 1-0
20 Aug 1997   Colombia vs Bolivia 3-0
20 Aug 1997   Ecuador vs Paraguay 2-1
20 Aug 1997   Uruguay vs Chile 1-0
20 Aug 1997   Venezuela vs Peru 0-3
10 Sep 1997   Chile vs Argentina 1-2
10 Sep 1997   Colombia vs Venezuela 1-0
10 Sep 1997   Paraguay vs Bolivia 2-1
10 Sep 1997   Peru vs Uruguay 2-1
12 Oct 1997   Argentina vs Uruguay 0-0
12 Oct 1997   Chile vs Peru 4-0
12 Oct 1997   Ecuador vs Bolivia 1-0
12 Oct 1997   Paraguay vs Venezuela 1-0
16 Nov 1997   Argentina vs Colombia 1-1
16 Nov 1997   Chile vs Bolivia 3-0
16 Nov 1997   Peru vs Paraguay 1-0
16 Nov 1997   Uruguay vs Ecuador 5-3

	P	W	D	L	F	A	Pts
Argentina	16	8	6	2	23	13	30
Paraguay	16	9	2	5	21	14	29
Colombia	16	8	4	4	23	15	28
Chile	16	7	4	5	32	18	25
Peru	16	7	4	5	19	20	25
Ecuador	16	6	3	7	22	21	21
Uruguay	16	6	3	7	18	21	21
Bolivia	16	4	5	7	18	21	17
Venezuela	16	0	3	13	8	41	3

Argentina, Paraguay, Colombia and Chile qualified for Finals

AFRICA

ROUND ONE

31 May 1996   Mauritania vs Burkina Faso 0-0
16 Jun 1996   Burkina Faso vs Mauritania 2-0

Burkina Faso won 2-0 on aggregate and qualified for Round Two

1 Jun 1996   Uganda vs Angola 0-2
16 Jun 1996   Angola vs Uganda 3-1

Angola won 5-1 on aggregate and qualified for Round Two

1 Jun 1996   Sudan vs Zambia 2-0
16 Jun 1996   Zambia vs Sudan 3-0

Zambia won 3-2 on aggregate and qualified for Round Two

1 Jun 1996   Malawi vs South Africa 0-1
16 Jun 1996   South Africa vs Malawi 3-0

South Africa won 4-0 on aggregate and qualified for Round Two

1 Jun 1996   Guinea Bissau vs Guinea 3-2
16 Jun 1996   Guinea vs Guinea Bissau 3-1

Guinea won 5-4 on aggregate and qualified for Round Two

1 Jun 1996   Gambia vs Liberia 2-1
23 Jun 1996   Liberia vs Gambia 4-0

Liberia won 5-2 on aggregate and qualified for Round Two

| 1 Jun 1996 | Namibia vs Mozambique | 2-0 |
| 16 Jun 1996 | Mozambique vs Namibia | 1-1 |

Namibia won 3-1 on aggregate and qualified for Round Two

| 2 Jun 1996 | Swaziland vs Gabon | 0-1 |
| 16 Jun 1996 | Gabon vs Swaziland | 2-0 |

Gabon won 3-0 on aggregate and qualified for Round Two

| 2 Jun 1996 | Mauritius vs Zaire | 1-5 |
| 16 Jun 1996 | Zaire vs Mauritius | 2-0 |

Zaire won 7-1 on aggregate and qualified for Round Two

| 2 Jun 1996 | Madagascar vs Zimbabwe | 1-2 |
| 16 Jun 1996 | Zimbabwe vs Madagascar | 2-2 |

Zimbabwe won 4-3 on aggregate and qualified for Round Two

| 2 Jun 1996 | Rwanda vs Tunisia | 1-3 |
| 16 Jun 1996 | Tunisia vs Rwanda | 2-0 |

Tunisia won 5-1 on aggregate and qualified for Round Two

| 2 Jun 1996 | Congo vs Ivory Coast | 2-0 |
| 16 Jun 1996 | Ivory Coast vs Congo | 1-1 |

Congo won 3-1 on aggregate and qualified for Round Two

| 2 Jun 1996 | Kenya vs Algeria | 3-1 |
| 14 Jun 1996 | Algeria vs Kenya | 1-0 |

Kenya won 3-2 on aggregate and qualified for Round Two

| 2 Jun 1996 | Burundi vs Sierra Leone | 1-0 |
| 16 Jun 1996 | Sierra Leone vs Burundi | 0-1 |

Burundi won 2-0 on aggregate and qualified for Round Two

| 2 Jun 1996 | Togo vs Senegal | 2-1 |
| 15 Jun 1996 | Senegal vs Togo | 1-1 |

Togo won 3-2 on aggregate and qualified for Round Two

| 8 Jun 1996 | Tanzania vs Ghana | 0-0 |
| 17 Jun 1996 | Ghana vs Tanzania | 2-1 |

Ghana won 2-1 on aggregate and qualified for Round Two

ROUND TWO

GROUP 1

9 Nov 1996	Nigeria vs Burkina Faso	2-0
10 Nov 1996	Guinea vs Kenya	3-1
12 Jan 1997	Kenya vs Nigeria	1-1
12 Jan 1997	Burkina Faso vs Guinea	0-2
5 Apr 1997	Nigeria vs Guinea	2-1
5 Apr 1997	Kenya vs Burkina Faso	4-3
27 Apr 1997	Burkina Faso vs Nigeria	1-2
27 Apr 1997	Kenya vs Guinea	1-0
7 Jun 1997	Nigeria vs Kenya	3-0
8 Jun 1997	Guinea vs Burkina Faso	3-1
17 Aug 1997	Guinea vs Nigeria	1-0
17 Aug 1997	Burkina Faso vs Kenya	2-4

	P	W	D	L	F	A	Pts
Nigeria	6	4	1	1	10	4	13
Guinea	6	4	0	2	10	5	12
Kenya	6	3	1	2	11	12	10
Burkina Faso	6	0	0	6	7	17	0

Nigeria qualified for Finals

GROUP 2

8 Nov 1996	Egypt vs Namibia	7-1
10 Nov 1996	Liberia vs Tunisia	0-1
11 Jan 1997	Namibia vs Liberia	0-0
12 Jan 1997	Tunisia vs Egypt	1-0

6 Apr 1997	Liberia vs Egypt	1-0
6 Apr 1997	Namibia vs Tunisia	1-2
26 Apr 1997	Namibia vs Egypt	2-3
27 Apr 1997	Tunisia vs Liberia	2-0
8 Jun 1997	Liberia vs Namibia	1-2
8 Jun 1997	Egypt vs Tunisia	0-0
17 Aug 1997	Egypt vs Liberia	5-0
17 Aug 1997	Tunisia vs Namibia	4-0

	P	W	D	L	F	A	Pts
Tunisia	6	5	1	0	10	1	16
Egypt	6	3	1	2	15	5	10
Liberia	6	1	1	4	2	10	4
Namibia	6	1	1	4	6	17	4

Tunisia qualified for Finals

GROUP 3

9 Nov 1996	South Africa vs Zaire	1-0
10 Nov 1996	Congo vs Zambia	1-0
11 Jan 1997	Zambia vs South Africa	0-0
12 Jan 1997	Zaire vs Congo	1-1
6 Apr 1997	Congo vs South Africa	2-0
6 Apr 1997	Zaire vs Zambia	2-2
27 Apr 1997	Zambia vs Congo	3-0
27 Apr 1997	Zaire vs South Africa	1-2
8 Jun 1997	Congo vs Congo DR	1-0

N.B. Congo DR was formerly Zaire

8 Jun 1997	South Africa vs Zambia	3-0
17 Aug 1997	South Africa vs Congo	1-0
17 Aug 1997	Zambia vs Congo DR	2-0

	P	W	D	L	F	A	Pts
South Africa	6	4	1	1	7	3	13
Congo	6	3	1	2	5	5	10
Zambia	6	2	2	2	7	6	8
Congo DR	6	0	2	4	4	9	2

South Africa qualified for Finals

GROUP 4

10 Nov 1996	Angola vs Zimbabwe	2-1
10 Nov 1996	Togo vs Cameroon	2-4
12 Jan 1997	Cameroon vs Angola	0-0
12 Jan 1997	Zimbabwe vs Togo	3-0
6 Apr 1997	Angola vs Togo	3-1
6 Apr 1997	Cameroon vs Zimbabwe	1-0
27 Apr 1997	Zimbabwe vs Angola	0-0
27 Apr 1997	Cameroon vs Togo	2-0
8 Jun 1997	Angola vs Cameroon	1-1
8 Jun 1997	Togo vs Zimbabwe	2-1
17 Aug 1997	Togo vs Angola	1-1
17 Aug 1997	Zimbabwe vs Cameroon	1-2

	P	W	D	L	F	A	Pts
Cameroon	6	4	2	0	10	4	14
Angola	6	2	4	0	7	4	10
Zimbabwe	6	1	1	4	6	7	4
Togo	6	1	1	4	6	14	4

Cameroon qualified for Finals

GROUP 5

| 9 Nov 1996 | Morocco vs Sierra Leone | 4-0 |

220

| | | 10 Nov 1996 | Gabon vs Ghana | 1-1 |

10 Nov 1996	Gabon vs Ghana 1-1
11 Jan 1997	Sierra Leone vs Gabon 1-0
12 Jan 1997	Ghana vs Morocco 2-2
5 Apr 1997	Sierra Leone vs Ghana 1-1
6 Apr 1997	Gabon vs Morocco 0-4
26 Apr 1997	Sierra Leone vs Morocco 0-1
27 Apr 1997	Ghana vs Gabon 3-0
8 Jun 1997	Gabon vs Sierra Leone .... Postponed
8 Jun 1997	Morocco vs Ghana 1-0
17 Aug 1997	Morocco vs Gabon 2-0
17 Aug 1997	Ghana vs Sierra Leone 0-2

Gabon vs Sierra Leone was not played

	P	W	D	L	F	A	Pts
Morocco	6	5	1	0	14	2	16
Sierra Leone	5	2	1	2	4	6	7
Ghana	6	1	3	2	7	7	6
Gabon	5	0	1	4	1	11	1

Morocco qualified for Finals

ASIA

ROUND ONE

GROUP 1

Following matches all played in Malaysia

16 Mar 1997	Chinese Taipei vs Saudi Arabia 0-2
16 Mar 1997	Malaysia vs Bangladesh 2-0
18 Mar 1997	Bangladesh vs Chinese Taipei 1-3
18 Mar 1997	Malaysia vs Saudi Arabia 0-0
20 Mar 1997	Bangladesh vs Saudi Arabia 1-4
20 Mar 1997	Malaysia vs Chinese Taipei 2-0

Following matches all played in Jeddah, Saudi Arabia

27 Mar 1997	Chinese Taipei vs Malaysia 0-0
27 Mar 1997	Saudi Arabia vs Bangladesh 3-0
29 Mar 1997	Chinese Taipei vs Bangladesh 1-2
29 Mar 1997	Saudi Arabia vs Malaysia 3-0
31 Mar 1997	Bangladesh vs Malaysia 0-1
31 Mar 1997	Saudi Arabia vs Chinese Taipei 6-0

	P	W	D	L	F	A	Pts
Saudi Arabia	6	5	1	0	18	1	16
Malaysia	6	3	2	1	5	3	11
Chinese Taipei	6	1	1	4	4	13	4
Bangladesh	6	1	0	5	4	14	3

Saudi Arabia qualified for Round Two

GROUP 2

Following matches all played in Damascus, Syria

2 Jun 1997	Syria vs Kyrgyzstan .... Abandoned
2 Jun 1997	Maldives vs Iran 0-17
4 Jun 1997	Syria vs Maldives 12-0
4 Jun 1997	Kyrgyzstan vs Iran 0-7
6 Jun 1997	Syria vs Iran 0-1
6 Jun 1997	Kyrgyzstan vs Maldives 3-0

Following matches all played in Tehran, Iran

9 Jun 1997	Iran vs Kyrgyzstan 3-1
9 Jun 1997	Maldives vs Syria 0-12
11 Jun 1997	Iran vs Maldives 9-0
11 Jun 1997	Kyrgyzstan vs Syria 2-1

| 15 Jun 1997 | Iran vs Syria .... 2-2 |
| 15 Jun 1997 | Maldives vs Kyrgyzstan .... 0-6 |

	P	W	D	L	F	A	Pts
Iran	6	5	1	0	39	3	16
Kyrgyzstan	6	3	0	2	12	11	9
Syria	5	2	1	2	27	5	7
Maldives	6	0	0	6	0	59	0

Iran qualified for Round Two

GROUP 3

Following matches all played in Manama

8 Apr 1997	Jordan vs United Arab Emirates 0-0
11 Apr 1997	Bahrain vs United Arab Emirates 1-2
14 Apr 1997	Bahrain vs Jordan 1-0

Following matches all played in Sharjah

19 Apr 1997	Jordan vs Bahrain 4-1
22 Apr 1997	United Arab Emirates vs Bahrain 3-0
26 Apr 1997	United Arab Emirates vs Jordan 2-0

	P	W	D	L	F	A	Pts
United Arab Emirates	4	3	1	0	7	1	10
Jordan	4	1	1	2	4	4	4
Bahrain	4	1	0	3	3	9	3

United Arab Emirates qualified for Round Two

GROUP 4

Following matches all played in Muscat

23 Mar 1997	Nepal vs Macao 1-1
23 Mar 1997	Oman vs Japan 0-1
25 Mar 1997	Macao vs Japan 0-10
25 Mar 1997	Oman vs Nepal 1-0
27 Mar 1997	Nepal vs Japan 0-6
27 Mar 1997	Oman vs Macao 4-0

Following matches all played in Tokyo, Japan

22 Jun 1997	Japan vs Macao 10-0
22 Jun 1997	Nepal vs Oman 0-6
25 Jun 1997	Japan vs Nepal 3-0
25 Jun 1997	Macao vs Oman 0-2
28 Jun 1997	Japan vs Oman 1-1
28 Jun 1997	Macao vs Nepal 2-1

	P	W	D	L	F	A	Pts
Japan	6	5	1	0	31	1	16
Oman	6	4	1	1	14	2	13
Nepal	6	1	1	4	3	28	4
Macao	6	0	1	5	2	19	1

Japan qualified for Round Two

GROUP 5

6 Apr 1997	Indonesia vs Cambodia 8-0
13 Apr 1997	Indonesia vs Yemen 0-0
20 Apr 1997	Cambodia vs Yemen 0-1
27 Apr 1997	Cambodia vs Indonesia 1-1
9 May 1997	Yemen vs Uzbekistan 0-1
16 May 1997	Yemen vs Cambodia 7-0
25 May 1997	Uzbekistan vs Cambodia 6-0
1 Jun 1997	Indonesia vs Uzbekistan 1-1
13 Jun 1997	Yemen vs Indonesia 1-1
20 Jun 1997	Uzbekistan vs Indonesia 3-0

| 29 Jun 1997 | Cambodia vs Uzbekistan | 1-4 |
| 13 Jul 1997 | Uzbekistan vs Yemen | 5-1 |

	P	W	D	L	F	A	Pts
Uzbekistan	6	5	1	0	20	3	16
Yemen	6	2	2	2	10	7	8
Indonesia	6	1	4	1	11	6	7
Cambodia	6	0	1	5	2	27	1

Uzbekistan qualified for Round Two

GROUP 6

23 Feb 1997	Hong Kong vs South Korea	0-2
2 Mar 1997	Thailand vs South Korea	1-3
9 Mar 1997	Thailand vs Hong Kong	2-0
16 Mar 1997	Hong Kong vs Thailand	3-2
28 May 1997	South Korea vs Hong Kong	4-0
1 Jun 1997	South Korea vs Thailand	0-0

	P	W	D	L	F	A	Pts
South Korea	4	3	1	0	9	1	10
Thailand	4	1	1	2	5	6	4
Hong Kong	4	1	0	3	3	10	3

South Korea qualified for Round Two

GROUP 7

13 Apr 1997	Lebanon vs Singapore	1-1
26 Apr 1997	Singapore vs Kuwait	0-1
8 May 1997	Kuwait vs Lebanon	2-0
24 May 1997	Singapore vs Lebanon	1-2
5 Jun 1997	Kuwait vs Singapore	4-0
22 Jun 1997	Lebanon vs Kuwait	1-3

	P	W	D	L	F	A	Pts
Kuwait	4	4	0	0	10	1	12
Lebanon	4	1	1	2	4	7	4
Singapore	4	0	1	3	2	8	1

Kuwait qualified for Round Two

GROUP 8

4 May 1997	Turkmenistan vs China	1-4
4 May 1997	Tajikistan vs Vietnam	4-0
11 May 1997	Vietnam vs China	1-3
11 May 1997	Turkmenistan vs Tajikistan	1-2
18 May 1997	Turkmenistan vs Vietnam	2-1
18 May 1997	Tajikistan vs China	0-1
1 Jun 1997	Vietnam vs Tajikistan	0-4
1 Jun 1997	China vs Turkmenistan	1-0
8 Jun 1997	China vs Tajikistan	0-0
8 Jun 1997	Vietnam vs Turkmenistan	0-4
22 Jun 1997	China vs Vietnam	4-0
22 Jun 1997	Tajikistan vs Turkmenistan	5-0

	P	W	D	L	F	A	Pts
China	6	5	1	0	13	2	16
Tajikistan	6	4	1	1	15	2	13
Turkmenistan	6	2	0	4	8	13	6
Vietnam	6	0	0	6	2	21	0

China qualified for Round Two

GROUP 9

| 11 May 1997 | Kazakhstan vs Pakistan | 3-0 |
| 23 May 1997 | Pakistan vs Iraq | 2-6 |

6 Jun 1997	Iraq vs Kazakhstan	1-2
11 Jun 1997	Pakistan vs Kazakhstan	0-7
20 Jun 1997	Iraq vs Pakistan	6-1
29 Jun 1997	Kazakhstan vs Iraq	3-1

	P	W	D	L	F	A	Pts
Kazakhstan	4	4	0	0	15	2	12
Iraq	4	2	0	2	14	8	6
Pakistan	4	0	0	4	3	22	0

Kazakhstan qualified for Round Two

GROUP 10

20 Sep 1996	Qatar vs Sri Lanka	3-0
21 Sep 1996	India vs Philippines	2-0
23 Sep 1996	Qatar vs Philippines	5-0
24 Sep 1996	Sri Lanka vs India	1-1
26 Sep 1996	Philippines vs Sri Lanka	0-3
27 Sep 1996	Qatar vs India	6-0

	P	W	D	L	F	A	Pts
Qatar	3	3	0	0	14	0	9
Sri Lanka	3	1	1	1	4	4	4
India	3	1	1	1	3	7	4
Philippines	3	0	0	3	0	10	0

Qatar qualified for Round Two

ROUND TWO

GROUP A

13 Sep 1997	China vs Iran	2-4
14 Sep 1997	Saudi vs Kuwait	2-1
19 Sep 1997	Iran vs Saudi Arabia	1-1
19 Sep 1997	Qatar vs Kuwait	0-2
26 Sep 1997	Kuwait vs Iran	1-1
26 Sep 1997	Qatar vs China	1-1
3 Oct 1997	China vs Saudi Arabia	1-0
3 Oct 1997	Iran vs Qatar	3-0
10 Oct 1997	Kuwait vs China	1-2
11 Oct 1997	Saudi Arabia vs Qatar	1-0
17 Oct 1997	Iran vs China	4-1
17 Oct 1997	Kuwait vs Saudi Arabia	2-1
24 Oct 1997	Kuwait vs Qatar	0-1
24 Oct 1997	Saudi Arabia vs Iran	1-0
31 Oct 1997	China vs Qatar	2-3
31 Oct 1997	Iran vs Kuwait	0-0
6 Nov 1997	Saudi Arabia vs China	1-1
7 Nov 1997	Qatar vs Iran	2-0
12 Nov 1997	China vs Kuwait	1-0
12 Nov 1997	Qatar vs Saudi Arabia	0-1

	P	W	D	L	F	A	Pts
Saudi Arabia	8	4	2	2	8	6	14
Iran	8	3	3	2	13	8	12
China	8	3	2	3	11	14	11
Qatar	8	3	1	4	7	10	10
Kuwait	8	2	2	4	7	8	8

Saudi Arabia qualified for Finals

Iran qualified for Play-off

GROUP B

| 6 Sep 1997 | South Korea vs Kazakhstan | 3-0 |

7 Sep 1997	Japan vs Uzbekistan	6-3
12 Sep 1997	South Korea vs Uzbekistan	2-1
12 Sep 1997	United Arab Emirates vs Kazakhstan	4-0
19 Sep 1997	United Arab Emirates vs Japan	0-0
20 Sep 1997	Kazakhstan vs Uzbekistan	1-1
27 Sep 1997	Uzbekistan vs United Arab Emirates	2-3
28 Sep 1997	Japan vs South Korea	1-2
4 Oct 1997	South Korea vs United Arab Emirates	3-0
4 Oct 1997	Kazakhstan vs Japan	1-1
11 Oct 1997	Uzbekistan vs Japan	1-1
11 Oct 1997	Kazakhstan vs South Korea	1-1
18 Oct 1997	Uzbekistan vs South Korea	1-5
18 Oct 1997	Kazakhstan vs United Arab Emirates	3-0
25 Oct 1997	Uzbekistan vs Kazakhstan	4-0
26 Oct 1997	Japan vs United Arab Emirates	1-1
1 Nov 1997	South Korea vs Japan	0-2
2 Nov 1997	United Arab Emirates vs Uzbekistan	0-0
8 Nov 1997	Japan vs Kazakhstan	5-1
9 Nov 1997	United Arab Emirates vs South Korea	1-3

	P	W	D	L	F	A	Pts
South Korea	8	6	1	1	19	7	19
Japan	8	3	4	1	17	9	13
United Arab Emirates	8	2	3	3	9	12	9
Uzbekistan	8	1	3	4	13	18	6
Kazakhstan	8	1	3	4	7	19	6

South Korea qualified for Finals

Japan qualified for Play-off

PLAY-OFF (in Malaysia)

16 Nov 1997	Japan vs Iran	3-2

Japan won by Golden Goal and qualified for Finals

Iran played Oceania winners in qualification Play-off

ASIA-OCEANIA PLAY-OFF

22 Nov 1997	Iran vs Australia	1-1
29 Nov 1997	Australia vs Iran	2-2

Iran qualified for Finals on Away Goals

CONCACAF

ROUND ONE

CARIBBEAN ZONE

24 Mar 1996	Dominican Republic vs Aruba	3-2
31 Mar 1996	Aruba vs Dominican Republic	1-3

Dominican Republic qualified for Round Two

29 Mar 1996	Guyana vs Grenada	1-2
7 Apr 1996	Grenada vs Guyana	6-0

Grenada qualified for Round Two

10 Mar 1996	Dominica vs Antigua	3-3
31 Mar 1996	Antigua vs Dominica	1-3

Dominica qualified for Round Two

St. Kitts & Nevis walk over vs Bahamas (withdrew)

St. Kitts & Nevis qualified for Round Two

ROUND TWO

CARIBBEAN ZONE

31 Mar 1996	Surinam vs Jamaica	0-1

21 Apr 1996	Jamaica vs Surinam	1-0

Jamaica qualified for Round Three

4 May 1996	Puerto Rico vs St. Vincent	1-2
12 May 1996	St. Vincent vs Puerto Rico	7-0

St. Vincent qualified for Round Three

5 May 1996	St. Kitts & Nevis vs St. Lucia	5-1
19 May 1996	St. Lucia vs St. Kitts & Nevis	0-1

St. Kitts & Nevis qualified for Round Three

12 May 1996	Cayman vs Cuba	0-1
14 May 1996	Cuba vs Cayman	5-0

Cuba qualified for Round Three

12 May 1996	Haiti vs Grenada	6-1
18 May 1996	Grenada vs Haiti	0-1

Haiti qualified for Round Three

14 May 1996	Dominica vs Barbados	0-1
19 May 1996	Barbados vs Dominica	1-0

Barbados qualified for Round Three

4 May 1996	Dominican Rep. vs Netherlands Antilles	2-1
11 May 1996	Netherlands Antilles vs Dominican Rep.	0-0

Dominican Republic qualified for Round Three

Trinidad & Tobago walk over vs Bermuda (withdrew)

Trinidad & Tobago qualified for Round Three

ROUND THREE

CARIBBEAN ZONE

10 Jun 1996	Cuba vs Haiti	6-1
30 Jun 1996	Haiti vs Cuba	1-1

Cuba qualified for Semi-Final Round

23 Jun 1996	St. Kitts & Nevis vs St. Vincent	2-2
30 Jun 1996	St. Vincent vs St. Kitts & Nevis	0-0

St. Vincent qualified for Semi-Final Round on Away Goals

23 Jun 1996	Barbados vs Jamaica	0-1
30 Jun 1996	Jamaica vs Barbados	2-0

Jamaica qualified for Semi-Final Round

15 Jun 1996	Dominican Rep. vs Trinidad & Tobago	1-4
23 Jun 1996	Trinidad & Tobago vs Domincan Rep.	8-0

Trinidad & Tobago qualified for Semi-Final Round

CENTRAL AMERICAN ZONE

5 May 1996	Nicaragua vs Guatemala	0-1
10 May 1996	Guatemala vs Nicaragua	2-1

Guatemala qualified for Semi-Final Round

2 Jun 1996	Belize vs Panama	1-2
9 Jun 1996	Panama vs Belize	4-1

Panama qualified for Semi-Final Round

SEMI-FINAL ROUND

GROUP 1

1 Sep 1996	Trinidad & Tobago vs Costa Rica	0-1
6 Oct 1996	Trinidad & Tobago vs Guatemala	1-1
16 Oct 1996	Guatemala vs Costa Rica	Postponed
25 Oct 1996	Guatemala vs Trinidad & Tobago	Postponed
3 Nov 1996	USA vs Guatemala	2-0
10 Nov 1996	USA vs Trinidad & Tobago	2-0
17 Nov 1996	Costa Rica vs Guatemala	3-0

24 Nov 1996	Trinidad & Tobago vs USA	0-1
24 Nov 1996	Guatemala vs Costa Rica	1-0
1 Dec 1996	Costa Rica vs USA	2-1
8 Dec 1996	Guatemala vs Trinidad & Tobago	2-1
14 Dec 1996	USA vs Costa Rica	2-1
21 Dec 1996	Costa Rica vs Trinidad & Tobago	2-1
21 Dec 1996	Guatemala vs USA	2-2

	P	W	D	L	F	A	Pts
USA	6	4	1	1	10	5	13
Costa Rica	6	4	0	2	9	5	12
Guatemala	6	2	2	2	6	9	8
Trinidad & Tobago	6	0	1	5	3	9	1

USA and Costa Rica qualified for Final Round

GROUP 2

30 Aug 1996	Canada vs Panama	3-1
8 Sep 1996	Cuba vs El Salvador	0-5
22 Sep 1996	Cuba vs Panama	3-1
6 Oct 1996	Panama vs El Salvador	1-1
10 Oct 1996	Canada vs Cuba	2-0
13 Oct 1996	Cuba vs Canada	0-2
27 Oct 1996	Panama vs Canada	0-0
3 Nov 1996	Canada vs El Salvador	1-0
10 Nov 1996	El Salvador vs Panama	3-2
1 Dec 1996	El Salvador vs Cuba	3-0
15 Dec 1996	Panama vs Cuba	3-1
15 Dec 1996	El Salvador vs Canada	0-2

	P	W	D	L	F	A	Pts
Canada	6	5	1	0	10	1	16
El Salvador	6	3	1	2	12	6	10
Panama	6	1	2	3	8	11	5
Cuba	6	1	0	5	4	16	3

Canada and El Salvador qualified for Final Round

GROUP 3

15 Sep 1996	Jamaica vs Honduras	3-0
15 Sep 1996	St. Vincent vs Mexico	0-3
21 Sep 1996	Honduras vs Mexico	2-1
23 Sep 1996	St. Vincent vs Jamaica	1-2
13 Oct 1996	St. Vincent vs Honduras	1-4
16 Oct 1996	Mexico vs Jamaica	2-1
27 Oct 1996	Honduras vs Jamaica	0-0
30 Oct 1996	Mexico vs St. Vincent	5-1
6 Nov 1996	Mexico vs Honduras	3-1
10 Nov 1996	Jamaica vs St. Vincent	5-0
17 Nov 1996	Honduras vs St. Vincent	11-3
17 Nov 1996	Jamaica vs Mexico	1-0

	P	W	D	L	F	A	Pts
Jamaica	6	4	1	1	12	3	13
Mexico	6	4	0	2	14	6	12
Honduras	6	3	1	2	18	11	10
St. Vincent	6	0	0	6	6	30	0

Jamaica and Mexico qualified for Final Round

FINAL ROUND

2 Mar 1997	Mexico vs Canada	4-0
2 Mar 1997	Jamaica vs USA	0-0
16 Mar 1997	USA vs Canada	3-0

16 Mar 1997	Costa Rica vs Mexico	0-0
23 Mar 1997	Costa Rica vs USA	3-2
6 Apr 1997	Canada vs El Salvador	0-0
13 Apr 1997	Mexico vs Jamaica	6-0
20 Apr 1997	USA vs Mexico	2-2
27 Apr 1997	Canada vs Jamaica	0-0
4 May 1997	El Salvador vs Costa Rica	2-1
11 May 1997	Costa Rica vs Jamaica	3-1
18 May 1997	Jamaica vs El Salvador	1-0
1 Jun 1997	Canada vs Costa Rica	1-0
8 Jun 1997	El Salvador vs Mexico	0-1
29 Jun 1997	El Salvador vs USA	1-1
10 Aug 1997	Costa Rica vs El Salvador	0-0
7 Sep 1997	USA vs Costa Rica	1-0
7 Sep 1997	Jamaica vs Canada	1-0
14 Sep 1997	Jamaica vs Costa Rica	1-0
14 Sep 1997	El Salvador vs Canada	4-1
3 Oct 1997	USA vs Jamaica	1-1
5 Oct 1997	Mexico vs El Salvador	5-0
12 Oct 1997	Canada vs Mexico	2-2
2 Nov 1997	Mexico vs USA	0-0
9 Nov 1997	Canada vs USA	0-3
9 Nov 1997	El Salvador vs Jamaica	2-2
9 Nov 1997	Mexico vs Costa Rica	3-3
16 Nov 1997	Jamaica vs Mexico	0-0
16 Nov 1997	Costa Rica vs Canada	3-1
16 Nov 1997	USA vs El Salvador	4-2

	P	W	D	L	F	A	Pts
Mexico	10	4	6	0	23	7	18
USA	10	4	5	1	17	9	17
Jamaica	10	3	5	2	7	12	14
Costa Rica	10	3	3	4	13	12	12
El Salvador	10	2	4	4	11	16	10
Canada	10	1	3	6	5	20	6

Mexico, USA and Jamaica qualified for Finals

FULL RECORD OF FINAL
SERIES GAMES

A country-by-country listing in alphabetical order

ALGERIA
SPAIN 1982
GROUP MATCHES – GROUP 2

16/6/82 **ALGERIA**.........(0) **2** **WEST GERMANY** . (0) 1 42000
Madjer, Belloumi *Rummenigge*

21/6/82 **AUSTRIA** ....(0) **2** **ALGERIA** .... (0) **0** 22000
Schachner, Krankl

24/6/82 **ALGERIA**.........(3) **3** **CHILE** .... (0) 2 16000
Assad 2, Bensoula *Neira (pen), Letelier*

MEXICO 1986
GROUP MATCHES – GROUP D

3/6/86 **ALGERIA**.........(0) **1** **NORTHERN IRELAND**(1) 1 22000
Zidane *Whiteside*

6/6/86 **BRAZIL**...........(0) **1** **ALGERIA** .... (0) **0** 48000
Careca

12/6/86 **ALGERIA**.........(0) **0** **SPAIN** .... (2) 3 23980

ARGENTINA
URUGUAY 1930
GROUP MATCHES – GROUP 1

15/7/30 **ARGENTINA**......(0) **1** **FRANCE** ...... (0) **0** 3000
Monti

19/7/30 **ARGENTINA**......(3) **6** **MEXICO** ...... (0) 3 5000
Stabile 3, Varallo 2, Zumelzu *Lopez, Rosas (F), Rosas (M)*

22/7/30 **ARGENTINA**......(2) **3** **CHILE** .... (1) 1 1000
Stabile 2, Evaristo (M) *Subiabre*

Semi-Final

26/7/30 **ARGENTINA**......(1) **6** **USA**.............. (0) 1 80000
Monti, Scopelli, Stabile 2, Peucelle 2 *Brown*

Final

30/7/30 **URUGUAY** ....(1) **4** **ARGENTINA** ...... (2) 2 93000
Dorado, Cea, Iriarte, Castro *Peucelle, Stabile*

ITALY 1934

First Round

27/5/34 **SWEDEN** ....(1) **3** **ARGENTINA** ...... (1) 2 N.R.
Jonasson 2, Kroon *Belis. Galateo*

SWEDEN 1958
GROUP MATCHES – GROUP 1

8/6/58 **WEST GERMANY** ..(2) **3** **ARGENTINA** ...... (1) 1 31156
Rahn 2, Schmidt *Corbatta*

11/6/58 **ARGENTINA**......(1) **3** **NORTHERN IRELAND**(1) 1 14174
Corbatta 2 (1 pen), Menendez *McParland*

15/6/58 **CZECHOSLOVAKIA**..(3) **6** **ARGENTINA** ...... (1) 1 16418
Dvorak, Zikan 2, Feureisl, Hovorka *Corbatta*

CHILE 1962
GROUP MATCHES – GROUP 4

30/5/62 **ARGENTINA**......(1) **1** **BULGARIA** .... (0) **0** 7134
Facundo

2/6/62 **ENGLAND**.........(2) **3** **ARGENTINA** ...... (0) 1 9794
Flowers (pen), Charlton, Greaves *Sanfilippo*

6/6/62 **ARGENTINA**......(0) **0** **HUNGARY**........ (0) **0** 7945

ENGLAND 1966
GROUP MATCHES – GROUP 2

13/7/66 **ARGENTINA**......(0) **2** **SPAIN** ...... (0) 1 47982
Artime 2 *Pirri*

16/7/66 **ARGENTINA**......(0) **0** **WEST GERMANY** . (0) **0** 51,419

19/7/66 **ARGENTINA**......(0) **2** **SWITZERLAND**.... (0) **0** 31443
Artime, Onega

Quarter-Final

23/7/66 **ENGLAND**.........(0) **1** **ARGENTINA** ...... (0) **0** 90584
Hurst

WEST GERMANY 1974
GROUP MATCHES – GROUP 4

15/6/74 **POLAND**..........(2) **3** **ARGENTINA** ...... (0) 2 32700
Lato 2, Szarmach *Heredia, Babington*

19/6/74 **ARGENTINA**......(1) **1** **ITALY**............ (1) 1 70100
Houseman *Perfumo (o.g.)*

23/6/74 **ARGENTINA**......(2) **4** **HAITI**............ (0) 1 25900
Yazalde 2, Houseman, Ayala *Sanon*

GROUP MATCHES – GROUP A

Quarter-Finals

26/6/74 **HOLLAND**.........(2) **4** **ARGENTINA** ...... (0) **0** 55000
Cruyff 2, Krol, Rep

30/6/74 **BRAZIL**...........(1) **2** **ARGENTINA** ...... (1) 1 29400
Rivelino, Jairzinho *Brindisi*

3/7/74 **ARGENTINA**......(1) **1** **EAST GERMANY** .. (1) 1 54200
Houseman *Streich*

ARGENTINA 1978
GROUP MATCHES – GROUP 1

2/6/78 **ARGENTINA**......(1) **2** **HUNGARY**........ (1) 1 77000
Luque, Alonso *Csapo*

6/6/78 **ARGENTINA**......(1) **2** **FRANCE** ...... (0) 1 77216
Passarella (pen), Luque *Platini*

10/6/78 **ITALY**.............(0) **1** **ARGENTINA** ...... (0) **0** 77260
Bettega

GROUP MATCHES – GROUP B

Quarter-Finals

14/6/78 **ARGENTINA** ......(1) **2** **POLAND** ...... (0) **0** 40000
Kempes 2

18/6/78 **ARGENTINA**......(0) **0** **BRAZIL** ...... (0) **0** 46000

21/6/78 **ARGENTINA**......(2) **6** **PERU**............ (0) **0** 40567
Kempes 2, Tarantini, Luque 2, Houseman

Final

25/6/78 **ARGENTINA**......(1) **3** **HOLLAND** ...... (0) 1 77260
Kempes 2, Bertoni *Nanninga*

(After Extra Time)

SPAIN 1982
GROUP MATCHES – GROUP 3

13/6/82 **BELGIUM** ....(0) **1** **ARGENTINA** ...... (0) **0** 95000
Van Den Bergh

18/6/82 **ARGENTINA**......(2) **4** **HUNGARY**........ (0) 1 32093
Bertoni, Ardiles, Maradona 2 *Poloskei*

23/6/82 **ARGENTINA**......(1) **2** **EL SALVADOR**..... (0) **0** 32000
Passarella (pen), Bertoni

GROUP MATCHES – GROUP C

Quarter-Finals

29/6/82 **ITALY** ....(0) **2** **ARGENTINA** ...... (0) 1 43000
Tardelli, Cabrini *Passarella*

2/7/82 **BRAZIL**...........(1) **3** **ARGENTINA** ...... (0) 1 44000
Zico, Serginho, Junior *Diaz*

MEXICO 1986
GROUP MATCHES – GROUP A

2/6/86 **ARGENTINA**......(2) **3** **SOUTH KOREA** .... (0) 1 60000
Valdano 2, Ruggeri *Park Chang Sun*

5/6/86 **ITALY** ....(1) **1** **ARGENTINA** ...... (1) 1 32000
Altobelli (pen) *Maradona*

10/6/86 **ARGENTINA**......(1) **2** **BULGARIA** ...... (0) **0** 65000
Valdano, Burruchaga

Second Round

16/6/86 **ARGENTINA**......(1) **1** **URUGUAY**........ (0) **0** 26000
Pasculli

Quarter-Final

22/6/86 **ARGENTINA**......(0) **2** **ENGLAND**........ (0) 1 114580
Maradona 2 *Lineker*

Semi-Final

25/6/86 **ARGENTINA**.......(0) **2** **BELGIUM** ....(0) **0** 110420
Maradona 2

Final

29/6/86 **ARGENTINA**.......(1) **3** **WEST GERMANY**...(0) **2** 114590
Brown, Valdano, Burruchago   Rummenegge, Voeller

ITALY 1990
GROUP MATCHES – GROUP B

8/6/90 **ARGENTINA**......(0) **0** **CAMEROON** ....(0) **1** 73780
F. Biyick
13/6/90 **ARGENTINA**......(1) **2** **USSR**.............(0) **0** 55759
Troglio, Burruchaga
18/6/90 **ARGENTINA**......(0) **1** **ROMANIA**........(0) **1** 52733
Monzon   Balint

Second Round

24/6/90 **BRAZIL**...........(0) **0** **ARGENTINA** ....(0) **1** 61381
Caniggia

Quarter-Final

30/6/90 **ARGENTINA**......(0) **0** **YUGOSLAVIA** ......(0) **0** 33971
(After Extra Time – Argentina won 3-2 on penalties)

Semi-Final

3/7/90 **ARGENTINA**......(0) **1** **ITALY**............(1) **1** 59978
Caniggia   Schillaci
(After Extra Time – Argentina won 4-3 on penalties)

Final

8/7/90 **ARGENTINA**......(0) **0** **WEST GERMANY**...(0) **1** 73603
Brehme (pen)

U.S.A. 1994
GROUP MATCHES – GROUP D

21/6/94 **ARGENTINA**.......(2) **4** **GREECE**..........(0) **0** 53486
Batistuta 3, Maradona
25/6/94 **ARGENTINA**.......(2) **2** **NIGERIA** ....(1) **1** 54453
Caniggia 2   Siasia
30/6/94 **ARGENTINA**......(0) **0** **BULGARIA** ....(0) **2** 63998
Stoichkov, Sirakov

Second Round

3/7/94 **ROMANIA** ....(2) **3** **ARGENTINA** ....(1) **2** 90469
Dumitrescu 2, Hagi   Batistuta (pen), Balbo

FRANCE 1998
GROUP MATCHES – GROUP H

14/6/98 **ARGENTINA**.......(1) **1** **JAPAN** ....(0) **0** 33400
Batistuta
21/6/98 **ARGENTINA**.......(1) **5** **JAMAICA**.........(0) **0** 48500
Ortega 2, Batistuta 3 (1 pen)
26/6/98 **ARGENTINA**.......(1) **1** **CROATIA**.........(0) **0** 35000
Pineda

Second Round

30/6/98 **ARGENTINA**.......(2) **2** **ENGLAND**........(2) **2** 35000
Batistuta (pen), Zanetti   Shearer (pen), Owen

Quarter-Finals

4/7/98 **HOLLAND**.........(1) **2** **ARGENTINA** ....(1) **1** 55000
Kluivert, Bergkamp   Lopez

AUSTRALIA
WEST GERMANY 1974
GROUP MATCHES – GROUP 1

14/6/74 **EAST GERMANY**...(0) **2** **AUSTRALIA** ....(0) **0** 17000
Curran (o.g.), Streich
18/6/74 **WEST GERMANY** ..(2) **3** **AUSTRALIA** ....(0) **0** 53300
Overath, Cullman, Muller
22/6/74 **AUSTRALIA**.......(0) **0** **CHILE** ....(0) **0** 14000

AUSTRIA
ITALY 1934

First Round

27/5/34 **AUSTRIA** ....(1) **3** **FRANCE** ....(1) **2** N.R.
Sindelar, Schall, Bican   Nicolas, Verriest (pen)
(After Extra Time)

Second Round

31/5/34 **AUSTRIA** ....(1) **2** **HUNGARY**.........(0) **1** N.R.
Horwath, Zischek   Sarosi (pen)

Semi-Final

3/6/34 **ITALY** ....(1) **1** **AUSTRIA**.........(0) **0** 60000
Guaita

SWITZERLAND 1954
GROUP MATCHES – GROUP 3

16/6/54 **AUSTRIA** ....(1) **1** **SCOTLAND**........(0) **0** 25000
Probst
19/6/54 **AUSTRIA** ....(4) **5** **CZECHOSLOVAKIA**..(0) **0** 21000
Stojaspal 2, Probst 3

Quarter-Final

26/6/54 **AUSTRIA** ....(5) **7** **SWITZERLAND**.....(4) **5** 31000
A. Koerner 2, Ocwirk, Wagner 3 Ballaman 2, Hugi 2, Hanappi (o.g.)
Probst

Semi-Final

30/6/54 **WEST GERMANY** ..(1) **6** **AUSTRIA**.........(0) **1** 58000
Schaefer, Morlock, F. Walter 2 (pens), Probst
O. Walter 2

SWEDEN 1958
GROUP MATCHES – GROUP 4

8/6/58 **BRAZIL**...........(1) **3** **AUSTRIA**.........(0) **0** 21000
Mazzola 2, N. Santos
11/6/58 **USSR** ....(1) **2** **AUSTRIA**.........(0) **0** 21239
Ilyin, V. Ivanov
15/6/58 **ENGLAND** ....(0) **2** **AUSTRIA**.........(1) **2** 16800
Haynes, Kevan   Koller, Koerner

ARGENTINA 1978
GROUP MATCHES – GROUP 3

3/6/78 **AUSTRIA** ....(1) **2** **SPAIN**...........(0) **1** 49317
Schachner, Krankl   Dani
7/6/78 **AUSTRIA** ....(1) **1** **SWEDEN**.........(0) **0** 46000
Krankl (pen)
11/6/78 **BRAZIL**...........(1) **1** **AUSTRIA**.........(0) **0** 40000
Roberto

GROUP MATCHES – GROUP A

Quarter-Finals

14/6/78 **HOLLAND**........ (3) **5** **AUSTRIA**.........(0) **1** 15000
Brandts, Rensenbrink (pen), Rep 2, Obermayer
Van Der Kerkhof
18/6/78 **ITALY** ....(1) **1** **AUSTRIA**.........(0) **0** 50000
Rossi
21/6/78 **AUSTRIA** ....(0) **3** **WEST GERMANY**...(1) **2** 20000
Vogts (o.g), Krankl 2   Rummenigge, Holzenbein

SPAIN 1982
GROUP MATCHES – GROUP 2

17/6/82 **AUSTRIA** ....(1) **1** **CHILE** ....(0) **0** 22500
Schachner
21/6/82 **AUSTRIA** ....(0) **2** **ALGERIA**.........(0) **0** 22000
Schachner, Krankl
25/6/82 **WEST GERMANY** ..(1) **1** **AUSTRIA**.........(0) **0** 41000
Hrubesch

GROUP D

Quarter-Finals

28/6/82 **FRANCE**..........(1) **1** **AUSTRIA**.........(0) **0** 37000
Genghini

1/7/82 **NORTHERN IRELAND**(1)**2** **AUSTRIA**........ (0) **2** 20000
  Hamilton 2   Pezzey, Hintermaier

ITALY 1990
GROUP MATCHES – GROUP A

9/6/90 **ITALY** ....(0) **1** **AUSTRIA**........ (0) **0** 72303
  Schillaci
15/6/90 **AUSTRIA** ....(0) **0** **CZECHOSLOVAKIA** . (1) **1** 38962
                                    Bilek (pen)
19/6/90 **AUSTRIA** ....(0) **2** **USA**............. (0) **1** 34857
  Ogris, Rodax   Murray

FRANCE 1998
GROUP MATCHES – GROUP B

11/6/98 **CAMEROON**.......(0) **1** **AUSTRIA**........ (0) **1** 37500
  Njanka   Polster
17/6/98 **CHILE** ....(0) **1** **AUSTRIA**........ (0) **1** 30392
  Salas   Vastic
23/6/98 **ITALY** ....(0) **2** **AUSTRIA**........ (0) **1** 75000
  Vieri, R. Baggio   Herzog (pen)

BELGIUM
URUGUAY 1930
GROUP MATCHES – GROUP 4

13/7/30 **USA** ....(2) **3** **BELGIUM** .... (0) **0** 10000
  McGhee 2, Patenaude
20/7/30 **PARAGUAY** ....(1) **1** **BELGIUM** .... (0) **0** 900
  Pena

ITALY 1934
First Round

27/5/34 **GERMANY** ....(1) **5** **BELGIUM** .... (2) **2** 8000
  Conen 3, Kobierski 2   Voorhoof 2

FRANCE 1938
First Round

5/6/38 **FRANCE**..........(2) **3** **BELGIUM** .... (1) **1** N.R.
  Veinante, Nicolas 2   Isemborghs

SWITZERLAND 1954
GROUP MATCHES – GROUP 4

17/6/54 **ENGLAND**........(2) **4** **BELGIUM** .... (1) **4** 14000
  Broadis 2, Lofthouse 2   Anoul 2, Coppens, Dickinson (o.g.)
(After Extra Time)
20/6/54 **ITALY** ....(1) **4** **BELGIUM** .... (0) **1** 24000
  Pandolfini (pen), Galli, Frignani   Anoul
  Lorenzi

MEXICO 1970
GROUP MATCHES – GROUP 1

3/6/70 **BELGIUM** ....(1) **3** **EL SALVADOR**..... (0) **0** 92000
  Van Moer 2, Lambert (pen)
6/6/70 **USSR** ....(1) **4** **BELGIUM** .... (0) **1** 59000
  Byshovets, Asatiani, Khmelnitsky   Lambert
11/6/70 **MEXICO** ....(1) **1** **BELGIUM** .... (0) **0** 105000
  Pena (pen)

SPAIN 1982
GROUP MATCHES – GROUP 3

13/6/82 **BELGIUM** ....(0) **1** **ARGENTINA** ...... (0) **0** 95000
  Van Den Bergh
19/6/82 **BELGIUM** ....(1) **1** **EL SALVADOR**..... (0) **0** 15000
  Coeck
22/6/82 **BELGIUM** ....(0) **1** **HUNGARY**........ (1) **1** 37000
  Czerniatynski   Varga

GROUP MATCHES – GROUP A
Quarter-Finals

28/6/82 **POLAND**..........(2) **3** **BELGIUM** ...... (0) **0** 65000
  Boniek 3
1/7/82 **USSR** ....(0) **1** **BELGIUM** ...... (0) **0** 45000
  Oganesian

MEXICO 1986
GROUP MATCHES – GROUP B

3/6/86 **BELGIUM** ....(1) **1** **MEXICO** .... (2) **2** 110000
  Van Den Bergh   Quirante, Sanchez
8/6/86 **IRAQ**.............(0) **1** **BELGIUM** .... (2) **2** 20000
  Rahdi   Scifo, Claesen (pen)
11/6/86 **PARAGUAY** ....(0) **2** **BELGIUM** .... (1) **2** 16000
  Cabanas 2   Vercauteren, Veyt
Second Round
15/6/86 **USSR** ....(1) **3** **BELGIUM** .... (0) **4** 32277
  Belanov 3 (1pen)   Scifo, Ceulemans, De Mol, Claesen
(After Extra Time)
Quarter-Final
22/6/86 **BELGIUM** ....(1) **1** **SPAIN**............ (1) **1** 45000
  Ceulemans   Senor
(After Extra Time – Belgium won 5-4 on penalties)
Semi-Final
25/6/86 **ARGENTINA** ......(0) **2** **BELGIUM** ...... (0) **0** 110420
  Maradona 2
Third place play-off
28/6/86 **BELGIUM** ....(1) **2** **FRANCE** .... (2) **4** 21000
  Ceulemans, Claeson   Ferrari, Papin, Genghini, Amoros (pen)
(After Extra Time)

ITALY 1990
GROUP MATCHES – GROUP E

12/6/90 **BELGIUM** ....(0) **2** **SOUTH KOREA** .... (0) **0** 32486
  Degryse, De Wolf
17/6/90 **BELGIUM** ....(2) **3** **URUGUAY**........ (0) **1** 33759
  Clijsters, Scifo, Ceulemans   Bengoechea
21/6/90 **BELGIUM** ....(1) **1** **SPAIN**............ (2) **2** 35950
  Vervoort   Michel (pen), Gorriz
Second Round
26/6/90 **ENGLAND**........(0) **1** **BELGIUM** .... (0) **0** 34520
  Platt
(After Extra Time)

U.S.A. 1994
GROUP MATCHES – GROUP F

19/6/94 **BELGIUM** ....(1) **1** **MOROCCO** .... (0) **0** 60790
  Degryse
25/6/94 **BELGIUM** ....(0) **1** **HOLLAND** .... (0) **0** 62387
  Albert
29/6/94 **BELGIUM** ....(0) **0** **SAUDI ARABIA** ... (1) **1** 52959
                                    Owairan
Second Round
2/7/94 **GERMANY** ....(3) **3** **BELGIUM** .... (1) **2** 60246
  Voller 2, Klinsmann   Grun, Albert

FRANCE 1998
GROUP MATCHES – GROUP E

13/6/98 **HOLLAND**.........(0) **0** **BELGIUM** .... (0) **0** 75000
20/6/98 **BELGIUM** ....(1) **2** **MEXICO** .... (0) **2** 34750
  Wilmots 2   Garcia Aspe (pen), Blanco
25/6/98 **BELGIUM** ....(1) **1** **SOUTH KOREA** .... (0) **1** 48500
  Nilis   Yoo

228

BOLIVIA
URUGUAY 1930
GROUP MATCHES – GROUP 2

17/7/30 **YUGOSLAVIA**......(0) **4 BOLIVIA** ....(0) **0**   800
Beck 2, Marianovic, Vujadinovic
20/7/30 **BRAZIL**...........(1) **4 BOLIVIA** ....(0) **0** 1200
Visintainer 2, Neto 2

BRAZIL 1950
GROUP MATCHES – GROUP 4

2/7/50 **URUGUAY** ....(4) **8 BOLIVIA** ....(0) **0** 5284
Schiaffino 4, Miguez 2, Vidal, Ghiggia

U.S.A. 1994
GROUP MATCHES – GROUP C

17/6/94 **GERMANY**........(0) **1 BOLIVIA** ....(0) **0** 63117
Klinsmann
23/6/94 **SOUTH KOREA**.....(0) **0 BOLIVIA** ....(0) **0** 53456
27/6/94 **BOLIVIA**..........(0) **1 SPAIN**...........(1) **3** 63089
Sanchez   *Guardiola (pen), Caminero*

BRAZIL
URUGUAY 1930
GROUP MATCHES – GROUP 2

14/7/30 **YUGOSLAVIA**......(2) **2 BRAZIL** ....(0) **1** 5000
Tirnanic, Beck   *Neto*
20/7/30 **BRAZIL**...........(1) **4 BOLIVIA** ....(0) **0** 1200
Visintainer 2, Neto 2

ITALY 1934
First Round

27/5/34 **SPAIN**...........(3) **3 BRAZIL** ....(1) **1** N.R.
Iraragorri (pen), Langara 2   *Silva*

FRANCE 1938
First Round

5/6/38 **BRAZIL**...........(3) **6 POLAND** ....(1) **5** N.R.
Leonidas 4, Peracio, Romeo   *Willimowski 4, Piontek*
(After Extra Time)

Second Round

12/6/38 **BRAZIL**...........(1) **1 CZECHOSLOVAKIA**..(1) **1** 25000
Leonidas   *Nejedly (pen)*
(After Extra Time)

Replay

14/6/38 **BRAZIL**...........(0) **2 CZECHOSLOVAKIA**..(1) **1** N.R.
Leonidas, Roberto   *Kopecky*

Semi-Final

16/6/38 **ITALY** ....(2) **2 BRAZIL** ....(0) **1** 35000
Colaussi, Meazza (pen)   *Romeo*

BRAZIL 1950
GROUP MATCHES – GROUP 1

24/6/50 **BRAZIL**...........(1) **4 MEXICO** ....(0) **0** 81649
Ademir 2, Jair, Baltazar
28/6/50 **BRAZIL**...........(2) **2 SWITZERLAND**....(1) **2** 42032
Alfredo, Baltazar   *Fatton, Tamini*
1/7/50 **BRAZIL**...........(1) **2 YUGOSLAVIA** .....(0) **0** 142409
Ademir, Zizinho

GROUP MATCHES – FINAL POOL

3/7/50 **BRAZIL**...........(3) **7 SWEDEN**..........(0) **1** 138886
Ademir 4, Chico 2, Maneca   *Andersson (pen)*
13/7/50 **BRAZIL**...........(3) **6 SPAIN**...........(0) **1** 152772
Jair 2, Chico 2, Zinzinho, Parra (o.g.) *Igoa*

16/7/50 **URUGUAY** ....(0) **2 BRAZIL** ....(0) **1** 199854
Schiaffino, Ghiggia   *Friaca*

SWITZERLAND 1954
GROUP MATCHES – GROUP 1

16/6/54 **BRAZIL**...........(4) **5 MEXICO** ....(0) **0** 12500
Baltazar, Didi, Pinga 2, Julinho
19/6/54 **BRAZIL**...........(0) **1 YUGOSLAVIA** .....(0) **1** 21000
Didi   *Zebec*
(After Extra Time)

Quarter-Final

27/6/54 **HUNGARY** ....(1) **4 BRAZIL** ....(1) **2** 40000
Hidegkuti 2, Kocsis, Lantus (pen) *D. Santos (pen), Julinho*

SWEDEN 1958
GROUP MATCHES – GROUP 4

8/6/58 **BRAZIL**...........(1) **3 AUSTRIA**.........(0) **0** 21000
Mazzola 2, N. Santos
11/6/58 **ENGLAND** ....(0) **0 BRAZIL** ....(0) **0** 40895
15/6/58 **BRAZIL**...........(1) **2 USSR**...........(0) **0** 50928
Vava 2

Quarter-Final

19/6/58 **BRAZIL**...........(0) **1 WALES** ....(0) **0** 25923
Pele

Semi-Final

24/6/58 **BRAZIL**...........(2) **5 FRANCE** ....(1) **2** 27100
Vava, Didi, Pele 3   *Fontaine, Piantoni*

Final

29/6/58 **BRAZIL**...........(2) **5 SWEDEN**..........(1) **2** 49733
Vava 2, Pele 2, Zagalo   *Liedholm, Simonsson*

CHILE 1962
GROUP MATCHES – GROUP 3

30/5/62 **BRAZIL**...........(0) **2 MEXICO** ....(0) **0** 10484
Zagalo, Pele
2/6/62 **BRAZIL**...........(0) **0 CZECHOSLOVAKIA**..(0) **0** 14903
6/6/62 **BRAZIL**...........(0) **2 SPAIN**...........(1) **1** 18715
Amarildo 2   *Adelardo*

Quarter-Final

10/6/62 **BRAZIL**...........(1) **3 ENGLAND** ....(1) **1** 17736
Garrincha 2, Vava   *Hitchens*

Semi-Final

13/6/62 **BRAZIL**...........(2) **4 CHILE** ....(1) **2** 76594
Garrincha 2, Vava 2   *Toro, L.. Sanchez (pen)*

Final

17/6/62 **BRAZIL**...........(1) **3 CZECHOSLOVAKIA**..(1) **1** 68679
Amarildo, Zito, Vava   *Masopust*

ENGLAND 1966
GROUP MATCHES – GROUP 3

12/7/66 **BRAZIL**...........(1) **2 BULGARIA** ....(0) **0** 52847
Pele, Garrincha
15/7/66 **HUNGARY** ....(1) **3 BRAZIL** ....(1) **1** 57455
Bene, Farkas, Meszoly (pen)   *Tostao*
19/7/66 **PORTUGAL**........(2) **3 BRAZIL** ....(0) **1** 62204
Simoes, Eusebio 2   *Rildo*

MEXICO 1970
GROUP MATCHES – GROUP 3

3/6/70 **BRAZIL**...........(1) **4 CZECHOSLOVAKIA**..(1) **1** 52000
Rivelino, Pele, Jairzinho 2   *Petras*
7/6/70 **BRAZIL**...........(0) **1 ENGLAND**.........(0) **0** 66000
Jairzinho
10/6/70 **BRAZIL**...........(2) **3 ROMANIA**........(1) **2** 50000
Pele 2, Jairzinho   *Dumitrche, Dembrovski*

Quarter-Final

14/6/70 **BRAZIL**...........(2) **4 PERU**............(1) **2** 54000
Rivelino, Tostao 2, Jairzinho *Gallardo, Cubillas*

229

Semi-Final

17/6/70 **BRAZIL**..........(1) **3** **URUGUAY**........ (1) **1** 51000
  Clodoaldo, Jairzinho, Rivelino   *Cubillas*

Final

21/6/70 **BRAZIL**..........(1) **4** **ITALY**........... (1) **1** 107000
  Pele, Gerson, Jairzinho, Carlos Alberto *Boninsegna*

WEST GERMANY 1974
GROUP MATCHES – GROUP 2

13/6/74 **BRAZIL**..........(0) **0** **YUGOSLAVIA**..... (0) **0** 62000
18/6/74 **BRAZIL**..........(0) **0** **SCOTLAND**....... (0) **0** 62000
22/6/74 **BRAZIL**..........(1) **3** **ZAIRE**.......... (0) **0** 36200
  Jairzinho, Rivelino, Valdomiro

GROUP MATCHES – GROUP A

Quarter-Finals

26/6/74 **BRAZIL**..........(0) **1** **EAST GERMANY**.. (0) **0** 59700
  Rivelino
30/6/74 **BRAZIL**..........(1) **2** **ARGENTINA**...... (1) **1** 39400
  Rivelino, Jairzinho   *Brindisi*
3/7/74 **HOLLAND**........(0) **2** **BRAZIL**.......... (0) **0** 53700
  Neeskens, Cruyff

Third Place Play-Off

6/7/74 **POLAND**..........(0) **1** **BRAZIL**.......... (0) **0** 79000
  Lato

ARGENTINA 1978
GROUP MATCHES – GROUP 3

3/6/78 **SWEDEN**.........(1) **1** **BRAZIL**.......... (1) **1** 38000
  Sjoberg   *Reinaldo*
7/6/78 **BRAZIL**..........(0) **0** **SPAIN**.......... (0) **0** 49317
11/6/78 **BRAZIL**..........(1) **1** **AUSTRIA**........ (0) **0** 40000

GROUP MATCHES – GROUP B

Quarter-Finals

14/6/78 **BRAZIL**..........(2) **3** **PERU**........... (0) **0** 40000
  Dirceu 2, Zico (pen)
18/6/78 **ARGENTINA**......(0) **0** **BRAZIL**.......... (0) **0** 46000
21/6/78 **BRAZIL**..........(1) **3** **POLAND**........ (1) **1** 44000
  Nelinho, Roberto 2   *Lato*

Third Place Play-Off

24/6/78 **BRAZIL**..........(0) **2** **ITALY**........... (1) **1** 76609
  Nelinho, Dirceu   *Causio*

SPAIN 1982
GROUP MATCHES – GROUP 6

14/6/82 **BRAZIL**..........(0) **2** **USSR**........... (1) **1** 68000
  Socrates, Eder   *Bal*
18/6/82 **BRAZIL**..........(1) **4** **SCOTLAND**....... (1) **1** 47374
  Zico, Oscar, Eder, Falcao   *Narey*
23/6/82 **BRAZIL**..........(2) **4** **NEW ZEALAND**... (0) **0** 43000
  Zico 2, Falcao, Serginho

GROUP MATCHES – GROUP C

Quarter-Finals

2/7/82 **BRAZIL**..........(1) **3** **ARGENTINA**...... (0) **1** 44000
  Zico 2, Falcao, Serginho   *Diaz*
5/7/82 **ITALY**...........(2) **3** **BRAZIL**.......... (1) **2** 44000
  Rossi 3   *Socrates, Falcao*

MEXICO 1986
GROUP MATCHES – GROUP D

1/6/86 **SPAIN**...........(0) **0** **BRAZIL**.......... (0) **1** 35748
  Socrates
6/6/86 **BRAZIL**..........(0) **1** **ALGERIA**........ (0) **0** 48000
  Careca
12/6/86 **NORTHERN IRELAND**(0)**0** **BRAZIL**.......... (2) **3** 51000
  Careca 2, Josimar

Second Round

16/6/86 **BRAZIL**..........(1) **4** **POLAND**........ (0) **0** 4500
  Socrates (pen), Josimar, Edinho, Careca (pen)

Quarter-Final

21/6/86 **BRAZIL**..........(1) **1** **FRANCE**........ (1) **1** 6577?
  Careca   *Platini*
(After Extra Time – France Won 4-3 on Penalties)

ITALY 1990
GROUP MATCHES – GROUP C

10/6/90 **BRAZIL**..........(1) **2** **SWEDEN**........ (0) **1** 6262?
  Careca 2   *Brolin*
16/6/90 **BRAZIL**..........(1) **1** **COSTA RICA**.... (0) **0** 5800?
  Muller
20/6/90 **BRAZIL**..........(0) **1** **SCOTLAND**....... (0) **0** 6250?
  Muller

Second Round

24/6/90 **BRAZIL**..........(0) **0** **ARGENTINA**...... (0) **1** 6138?
  Caniggia

U.S.A. 1994
GROUP MATCHES – GROUP B

20/6/94 **BRAZIL**..........(1) **2** **RUSSIA**........ (0) **0** 81061?
  Romario, Rai (pen)
24/6/94 **BRAZIL**..........(1) **3** **CAMEROON**..... (0) **0** 83401?
  Romario, Marcio Santos, Bebeto
28/6/94 **BRAZIL**..........(0) **1** **SWEDEN**........ (1) **1** 77217?
  Romario   *K. Anderson*

Second Round

4/7/94 **BRAZIL**..........(0) **1** **USA**........... (0) **0** 84147?
  Bebeto

Quarter-Final

9/7/94 **HOLLAND**........(0) **2** **BRAZIL**.......... (0) **3** 63998?
  Bergkamp, Winter   *Romario, Bebeto, Branco*

Semi-Final

13/7/94 **SWEDEN**.........(0) **0** **BRAZIL**.......... (0) **1** 84569?
  Romario

Final

17/7/94 **BRAZIL**..........(0) **0** **ITALY**........... (0) **0** 94194
(After Extra Time – Brazil won 3-2 on Penalties)

FRANCE 1998
GROUP MATCHES – GROUP A

10/6/98 **BRAZIL**..........(1) **2** **SCOTLAND**....... (1) **1** 80000
  Sampaio, Boyd (og)   *Collins (pen)*
16/6/98 **BRAZIL**..........(2) **3** **MOROCCO**....... (0) **0** 33266
  Ronaldo, Rivaldo, Bebeto
23/6/98 **BRAZIL**..........(0) **1** **NORWAY** .... (0) **2** 55500
  Bebeto   *T.A. Flo, Rekdal (pen)*

Second Round

27/6/98 **BRAZIL**..........(3) **4** **CHILE** .... (0) **1** 48500
  Sampaio 2, Ronaldo 2 (1 pen)   *Salas*

Quarter-Final

3/7/98 **BRAZIL**..........(2) **3** **DENMARK** .... (1) **2** 40000
  Bebeto, Rivaldo 2   *Jorgensen, B. Laudrup*

Semi-Final

7/7/98 **BRAZIL**..........(0) **1** **HOLLAND** .... (0) **1** 54000
  Ronaldo   *Kluivert*
(After Extra Time – Brazil won 4-2 on Penalties)

Final

12/7/98 **BRAZIL**..........(0) **0** **FRANCE** .... (2) **3** 75000
  Zidane 2, Petit

BULGARIA
CHILE 1962
GROUP MATCHES – GROUP 4

30/5/62 **ARGENTINA**.......(1) **1** **BULGARIA** ....(0) **0** 7134
Facundo

3/6/62 **HUNGARY** ....(4) **6** **BULGARIA** ....(0) **1** 7442
Albert 3, Tichy 2, Solymosi   *Sokolov*

7/6/62 **ENGLAND** ....(0) **0** **BULGARIA** ....(0) **0** 7945

ENGLAND 1966
GROUP MATCHES – GROUP 3

12/7/66 **BRAZIL**...........(1) **2** **BULGARIA** ....(0) **0** 52847
Pele, Garrincha

16/7/66 **PORTUGAL**........(2) **3** **BULGARIA** ....(0) **0** 57455
Vutzov (o.g.) Eusebio, Torres

20/7/66 **HUNGARY** ....(2) **3** **BULGARIA** ....(1) **1** 22064
Davidov (o.g.), Meszoly, Bene   *Asparoukhov*

MEXICO 1970
GROUP MATCHES – GROUP 4

2/6/70 **PERU** ....(0) **3** **BULGARIA** ....(1) **2** 14000
Gallardo, Chumpitaz, Cubillas   *Dermendjiev, Bonev*

7/6/70 **WEST GERMANY** ..(2) **5** **BULGARIA** ....(1) **2** 12700
Libuda, Muller 3 (1 pen), Seeler   *Nikodimov, Kolev*

11/6/70 **BULGARIA** ....(1) **1** **MOROCCO** ....(0) **1** 12200
Jetchev   *Ghazouani*

WEST GERMANY 1974
GROUP MATCHES – GROUP 3

15/6/74 **SWEDEN** ....(0) **0** **BULGARIA** ....(0) **0** 23300

19/6/74 **BULGARIA** ....(0) **1** **URUGUAY**.........(0) **1** 13400
Bonev   *Pavoni*

23/6/74 **HOLLAND**.........(2) **4** **BULGARIA** ....(0) **1** 53300
Neeskens (2 pens), Rep, De Jong   *Krol (o.g.)*

MEXICO 1986
GROUP MATCHES – GROUP A

31/5/86 **BULGARIA** ....(0) **1** **ITALY**.............(1) **1** 95000
Sirakov   *Altobelli*

5/6/86 **SOUTH KOREA**.....(0) **1** **BULGARIA** ....(1) **1** 45000
Kim Jong Boo   *Getov*

10/6/86 **ARGENTINA**.......(1) **2** **BULGARIA** ....(0) **0** 65000
Valdano, Burruchaga

Second Round

15/6/86 **MEXICO** ....(1) **2** **BULGARIA** ....(0) **0** 114580
Negrete, Servin

U.S.A. 1994
GROUP MATCHES – GROUP D

21/6/94 **NIGERIA**..........(2) **3** **BULGARIA** ....(0) **0** 44932
Yekini, Amokachi, Amunike

26/6/94 **BULGARIA** ....(1) **4** **GREECE**...........(0) **0** 63160
Stoichkov (2 pens), Lechkov, Borimirov

30/6/94 **ARGENTINA**......(0) **0** **BULGARIA** ....(0) **2** 63998
              Stoichkov, Sirakov

Second Round

5/7/94 **MEXICO** ....(1) **1** **BULGARIA** ....(1) **1** 71030
Garcia Aspe (pen)   *Stoichkov*

(After Extra Time – Bulgaria won 3-1 on penalties)

Quarter-Final

10/7/94 **BULGARIA** ....(0) **2** **GERMANY** ....(0) **1** 72416
Stoichkov, Lechkov   *Matthaus (pen)*

Semi-Final

13/7/94 **BULGARIA** ....(1) **1** **ITALY**.............(2) **2** 77094
Stoichkov (pen)   *R. Baggio 2*

Third Place Play-Off

16/7/94 **BULGARIA** ....(0) **0** **SWEDEN**.........(4) **4** 83716
           Brolin, Mild, Larsson, K. Anderson

FRANCE 1998
GROUP MATCHES – GROUP D

12/6/98 **PARAGUAY** ......(0) **0** **BULGARIA** ....(0) **0** 27650

19/6/98 **NIGERIA**..........(1) **1** **BULGARIA** ....(0) **0** 48500
Ikpeba

24/6/98 **SPAIN**............(2) **6** **BULGARIA** ....(0) **1** 40500
Hierro (pen), Luis Enrique,   *Kostadinov*
Morientes 2, Kiko 2

CAMEROON
SPAIN 1982
GROUP MATCHES – GROUP 1

15/6/82 **PERU** ....(0) **0** **CAMEROON** ......(0) **0** 11000

19/6/82 **POLAND**..........(0) **0** **CAMEROON** ......(0) **0** 19000

23/6/82 **ITALY** ....(0) **1** **CAMEROON** ......(0) **1** 20000
Graziani   *M'Bida*

ITALY 1990
GROUP MATCHES – GROUP B

8/6/90 **ARGENTINA**.......(0) **0** **CAMEROON** ......(0) **1** 73780
             F. Biyick

14/6/90 **CAMEROON**.......(0) **2** **ROMANIA**.........(0) **1** 38687
Milla 2   *Balint*

18/6/90 **CAMEROON**......(0) **0** **USSR**.............(2) **4** 37307
             Protasov, Zygmantovich, Zavarov
             Dobrovolsky

Second Round

23/6/90 **CAMEROON**.......(0) **2** **COLOMBIA** ....(0) **1** 50026
Milla 2   *Redin*

(After Extra Time)

1/7/90 **ENGLAND** ....(1) **3** **CAMEROON** ......(0) **2** 55205
Platt, Lineker (2 pens)   *Kunde (pen), Ekeke*

(After Extra Time)

U.S.A. 1994
GROUP MATCHES – GROUP B

19/6/94 **CAMEROON**......(1) **2** **SWEDEN**.........(1) **2** 83959
Embe, Omam-Biyik   *Ljung, Dahlin*

24/6/94 **BRAZIL**...........(1) **3** **CAMEROON** ......(0) **0** 83401
Romario, Marcio Santos, Bebeto

28/6/94 **RUSSIA** ....(3) **6** **CAMEROON** ......(0) **1** 74914
Salenko 5, Radchenko   *Milla*

FRANCE 1998
GROUP MATCHES – GROUP B

11/6/98 **CAMEROON**......(0) **1** **AUSTRIA**.........(0) **1** 37500
Njanka   *Polster*

17/6/98 **ITALY** ....(1) **3** **CAMEROON** ......(0) **0** 35000
Di Biagio, Vieri 2

23/6/98 **CHILE** ....(1) **1** **CAMEROON** ......(0) **1** 39000
Sierra   *Mboma*

CANADA
MEXICO 1986
GROUP MATCHES – GROUP C

1/6/86 **CANADA** ....(0) **0** **FRANCE** ....(0) **1** 65000
             Papin

6/6/86 **HUNGARY** ....(1) **2** **CANADA**..........(0) **0** 13800
Esterhazy, Detan

9/6/86 **USSR** ....(0) **2** **CANADA**..........(0) **0** 14200
Blokhin, Zavarov

CHILE
URUGUAY 1930
GROUP MATCHES – GROUP 1

16/7/30 **CHILE** ....(1) **3** **MEXICO** ....(0) **0** 500
Vidal, Subiabre 2

19/7/30 CHILE . . . .(0) 1 FRANCE . . . . (0) 0 2000
Subiabre

22/7/30 ARGENTINA. . . . . . .(2) 3 CHILE . . . . (1) 1 1000
Stabile 2, M. Evaristo   Subriabre

BRAZIL 1950
GROUP MATCHES – GROUP 2

25/6/50 ENGLAND. . . . .(1) 2 CHILE . . . . (0) 0 29703
Mortenson, Mannion

29/6/50 SPAIN. . . . .(2) 2 CHILE . . . . (0) 0 19700
Basora, Zarra

2/7/50 CHILE . . . .(2) 5 USA. . . . . (0) 2 8501
Robledo, Cremaschi 3, Prieto   Pariani, J. Souza

CHILE 1962
GROUP MATCHES – GROUP 2

30/5/62 CHILE . . . .(1) 3 SWITZERLAND. . . . (1) 1 65006
L. Sanchez 2, Ramirez   Wuthrich

2/6/62 CHILE . . . .(0) 2 ITALY. . . . . (0) 0 66057
Ramirez, Toro

6/6/62 WEST GERMANY . .(1) 2 CHILE . . . . (0) 0 67224
Szymaniak (pen), Seeler

Quarter-Final

10/6/62 CHILE . . . .(2) 2 USSR. . . . . (1) 1 17208
L. Sanchez, Rojas   Chislenko

Semi-Final

13/6/62 BRAZIL. . . . .(2) 4 CHILE . . . . (1) 2 76594
Garrincha 2, Vara 2   Toro, L. Sanchez (pen)

Third Place Play-Off

16/6/62 CHILE . . . .(0) 1 YUGOSLAVIA . . . . . (0) 0 66697
Rojas

ENGLAND 1966
GROUP MATCHES – GROUP 4

13/6/66 ITALY . . . .(1) 2 CHILE . . . . (0) 0 30956
·Mazzola, Barison

15/6/66 CHILE . . . .(1) 1 NORTH KOREA . . . (0) 1 15887
Marcos (pen)   Pak Seung Jin

20/6/66 USSR . . . .(1) 2 CHILE . . . . (1) 1 22590
Porkujan 2   Marcos

WEST GERMANY 1974
GROUP MATCHES – GROUP 1

14/6/74 WEST GERMANY . .(1) 1 CHILE . . . . (0) 0 83168
Breitner

18/6/74 EAST GERMANY . . .(0) 1 CHILE . . . . (0) 1 27300
Hoffman   Ahumada

22/6/74 CHILE . . . .(0) 0 AUSTRALIA . . . . . . (0) 0 14000

SPAIN 1982
GROUP MATCHES – GROUP 2

17/6/82 AUSTRIA . . . .(1) 1 CHILE . . . . (0) 0 22300
Schachner

20/6/82 WEST GERMANY . .(1) 4 CHILE . . . . (0) 1 42000
Rummenigge 3, Reinders   Moscoso

24/6/82 ALGERIA. . . . .(3) 3 CHILE . . . . (0) 2 16000
Assad 2, Bensoula   Neira (pen), Letelier

FRANCE 1998
GROUP MATCHES – GROUP B

11/6/98 ITALY . . . .(1) 2 CHILE . . . . (1) 2 31800
Vieri, R. Baggio (pen)   Salas 2

17/6/98 CHILE . . . .(0) 1 AUSTRIA. . . . . (0) 1 30392
Salas   Vastic

23/6/98 CHILE . . . .(1) 1 CAMEROON . . . . . . (0) 1 39000
Sierra   Mboma

Second Round

27/6/98 BRAZIL. . . . .(3) 4 CHILE . . . . (0) 1 48500
Sampaio 2, Ronaldo 2 (1 pen) Salas

COLOMBIA
CHILE 1962
GROUP MATCHES – GROUP 1

30/5/62 URUGUAY . . . .(0) 2 COLOMBIA . . . . (1) 1 7908
Cubilla, Sasia   Zaluaga

3/6/62 USSR . . . .(3) 4 COLOMBIA . . . . (1) 4 8040
Ivamov 2, Chislenko, Ponedelnik Aceros, Coll, Roda, Klinger

7/6/62 YUGOSLAVIA . . . . . .(2) 5 COLOMBIA . . . . (0) 0 716
Galic, Jerkovic 3, Melic

ITALY 1990
GROUP MATCHES – GROUP D

9/6/90 U.A.E. . . . .(0) 0 COLOMBIA . . . . (0) 2 30791
Redin, Valderrama

14/6/90 YUGOSLAVIA . . . . . .(0) 1 COLOMBIA . . . . (0) 0 32257
Jozic

19/6/90 WEST GERMANY . . .(0) 1 COLOMBIA . . . . (0) 1 72510
Littbarski   Rincon

Second Round

23/6/90 CAMEROON . . . .(0) 2 COLOMBIA . . . . (0) 1 50026
Milla 2   Redin

U.S.A. 1994
GROUP MATCHES – GROUP A

19/6/94 COLOMBIA. . . . .(1) 1 ROMANIA. . . . . (2) 3 91865
Valencia   Raducioiu 2, Hagi

24/6/94 USA . . . .(1) 2 COLOMBIA . . . . (0) 1 93194
Escobar (o.g.), Stewart   Valencia

28/6/94 SWITZERLAND . . . .(0) 0 COLOMBIA . . . . (1) 2 83769
Gaviria, Lozano

FRANCE 1998
GROUP MATCHES – GROUP G

15/6/98 ROMANIA . . . .(1) 1 COLOMBIA . . . . (0) 0 37572
Ilie

22/6/98 COLOMBIA. . . . .(0) 1 TUNISIA . . . . (0) 0 35000
Preciado

26/6/98 COLOMBIA. . . . .(0) 0 ENGLAND . . . . (2) 2 41275
Anderton, Beckham

COSTA RICA
ITALY 1990
GROUP MATCHES – GROUP C

11/6/90 COSTA RICA. . . . . . .(0) 1 SCOTLAND . . . . (0) 0 30867
Cayasso

16/6/90 BRAZIL. . . . .(1) 1 COSTA RICA . . . . . . (0) 0 38007
Muller

20/6/90 SWEDEN . . . .(1) 1 COSTA RICA . . . . . . (0) 2 30223
Ekstrom   Flores, Medford

Second Round

23/6/90 CZECHOSLOVAKIA. .(1) 4 COSTA RICA . . . . . . (0) 1 47673
Skuhravy 3, Kubik   Gonzalez

CROATIA
FRANCE 1998
GROUP MATCHES – GROUP H

14/6/98 JAMAICA. . . . .(1) 1 CROATIA. . . . . (1) 3 38058
Earle   Stanic, Prosinecki, Suker

20/6/98 JAPAN . . . .(0) 0 CROATIA. . . . . (0) 1 39000
Suker

26/6/98 ARGENTINA. . . . . . .(1) 1 CROATIA. . . . . (0) 0 35000
Pineda

Second Round

30/6/98 ROMANIA . . . .(0) 0 CROATIA. . . . . (1) 1 34700
Suker (pen)

232

Quarter-Final

4/7/98 **GERMANY** . . . . (0) **0**   **CROATIA** . . . .(1) **3** 39100
                                Jarni, Vlaovic, Suker

Semi-Final

8/7/98 **FRANCE** . . . . (0) **2**   **CROATIA** . . . .(0) **1** 76000
      Thuram 2   *Suker*

Third-Place Play-off

11/7/98 **HOLLAND** . . . .(1) **1**   **CROATIA** . . . .(2) **2** 44000
      Zenden   *Prosinecki, Suker*

CUBA
FRANCE 1938
GROUP MATCHES – GROUP 1

First Round

5/6/38 **CUBA** . . . .(0) **3**   **ROMANIA** . . . .(1) **3** 6000
      Tunas, Maquina, Sosa   *Convaci, Baratki, Dobai*

Replay

9/6/38 **CUBA** . . . .(0) **2**   **ROMANIA** . . . .(1) **1** 5000
      Socorro, Maquina   *Dobai*

Second Round

12/6/38 **SWEDEN** . . . .(4) **8**   **CUBA** . . . .(0) **0** N.R.
      Anderson, Jonasson, Wetterstroem 4
      Nyberg, Keller

CZECHOSLOVAKIA
ITALY 1934
GROUP MATCHES – GROUP 1

First Round

27/5/34 **CZECHOSLOVAKIA** . .(0) **2**   **ROMANIA** . . . .(1) **1** N.R.
      Puc, Nejedly   *Dobai*

Second Round

31/5/34 **CZECHOSLOVAKIA** . .(1) **3**   **SWITZERLAND** . . . . .(1) **2** N.R.
      Svoboda, Sobotka, Nejedly   *Kielholtz, Abegglen*

Semi-Final

3/6/34 **CZECHOSLOVAKIA** . .(1) **3**   **GERMANY** . . . .(0) **1** 10000
      Nejedly 2, Krcil   *Noack*

Final

10/6/34 **ITALY** . . . .(0) **2**   **CZECHOSLOVAKIA** . .(0) **1** 55000
      Orsi, Schiavio

(After Extra Time)

FRANCE 1938
GROUP MATCHES – GROUP 1

First Round

5/6/38 **CZECHOSLOVAKIA** . .(0) **3**   **HOLLAND** . . . .(0) **0** N.R.
      Kostalek, Boucek, Nejedly

(After Extra Time)

Second Round

12/6/38 **BRAZIL** . . . .(1) **1**   **CZECHOSLOVAKIA** . .(1) **1** 25000
      Leonidas   *Nejedly (pen)*

(After Extra Time)

Replay

14/6/38 **BRAZIL** . . . .(0) **2**   **CZECHOSLOVAKIA** . .(1) **1** N.R.
      Leonidas, Roberto   *Kopecky*

SWITZERLAND 1954
GROUP MATCHES – GROUP 3

16/6/38 **URUGUAY** . . . .(0) **2**   **CZECHOSLOVAKIA** . .(0) **0** 20500
      Miguez, Schiaffino

19/6/38 **AUSTRIA** . . . .(4) **5**   **CZECHOSLOVAKIA** . .(0) **0** 21000
      Stojaspal 2, Probst 3

SWEDEN 1958
GROUP MATCHES – GROUP 1

8/6/58 **NORTHERN IRELAND**(1)**1**   **CZECHOSLOVAKIA** . .(0) **0** 10647
      Cush

11/6/58 **WEST GERMANY** . .(1) **2**   **CZECHOSLOVAKIA** . .(0) **2** 25000
      Schaefer, Rahn   *Dvorak (pen), Zikan*

15/6/58 **CZECHOSLOVAKIA** . .(3) **6**   **ARGENTINA** . . . .(1) **1** 16418
      Dvorak, Zikan 2, Feureisl, Hovorka 2 *Corbatta*

Play-Off

17/6/58 **NORTHERN IRELAND**(1)**2**   **CZECHOSLOVAKIA** . .(1) **1** 6196
      McParland 2   *Zikan*

(After Extra Time)

CHILE 1962
GROUP MATCHES – GROUP 3

31/5/62 **CZECHOSLOVAKIA** . .(0) **1**   **SPAIN** . . . .(0) **0** 12700
      Stibranyi

2/6/62 **BRAZIL** . . . .(0) **0**   **CZECHOSLOVAKIA** . .(0) **0** 14903

7/6/62 **MEXICO** . . . .(2) **3**   **CZECHOSLOVAKIA** . .(1) **1** 10648
      Diaz, Del Aguila, H. Hernandez (pen) *Masek*

Quarter-Final

10/6/62 **CZECHOSLOVAKIA** . .(1) **1**   **HUNGARY** . . . .(0) **0** 11690
      Scherer

Semi-Final

13/6/62 **CZECHOSLOVAKIA** . .(0) **3**   **YUGOSLAVIA** . . . . . .(0) **1** 5890
      Kadraba, Scherer 2 (1 pen) *Jerkovic*

Final

17/6/62 **BRAZIL** . . . .(1) **3**   **CZECHOSLOVAKIA** . .(1) **1** 68679
      Amarildo, Zito, Vava   *Masopust*

MEXICO 1970
GROUP MATCHES – GROUP 3

3/6/70 **BRAZIL** . . . .(1) **4**   **CZECHOSLOVAKIA** . .(1) **1** 52000
      Rivelino, Pele, Jairzinho 2 *Petras*

6/6/70 **ROMANIA** . . . .(0) **2**   **CZECHOSLOVAKIA** . .(1) **1** 56000
      Neagu, Dumitrache (pen) *Petras*

11/6/70 **ENGLAND** . . . .(0) **1**   **CZECHOSLOVAKIA** . .(0) **0** 49000
      Clarke (pen)

SPAIN 1982
GROUP MATCHES – GROUP 4

17/6/82 **CZECHOSLOVAKIA** . .(1) **1**   **KUWAIT** . . . .(0) **1** 25000
      Panenka (pen)   *Al Dakhed*

20/6/82 **ENGLAND** . . . .(0) **2**   **CZECHOSLOVAKIA** . .(0) **0** 41123
      Francis, Barmos (o.g.)

24/6/82 **FRANCE** . . . .(0) **1**   **CZECHOSLOVAKIA** . .(0) **1** N.R.
      Six   *Panenka (pen)*

ITALY 1990
GROUP MATCHES – GROUP A

10/6/90 **USA** . . . .(0) **1**   **CZECHOSLOVAKIA** . .(2) **5** 33266
      Caligiuri   *Skuhravy 2, Bilek (pen), Hasek, Luhovy*

15/6/90 **AUSTRIA** . . . .(0) **0**   **CZECHOSLOVAKIA** . .(1) **1** 38962
                 Bilek (pen)

19/6/90 **ITALY** . . . .(1) **2**   **CZECHOSLOVAKIA** . .(0) **0** 73303
      Schillaci, Baggio

Second Round

23/6/90 **CZECHOSLOVAKIA** . .(1) **4**   **COSTA RICA** . . . .(0) **1** 47673
      Skuhravy 3, Kubik   *Gonzalez*

Quarter-Final

1/7/90 **CZECHOSLOVAKIA** . .(0) **0**   **WEST GERMANY** . . .(1) **1** 73347
                  Matthaus

DENMARK

MEXICO 1986

GROUP MATCHES – GROUP E

4/6/86 **SCOTLAND**........(0) **0**   **DENMARK** .... (0) **1** 18000
                        Elkjaer

8/6/86 **DENMARK** ....(2) **6**   **URUGUAY** .... (1) **1** 26500
      Elkjaer 3, Lerby, Laudrup, J. Olsen   *Francescoli*

13/6/86 **DENMARK** ....(1) **2**   **WEST GERMANY** .. (0) **0** 36000
      J. Olsen (pen), Eriksen

Second Round

18/6/86 **DENMARK** ....(1) **1**   **SPAIN** .... (1) **5** 38500
      J. Olsen (pen)   *Butragueno 4 (1 pen), Goicoechea (pen)*

FRANCE 1998

GROUP MATCHES – GROUP C

12/6/98 **SAUDI ARABIA** ....(0) **0**   **DENMARK** .... (0) **1** 38140
                      Rieper

18/6/98 **SOUTH AFRICA** ....(0) **1**   **DENMARK** .... (1) **1** 36500
      McCarthy   *Nielsen*

24/6/98 **FRANCE** ....(1) **2**   **DENMARK** .... (1) **1** 43500
      Djorkaeff (pen), Petit   *M. Laudrup (pen)*

Second Round

28/6/98 **NIGERIA** ....(0) **1**   **DENMARK** .... (2) **4** 80000
      Babangida   *Moller, B. Laudrup, Sand, Helveg*

Quarter-Final

3/7/98 **BRAZIL** ....(2) **3**   **DENMARK** .... (1) **2** 40000
      Bebeto, Rivaldo 2   *Jorgensen, B. Laudrup*

DUTCH EAST INDIES

FRANCE 1938

First Round

5/6/38 **HUNGARY** ....(4) **6**   **DUTCH EAST INDIES** (0) **0**   N.R.
      Kohut, Toldi, Sarosi 2, Szengeller 2

EAST GERMANY

WEST GERMANY 1974

GROUP MATCHES – GROUP 1

14/6/74 **EAST GERMANY** ...(0) **2**   **AUSTRALIA** ...... (0) **0** 17000
      Curran (o.g.), Streich

18/6/74 **EAST GERMANY** ...(0) **1**   **CHILE** .... (0) **1** 27300
      Hoffman   *Ahumada*

22/6/74 **EAST GERMANY** .. (0) **1**   **WEST GERMANY** .. (0) **0** 60000
      Sparwasser

GROUP MATCHES – GROUP A

Quarter-Finals

26/6/74 **BRAZIL** ....(0) **1**   **EAST GERMANY** .. (0) **0** 59700
      Rivelino

30/6/74 **HOLLAND**.........(1) **2**   **EAST GERMANY** .. (0) **0** 69600
      Neeskens, Rensenbrink

3/7/74 **ARGENTINA**.......(1) **1**   **EAST GERMANY** .. (1) **1** 54200
      Houseman   *Streich*

EGYPT

ITALY 1934

First Round

27/5/34 **HUNGARY** ....(2) **4**   **EGYPT**........... (1) **2**   N.R.
      Teleky, Toldi 2, Vincze   *Fawzi 2*

ITALY 1990

GROUP MATCHES – GROUP F

12/6/90 **HOLLAND**.........(0) **1**   **EGYPT**........... (0) **1** 33288
      Kieft   *Abdel-Ghani (pen)*

17/6/90 **EIRE** ....(0) **0**   **EGYPT**........... (0) **0** 33288

21/6/90 **ENGLAND**........(0) **1**   **EGYPT** .... (0) **0** 34959
      Wright

EIRE

ITALY 1990

GROUP MATCHES – GROUP F

11/6/90 **ENGLAND**........(1) **1**   **EIRE**............. (0) **1** 35238
      Lineker   *Sheedy*

17/6/90 **EIRE** ....(0) **0**   **EGYPT** .... (0) **0** 33288

21/6/90 **EIRE** ....(0) **1**   **HOLLAND** .... (1) **1** 33288
      Quinn   *Gullit*

Second Round

25/6/90 **EIRE** ....(0) **0**   **ROMANIA**........ (0) **0** 31818
      (After Extra Time – Eire won 5-4 on penalties)

30/6/90 **ITALY** ....(1) **1**   **EIRE**............. (0) **0** 73303
      Schillaci

U.S.A. 1994

GROUP MATCHES – GROUP E

18/6/94 **ITALY** ....(0) **0**   **EIRE**............. (1) **1** 74826
                      Houghton

24/6/94 **MEXICO** ....(1) **2**   **EIRE**............. (0) **1** 61219
      Luis Garcia 2   *Aldridge*

28/6/94 **EIRE** ....(0) **0**   **NORWAY** .... (0) **0** 76322

Second Round

4/7/94 **HOLLAND** ....(2) **2**   **EIRE**............. (0) **0** 61355
      Bergkamp, Jonk

EL SALVADOR

MEXICO 1970

GROUP MATCHES – GROUP 1

3/6/70 **BELGIUM** ....(1) **3**   **EL SALVADOR**..... (0) **0** 92000
      Van Moer 2, Lambert (pen)

7/6/70 **MEXICO** ....(1) **4**   **EL SALVADOR**..... (0) **0** 103000
      Valdivia 2, Fragoso, Basaguran

10/6/70 **USSR** ....(0) **2**   **EL SALVADOR**..... (0) **0** 89000
      Byshovets

SPAIN 1982

GROUP MATCHES – GROUP 3

15/6/82 **HUNGARY** ....(3) **10**   **EL SALVADOR** .... (0) **1** 23000
      Nyilasi 2, Fazekas 2, Poloskei, Toth,   *Zapata*
      Kiss 3, Szentes

19/6/82 **BELGIUM** ....(1) **1**   **EL SALVADOR** .... (0) **0** 15000
      Coeck

23/6/82 **ARGENTINA**......(1) **2**   **EL SALVADOR** .... (0) **0** 32000
      Passarella (pen), Bertoni

ENGLAND

BRAZIL 1950

GROUP MATCHES – GROUP 2

25/6/50 **ENGLAND**........(1) **2**   **CHILE** .... (0) **0** 29703
      Mortenson, Mannion

29/6/50 **USA** ....(1) **1**   **ENGLAND**....... (0) **0** 10151
      Gaetjens

2/7/50 **SPAIN**............(0) **1**   **ENGLAND**....... (0) **0** 74462
      Zarra

SWITZERLAND 1954

GROUP MATCHES – GROUP 4

17/6/54 **ENGLAND**........(2) **4**   **BELGIUM** .... (1) **4** 14000
      Broadis 2, Lofthouse 2   *Anoul 2, Coppens, Dickinson (o.g.)*

(After Extra Time)

20/6/54 **ENGLAND** . . . .(1) **2** **SWITZERLAND** . . . . .(0) **0** 43500
Mullen, Wilshaw

Quarter-Final

26/6/54 **URUGUAY** . . . .(2) **4** **ENGLAND** . . . .(1) **2** 50000
Borges, Varela, Schiaffino, Ambrois   Lofthouse, Finney

SWEDEN 1958
GROUP MATCHES – GROUP 4

8/6/58 **ENGLAND** . . . .(0) **2** **USSR** . . . .(1) **2** 49348
Kevan, Finney (pen)   Simonian, Ivanov (A)
11/6/58 **ENGLAND** . . . .(0) **0** **BRAZIL** . . . .(0) **0** 40895
15/6/58 **ENGLAND** . . . .(0) **2** **AUSTRIA** . . . .(1) **2** 16800
Haynes, Kevan   Koller, Koerner
17/6/58 **USSR** . . . .(0) **1** **ENGLAND** . . . .(0) **0** 23182
Ilyin

CHILE 1962
GROUP MATCHES – GROUP 4

31/5/62 **HUNGARY** . . . .(1) **2** **ENGLAND** . . . .(0) **1** 7938
Tichy, Albert   Flowers (pen)
2/6/62 **ENGLAND** . . . .(2) **3** **ARGENTINA** . . . .(0) **1** 9794
Flowers (pen), Charlton, Greaves   Sanfilippo
7/6/62 **ENGLAND** . . . .(0) **0** **BULGARIA** . . . .(0) **0** 5700

Quarter-Final

10/6/62 **BRAZIL** . . . .(1) **3** **ENGLAND** . . . .(1) **1** 17736
Garrincha 2, Vava   Hitchens

ENGLAND 1966
GROUP MATCHES – GROUP 1

11/7/66 **ENGLAND** . . . .(0) **0** **URUGUAY** . . . .(0) **0** 87148
13/7/66 **ENGLAND** . . . .(1) **2** **MEXICO** . . . .(0) **0** 92570
Charlton, Hunt
20/7/66 **ENGLAND** . . . .(1) **2** **FRANCE** . . . .(0) **0** 98270
Hunt 2

Quarter-Final

23/7/66 **ENGLAND** . . . .(0) **1** **ARGENTINA** . . . .(0) **0** 90584
Hurst

Semi-Final

26/7/66 **ENGLAND** . . . .(1) **2** **PORTUGAL** . . . .(0) **1** 94493
Charlton 2   Eusebio (pen)

Final

30/7/66 **ENGLAND** . . . .(1) **4** **WEST GERMANY** . . .(1) **2** 96924
Husrt 3, Peters   Haller, Weber

(After Extra Time)

MEXICO 1970
GROUP MATCHES – GROUP 3

2/5/70 **ENGLAND** . . . .(0) **1** **RUMANIA** . . . .(0) **0** 50000
Hurst
7/6/70 **BRAZIL** . . . .(0) **1** **ENGLAND** . . . .(0) **0** 66000
Jairzinho
11/6/70 **ENGLAND** . . . .(0) **1** **CZECHOSLOVAKIA** . .(0) **0** 49000
Clarke (pen)

Quarter-Final

14/6/70 **WEST GERMANY** . .(0) **3** **ENGLAND** . . . .(1) **2** 24000
Beckenbauer, Seeler, Muller   Mullery, Peters

(After Extra Time)

SPAIN 1982
GROUP MATCHES – GROUP 4

16/6/82 **ENGLAND** . . . .(1) **3** **FRANCE** . . . .(1) **1** 44172
Robson 2, Mariner   Soler
20/6/82 **ENGLAND** . . . .(0) **2** **CZECHOSLOVAKIA** . .(0) **0** 41123
Francis, Barmos (o.g.)

25/6/82 **ENGLAND** . . . .(1) **1** **KUWAIT** . . . .(0) **0** 39700
Francis

GROUP MATCHES – GROUP B

Quarter-Final

29/6/82 **ENGLAND** . . . .(0) **0** **WEST GERMANY** . . .(0) **0** 75000
5/7/82 **ENGLAND** . . . .(0) **0** **SPAIN** . . . .(0) **0** 75000

MEXICO 1986
GROUP MATCHES – GROUP F

3/6/86 **PORTUGAL** . . . .(0) **1** **ENGLAND** . . . .(0) **0** 23000
Carlos Manuel
6/6/86 **ENGLAND** . . . .(0) **0** **MOROCCO** . . . .(0) **0** 20200
11/6/86 **ENGLAND** . . . .(3) **3** **POLAND** . . . .(0) **0** 22700
Lineker 3

Second Round

18/6/86 **ENGLAND** . . . .(1) **3** **PARAGUAY** . . . .(0) **0** 98728
Lineker 2, Beardsley

Semi-Final

22/6/86 **ARGENTINA** . . . . . .(0) **2** **ENGLAND** . . . .(0) **1** 114580
Maradona 2   Lineker

ITALY 1990
GROUP MATCHES – GROUP F

11/6/90 **ENGLAND** . . . .(1) **1** **EIRE** . . . .(0) **1** 35238
Lineker   Sheedy
16/6/90 **ENGLAND** . . . .(0) **0** **HOLLAND** . . . .(0) **0** 35267
21/6/90 **ENGLAND** . . . .(0) **1** **EGYPT** . . . .(0) **0** 34959
Wright

Second Round

26/6/90 **ENGLAND** . . . .(0) **1** **BELGIUM** . . . .(0) **0** 34520
Platt

(After Extra Time)

Quarter-Final

1/7/90 **ENGLAND** . . . .(1) **3** **CAMEROON** . . . .(0) **2** 55205
Platt, Lineker, (2 pens)   Kunde (pen), Ekeke

(After Extra Time)

Semi-Final

4/7/90 **WEST GERMANY** . .(0) **1** **ENGLAND** . . . .(0) **1** 62628
Brehme   Lineker

(After Extra Time – West Germany won 4-3 on penalties)

Third Place Play-Off

7/7/90 **ITALY** . . . .(0) **2** **ENGLAND** . . . .(0) **1** 51426
Baggio, Schillaci (pen)   Platt

FRANCE 1998
GROUP MATCHES – GROUP G

15/6/98 **ENGLAND** . . . .(1) **2** **TUNISIA** . . . .(0) **0** 54587
Shearer, Scholes
22/6/98 **ROMANIA** . . . .(0) **2** **ENGLAND** . . . .(0) **1** 37500
Moldovan, Petrescu   Owen
26/6/98 **COLOMBIA** . . . .(0) **0** **ENGLAND** . . . .(2) **2** 35000
Anderton, Beckham

Second Round

30/6/98 **ARGENTINA** . . . . . .(2) **2** **ENGLAND** . . . .(2) **2** 35000
Batistuta (pen), Zanetti   Shearer (pen), Owen

FRANCE
URUGUAY 1930
GROUP MATCHES – GROUP 1

13/7/30 **FRANCE** . . . .(3) **4** **MEXICO** . . . .(0) **1** 1000
Laurent, Langiller, Maschinot 2   Carreno
15/7/30 **ARGENTINA** . . . . . .(0) **1** **FRANCE** . . . .(0) **0** 3000
Monti

235

19/7/30 **CHILE** . . . .(0) **1** **FRANCE** . . . . (0) **0** 2000
Subiabre

ITALY 1934
First Round
27/5/34 **AUSTRIA** . . . .(1) **3** **FRANCE** . . . . (1) **2** N.R.
Sindelar, Schall, Bican   *Nicholas, Verriest (pen)*
(After Extra Time)

FRANCE 1938
First Round
5/6/38 **FRANCE** . . . .(2) **3** **BELGIUM** . . . . . . (1) **1** N.R.
Veinante, Nicolas 2   *Isemborghs*
Second Round
12/6/38 **ITALY** . . . .(1) **3** **FRANCE** . . . . (1) **1** 58000
Colaussi, Piola 2   *Heisserer*

SWITZERLAND 1954
GROUP MATCHES – GROUP 1
16/6/54 **YUGOSLAVIA** . . . . . .(1) **1** **FRANCE** . . . . (0) **0** 16000
Milutinovic
19/6/54 **FRANCE** . . . .(1) **3** **MEXICO** . . . . (0) **2** 19000
Vincent, Cardenas (o.g.) Kopa (pen)   *Naranjo, Balcazar*

SWEDEN 1958
GROUP MATCHES – GROUP 2
8/6/58 **FRANCE** . . . .(2) **7** **PARAGUAY** . . . . (2) **3** 16518
Fontaine 3, Piantoni, Kopa, Wisnieski   *Amarilla 2 (1 pen), Romero*
Vincent
11/6/58 **YUGOSLAVIA** . . . . . .(1) **3** **FRANCE** . . . . (1) **2** 12217
Petakovic, Veselinovic 2   *Fontaine 2*
15/6/58 **FRANCE** . . . .(2) **2** **SCOTLAND** . . . . (0) **1** 13554
Kopa, Fontaine   *Baird*
Quarter-Final
19/6/58 **FRANCE** . . . .(1) **4** **NORTHERN IRELAND**(0) **0** 11800
Wisnieski, Fontaine 2, Piantoni
Semi-Final
24/6/58 **BRAZIL** . . . .(2) **5** **FRANCE** . . . . (1) **2** 27100
Vava, Didi, Pele 3   *Fontaine, Piantoni*
Third Place Play-Off
28/6/58 **FRANCE** . . . .(3) **6** **WEST GERMANY** . . (1) **3** 32482
Fontaine 4, Kopa (pen), Douis   *Cierlarczyk, Rahn, Schaefer*

ENGLAND 1966
GROUP MATCHES – GROUP 1
13/7/66 **FRANCE** . . . .(0) **1** **MEXICO** . . . . (0) **1** 69237
Hausser   *Borja*
15/7/66 **URUGUAY** . . . .(2) **2** **FRANCE** . . . . (1) **1** 45662
Rocha, Cortes   *De Bourgoing (pen)*
20/7/66 **ENGLAND** . . . .(1) **2** **FRANCE** . . . . (0) **0** 98270
Hunt 2

ARGENTINA 1978
GROUP MATCHES – GROUP 1
2/6/78 **FRANCE** . . . .(1) **1** **ITALY** . . . . (1) **2** 42375
Lacombe   *Rossi, Zaccarelli*
6/6/78 **ARGENTINA** . . . .(1) **2** **FRANCE** . . . . (0) **1** 77216
Passarella (pen), Luque   *Platini*
10/6/78 **FRANCE** . . . .(3) **3** **HUNGARY** . . . . (1) **1** 28000
Lopez, Berdoll, Rocheteau   *Zambori*

SPAIN 1982
GROUP MATCHES – GROUP 4
16/6/82 **ENGLAND** . . . .(1) **3** **FRANCE** . . . . (1) **1** 44172
Robson 2, Mariner   *Soler*
21/6/82 **FRANCE** . . . .(2) **4** **KUWAIT** . . . . (0) **1** 30034
Genghini, Platini, Six, Bossis   *Al Buloushi*

24/6/82 **FRANCE** . . . .(0) **1** **CZECHOSLOVAKIA** . (0) **1** N.R.
Six   *Panenka (pen)*

GROUP MATCHES – GROUP D
Quarter-Finals
28/6/82 **FRANCE** . . . .(1) **1** **AUSTRIA** . . . . (0) **0** 37000
Genghini
4/7/82 **FRANCE** . . . .(1) **4** **NORTHERN IRELAND**(0) **1** 37000
Giresse 2, Rocheteau 2   *Armstrong*
(After Extra Time)
Semi-Final
8/7/82 **WEST GERMANY** . .(1) **3** **FRANCE** . . . . (1) **3** 63000
Littbarski, Rummenige, Fischer   *Platini (pen),Tresor, Giresse*
(After Extra Time – West Germany won 5-4 on penalties)
Third Place Play-Off
10/7/82 **POLAND** . . . .(2) **3** **FRANCE** . . . . (1) **2** 28000
Szarmach, Majewski, Kupcewicz   *Girard, Couriol*

MEXICO 1986
GROUP MATCHES – GROUP C
1/6/86 **CANADA** . . . .(0) **0** **FRANCE** . . . . (0) **1** 65000
    Papin
5/6/86 **FRANCE** . . . .(0) **1** **USSR** . . . . (0) **1** 36540
Fernandez   *Rats*
9/6/86 **HUNGARY** . . . .(0) **0** **FRANCE** . . . . (2) **3** 31420
    Stopyra, Tigana, Rocheteau
Second Round
17/6/86 **ITALY** . . . .(0) **0** **FRANCE** . . . . (1) **2** 70000
    Platini, Stopyra
Quarter-Final
21/6/86 **BRAZIL** . . . .(1) **1** **FRANCE** . . . . (1) **1** 65777
Careca   *Platini*
(After Extra Time – France won 4-3 on penalties)
Semi-Final
25/6/86 **FRANCE** . . . .(0) **0** **WEST GERMANY** . . (1) **2** 45000
    Brehme, Voeller
Third Place Play-Off
28/6/86 **BELGIUM** . . . .(1) **2** **FRANCE** . . . . (2) **4** 21000
Ceulemans, Classen   *Ferrari, Papin, Genghini, Amoros (pen)*
(After Extra Time)

FRANCE 1998
GROUP MATCHES – GROUP C
12/6/98 **FRANCE** . . . .(1) **3** **SOUTH AFRICA** . . . (0) **0** 55077
Dugarry, Issa (og), Henry
18/6/98 **FRANCE** . . . .(1) **4** **SAUDI ARABIA** . . . (0) **0** 75000
Henry 2, Trezeguet, Lizarazu
24/6/98 **FRANCE** . . . .(1) **2** **DENMARK** . . . . (1) **1** 43500
Djorkaeff (pen), Petit
Second Round
28/6/98 **FRANCE** . . . .(0) **1** **PARAGUAY** . . . . (0) **0** 41275
Blanc
('Golden Goal' scored during Extra Time)
Quarter-Final
3/7/98 **ITALY** . . . .(0) **0** **FRANCE** . . . . (0) **0** 77000
(After Extra Time – France won 4-3 on Penalties)
Semi-Final
8/7/98 **FRANCE** . . . .(0) **2** **CROATIA** . . . . (0) **1** 76000
Thuram 2
Final
12/7/98 **BRAZIL** . . . .(0) **0** **FRANCE** . . . . (2) **3** 75000
    Zidane 2, Petit

GERMANY (PRE-WAR)
ITALY 1934

First Round

27/5/34 **GERMANY** . . . .(1) **5** **BELGIUM** . . . .(2) **2** 8000
Conen 3, Kobierski 2   Voorhoof 2

Second Round

31/5/34 **GERMANY** . . . .(1) **2** **SWEDEN**. . . . .(0) **1** 3000
Hohmann 2   Dunker

Semi-Final

3/6/34 **CZECHOSLOVAKIA**. .(1) **3** **GERMANY** . . . .(0) **1** 10000
Nejedly 2, Krcil   Noack

Third Place Play-Off

7/6/54 **GERMANY** . . . .(3) **3** **AUSTRIA** . . . .(1) **2** 7000
Lehner 2, Conen   Howarth, Seszta

FRANCE 1938

First Round

4/6/38 **SWITZERLAND** . . . .(1) **1** **GERMANY** . . . .(1) **1** 30000
Abegglen   Gauchel

(After Extra Time)

Replay

9/6/38 **SWITZERLAND** . . . .(0) **4** **GERMANY** . . . .(2) **2** 22000
Wallascher, Bickel, Abegglen 2   Haunemann, Loertscher (o.g.)

GERMANY (Unified)
U.S.A. 1994
GROUP MATCHES – GROUP C

17/6/94 **GERMANY** . . . .(0) **1** **BOLIVIA** . . . .(0) **0** 63117
Klinsmann

21/6/94 **GERMANY** . . . .(0) **1** **SPAIN**. . . . .(1) **1** 63113
Klinsmann   Goikoetxea

27/6/94 **GERMANY** . . . .(3) **3** **SOUTH KOREA** . . . .(0) **2** 63998
Klinsmann 2, Riedle   Hwang Sun-Hong, Hong Myung-Bo

Second Round

2/7/94 **GERMANY** . . . . (3) **3** **BELGIUM** . . . .(1) **2** 60246
Voller 2, Klinsmann   Grun, Albert

Quarter-Final

10/7/94 **BULGARIA** . . . .(0) **2** **GERMANY** . . . .(0) **1** 72416
Stoichkov, Lechkov   Matthaus (pen)

FRANCE 1998
GROUP MATCHES – GROUP F

15/6/98 **GERMANY** . . . .(1) **2** **USA**. . . . .(0) **0** 43875
Moller, Klinsmann

21/6/98 **GERMANY** . . . .(0) **2** **YUGOSLAVIA** . . . . . .(1) **2** 40775
Tarnat, Bierhoff   Mijatovic, Stoijkovic

25/6/98 **GERMANY** . . . .(0) **2** **IRAN**. . . . .(0) **0** 35000
Bierhoff, Klinsmann

Second Round

29/6/98 **GERMANY** . . . .(0) **2** **MEXICO** . . . .(0) **1** 35000
Klinsmann, Bierhoff   Hernandez

Quarter-Final

4/7/98 **GERMANY** . . . .(0) **0** **CROATIA**. . . . .(1) **3** 39100
Jarni, Vlaovic, Suker

GREECE
U.S.A. 1994
GROUP MATCHES – GROUP D

21/6/94 **ARGENTINA**. . . . . . .(2) **4** **GREECE** . . . .(0) **0** 53486
Batistuta 3, Maradona

26/6/94 **BULGARIA** . . . .(1) **4** **GREECE**. . . . .(0) **0** 63160
Stoichkov (2 pens), Lechkov, Borimirov

30/6/94 **GREECE** . . . .(0) **0** **NIGERIA** . . . .(1) **2** 53001
George, Amokachi

HAITI
WEST GERMANY 1974
GROUP MATCHES – GROUP 4

15/6/74 **ITALY** . . . .(0) **3** **HAITI**. . . . .(0) **1** 53000
Rivera, Benetti, Anastasi   Sanon

19/6/74 **POLAND**. . . . .(5) **7** **HAITI**. . . . .(0) **0** 25300
Lato 2, Deyna, Szarmach 3, Gorgon

23/6/74 **ARGENTINA**. . . . . . .(2) **4** **HAITI**. . . . .(0) **1** 25900
Yazalde 2, Houseman, Ayala   Sanon

HOLLAND
ITALY 1934

First Round

27/5/34 **SWITZERLAND** . . . .(2) **3** **HOLLAND** . . . .(1) **2** N.R.
Kielholtz 2, Abegglen   Smit, Vente

FRANCE 1938

First Round

5/6/38 **CZECHOSLOVAKIA**. .(0) **3** **HOLLAND** . . . .(0) **0** N.R.
Kostalek, Boucek, Nejedly   Smit, Vente

(After Extra Time)

WEST GERMANY 1974
GROUP MATCHES – GROUP 3

15/6/74 **HOLLAND**. . . . .(1) **2** **URUGUAY**. . . . .(0) **0** 55000
Rep 2

19/6/74 **HOLLAND**. . . . .(0) **0** **SWEDEN**. . . . .(0) **0** 53700

23/6/74 **HOLLAND**. . . . .(2) **4** **BULGARIA** . . . .(0) **1** 13400
Neeskens 2 (2 pens), Rep, De Jong   Krol (o.g.)

GROUP MATCHES – GROUP A

Quarter-Finals

26/6/74 **HOLLAND**. . . . .(2) **4** **ARGENTINA** . . . .(0) **0** 55000
Cruyff 2, Krol, Rep

30/6/74 **HOLLAND**. . . . .(1) **2** **EAST GERMANY** . . .(0) **0** 69600
Neeskens, Rensenbrink

3/7/74 **HOLLAND**. . . . .(0) **2** **BRAZIL**. . . . .(0) **0** 53700
Neeskens, Cruyff

Final

7/7/74 **WEST GERMANY** . .(2) **2** **HOLLAND** . . . .(1) **1** 77833
Breitner (pen), Muller   Neeskens (pen)

ARGENTINA 1978
GROUP MATCHES – GROUP 4

3/6/78 **IRAN**. . . . .(0) **0** **HOLLAND** . . . .(1) **3** 42000
Rensenbrink 3 (2 pens)

7/6/78 **HOLLAND**. . . . .(0) **0** **PERU** . . . .(0) **0** 30000

11/6/78 **SCOTLAND**. . . . . . .(1) **3** **HOLLAND** . . . .(1) **2** 40000
Dalglish, Gemmill 2 (1 pen)   Rensenbrink (pen), Rep

GROUP MATCHES – GROUP A

Quarter-Finals

14/6/78 **AUSTRIA** . . . .(0) **1** **HOLLAND** . . . .(3) **5** 15000
Obermayer   Brandts, Rensenbrink (pen), Rep 2,
      W. Van Der Kerkhof

18/6/78 **HOLLAND**. . . . .(1) **2** **WEST GERMANY** . . .(1) **2** 46000
Haan, R. Van Der Kerkhof   Abramczik 2

21/6/78 **HOLLAND**. . . . .(0) **2** **ITALY**. . . . .(1) **1** 70000
Brandts, Haan   Brandts (o.g)

Final

25/6/78 **ARGENTINA**. . . . . . .(1) **3** **HOLLAND** . . . .(0) **1** 77260
Kempes 2, Bertoni   Nanninga

(After extra time)

ITALY 1990
GROUP MATCHES – GROUP F

12/6/90 **HOLLAND**.........(0) **1** **EGYPT**...........(0) **1** 33288
Kieft   Abdel-Ghani (pen)
16/6/90 **ENGLAND**.........(0) **0** **HOLLAND**........(0) **0** 35267
21/6/90 **EIRE**.............(0) **1** **HOLLAND**........(1) **1** 33288
Quinn   Gullit

Second Round

24/6/90 **WEST GERMANY** ..(0) **2** **HOLLAND**........(0) **1** 74559
Klinsmann, Brehme   Koeman (pen)

U.S.A 1994
GROUP MATCHES – GROUP F

20/6/94 **HOLLAND**........(0) **2** **SAUDI ARABIA** ... (1) **1** 52535
Jonk, Taument   Amin
25/6/94 **BELGIUM** ....(0) **1** **HOLLAND**........(0) **0** 62387
Albert
29/6/94 **MOROCCO** ....(0) **1** **HOLLAND**........(1) **2** 60578
Nader   Bergkamp, Roy

Second Round

4/7/94 **HOLLAND**.........(2) **2** **EIRE**............(0) **0** 61355
Bergkamp, Jonk

Quarter-Final

9/7/94 **HOLLAND**.........(0) **2** **BRAZIL** ....(0) **3** 63998
Bergkamp, Winter   Romario, Bebeto, Branco

FRANCE 1998
GROUP MATCHES – GROUP E

13/6/98 **HOLLAND**.........(0) **0** **BELGIUM** ....(0) **0** 75000
20/6/98 **HOLLAND**.........(2) **5** **SOUTH KOREA** .... (0) **0** 60000
Cocu, Overmars, Bergkamp,
Van Hooijdonk, De Boer
25/6/98 **HOLLAND**.........(2) **2** **MEXICO** ....(0) **2** 35500
Cocu, R. De Boer   Pelaez, Hernandez

Second Round

29/6/98 **HOLLAND**.........(1) **2** **YUGOSLAVIA** ..... (0) **1** 35000
Bergkamp, Davids   Komljenovic

Quarter-Final

4/7/98 **HOLLAND**.........(1) **2** **ARGENTINA** ...... (1) **1** 55000
Kluivert, Bergkamp   Lopez

Semi-Final

7/7/98 **BRAZIL**...........(0) **1** **HOLLAND**........(0) **1** 54000
Ronaldo   Kluivert
(After Extra Time – Brazil won 4-2 on penalties)

Third Place Play-off

11/7/98 **HOLLAND**.........(1) **1** **CROATIA**........(2) **2** 44000
Zenden   Prosinecki, Suker

HONDURAS
SPAIN 1982
GROUP MATCHES – GROUP 5

16/6/82 **SPAIN**............(0) **1** **HONDURAS** ...... (1) **1** 49562
Ufarte (pen)   Zelaya
21/6/82 **HONDURAS**.......(0) **1** **NORTHERN IRELAND**(1) **1** 15000
Laing   Armstrong
24/6/82 **YUGOSLAVIA**......(0) **1** **HONDURAS** ...... (0) **0** 25000
Petrovic

HUNGARY
ITALY 1934

First Round

27/5/34 **HUNGARY** ....(2) **4** **EGYPT**...........(1) **2** N.R.
Teleky, Toldi 2, Vincze   Fawzi 2

Second Round

31/5/34 **AUSTRIA** ....(1) **2** **HUNGARY**........(0) **1** N.R.
Horwath, Zischek   Sarosi (pen)

FRANCE 1938

First Round

5/6/38 **HUNGARY** ....(4) **6** **DUTCH EAST INDIES**(0) **0** N.R.
Kohut, Toldi, Sarosi 2, Szengeller 2

Second Round

12/6/38 **HUNGARY** ....(1) **2** **SWITZERLAND**.... (0) **0** N.R.
Szengeller 2

Semi-Final

16/6/38 **HUNGARY** ....(3) **5** **SWEDEN**.........(1) **1** 17000
Szengeller 3, Titkos, Sarosi   Nyberg

Final

19/6/38 **ITALY** ....(3) **4** **HUNGARY**........(1) **2** 55000
Colaussi 2, Piola 2   Titkos, Sarosi

SWITZERLAND 1954
GROUP MATCHES – GROUP 2

17/6/54 **HUNGARY** ....(4) **9** **SOUTH KOREA** .... (0) **0** 13000
Czibor, Kocsis 3, Puskas 2, Lantos
Palotas 2
20/6/54 **HUNGARY** ....(3) **8** **WEST GERMANY** .. (1) **3** 56000
Hidegkuti 2, Kocsis 4, Puskas 2, Toth   Pfaff, Hermann, Rahn

Quarter-Final

27/6/54 **HUNGARY** ....(1) **4** **BRAZIL** ....(1) **2** 40000
Hidegkuti 2, Kocsis, Lantos (pen)   D. Santos (pen), Julinho

Semi-Final

30/6/54 **HUNGARY** ....(1) **4** **URUGUAY** ....(0) **2** 37000
Czibor, Hidegkuti, Kocsis 2   Hohberg 2
(After Extra Time)

Final

4/7/54 **WEST GERMANY** ..(2) **3** **HUNGARY**........(2) **2** 60000
Morlock, Rahn 2   Puskas, Czibor

SWEDEN 1958
GROUP MATCHES – GROUP 3

8/6/58 **WALES**...........(1) **1** **HUNGARY**........(1) **1** 15343
J. Charles   Bozsik
12/6/58 **SWEDEN** ....(1) **2** **HUNGARY**........(0) **1** 38850
Hamrin 2   Tichy
15/6/58 **HUNGARY** ....(1) **4** **MEXICO** ....(0) **0** 13310
Tichy 2, Sandor, Bencsics

Play-Off

17/6/58 **WALES**...........(0) **2** **HUNGARY**........(1) **1** 2832
Allchurch, Medwin   Tichy

CHILE 1962
GROUP MATCHES – GROUP 4

31/5/62 **HUNGARY** ....(1) **2** **ENGLAND** ....(0) **1** 7938
Tichy, Albert   Flowers (pen)
3/6/62 **HUNGARY** ....(4) **6** **BULGARIA** ....(0) **1** 7442
Albert 3, Tichy 2, Solymosi   Sokolov
6/6/62 **ARGENTINA**.......(0) **0** **HUNGARY**........(0) **0** 7945

Quarter-Final

10/6/62 **CZECHOSLOVAKIA**..(1) **1** **HUNGARY**........(0) **0** 11690
Scherer

ENGLAND 1966
GROUP MATCHES – GROUP 3

13/7/66 **PORTUGAL**........(1) **3** **HUNGARY**........(0) **1** 37311
Augusto 2, Torres   Bene
15/7/66 **HUNGARY** ....(1) **3** **BRAZIL** ....(1) **1** 57455
Bene, Farkas, Meszoly (pen)   Tostao
20/7/66 **HUNGARY** ....(2) **3** **BULGARIA** .... (1) **1** 22064
Davidov (o.g.), Meszoly, Bene Asparoukhov

Quarter-Final

23/7/66 **USSR** . . . .(1) **2** **HUNGARY**. . . . .(0) **1** 26844
Chislenko, Porkujan   *Bene*

ARGENTINA 1978
GROUP MATCHES – GROUP 1

2/6/78 **ARGENTINA**. . . . . .(1) **2** **HUNGARY**. . . . . .(1) **1** 77000
Luque, Alonso   *Csapo*

6/6/78 **ITALY** . . . .(2) **3** **HUNGARY**. . . . .(0) **1** 32000
Rossi, Bettega, Benetti   *Toth (pen)*

10/6/78 **FRANCE** . . . .(3) **3** **HUNGARY**. . . . . . .(1) **1** 28000
Lopez, Berdoll, Rocheteau   *Zambori*

SPAIN 1982
GROUP MATCHES – GROUP 3

15/6/82 **HUNGARY** . . . .(3) **10** **EL SALVADOR** . . . .(0) **1** 23000
Nyilasi 2, Fazekas 2, Paloskei, Toth   *Zapata*
Kiss 3, Szentes

18/6/82 **ARGENTINA**. . . . . .(2) **4** **HUNGARY**. . . . . . .(0) **1** 32093
Bertoni, Ardiles, Maradona 2   *Poloskei*

22/6/82 **BELGIUM**. . . . .(0) **1** **HUNGARY**. . . . . . .(1) **1** 37000
Czerniatynski   *Varga*

MEXICO 1986
GROUP MATCHES – GROUP C

2/6/86 **USSR** . . . .(3) **6** **HUNGARY**. . . . .(0) **0** 16600
Yakovenko, Aleinikov, Belanov (pen)
Yaremchuck 2, Rodionov

6/6/86 **HUNGARY** . . . .(1) **2** **CANADA**. . . . .(0) **0** 13800
Esterhazy, Detari

9/6/86 **HUNGARY** . . . .(0) **0** **FRANCE** . . . .(2) **3** 31420
    Stopyra, Tigana, Rocheteau

IRAN
ARGENTINA 1978
GROUP MATCHES – GROUP 4

3/6/78 **IRAN**. . . . .(0) **0** **HOLLAND** . . . .(1) **3** 42000
    Rensenbrink 3 (2 pens)

7/6/78 **SCOTLAND**. . . . . . .(1) **1** **IRAN** . . . .(1) **1** 8000
Eskandarian (o.g.)   *Danaiford*

11/6/78 **PERU** . . . .(3) **4** **IRAN** . . . .(1) **1** 25000
Velasquez, Cubillas 3 (2 pens)   *Rowshan*

FRANCE 1998
GROUP MATCHES – GROUP F

14/6/98 **YUGOSLAVIA**. . . . . .(0) **1** **IRAN** . . . .(0) **0** 30392
Mihailovic

21/6/98 **USA** . . . .(0) **1** **IRAN** . . . .(1) **2** 44000
McBride   *Estili, Mahdavikia*

25/6/98 **GERMANY** . . . .(0) **2** **IRAN** . . . .(0) **0** 35000
Bierhoff, Klinsmann

IRAQ
MEXICO 1986
GROUP MATCHES – GROUP B

4/6/86 **PARAGUAY** . . . .(1) **1** **IRAQ**. . . . .(0) **0** 24000
Romero

8/6/86 **IRAQ**. . . . .(0) **1** **BELGIUM** . . . .(2) **2** 20000
Rahdi   *Scifo, Claesen (pen)*

11/6/86 **IRAQ**. . . . .(0) **0** **MEXICO** . . . .(0) **1** 103762
    Quirarte

ISRAEL
MEXICO 1970
GROUP MATCHES – GROUP 2

2/6/70 **URUGUAY** . . . .(1) **2** **ISRAEL** . . . .(0) **0** 20000
Maneiro, Mujica

7/6/70 **SWEDEN** . . . .(0) **1** **ISRAEL** . . . .(0) **1** 9000
Turesson   *Spiegler*

11/6/70 **ITALY** . . . .(0) **0** **ISRAEL** . . . .(0) **0** 9000

ITALY
ITALY 1934

First Round

27/5/34 **ITALY** . . . .(3) **7** **USA**. . . . .(0) **1** 30000
Schiavio 3, Orsi 2, Meazza, Ferrari   *Donelli*

Second Round

31/5/34 **ITALY** . . . .(0) **1** **SPAIN** . . . .(0) **1** 35000
Ferrari   *Regueiro*

(After Extra Time)

Replay

1/6/34 **ITALY** . . . .(1) **1** **SPAIN** . . . .(0) **0** 43000
Meazza

Semi-Final

3/6/34 **ITALY** . . . .(1) **1** **AUSTRIA**. . . . .(0) **0** 60000
Guaita

Final

10/6/34 **ITALY** . . . .(0) **2** **CZECHOSLOVAKIA**. .(0) **1** 55000
Orsi, Schiavio   *Puc*

(After Extra Time)

FRANCE 1938

First Round

5/6/38 **ITALY** . . . .(1) **2** **NORWAY** . . . .(0) **1** N.R.
Ferrari, Piola   *Brustad*

(After Extra Time)

Second Round

12/6/38 **ITALY** . . . .(1) **3** **FRANCE** . . . .(1) **1** 58000
Colaussi, Piola 2   *Heisserer*

Semi-Final

16/6/38 **ITALY** . . . .(2) **2** **BRAZIL** . . . .(0) **1** 35000
Colaussi, Meazza (pen)   *Romeo*

Final

19/6/38 **ITALY** . . . .(3) **4** **HUNGARY**. . . . .(1) **2** 55000
Colaussi 2, Piola 2   *Titkos, Sarosi*

BRAZIL 1950
GROUP MATCHES – GROUP 3

25/6/50 **SWEDEN** . . . .(2) **3** **ITALY**. . . . .(1) **2** 56502
Jeppson 2, Anderson   *Carapellese, Muccinelli*

2/7/50 **ITALY** . . . .(1) **2** **PARAGUAY**. . . . . . .(0) **0** 25811
Carapellese, Pandolfini

SWITZERLAND 1954
GROUP MATCHES – GROUP 4

17/6/54 **SWITZERLAND** . . . .(1) **2** **ITALY**. . . . .(1) **1** 40500
Ballaman, Hugi   *Boniperti*

20/6/54 **ITALY** . . . .(1) **4** **BELGIUM** . . . .(0) **1** 24000
Pandolfini (pen), Galli, Frignani   *Anoul*
Lorenzi

Play-Off

23/6/54 **SWITZERLAND** . . . .(1) **4** **ITALY**. . . . .(0) **1** 29000
Hugi 2, Ballaman, Fatton   *Nesti*

CHILE 1962
GROUP MATCHES – GROUP 2

31/5/62 **WEST GERMANY** . .(0) **0** **ITALY**. . . . .(0) **0** 65440

2/6/62 **CHILE** . . . .(2) **2** **ITALY**. . . . .(0) **0** 66057
Ramirez, Toro

7/6/62 **ITALY** . . . .(1) **3** **SWITZERLAND**. . . . .(0) **0** 59828
Mora, Bulgarelli 2

ENGLAND 1966
GROUP MATCHES – GROUP 4

13/7/66 **ITALY** ....(1) **2** **CHILE** ....(0) **0** 30956
  Mazzola, Barison
16/7/66 **USSR** ....(0) **1** **ITALY**...........(0) **0** 31989
  Chislenko
19/7/66 **NORTH KOREA**.....(1) **1** **ITALY** ....(0) **0** 18727
  Pak Doo Ik

MEXICO 1970
GROUP MATCHES – GROUP 2

3/6/70 **ITALY** ....(1) **1** **SWEDEN**.........(0) **0** 14000
  Domenghini
6/6/70 **URUGUAY** ....(0) **0** **ITALY** ....(0) **0** 30000
11/6/70 **ITALY** ....(0) **0** **ISRAEL** ....(0) **0** 9000

Quarter-Final

14/6/70 **ITALY** ....(1) **4** **MEXICO** ....(1) **1** 24000
  Domenghini, Riva 2, Rivera

Semi-Final

17/6/70 **ITALY** ....(1) **4** **WEST GERMANY**..(0) **3** 80000
  Boninsegna, Burgnich, Riva, Rivera   Schnellinger, Muller 2
  (After Extra Time)

Final

21/6/70 **BRAZIL**...........(1) **4** **ITALY**...........(1) **1** 107000
  Pele, Gerson, Jairzinho, Carlos Alberto Boninsegna

WEST GERMANY 1974
GROUP MATCHES – GROUP 4

15/6/70 **ITALY** ....(0) **3** **HAITI**...........(0) **1** 53000
  Rivera, Benetti, Anastasi   Sanon
19/6/70 **ARGENTINA**......(1) **1** **ITALY**...........(1) **1** 70100
  Houseman   Perfumo (o.g.)
23/6/70 **POLAND**.........(2) **2** **ITALY**...........(0) **1** 70100
  Szarmach, Deyna   Capello

ARGENTINA 1978
GROUP MATCHES – GROUP 1

2/6/78 **FRANCE**.........(1) **1** **ITALY**...........(1) **2** 42373
  Lacombe   Rossi, Zaccarelli
6/6/78 **ITALY** ....(2) **3** **HUNGARY**......(0) **1** 32000
  Rossi, Bettega, Benetti   Toth (pen)
10/6/78 **ITALY** ....(0) **1** **ARGENTINA**......(0) **0** 77260
  Bettega

GROUP MATCHES – GROUP A

Quarter-Finals

14/6/78 **WEST GERMANY** ..(0) **0** **ITALY**...........(0) **0** 60000
18/6/78 **ITALY** ....(1) **1** **AUSTRIA**.........(0) **0** 50000
  Rossi
21/6/78 **HOLLAND**.........(0) **2** **ITALY**...........(1) **1** 70000
  Brandts, Haan   Brandts (o.g.)

Third Place Play-Off

24/6/78 **BRAZIL**...........(0) **2** **ITALY**...........(1) **1** 76609
  Nelinho, Dirceu   Causio

SPAIN 1982
GROUP MATCHES – GROUP 1

14/6/82 **ITALY** ....(0) **0** **POLAND** ....(0) **0** 33000
18/6/82 **ITALY** ....(1) **1** **PERU** ....(0) **1** 25000
  Conti   Diaz
23/6/82 **ITALY** ....(0) **1** **CAMEROON** ......(0) **1** 20000
  Graziani   M'Bida

GROUP MATCHES – GROUP C

Quarter-Finals

29/6/82 **ITALY** ....(0) **2** **ARGENTINA** ......(0) **1** 43000
  Tardelli, Cabrini   Passarella

5/7/82 **ITALY** ....(2) **3** **BRAZIL** ....(1) **2** 44000
  Rossi 3   Socrates, Falcao

Semi-Final

8/7/82 **ITALY** ....(1) **2** **POLAND** ....(0) **0** 50000
  Rossi 2

Final

11/7/82 **ITALY** ....(0) **3** **WEST GERMANY** ..(0) **1** 90000
  Rossi, Tardelli, Altobelli   Breitner

MEXICO 1986
GROUP MATCHES – GROUP A

31/5/86 **BULGARIA** ....(0) **1** **ITALY**...........(1) **1** 95000
  Sirakov   Altobelli
5/6/86 **ITALY** ....(1) **1** **ARGENTINA**......(1) **1** 32000
  Altobelli (pen)   Maradona
10/6/86 **SOUTH KOREA**.....(0) **2** **ITALY**...........(1) **3** 20000
  Choi Soon-Hoo, Huh Jung-Moo   Atobelli 3

Second Round

17/6/86 **ITALY** ....(0) **0** **FRANCE** ....(1) **2** 70000
  Platini, Stopyra

ITALY 1990
GROUP MATCHES – GROUP A

9/6/90 **ITALY** ....(0) **1** **AUSTRIA**.........(0) **0** 72303
  Schillaci
14/6/90 **ITALY** ....(1) **1** **USA**............(0) **0** 73423
  Giannini
19/6/90 **ITALY** ....(1) **2** **CZECHOSLOVAKIA** .(0) **0** 73303
  Schillaci, Baggio

Second Round

25/6/90 **ITALY** ....(0) **2** **URUGUAY** ....(0) **0** 73303
  Schillaci, Serena

Quarter-Final

30/6/90 **ITALY** ....(1) **1** **EIRE**............(0) **0** 73303
  Schillaci

Semi-Final

3/7/90 **ARGENTINA**......(0) **1** **ITALY**...........(1) **1** 59978
  Caniggia   Schillaci
  (After Extra Time – Argentina won 4-3 on penalties)

Third Place Play-Off

7/7/90 **ITALY** ....(0) **2** **ENGLAND** ....(0) **1** 51426
  Baggio, Schillaci (pen)   Platt

U.S.A. 1994
GROUP MATCHES – GROUP E

18/6/94 **ITALY** ....(0) **0** **EIRE**............(1) **1** 74826
  Houghton
23/6/94 **ITALY** ....(0) **1** **NORWAY** ....(0) **0** 74624
  D. Baggio
28/6/94 **ITALY** ....(0) **1** **MEXICO** ....(0) **1** 53186
  Massaro   Bernal

Second Round

5/7/94 **NIGERIA**..........(1) **1** **ITALY**...........(0) **2** 54367
  Amunike   R. Baggio 2 (1 pen)

Quarter-Final

9/7/94 **ITALY** ....(1) **2** **SPAIN** ....(0) **1** 54605
  D. Baggio, R. Baggio   Caminero

Semi-Final

13/7/94 **BULGARIA** ....(1) **1** **ITALY**...........(2) **2** 77094
  Stoichkov (pen)   R. Baggio 2

Final

17/7/94 **BRAZIL**...........(0) **0** **ITALY**...........(0) **0** 94194
  (After Extra Time – Brazil won 3-2 on penalties)

FRANCE 1998
GROUP MATCHES – GROUP B

11/6/98 **ITALY** . . . .(1) **2** **CHILE** . . . .(1) **2** 31800
Vieri, R. Baggio (pen)   *Salas 2*
17/6/98 **ITALY** . . . .(1) **3** **CAMEROON** . . . .(0) **0** 35000
Di Biagio, Vieri 2
23/6/98 **ITALY** . . . .(0) **2** **AUSTRIA** . . . .(0) **1** 75000
Vieri, R. Baggio

Second Round

27/6/98 **ITALY** . . . .(1) **1** **NORWAY** . . . .(0) **0** 59500
Vieri

Quarter-Final

3/7/98 **ITALY** . . . .(0) **0** **FRANCE** . . . .(0) **0** 77000
(After Extra Time – France won 4-3 on penalties)

JAMAICA
FRANCE 1998
GROUP MATCHES – GROUP H

14/6/98 **JAMAICA**. . . . .(1) **1** **CROATIA**. . . . .(1) **3** 38058
Earle   *Stanic, Prosinecki, Suker*
21/6/98 **ARGENTINA**. . . . . . (1) **5** **JAMAICA**. . . . .(0) **0** 48500
Ortega 2, Batistuta 3 (1 pen)
26/6/98 **JAPAN** . . . .(0) **1** **JAMAICA** . . . .(1) **2** 43500
Nakayama   *Whitmore 2*

JAPAN
FRANCE 1998

14/6/98 **ARGENTINA**. . . . . .(1) **1** **JAPAN** . . . .(0) **0** 33400
Batistuta
20/6/98 **JAPAN** . . . .(0) **0** **CROATIA**. . . . .(0) **1** 39000
Suker
26/6/98 **JAPAN** . . . .(0) **1** **JAMAICA** . . . .(1) **2** 43500
Nakayama   *Whitmore 2*

KUWAIT
SPAIN 1982
GROUP MATCHES – GROUP 4

17/6/82 **CZECHOSLOVAKIA**. .(1) **1** **KUWAIT** . . . .(0) **1** 25000
Panenka (pen)   *Al Dakheel*
21/6/82 **FRANCE** . . . .(2) **4** **KUWAIT** . . . .(0) **1** 30034
Genghini, Platini, Six, Bossis   *Al Buloushi*
25/6/82 **ENGLAND** . . . .(1) **1** **KUWAIT** . . . .(0) **0** 39700
Francis

MEXICO
URUGUAY 1930
GROUP MATCHES – GROUP 1

13/7/30 **FRANCE**. . . . .(3) **4** **MEXICO** . . . .(0) **1** 1000
Laurent, Langiller, Maschinot 2   *Carreno*
16/7/30 **CHILE** . . . .(1) **3** **MEXICO** . . . .(0) **0** 500
Vidal, Subiabre 2
19/7/30 **ARGENTINA**. . . . . .(3) **6** **MEXICO** . . . .(0) **3** 5000
Stabile 3, Varallo 2, Zumelzu   *Lopez, F. Rosas, M. Rosas*

BRAZIL 1950
GROUP MATCHES – GROUP 1

24/6/50 **BRAZIL**. . . . .(1) **4** **MEXICO** . . . .(0) **0** 81649
Ademir 2, Jair, Baltazar
29/6/50 **YUGOSLAVIA**. . . . . .(2) **4** **MEXICO** . . . .(0) **1** 11678
Bobek, Cajkowski 2, Tomasevic   *Casarin*
2/7/50 **SWITZERLAND** . . . .(2) **2** **MEXICO** . . . .(0) **1** 3580
Bader, Fatton   *Velasquez*

SWITZERLAND 1954
GROUP MATCHES – GROUP 1

16/6/54 **BRAZIL**. . . . .(4) **5** **MEXICO** . . . .(0) **0** 12500
Baltazar, Didi, Pinga 2, Julinho
19/6/54 **FRANCE**. . . . .(1) **3** **MEXICO** . . . .(0) **2** 19000
Vincent, Cardenas (o.g.), Kopa (pen)   *Naranjo, Balcazar*

SWEDEN 1958
GROUP MATCHES – GROUP 3

8/6/58 **SWEDEN** . . . .(1) **3** **MEXICO** . . . .(0) **0** 34107
Simonsson 2, Liedholm (pen)
11/6/58 **WALES** . . . .(1) **1** **MEXICO** . . . .(1) **1** 15150
Allchurch   *Belmonte*
15/6/58 **HUNGARY** . . . .(1) **4** **MEXICO** . . . .(0) **0** 13310
Tichy 2, Sandor, Bencsics

CHILE 1962
GROUP MATCHES – GROUP 3

30/5/62 **BRAZIL**. . . . .(0) **2** **MEXICO** . . . .(0) **0** 10484
Zagalo, Pele
3/6/62 **SPAIN** . . . .(0) **1** **MEXICO** . . . .(0) **0** 11875
Peiro
7/6/62 **MEXICO** . . . .(2) **3** **CZECHOSLOVAKIA**. .(1) **1** 10648
Diaz, Del Aguila, H. Hernandez (pen)   *Masek*

ENGLAND 1966
GROUP MATCHES – GROUP 1

13/7/66 **FRANCE**. . . . .(0) **1** **MEXICO** . . . .(0) **1** 69237
Hausser   *Borja*
16/7/66 **ENGLAND** . . . .(1) **2** **MEXICO** . . . .(0) **0** 92570
Charlton, Hunt
19/7/66 **URUGUAY** . . . .(0) **0** **MEXICO** . . . .(0) **0** 61112

MEXICO 1970
GROUP MATCHES – GROUP 1

31/5/70 **MEXICO** . . . .(0) **0** **USSR**. . . . .(0) **0** 107000
7/6/70 **MEXICO** . . . .(1) **4** **EL SALVADOR**. . . . .(0) **0** 103000
Valdivia 2, Fragoso, Basaguren
11/6/70 **MEXICO** . . . .(1) **1** **BELGIUM** . . . .(0) **0** 105000
Pena (pen)

Quarter-Final

14/6/70 **ITALY** . . . .(1) **4** **MEXICO** . . . .(1) **1** 24000
Domenghini, Riva 2, Rivera   *Gonzales*

ARGENTINA 1978
GROUP MATCHES – GROUP 2

2/6/78 **TUNISIA**. . . . .(0) **3** **MEXICO** . . . .(1) **1** 25000
Kabbi, Goummidh, Dhouib   *Vazquez*
6/6/78 **MEXICO** . . . .(0) **0** **WEST GERMANY**. . .(4) **6** 46000
D. Muller, H. Muller, Rummenigge 2 Flohe 2
10/6/78 **MEXICO** . . . .(0) **1** **POLAND** . . . .(1) **3** 25000
Rangel   *Boniek 2, Deyna*

MEXICO 1986
GROUP MATCHES – GROUP B

3/6/86 **BELGIUM** . . . .(1) **1** **MEXICO** . . . .(2) **2** 110000
Van Den Bergh   *Quirarte, Sanchez*
7/6/86 **MEXICO** . . . .(1) **1** **PARAGUAY**. . . . . . .(0) **1** 114600
Flores   *Romero*
11/6/86 **IRAQ**. . . . .(0) **0** **MEXICO** . . . .(0) **1** 103762
Quirarte

Second Round

15/6/86 **MEXICO** . . . .(1) **2** **BULGARIA** . . . .(0) **0** 114580
Negrete, Servin

21/6/86 **WEST GERMANY** . . (0) **0** **MEXICO** . . . . (0) **0** 114580

(After Extra Time – West Germany won 4-1 on penalties)

U.S.A. 1994
GROUP MATCHES – GROUP E

19/6/94 **NORWAY** . . . . (0) **1** **MEXICO** . . . . (0) **0** 52359
Rekdal

24/6/94 **MEXICO** . . . . (1) **2** **EIRE** . . . . (0) **1** 61219
Luis Garcia 2   Aldridge

28/6/94 **ITALY** . . . . (0) **1** **MEXICO** . . . . (0) **1** 53186
Massaro   Bernal

Second Round

5/7/94 **MEXICO** . . . . (1) **1** **BULGARIA** . . . . . . (1) **1** 71030
Garcia Aspe (pen)   Stoichkov

(After Extra Time – Bulgaria won 3-1 on penalties)

FRANCE 1998
GROUP MATCHES – GROUP E

13/6/98 **SOUTH KOREA** . . . . (1) **1** **MEXICO** . . . . (0) **3** 37588
Ha Seok-Ju   Pelaez, Hernandez 2

20/6/98 **BELGIUM** . . . . (1) **2** **MEXICO** . . . . (0) **2** 34750
Wilmots 2   Garcia Aspe (pen), Blanco

25/6/98 **HOLLAND** . . . . (2) **2** **MEXICO** . . . . (0) **2** 35500
Cocu, R. De Boer   Pelaez, Hernandez

Second Round

29/6/98 **GERMANY** . . . . (0) **2** **MEXICO** . . . . (0) **1** 35000
Klinsmann, Bierhoff   Hernandez

MOROCCO
MEXICO 1970
GROUP MATCHES – GROUP 4

3/6/70 **WEST GERMANY** . . (0) **2** **MOROCCO** . . . . (1) **1** 9000
Seeler, Muller   Houmane

6/6/70 **PERU** . . . . (0) **3** **MOROCCO** . . . . (0) **0** 13500
Cubillas 2, Challe

11/6/70 **BULGARIA** . . . . (1) **1** **MOROCCO** . . . . (0) **1** 12200
Jetchev   Ghazouani

MEXICO 1986
GROUP MATCHES – GROUP F

2/6/86 **MOROCCO** . . . . (0) **0** **POLAND** . . . . (0) **0** 19000

6/6/86 **ENGLAND** . . . . (0) **0** **MOROCCO** . . . . (0) **0** 20200

11/6/86 **PORTUGAL** . . . . (0) **1** **MOROCCO** . . . . (2) **3** 28000
Diamantino   Khairi 2, K. Merry

Second Round

17/6/86 **MOROCCO** . . . . (0) **0** **WEST GERMANY** . . (0) **1** 19800
                             Matthaus

U.S.A. 1994
GROUP MATCHES – GROUP F

19/6/94 **BELGIUM** . . . . (1) **1** **MOROCCO** . . . . . . (0) **0** 60790
Degryse

25/6/94 **SAUDI ARABIA** . . . . (2) **2** **MOROCCO** . . . . (1) **1** 72404
Al Jaber (pen), Amin   Chaouchi

29/6/94 **MOROCCO** . . . . (0) **1** **HOLLAND** . . . . (1) **2** 60578
Nader   Bergkamp, Roy

FRANCE 1998
GROUP MATCHES – GROUP A

10/6/98 **MOROCCO** . . . . (1) **2** **NORWAY** . . . . (1) **2** 29750
Hadji, Hadda   Chippo (og), Eggen

16/6/98 **BRAZIL** . . . . (2) **3** **MOROCCO** . . . . (0) **0** 33266
Ronaldo, Rivaldo, Bebeto

23/6/98 **SCOTLAND** . . . . (0) **0** **MOROCCO** . . . . . . (1) **3** 35000
                             Bassir 2, Hadda

NEW ZEALAND
SPAIN 1982
GROUP MATCHES – GROUP 6

15/6/82 **SCOTLAND** . . . . (3) **5** **NEW ZEALAND** . . . (0) **2** 36000
Wark 2, Dalglish, Robertson, Archibald   Sumner, Wooddin

19/6/82 **USSR** . . . . (1) **3** **NEW ZEALAND** . . . (0) **0** 19000
Gavrilov, Blokhin, Baltacha

23/6/82 **BRAZIL** . . . . (2) **4** **NEW ZEALAND** . . . (0) **0** 43000
Zico 2, Falcao, Serginho

NIGERIA
U.S.A. 1994
GROUP MATCHES – GROUP D

21/6/94 **NIGERIA** . . . . (2) **3** **BULGARIA** . . . . . . (0) **0** 44932
Yekini, Amokachi, Amunike

25/6/94 **ARGENTINA** . . . . . . (2) **2** **NIGERIA** . . . . (1) **1** 54453
Caniggia   Siasia

30/6/94 **GREECE** . . . . (0) **0** **NIGERIA** . . . . (1) **2** 53001
                             George, Amokachi

Second Round

5/7/94 **NIGERIA** . . . . (1) **1** **ITALY** . . . . (0) **2** 54367
Amunike   R. Baggio 3 (1 pen)

FRANCE 1998
GROUP MATCHES – GROUP D

13/6/98 **SPAIN** . . . . (1) **2** **NIGERIA** . . . . (1) **3** 33257
Hierro, Raul   Adepoju, Lawal, Oliseh

19/6/98 **NIGERIA** . . . . (1) **1** **BULGARIA** . . . . . . (0) **0** 48500
Ikpeba

24/6/98 **NIGERIA** . . . . (1) **1** **PARAGUAY** . . . . . . (1) **3** 36500
Oruma   Ayala, Benitez, Cardoso

Second Round

28/6/98 **NIGERIA** . . . . (0) **1** **DENMARK** . . . . (2) **4** 80000
Babangida   Moller, B. Laudrup, Sand, Helveg

NORTH KOREA
ENGLAND 1966
GROUP MATCHES – GROUP 4

12/7/66 **USSR** . . . . (2) **3** **NORTH KOREA** . . . . (0) **0** 22568
Malafeev 2, Banishevski

15/7/66 **CHILE** . . . . (1) **1** **NORTH KOREA** . . . . (1) **1** 15887
Marcos (pen)   Pak Seung Jin

19/7/66 **NORTH KOREA** . . . . (1) **1** **ITALY** . . . . (0) **0** 18727
Pak Doo Ik

Quarter-Final

23/7/66 **PORTUGAL** . . . . (2) **5** **NORTH KOREA** . . . . (3) **3** 51780
Eusebio 4 (2 pens), Augusto Pak Seung Jin, Yang Sung Kook,
                             Li Dong Woon

NORTHERN IRELAND
SWEDEN 1958
GROUP MATCHES – GROUP 1

8/6/58 **NORTHERN IRELAND**(1)**1** **CZECHOSLOVAKIA** . (0) **0** 10647
Cush

11/6/58 **ARGENTINA** . . . . . . (1) **3** **NORTHERN IRELAND**(1)**1** 31156
Corbatta 2(1 pen), Menendez McParland

15/6/58 **WEST GERMANY** . . (1) **2** **NORTHERN IRELAND**(1)**2** 21990
Rahn, Seeler   McParland 2

Play-Off

17/6/58 **NORTHERN IRELAND**(1)**2** **CZECHOSLOVAKIA** . (1) **1** 6196
McParland 2   Zikan

(After Extra Time)

Quarter-Final

19/6/58 **FRANCE**..........(1) **4** **NORTHERN IRELAND**(0)**0** 11800
Wisnieski, Fontaine 2, Piantoni

SPAIN 1982
GROUP MATCHES – GROUP 5

17/6/82 **NORTHERN IRELAND**(0)**0** **YUGOSLAVIA**......(0) **0** 25000
21/6/82 **HONDURAS**.......(0) **1** **NORTHERN IRELAND**(1)**1** 15000
Laing   *Armstrong*
25/6/82 **NORTHERN IRELAND**(0)**1** **SPAIN**...........(0) **0** 49562
Armstrong

GROUP MATCHES – GROUP D

Quarter-Finals

1/7/82 **NORTHERN IRELAND**(1)**2** **AUSTRIA** ....(0) **2** 20000
Hamilton 2   *Pezzey, Hintermaier*
4/7/82 **FRANCE**...........(1) **4** **NORTHERN IRELAND**(0)**1** 37000
Giresse 2, Rocheteau 2   *Armstrong*

MEXICO 1986
GROUP MATCHES – GROUP D

3/6/86 **ALGERIA** ....(0) **1** **NORTHERN IRELAND**(1)**1** 22000
Zidane   *Whiteside*
7/6/86 **NORTHERN IRELAND**(0)**1** **SPAIN**...........(2) **2** 28200
Clarke   *Butragueno, Salinas*
12/6/86 **NORTHERN IRELAND**(0)**0** **BRAZIL**..........(2) **3** 51000
         Careca 2, Josimar

NORWAY
FRANCE 1938

First Round

5/6/38 **ITALY** ....(1) **2** **NORWAY** ....(0) **1** N.R.
Ferrari, Piola   *Brustad*

(After Extra Time)

U.S.A. 1994
GROUP MATCHES – GROUP E

19/6/94 **NORWAY** ....(0) **1** **MEXICO** ....(0) **0** 52359
Rekdal
23/6/94 **ITALY** ....(0) **1** **NORWAY** ....(0) **0** 7462
D. Baggio
28/6/94 **EIRE** ....(0) **0** **NORWAY** ....(0) **0** 76322

FRANCE 1998
GROUP MATCHES – GROUP A

10/6/98 **MOROCCO** ....(1) **2** **NORWAY** ....(1) **2** 29750
Hadji, Hadda   *Chippo (og), Eggen*
16/6/98 **SCOTLAND**.......(0) **1** **NORWAY** ....(0) **1** 30236
Burley   *H. Flo*
23/6/98 **BRAZIL**..........(0) **1** **NORWAY** ....(0) **2** 55500
Bebeto   *T.A. Flo, Rekdal (pen)*

Second Round

27/6/98 **ITALY** ....(1) **1** **NORWAY** ....(0) **0** 59500
Vieri

PARAGUAY
URUGUAY 1930
GROUP MATCHES – GROUP 4

17/7/30 **USA** ....(2) **3** **PARAGUAY**.......(0) **0** 800
Patenaude 2, Florie
20/7/30 **PARAGUAY** ....(1) **1** **BELGIUM** ....(0) **0** 900
Pena

BRAZIL 1950
GROUP MATCHES – GROUP 3

29/6/50 **SWEDEN** ....(2) **2** **PARAGUAY**.......(1) **2** 7903
Sundqvist, Palmer   *A Lopez, F Lopez*
2/7/50 **ITALY** ....(1) **2** **PARAGUAY**.......(0) **0** 25811
Carapellese, Pandolfini

SWEDEN 1958
GROUP MATCHES – GROUP 2

8/6/58 **FRANCE**..........(2) **7** **PARAGUAY**.......(2) **3** 16518
Fontaine 3, Piantoni, Kopa, Wisnieski   *Amarilla 2 (1 pen), Romero*
Vincent
11/6/58 **PARAGUAY** ....(2) **3** **SCOTLAND**.......(1) **2** 11665
Aguero, Re, Parodi   *Mudie, Collins*
15/6/58 **YUGOSLAVIA**.....(2) **3** **PARAGUAY**.......(1) **3** 13103
Ognjanovic, Rajkov, Veselinovic   *Parodi, Aguero, Romero*

MEXICO 1986
GROUP MATCHES – GROUP B

4/6/86 **PARAGUAY** ....(1) **1** **IRAQ** ....(0) **0** 24000
Romero
7/6/86 **MEXICO** ....(1) **1** **PARAGUAY**.......(0) **1** 114600
Flores   *Romero*
11/6/86 **PARAGUAY** ....(0) **2** **BELGIUM** ....(1) **2** 16000
Cabanas 2   *Vercauteren, Veyt*

Second Round

18/6/86 **ENGLAND** ....(1) **3** **PARAGUAY**.......(0) **0** 98728
Lineker 2, Beardsley

FRANCE 1998
GROUP MATCHES – GROUP D

12/6/98 **PARAGUAY** ....(0) **0** **BULGARIA** ....(0) **0** 27650
19/6/98 **SPAIN**............(0) **0** **PARAGUAY**.......(0) **0** 35300
24/6/98 **NIGERIA**..........(1) **1** **PARAGUAY**.......(1) **3** 36500
Babangida   *Ayala, Benitez, Cardoso*

Second Round

28/6/98 **FRANCE**..........(0) **1** **PARAGUAY**.......(0) **0** 41275
Blanc

('Golden Goal' scored in Extra Time)

PERU
URUGUAY 1930
GROUP MATCHES – GROUP 3

14/7/30 **ROMANIA** ....(1) **3** **PERU**.............(0) **1** 300
Staucin 2, Barbu   *Souza*
18/7/30 **URUGUAY** ....(0) **1** **PERU**.............(0) **0** 70000
Castro

MEXICO 1970
GROUP MATCHES – GROUP 4

2/6/70 **PERU** ....(0) **3** **BULGARIA** ....(1) **2** 14000
Gallardo, Chumpitaz, Cubillas   *Dermendjiev, Bonev*
6/6/70 **PERU** ....(0) **3** **MOROCCO** ....(0) **0** 13500
Cubillas 2, Challe
10/6/70 **WEST GERMANY** ..(3) **3** **PERU**.............(0) **1** 18000
Muller 3   *Cubillas*

Quarter-Final

14/6/70 **BRAZIL**..........(2) **4** **PERU**.............(1) **2** 54000
Rivelino, Tostao 2, Jairzinho   *Gallardo, Cubillas*

ARGENTINA 1978
GROUP MATCHES – GROUP 4

3/6/78 **PERU** ....(1) **3** **SCOTLAND**.......(1) **1** 45000
Cueto, Cubillas 2   *Jordan*

| 7/6/68 | HOLLAND........(0) 0 | PERU...........(0) 0 | 30000 |
| 11/6/68 | PERU..........(3) 4 | IRAN..........(1) 1 | 25000 |

Velasquez, Cubillas 3 (2 pens) — Rowshan

GROUP MATCHES – GROUP B

Quarter-Finals

| 14/6/78 | BRAZIL..........(2) 3 | PERU.........(0) 0 | 40000 |

Dirceu 2, Zico (pen)

| 18/6/78 | PERU...........(0) 0 | POLAND.........(0) 1 | 35000 |

Szarmach

| 21/6/78 | ARGENTINA......(2) 6 | PERU..........(0) 0 | 40561 |

Kempes 2, Tarantini, Luque 2
Houseman

SPAIN 1982
GROUP MATCHES – GROUP 1

| 15/6/82 | PERU............(0) 0 | CAMEROON......(0) 0 | 11000 |
| 18/6/82 | ITALY...........(1) 1 | PERU..........(0) 1 | 25000 |

Conti — Diaz

| 22/6/82 | POLAND..........(0) 5 | PERU..........(0) 1 | 25000 |

Smolarek, Lato, Boniek, Buncol — La Rosa
Ciolek

POLAND
FRANCE 1938

First Round

| 5/6/38 | BRAZIL..........(3) 6 | POLAND.........(1) 5 | N.R. |

Leonidas 4, Peracio, Romero — Willimowski 4, Piontek

(After Extra Time)

WEST GERMANY 1974
GROUP MATCHES – GROUP 4

| 15/6/74 | POLAND.........(2) 3 | ARGENTINA......(0) 2 | 32700 |

Lato 2, Szarmach — Heredia, Babington

| 19/6/74 | POLAND.........(5) 7 | HAITI.........(0) 0 | 25300 |

Lato 2, Deyna, Szarmach 3, Gorgon

| 23/6/74 | POLAND.........(2) 2 | ITALY.........(0) 1 | 70100 |

Szarmach, Deyna — Capello

GROUP MATCHES – GROUP B

Quarter-Finals

| 26/6/74 | POLAND.........(1) 1 | SWEDEN.........(0) 0 | 45000 |

Lato

| 30/6/74 | POLAND.........(1) 2 | YUGOSLAVIA.....(1) 1 | 53200 |

Deyna (pen), Lato — Karasi

| 3/7/74 | WEST GERMANY..(0) 1 | POLAND........(0) 0 | 62000 |

Muller

Third Place Play-Off

| 6/7/74 | POLAND..........(0) 1 | BRAZIL.........(0) 0 | 79000 |

Lato

ARGENTINA 1978
GROUP MATCHES – GROUP 2

| 1/6/78 | WEST GERMANY..(0) 0 | POLAND.........(0) 0 | 77000 |
| 6/6/78 | POLAND..........(1) 1 | TUNISIA........(0) 0 | 15000 |

Lato

| 10/6/78 | MEXICO.........(0) 1 | POLAND.........(1) 3 | 25000 |

Rangel — Boniek 2, Deyna

GROUP MATCHES – GROUP B

Quarter-Finals

| 14/6/78 | ARGENTINA......(1) 2 | POLAND........(0) 0 | 40000 |

Kempes 2

| 18/6/78 | PERU...........(0) 0 | POLAND........(0) 1 | 35000 |

Szarmach

| 21/6/78 | BRAZIL..........(1) 3 | POLAND........(1) 1 | 44000 |

Nelinho, Roberto 2 — Lato

SPAIN 1982
GROUP MATCHES – GROUP 1

14/6/82	ITALY...........(0) 0	POLAND.........(0) 0	35000
19/6/82	POLAND..........(0) 0	CAMEROON......(0) 0	19000
22/6/82	POLAND..........(0) 5	PERU..........(0) 1	25000

Smolarek, Lato, Boniek, Buncol, — La Rosa
Ciolek

GROUP MATCHES – GROUP A

Quarter-Finals

| 28/6/82 | POLAND..........(2) 3 | BELGIUM.......(0) 0 | 65000 |

Boniek 3

| 4/7/82 | POLAND..........(0) 0 | USSR..........(0) 0 | 65000 |

Semi-Final

| 8/7/82 | ITALY...........(1) 2 | POLAND.........(0) 0 | 50000 |

Rossi 2

Third Place Play-Off

| 10/7/82 | POLAND..........(2) 3 | FRANCE.........(1) 2 | 28000 |

Szarmach, Majewski, Kupcewicz — Girard, Couriol

MEXICO 1986
GROUP MATCHES – GROUP F

| 2/6/86 | MOROCCO........(0) 0 | POLAND.........(0) 0 | 19000 |
| 7/6/86 | POLAND..........(0) 1 | PORTUGAL......(0) 0 | 19915 |

Smolarek

| 11/6/86 | ENGLAND........(3) 3 | POLAND........(0) 0 | 22700 |

Lineker 3

Second Round

| 16/6/86 | BRAZIL..........(1) 4 | POLAND........(0) 0 | 45000 |

Socrates (pen), Josimar, Edinho
Careca (pen)

PORTUGAL
ENGLAND 1966
GROUP MATCHES – GROUP 3

| 13/7/66 | PORTUGAL.......(1) 3 | HUNGARY.......(0) 1 | 37311 |

Augusto 2, Torres — Bene

| 16/7/66 | PORTUGAL.......(2) 3 | BULGARIA......(0) 0 | 33355 |

Vutzov (o.g.), Eusebio, Torres

| 19/7/66 | PORTUGAL.......(2) 3 | BRAZIL........(0) 1 | 62204 |

Simoes, Eusebio 2 — Rildo

Quarter-Final

| 23/7/66 | PORTUGAL.......(2) 5 | NORTH KOREA....(3) 3 | 51780 |

Eusebio 4 (2 pens), Augusto — Pak Seung Jin, Yang Sung Kook
Li Dong Woon

Semi-Final

| 26/7/66 | ENGLAND........(1) 2 | PORTUGAL......(0) 1 | 94493 |

R. Charlton 2 — Eusebio (pen)

Third Place Play-Off

| 28/7/66 | PORTUGAL.......(1) 2 | USSR..........(1) 1 | 87656 |

Eusebio (pen), Torres — Malafeev

MEXICO 1986
GROUP MATCHES – GROUP F

| 3/6/86 | PORTUGAL.......(0) 1 | ENGLAND.......(0) 0 | 23000 |

Carlos Manuel

| 7/6/86 | POLAND..........(0) 0 | PORTUGAL......(0) 0 | 19915 |

Smolarek

| 11/6/86 | PORTUGAL.......(0) 0 | MOROCCO.......(2) 3 | 28000 |

Diamantino — Khairi 2, K. Merry

ROMANIA
URUGUAY 1930
GROUP MATCHES – GROUP 3

| 14/7/30 | ROMANIA........(1) 3 | PERU..........(0) 1 | 360 |

Staucin 2, Barbu — Souza

22/7/30 **URUGUAY** . . . . (4) **4 ROMANIA** . . . . (0) **0** 80000
Dorado, Scarone, Anselmo, Cea

ITALY 1934
First Round

27/5/34 **CZECHOSLOVAKIA**. . (0) **2 ROMANIA** . . . . (0) **0** N.R.
Puc, Nejedly   *Dobai*

FRANCE 1938
First Round

5/6/38 **CUBA** . . . . (0) **3 ROMANIA** . . . . (1) **3** 6000
Tunas, Maquina, Sosa   *Covaci, Baratki, Dobai*

(After Extra Time)

Replay

9/6/38 **CUBA** . . . . (0) **2 ROMANIA** . . . . (1) **1** 5000
Socorro, Maquina   *Dobai*

MEXICO 1970
GROUP MATCHES – GROUP 3

2/6/70 **ENGLAND** . . . . (0) **1 ROMANIA** . . . . (0) **0** 50000
Hurst

6/6/70 **ROMANIA** . . . . (0) **2 CZECHOSLOVAKIA** . . (1) **1** 52000
Neagu, Dumitrache (pen)   *Petras*

10/6/70 **BRAZIL** . . . . (2) **3 ROMANIA** . . . . (1) **2** 50000
Pele 2, Jairzinho   *Dumitrache, Dembrovski*

ITALY 1990
GROUP MATCHES – GROUP B

9/6/90 **USSR** . . . . (0) **0 ROMANIA** . . . . (1) **2** 42960
     Lacatus 2 (1 pen)

14/6/90 **CAMEROON** . . . . . . (0) **2 ROMANIA** . . . . (0) **1** 38687
Milla 2   *Balint*

18/6/90 **ARGENTINA** . . . . . . (0) **1 ROMANIA** . . . . (0) **1** 52733
Monzon   *Balint*

Second Round

25/6/90 **EIRE** . . . . (0) **0 ROMANIA** . . . . (0) **0** 31818

(After Extra Time – Eire won 5-4 on penalties)

U.S.A. 1994
GROUP MATCHES – GROUP A

18/6/94 **COLOMBIA** . . . . (1) **1 ROMANIA** . . . . (2) **3** 91865
Valencia   *Raducioiu 2, Hagi*

22/6/94 **ROMANIA** . . . . (1) **1 SWITZERLAND** . . . . (1) **4** 61428
Hagi   *Sutter, Chapuisat, Knup, Bregy*

26/6/94 **USA** . . . . (0) **0 ROMANIA** . . . . (1) **1** 93869
     Petrescu

Second Round

3/7/94 **ROMANIA** . . . . (2) **3 ARGENTINA** . . . . . . (1) **2** 90469
Dumitrescu 2, Hagi   *Batistuta (pen), Balbo*

Quarter-Final

10/7/94 **ROMANIA** . . . . (0) **2 SWEDEN** . . . . (0) **2** 81715
Raducioiu 2   *Brolin, K. Andersson*

(After Extra Time – Sweden won 5-4 on Penalties)

FRANCE 1998
GROUP MATCHES – GROUP G

15/6/98 **ROMANIA** . . . . (1) **1 COLOMBIA** . . . . (0) **0** 37572
Ilie

22/6/98 **ROMANIA** . . . . (0) **2 ENGLAND** . . . . (0) **1** 37500
Moldovan, Petrescu   *Owen*

26/6/98 **ROMANIA** . . . . (0) **1 TUNISIA** . . . . (1) **1** 80000
Moldovan   *Souayeh (pen)*

Second Round

30/6/98 **ROMANIA** . . . . (0) **0 CROATIA** . . . . (1) **1** 34700
     Suker (pen)

RUSSIA
(See USSR for earlier games)
U.S.A. 1994
GROUP MATCHES – GROUP B

20/6/94 **BRAZIL** . . . . (1) **2 RUSSIA** . . . . (0) **0** 81061
Romario, Rai (pen)

24/6/94 **SWEDEN** . . . . (1) **3 RUSSIA** . . . . (1) **1** 71528
Brolin (pen), Dahlin 2   *Salenko*

28/6/94 **RUSSIA** . . . . (3) **6 CAMEROON** . . . . . . (0) **1** 74914
Salenko 5, Radchenko   *Milla*

SAUDI ARABIA
U.S.A. 1994
GROUP MATCHES – GROUP F

20/6/94 **HOLLAND** . . . . (0) **2 SAUDI ARABIA** . . . . (1) **1** 52535
Jonk, Taument   *Amin*

25/6/94 **SAUDI ARABIA** . . . . (2) **2 MOROCCO** . . . . (1) **1** 72404
Al Jaber (pen), Amin   *Chaouchi*

29/6/94 **BELGIUM** . . . . (0) **0 SAUDI ARABIA** . . . . (1) **1** 52959
     Owairan

Second Round

3/7/94 **SAUDI ARABIA** . . . . (0) **1 SWEDEN** . . . . (1) **3** 60277
Al Ghesheyan   *Dahlin, K. Andersson 2*

FRANCE 1998
GROUP MATCHES – GROUP C

12/6/98 **SAUDI ARABIA** . . . . (0) **0 DENMARK** . . . . (0) **1** 38140
     Rieper

18/6/98 **FRANCE** . . . . (1) **4 SAUDI ARABIA** . . . . (0) **0** 75000
Henry 2, Trezeguet, Lizarazu

24/6/98 **SOUTH AFRICA** . . . . (1) **2 SAUDI ARABIA** . . . . (1) **2** 34500
Bartlett 2 (1 pen)   *Al-Jaber (pen), Al-Thyniyan (pen)*

SCOTLAND
SWITZERLAND 1954
GROUP MATCHES – GROUP 3

16/6/54 **AUSTRIA** . . . . (1) **1 SCOTLAND** . . . . (0) **0** 25000
Probst

19/6/54 **URUGUAY** . . . . (2) **7 SCOTLAND** . . . . (0) **0** 34000
Borges 3, Miguez 2, Abbadie 2

SWEDEN 1958
GROUP MATCHES – GROUP 2

8/6/58 **YUGOSLAVIA** . . . . . . (1) **1 SCOTLAND** . . . . (0) **1** 9591
Petakovic   *Murray*

11/6/58 **PARAGUAY** . . . . (2) **3 SCOTLAND** . . . . (1) **2** 11665
Aguero, Re, Parodi   *Mudie, Collins*

15/6/58 **FRANCE** . . . . (2) **2 SCOTLAND** . . . . (0) **1** 13554
Kopa, Fontaine   *Baird*

WEST GERMANY 1974
GROUP MATCHES – GROUP 2

14/6/74 **SCOTLAND** . . . . (2) **2 ZAIRE** . . . . (0) **0** 27000
Lorimer, Jordan

18/6/74 **BRAZIL** . . . . (0) **0 SCOTLAND** . . . . (0) **0** 62000

22/6/74 **SCOTLAND** . . . . (0) **1 YUGOSLAVIA** . . . . . . (0) **1** 56000
Jordan   *Karasi*

ARGENTINA 1978
GROUP MATCHES – GROUP 4

3/6/78 **PERU** . . . . (1) **3 SCOTLAND** . . . . (1) **1** 45000
Cueto, Cubillas 2   *Jordan*

7/6/78 **SCOTLAND**........(1) **1** **IRAN** ....(0) **1** 8000
Eskandarian (o.g.)   *Danaiford*

11/6/78 **SCOTLAND**........(1) **3** **HOLLAND** ....(1) **2** 40000
Dalglish, Gemmill 2 (1 pen)   *Rensenbrink (pen), Rep*

SPAIN 1982
GROUP MATCHES – GROUP 6

15/6/82 **SCOTLAND**........(3) **5** **NEW ZEALAND** ...(0) **2** 36000
Wark 2, Dalglish, Robertson, Archibald   *Sumner, Wooddin*

18/6/82 **BRAZIL**...........(1) **4** **SCOTLAND** ....(1) **1** 47679
Zico, Oscar, Eder, Falcao   *Narey*

22/6/82 **SCOTLAND**........(1) **2** **USSR**............(0) **0** 45000
Jordan, Souness   *Chivadze, Shengelia*

MEXICO 1986
GROUP MATCHES – GROUP E

4/6/86 **SCOTLAND**........(0) **0** **DENMARK** ....(0) **1** 18000
   Elkjaer

8/6/86 **WEST GERMANY** ..(1) **2** **SCOTLAND** ....(1) **1** 30000
Voeller, Allofs   *Strachan*

13/6/86 **SCOTLAND**........(0) **0** **URUGUAY** ....(0) **0** 20000

ITALY 1990
GROUP MATCHES – GROUP C

11/6/90 **COSTA RICA**.......(0) **1** **SCOTLAND** ....(0) **0** 30867
Cayasso

16/6/90 **SWEDEN** ....(0) **1** **SCOTLAND** ....(1) **2** 31823
Stromberg   *McCall, Johnston (pen)*

20/6/90 **BRAZIL**...........(0) **1** **SCOTLAND** ....(0) **0** 62502
Muller

FRANCE 1998
GROUP MATCHES – GROUP A

10/6/98 **BRAZIL**...........(1) **2** **SCOTLAND** ....(1) **1** 80000
Sampaio, Boyd (og)   *Collins (pen)*

16/6/98 **SCOTLAND**........(0) **1** **NORWAY** ....(0) **1** 30236
Burley   *H. Flo*

23/6/98 **SCOTLAND**........(0) **0** **MOROCCO** ....(1) **3** 35000
   Bassir 2, Hadda

SOUTH AFRICA
FRANCE 1998
GROUP MATCHES – GROUP C

12/6/98 **FRANCE** ....(1) **3** **SOUTH AFRICA** ...(0) **0** 55077
Dugarry, Issa (og), Henry

18/6/98 **SOUTH AFRICA** ....(0) **1** **DENMARK** ....(1) **1** 36500
McCarthy   *Nielsen*

24/6/98 **SOUTH AFRICA** ....(1) **2** **SAUDI ARABIA** ... (1) **L** 34500
Bartlett 2 (1 pen)   *Al-Jaber (pen), Al-Thyniyan (pen)*

SOUTH KOREA
SWITZERLAND 1954
GROUP MATCHES – GROUP 2

17/6/54 **HUNGARY** ....(4) **9** **SOUTH KOREA** ....(0) **0** 13000
Czibor, Kocsis 3, Puskas 2, Lantos
Palotas 2

20/6/54 **TURKEY** ....(4) **7** **SOUTH KOREA** ....(0) **0** 4000
Burhan 3, Erol, Lefter, Suat 2

MEXICO 1986
GROUP MATCHES – GROUP A

2/6/86 **ARGENTINA**.......(2) **3** **SOUTH KOREA** ....(0) **1** 60000
Valdano 2, Ruggeri   *Park Chang Sun*

5/6/86 **SOUTH KOREA**.....(0) **1** **BULGARIA** ....(1) **1** 45000
Kim Jong Boo   *Getov*

10/6/86 **SOUTH KOREA**.....(0) **2** **ITALY**............(1) **3** 20000
Choi Soon-Hoo, Huh Jung-Moo   *Altobelli 3*

ITALY 1990
GROUP MATCHES – GROUP E

12/6/90 **BELGIUM** ....(0) **2** **SOUTH KOREA** ....(0) **0** 32486
Degryse, De Wolf

17/6/90 **SOUTH KOREA**.....(1) **1** **SPAIN** ....(1) **3** 32733
Kwan   *Gonzalez 3*

21/6/90 **SOUTH KOREA**.....(0) **0** **URUGUAY** ....(0) **1** 29039
   Fonseca

U.S.A. 1994
GROUP MATCHES – GROUP C

17/6/94 **SPAIN**...........(0) **2** **SOUTH KOREA** ....(0) **2** 56247
Salinas, Goikoetxea   *Hong Myung-Bo, Seo Jung-Won*

23/6/94 **SOUTH KOREA**.....(0) **0** **BOLIVIA** ....(0) **0** 53456

27/6/94 **GERMANY** ....(3) **3** **SOUTH KOREA** ....(0) **2** 63998
Klinsmann 2, Riedle   *Hwang Sun-Hong, Hong Myung-Bo*

FRANCE 1998
GROUP MATCHES – GROUP E

13/6/98 **SOUTH KOREA**.....(1) **1** **MEXICO** ....(0) **3** 37588
Ha Seok-Ju   *Pelaez, Hernandez 2*

20/6/98 **HOLLAND**..........(2) **5** **SOUTH KOREA** ....(0) **0** 60000
Cocu, Overmars, Bergkamp,
Van Hooijdonk, De Boer

25/6/98 **BELGIUM** ....(1) **1** **SOUTH KOREA** ....(0) **1** 48500
Nilis   *Yoo*

SPAIN
ITALY 1934
First Round

27/5/34 **SPAIN**...........(3) **3** **BRAZIL** ....(1) **1** N.R.
Iraragorri (pen), Langara 2   *Silva*

Second Round

31/5/34 **ITALY** ....(0) **1** **SPAIN** ....(1) **1** 35000
Ferrari   *Regueiro*

(After Extra Time)

Replay

1/6/34 **ITALY** ....(1) **1** **SPAIN** ....(0) **0** 43000
Meazza

BRAZIL 1950
GROUP MATCHES – GROUP 2

25/6/50 **SPAIN**............(0) **3** **USA**..............(1) **1** 9511
Basora 2, Zarra   *J. Souza*

29/6/50 **SPAIN**............(2) **2** **CHILE** ....(0) **0** 19790
Basora, Zarra

2/7/50 **SPAIN**............(0) **1** **ENGLAND** ....(0) **0** 74462
Zarra

GROUP MATCHES – FINAL POOL

9/7/50 **URUGUAY** ....(1) **2** **SPAIN** ....(2) **2** 44802
Ghiggia, Varela   *Basora 2*

13/7/50 **BRAZIL**...........(3) **6** **SPAIN** ....(0) **1** 152722
Jair 2, Chico 2, Zinzinho, Parra (o.g.)   *Igoa*

16/7/50 **SWEDEN** ....(2) **3** **SPAIN** ....(0) **1** 11227
Johansson, Mellberg, Palmer   *Zarra*

CHILE 1962
GROUP MATCHES – GROUP 3

31/5/62 **CZECHOSLOVAKIA**..(0) **1** **SPAIN** ....(0) **0** 12200
Stibranyi

3/6/62 **SPAIN**............(0) **1** **MEXICO** ....(0) **0** 11875
Peiro

6/6/62 **BRAZIL**..........(0) **2** **SPAIN**............(1) **1** 18715
Amarildo 2   *Adelardo*

ENGLAND 1966
GROUP MATCHES – GROUP 2

13/7/66 **ARGENTINA**......(0) **2** **SPAIN**............(0) **0** 47982
Artime 2   *Pirri*
15/7/66 **SPAIN**...........(0) **2** **SWITZERLAND**.....(1) **1** 32028
Sanchis, Amancio   *Quentin*
20/7/66 **WEST GERMANY**..(1) **2** **SPAIN**............(1) **1** 51875
Emmerich, Seeler   *Fuste*

ARGENTINA 1978
GROUP MATCHES – GROUP 3

3/6/78 **AUSTRIA**.........(1) **2** **SPAIN**............(1) **1** 49317
Schachner, Krankl   *Dani*
7/6/78 **BRAZIL**..........(0) **0** **SPAIN**............(0) **0** 40000
11/6/78 **SPAIN**...........(0) **1** **SWEDEN**...........(0) **0** 48000
Asensi

SPAIN 1982
GROUP MATCHES – GROUP 5

16/6/82 **SPAIN**...........(0) **1** **HONDURAS**.......(1) **1** 49562
Ufarte (pen)   *Zelaya*
20/6/82 **SPAIN**...........(1) **2** **YUGOSLAVIA**.....(1) **1** 48000
Juanito (pen), Saura   *Gudelj*
25/6/82 **NORTHERN IRELAND**(0) **1** **SPAIN**............(0) **0** 49562
Armstrong

GROUP MATCHES – GROUP B

Quarter-Finals

2/7/82 **WEST GERMANY**..(0) **2** **SPAIN**............(0) **1** 90089
Littbarski, Fischer   *Zamora*
5/7/82 **ENGLAND**........(0) **0** **SPAIN**............(0) **0** 75000

MEXICO 1986
GROUP MATCHES – GROUP D

1/6/86 **SPAIN**...........(0) **0** **BRAZIL**...........(0) **1** 35748
                             Socrates
7/6/86 **NORTHERN IRELAND**(0) **1** **SPAIN**............(2) **2** 28200
Clarke   *Butragueno, Salinas*
12/6/86 **ALGERIA** ....(0) **0** **SPAIN**............(2) **3** 23980
                         Caldere 2, Olaya

Second Round

18/6/86 **DENMARK**........(1) **1** **SPAIN**............(1) **5** 38500
J. Olsen (pen)   *Butragueno 4 (1 pen), Goicoetxea (pen)*

Quarter-Final

22/6/86 **BELGIUM**.........(1) **1** **SPAIN**............(1) **1** 45000
Ceulemans   *Senor*

(After Extra Time – Belgium won 5-4 on penalties)

ITALY 1990
GROUP MATCHES – GROUP E

13/6/90 **URUGUAY**........(0) **0** **SPAIN**............(0) **0** 35713
17/6/90 **SOUTH KOREA**.....(1) **1** **SPAIN**............(1) **3** 32733
Kwan   *Gonzalez 3*
21/6/90 **BELGIUM**.........(1) **1** **SPAIN**............(2) **2** 35950
Vervoort   *Michel (pen), Gorriz*

Second Round

26/6/90 **SPAIN**...........(0) **1** **YUGOSLAVIA**.....(0) **2** 35950
Salinas   *Stojkovic 2*

U.S.A. 1994
GROUP MATCHES – GROUP C

17/6/94 **SPAIN**...........(0) **2** **SOUTH KOREA**.....(0) **2** 56247
Salinas, Goikoetxea   *Hong Myung-Bo, Seo Jung-Won*

21/6/94 **GERMANY** ....(0) **1** **SPAIN**............(1) **1** 56247
Klinsmann   *Goikoetxea*
27/6/94 **BOLIVIA** ....(0) **1** **SPAIN**............(1) **3** 63089
Sanchez   *Guardiola (pen), Caminero 2*

Second Round

2/7/94 **SPAIN**...........(1) **3** **SWITZERLAND**.....(0) **0** 53121
Hierro, Luis Enrique, Beguiristain

Quarter Final

9/7/94 **ITALY** ....(1) **2** **SPAIN**............(0) **1** 54605
D. Baggio, R. Baggio   *Caminero*

FRANCE 1998
GROUP MATCHES – GROUP D

13/6/98 **SPAIN**...........(1) **2** **NIGERIA** ....(1) **3** 33257
Hierro, Raul   *Adepoju, Lawal, Oliseh*
19/6/98 **SPAIN**...........(0) **0** **PARAGUAY**........(0) **0** 35300
24/6/98 **SPAIN**...........(2) **6** **BULGARIA** ....(0) **1** 40500
Hierro (pen), Luis Enrique,   *Kostadinov,*
Morientes 2, Kiko 2

SWEDEN
ITALY 1934

First Round

27/5/34 **SWEDEN** ....(1) **3** **ARGENTINA**.......(1) **2** N.R.
Jonasson 2, Kroon   *Belis, Galateo*

Second Round

31/5/34 **GERMANY** ....(1) **2** **SWEDEN**...........(0) **1** 3000
Hohmann 2   *Dunker*

FRANCE 1938

First Round

SWEDEN RECEIVED A BYE

Second Round

12/6/38 **SWEDEN** ....(4) **8** **CUBA** ....(0) **0** N.R.
Andersson, Jonasson, Wetterstroem 4
Nyberg, Keller

Semi-Final

16/6/38 **HUNGARY** ....(3) **5** **SWEDEN**...........(1) **1** 17000
Szengeller 3, Titkos, Sarosi   *Nyberg*

Third Place Play-Off

19/6/38 **BRAZIL**..........(1) **4** **SWEDEN**...........(2) **2** N.R.
Romeu, Leonidas 2, Peracio   *Jonasson, Nyberg*

BRAZIL 1950
GROUP MATCHES – GROUP 3

25/6/50 **SWEDEN** ....(2) **3** **ITALY**............(1) **2** 56502
Jeppson 2, Anderson   *Carapellese, Muccinelli*
29/6/50 **SWEDEN** ....(2) **2** **PARAGUAY**........(1) **2** 7903
Sundqvist, Palmer   *A. Lopez, F. Lopez*

GROUP MATCHES – FINAL POOL

3/7/50 **BRAZIL**..........(3) **7** **SWEDEN**...........(0) **1** 138886
Ademir 4, Chico 2, Maneca   *Andersson (pen)*
13/7/50 **URUGUAY** ....(1) **3** **SWEDEN**...........(2) **2** 7987
Ghiggia, Miguez 2   *Palmer, Sundqvist*
16/7/50 **SWEDEN** ....(2) **3** **SPAIN**............(0) **1** 11227
Johansson, Mellberg, Palmer   *Zarra*

SWEDEN 1958
GROUP MATCHES – GROUP 3

8/6/58 **SWEDEN** ....(1) **3** **MEXICO** ....(0) **0** 34107
Simonsson 2, Liedholm (pen)
12/6/58 **SWEDEN** ....(1) **2** **HUNGARY**.........(0) **1** 38850
Hamrin 2   *Tichy*
15/6/58 **SWEDEN** ....(0) **0** **WALES** ....(0) **0** 29800

Quarter-Final

19/6/58 **SWEDEN** ....(0) **2** **USSR**.......... (0) **0** 31900
Hamrin, Simonsson

Semi-Final

24/6/58 **SWEDEN** ....(1) **3** **WEST GERMANY**.. (1) **1** 49471
Skoglund, Gren, Hamrin   Schaefer

Final

29/6/58 **BRAZIL**...........(2) **5** **SWEDEN**......... (1) **2** 49737
Vava 2, Pele, Hamrin   Liedholm, Simonsson

MEXICO 1970
GROUP MATCHES – GROUP 2

3/6/70 **ITALY** ....(1) **1** **SWEDEN** .... (0) **0** 14000
Domenghini

7/6/70 **SWEDEN** ....(0) **1** **ISRAEL** .... (0) **1** 9000
Turesson   Spiegler

10/6/70 **SWEDEN** ....(0) **1** **URUGUAY**....... (0) **0** 18000
Grahn

WEST GERMANY 1974
GROUP MATCHES – GROUP 3

15/6/74 **SWEDEN** ....(0) **0** **BULGARIA** ..... (0) **0** 23300

19/6/74 **HOLLAND**.........(0) **0** **SWEDEN**........ (0) **0** 53700

23/6/74 **SWEDEN** ....(0) **3** **URUGUAY** ...... (0) **0** 28300
Edstroem 2, Sandberg

GROUP MATCHES – GROUP B

Quarter-Finals

26/6/74 **POLAND**..........(1) **1** **SWEDEN**........ (0) **0** 45000
Lato

30/6/74 **WEST GERMANY** ..(0) **4** **SWEDEN**........ (1) **2** 67800
Overath, Bonhof, Grabowski   Edstroem, Sandberg
Hoeness (pen)

3/7/74 **SWEDEN** ....(1) **2** **YUGOSLAVIA** ..... (1) **1** 37700
Edstroem, Torstensson   Surjak

ARGENTINA 1978
GROUP MATCHES – GROUP 3

3/6/78 **SWEDEN** ....(1) **1** **BRAZIL** .... (1) **1** 38000
Sjoberg   Reinaldo

7/6/78 **AUSTRIA** ....(1) **1** **SWEDEN** .... (0) **0** 46000
Krankl (pen)

11/6/78 **SPAIN**............(0) **1** **SWEDEN**........ (0) **0** 48000
Asensi

ITALY 1990
GROUP MATCHES – GROUP C

10/6/90 **BRAZIL**...........(1) **2** **SWEDEN**........ (0) **1** 62628
Careca 2   Brolin

16/6/90 **SWEDEN** ....(0) **1** **SCOTLAND** .... (1) **2** 31823
Stromberg   McCall, Johnston (pen)

20/6/90 **SWEDEN** ....(1) **1** **COSTA RICA** ...... (0) **2** 30223
Ekstrom   Flores, Medford

U.S.A. 1994
GROUP MATCHES – GROUP B

19/4/94 **CAMEROON**.......(1) **2** **SWEDEN**......... (1) **2** 83959
Embe, Omam-Biyik   Ljung, Dahlin

24/6/94 **SWEDEN** ....(1) **3** **RUSSIA**......... (1) **1** 71528
Brolin (pen), Dahlin 2   Salenko (pen)

28/6/94 **BRAZIL**...........(0) **1** **SWEDEN**......... (1) **1** 77217
Romario   K. Andersson

Second Round

3/7/94 **SAUDI ARABIA** ....(0) **1** **SWEDEN**......... (1) **3** 60277
Al Ghesheyan   Dahlin, K. Andersson 2

Quarter-Final

10/7/94 **ROMANIA** ....(0) **2** **SWEDEN**......... (0) **2** 81715
Raducioiu 2   Brolin, K. Andersson

(After Extra Time – Sweden won 5-4 on penalties)

Semi-Final

13/7/94 **SWEDEN** ....(0) **0** **BRAZIL** .... (0) **1** 84569
    Romario

Third Place Play-Off

16/7/94 **BULGARIA** ....(0) **0** **SWEDEN**......... (4) **4** 83716
Brolin, Mild, Larsson, K. Andersson

SWITZERLAND
ITALY 1934
First Round

27/5/34 **SWITZERLAND** ....(2) **3** **HOLLAND** .... (1) **2** N.R.
Kielholtz 2, Abegglen   Smit, Vente

Second Round

31/5/34 **CZECHOSLOVAKIA**..(1) **3** **SWITZERLAND**.... (1) **2** N.R.
Svoboda, Sobotka, Nejedly   Kielhotz, Abegglen

FRANCE 1938
First Round

4/6/38 **SWITZERLAND** ....(1) **1** **GERMANY** .... (1) **1** 30000
Abegglen   Gauchel

(After Extra Time)

Replay

9/6/38 **SWITZERLAND** ....(0) **4** **GERMANY** .... (2) **2** 22000
Wallaschek, Bickel, Abegglen 2   Hahnemann, Loertscher (o.g.)

Second Round

12/6/38 **HUNGARY** ....(1) **2** **SWITZERLAND**.... (0) **0** N.R.
Szengeller 2

BRAZIL 1950
GROUP MATCHES – GROUP 1

25/6/50 **YUGOSLAVIA**......(3) **3** **SWITZERLAND**.... (0) **0** 7336
Tomasevic 2, Ognanov

28/6/50 **BRAZIL**...........(2) **2** **SWITZERLAND**... (1) **2** 42032
Alfredo, Baltazar   Fatton, Tamini

2/7/50 **SWITZERLAND** ....(2) **2** **MEXICO** .... (0) **1** 3580
Bader, Fatton   Velasquez

SWITZERLAND 1954
GROUP MATCHES – GROUP 4

17/6/54 **SWITZERLAND** ....(1) **2** **ITALY**............ (1) **1** 40500
Ballaman, Hugi   Boniperti

20/6/54 **ENGLAND**.........(1) **2** **SWITZERLAND**.... (0) **0** 43500
Mullen, Wilshaw

Play-Off

23/6/54 **SWITZERLAND** ....(1) **4** **ITALY**............ (1) **1** 29000
Hugi 2, Ballaman, Fatton   Nesti

Quarter-Final

26/6/54 **AUSTRIA** ....(5) **7** **SWITZERLAND**.... (4) **5** 31000
A Koerner 2, Ocwirk, Wagner 3   Ballaman 2, Hugi 2, Hanappi (o.g.)
Probst

CHILE 1962
GROUP MATCHES – GROUP 2

30/5/62 **CHILE** ....(1) **3** **SWITZERLAND**... (1) **1** 65006
L. Sanchez 2, Ramirez   Wuthrich

3/6/62 **WEST GERMANY** ..(1) **2** **SWITZERLAND**... (0) **1** 64992
Brulls, Seeler   Schneiter

7/6/62 **ITALY** ....(1) **3** **SWITZERLAND**... (0) **0** 59828
Mora, Bulgarelli 2

ENGLAND 1966
GROUP MATCHES – GROUP 2

12/7/66 **WEST GERMANY** ..(3) **5** **SWITZERLAND**.... (0) **0** 36127
Held, Haller 2 (1 pen), Beckenbauer

15/7/66 **SPAIN**. . . . .(0) **2** **SWITZERLAND**. . . . .(1) **1** 32028
Sanchis, Amancio   Quentin

19/7/66 **ARGENTINA**. . . . . .(0) **2** **SWITZERLAND**. . . . .(0) **0** 31443
Artime, Onega

U.S.A. 1994
GROUP MATCHES – GROUP A

18/6/94 **USA** . . . .(1) **1** **SWITZERLAND**. . . . .(1) **1** 73425
Wynalda   Bregy

22/6/94 **ROMANIA** . . . .(1) **1** **SWITZERLAND**. . . . .(1) **4** 61428
Hagi   Sutter, Chapuisat, Knup, Bregy

26/6/94 **SWITZERLAND** . . . .(0) **0** **COLOMBIA** . . . .(1) **2** 83769
                          Gaviria, Lozano

Second Round

2/7/94 **SPAIN**. . . . .(1) **3** **SWITZERLAND**. . . . .(0) **0** 53121
Hierro, Luis Enrique, Beguiristain

TUNISIA
ARGENTINA 1978
GROUP MATCHES – GROUP 2

2/6/78 **TUNISIA**. . . . .(0) **3** **MEXICO** . . . .(1) **1** 25000
Kaabi, Goummidh, Dhouib   Vazquez

6/6/78 **POLAND**. . . . .(1) **1** **TUNISIA**. . . . .(0) **0** 15000
Lato

10/6/78 **TUNISIA**. . . . .(0) **0** **WEST GERMANY** . .(0) **0** 35000

FRANCE 1998
GROUP MATCHES – GROUP G

15/6/98 **ENGLAND** . . . .(1) **2** **TUNISIA** . . . .(0) **0** 54587
Shearer, Scholes

22/6/98 **COLOMBIA**. . . . . . .(0) **1** **TUNISIA** . . . .(0) **0** 35000
Preciado

26/6/98 **ROMANIA** . . . .(0) **1** **TUNISIA** . . . .(1) **1** 80000
Moldovan   Souayeh (pen)

TURKEY
SWITZERLAND 1954
GROUP MATCHES – GROUP 2

17/6/54 **WEST GERMANY** . .(1) **4** **TURKEY**. . . . .(1) **1** 28000
Klodt, Morlock, Schaefer, O. Walter   Suat

20/6/54 **TURKEY**. . . . .(4) **7** **SOUTH KOREA** . . . . .(0) **0** 4000
Burhan 3, Erol, Lefter, Suat 2

Play-Off

23/6/54 **WEST GERMANY** . .(3) **7** **TURKEY**. . . . .(1) **2** 17000
Morlock 3, O. Walter, F. Walter   Mustafa, Lefter
Schaefer 2

UNITED ARAB EMIRATES (U.A.E.)
ITALY 1990
GROUP MATCHES – GROUP D

9/6/90 **U.A.E.**. . . . .(0) **0** **COLOMBIA** . . . .(0) **2** 30791
                          Redin, Valderrama

15/6/90 **WEST GERMANY** . .(2) **5** **U.A.E.**. . . . .(0) **1** 71167
Voeller 2, Klinsmann, Matthaus, Bein   Mubarek

19/6/90 **YUGOSLAVIA**. . . . . .(2) **4** **U.A.E.**. . . . .(1) **1** 27833
Susic, Pancev 2, Prosinecki   Jumaa

URUGUAY
URUGUAY 1930
GROUP MATCHES – GROUP 3

18/7/30 **URUGUAY** . . . .(0) **1** **PERU**. . . . .(0) **0** 70000
Castro

22/7/30 **URUGUAY** . . . .(4) **4** **ROMANIA**. . . . .(0) **0** 80000
Dorado, Scarone, Anselmo, Cea

Semi-Final

27/7/30 **URUGUAY** . . . .(3) **6** **YUGOSLAVIA** . . . . . .(1) **1** 93000
Cea 3, Anselmo 2, Iriarte   Seculic

Final

30/7/30 **URUGUAY** . . . .(1) **4** **ARGENTINA** . . . .(2) **2** 93000
Dorado, Cea, Iriarte, Castro   Peucelle, Stabile

BRAZIL 1950
GROUP MATCHES – GROUP 4

2/7/50 **URUGUAY** . . . .(4) **8** **BOLIVIA** . . . .(0) **0** 5284
Schiaffino 4, Miguez 2, Vidal, Ghiggia

GROUP MATCHES – FINAL POOL

9/7/50 **URUGUAY** . . . .(1) **2** **SPAIN**. . . . .(2) **2** 44802
Ghiggia, Varela   Basora 2

13/7/50 **URUGUAY** . . . .(1) **3** **SWEDEN**. . . . .(2) **2** 7987
Ghiggia, Miguez 2   Palmer, Sundqvist

16/7/50 **URUGUAY** . . . .(0) **2** **BRAZIL** . . . .(0) **1** 199854
Schiaffino, Ghiggia   Friaca

SWITZERLAND 1954
GROUP MATCHES – GROUP 3

16/6/54 **URUGUAY** . . . .(0) **2** **CZECHOSLOVAKIA** . .(0) **0** 20500
Miguez, Schiaffino

19/6/54 **URUGUAY** . . . .(2) **7** **SCOTLAND** . . . .(0) **0** 34000
Borges 3, Miguez 2, Abbadie 2

Quarter-Final

26/6/54 **URUGUAY** . . . .(2) **4** **ENGLAND** . . . .(1) **2** 50000
Borges, Varela, Schiaffino, Ambrois   Lofthouse, Finney

Semi-Final

30/6/54 **HUNGARY** . . . .(1) **4** **URUGUAY** . . . .(0) **2** 37000
Czibor, Hidegkuti, Kocsis 2   Hohberg 2

(After Extra Time)

Third Place Play-Off

3/7/54 **AUSTRIA** . . . .(1) **3** **URUGUAY**. . . . .(1) **1** 31000
Stojaspel (pen), Cruz (o.g.), Ocwirk   Hohberg

CHILE 1962
GROUP MATCHES – GROUP 1

30/5/62 **URUGUAY** . . . .(0) **2** **COLOMBIA** . . . .(1) **1** 7908
Cubilla, Sasia   Zaluaga

2/6/62 **YUGOSLAVIA**. . . . . .(2) **3** **URUGUAY**. . . . .(1) **1** 8829
Skoblar, Galic, Jerkovic   Cabrera

6/6/62 **USSR** . . . .(1) **2** **URUGUAY**. . . . .(0) **1** 9973
Mamikin, Ivanov   Sasia

ENGLAND 1966
GROUP MATCHES – GROUP 1

11/7/66 **ENGLAND** . . . .(0) **0** **URUGUAY**. . . . .(0) **0** 87148

15/7/66 **URUGUAY** . . . .(2) **2** **FRANCE** . . . .(1) **1** 45662
Rocha, Cortes   De Bourgoing (pen)

19/7/66 **URUGUAY** . . . .(0) **0** **MEXICO** . . . .(0) **0** 92570

Quarter-Final

23/7/66 **WEST GERMANY** . .(1) **4** **URUGUAY**. . . . .(0) **0** 33751
Held, Beckenbauer, Seeler, Haller

MEXICO 1970
GROUP MATCHES – GROUP 2

2/6/70 **URUGUAY** . . . .(1) **2** **ISRAEL** . . . .(0) **0** 20000
Maneiro, Mujica

6/6/70 **URUGUAY** . . . .(0) **0** **ITALY**. . . . .(0) **0** 30000

10/6/70 **SWEDEN** . . . .(0) **1** **URUGUAY**. . . . .(0) **0** 18000
Grahn

Quarter-Final

14/6/70 **URUGUAY** . . . .(0) **1** **USSR**. . . . .(0) **0** 45000
Esparrago

Semi-Final

17/6/70 **BRAZIL**............(1) **3** **URUGUAY**.......(1) **1** 51000
Clodoaldo, Jairzinho, Rivelino Cubillas

Third Place Play-Off

20/6/70 **WEST GERMANY**..(1) **1** **URUGUAY**.......(0) **0** 104000
Overath

WEST GERMANY 1974
GROUP MATCHES – GROUP 3

15/6/74 **HOLLAND**........(1) **2** **URUGUAY**.......(0) **0** 55000
Rep 2

19/6/74 **BULGARIA**........(0) **1** **URUGUAY**.......(0) **1** 13400
Bonev Pavoni

23/6/74 **SWEDEN**.........(0) **3** **URUGUAY**.......(0) **0** 28300
Edstroem 2, Sandberg

MEXICO 1986
GROUP MATCHES – GROUP E

4/6/86 **URUGUAY**........(1) **1** **WEST GERMANY**..(0) **1** 30500
Alzamendi Allofs

8/6/86 **DENMARK**.......(2) **6** **URUGUAY**.......(1) **1** 26500
Elkjaer 3, Lerby, Laudrup, J. Olsen Francescoli (pen)

13/6/86 **SCOTLAND**.......(0) **0** **URUGUAY**.......(0) **0** 20000

Second Round

16/6/86 **ARGENTINA**.......(1) **1** **URUGUAY**.......(0) **0** 26000
Pasculli

ITALY 1990
GROUP MATCHES – GROUP E

13/6/90 **URUGUAY**........(0) **0** **SPAIN**.........(0) **0** 35713

17/6/90 **BELGIUM**.........(2) **3** **URUGUAY**.......(0) **1** 33759
Clijsters, Scifo, Ceulemans Bengoechea

21/6/90 **SOUTH KOREA**....(0) **0** **URUGUAY**.......(0) **1** 29039
Fonseca

Second Round

25/6/90 **ITALY**...........(0) **2** **URUGUAY**.......(0) **0** 73300
Schillaci, Serena

USA
URUGUAY 1930
GROUP MATCHES – GROUP 4

13/7/30 **USA**.............(2) **3** **BELGIUM**........(0) **0** 10000
McGhee 2, Patenaude

17/7/30 **USA**.............(2) **3** **PARAGUAY**.......(0) **0** 800
Patenaude 2, Florie

Semi-Final

26/7/30 **ARGENTINA**.......(1) **6** **USA**...........(0) **1** 80000
Monti, Scopelli, Stabile 2, Paucelle 2 Brown

ITALY 1934

First Round

27/5/34 **ITALY**...........(3) **7** **USA**...........(0) **1** 30000
Schiavio 3, Orsi 2, Meazza, Ferrari Donelli

BRAZIL 1950
GROUP MATCHES – GROUP 2

25/6/50 **SPAIN**...........(0) **3** **USA**...........(1) **1** 9511
Basora 2, Zarra J. Souza

29/6/50 **USA**.............(1) **1** **ENGLAND**........(0) **0** 10151
Gaetjens

2/7/50 **CHILE**...........(2) **5** **USA**...........(0) **2** 8501
Robledo, Cremaschi 3, Prieto Pariani, J. Souza

ITALY 1990
GROUP MATCHES – GROUP A

10/6/90 **USA**.............(0) **1** **CZECHOSLOVAKIA**.(2) **5** 33266
Caligiuri Skuhravy 2, Bilek (pen), Hasek, Luhovy

14/6/90 **ITALY**............(0) **1** **USA**.............(0) **0** 73423
Giannini

19/6/90 **AUSTRIA**.........(0) **2** **USA**.............(0) **1** 34857
Ogris, Rodax Murray

U.S.A. 1994
GROUP MATCHES – GROUP A

18/6/94 **USA**.............(1) **1** **SWITZERLAND**....(1) **1** 73425
Wynalda Bregy

22/6/94 **USA**.............(1) **2** **COLOMBIA**.......(0) **1** 93194
Escobar (o.g.), Stewart Valencia

26/6/94 **USA**.............(0) **0** **ROMANIA**........(1) **1** 93869
Petrescu

Second Round

4/7/94 **BRAZIL**...........(0) **1** **USA**.............(0) **0** 84147
Bebeto

FRANCE 1998
GROUP MATCHES – GROUP F

15/6/98 **GERMANY**........(1) **2** **USA**.............(0) **0** 43875
Moller, Klinsmann

21/6/98 **USA**.............(0) **1** **IRAN**............(1) **2** 44000
McBride Estili, Mahdavikia

25/6/98 **USA**.............(0) **0** **YUGOSLAVIA**.....(1) **1** 39000
Komljenovic

USSR
(See Russia for 1994)
SWEDEN 1958
GROUP MATCHES – GROUP 4

8/6/58 **ENGLAND**.........(0) **2** **USSR**............(1) **2** 49348
Kevan, Finney (pen) Simonian, A. Ivanov

11/6/58 **USSR**............(1) **2** **AUSTRIA**.........(0) **0** 21239
Ilyin, V. Ivanov

15/6/58 **BRAZIL**...........(1) **2** **USSR**............(0) **0** 50928
Vava 2

Play-Off

17/6/58 **USSR**.............(0) **1** **ENGLAND**........(0) **0** 23182
Ilyin

Quarter-Final

19/6/58 **SWEDEN**.........(0) **2** **USSR**.............(0) **0** 31900
Hamrin, Simonsson

CHILE 1962
GROUP MATCHES – GROUP 1

31/5/62 **USSR**............(0) **2** **YUGOSLAVIA**.....(0) **0** 9622
Ivanov, Ponedelnik

3/6/62 **USSR**.............(3) **4** **COLOMBIA**.......(1) **4** 8040
Ivanov 2, Chislenko, Ponedelnik Aceros, Coll, Roda, Klinger

6/6/62 **USSR**.............(1) **2** **URUGUAY**........(0) **1** 9973
Mamikin, Ivanov Sasia

Quarter-Final

10/6/62 **CHILE**...........(2) **2** **USSR**............(1) **1** 17268
L. Sanchez, Rojas Chislenko

ENGLAND 1966
GROUP MATCHES – GROUP 4

12/7/66 **USSR**............(2) **3** **NORTH KOREA**....(0) **0** 22568
Malafeev 2, Banischevski

16/7/66 **USSR**............(0) **1** **ITALY**...........(0) **0** 31989
Chislenko

20/7/66 **USSR** . . . .(1) **2** **CHILE** . . . .(1) **1** 22590
Porkujan 2 *Marcos*

Quarter-Final

23/7/66 **USSR** . . . .(1) **2** **HUNGARY** . . . .(0) **1** 26844
Chislenko, Porkujan *Bene*

Semi-Final

25/7/66 **WEST GERMANY** . .(1) **2** **USSR** . . . .(0) **1** 43921
Haller, Beckenbauer *Porkujan*

Third Place Play-Off

28/7/66 **PORTUGAL** . . . . . .(1) **2** **USSR** . . . .(0) **1** 87696
Eusebio (pen), Torres *Malafeev*

MEXICO 1970
GROUP MATCHES – GROUP 1

31/5/70 **MEXICO** . . . .(0) **0** **USSR** . . . .(0) **0** 107000

6/6/70 **USSR** . . . .(1) **4** **BELGIUM** . . . .(0) **1** 59000
Byshovets 2, Asatiani, Khmelnitsky *Lambert*

10/6/70 **USSR** . . . .(0) **2** **EL SALVADOR** . . . . .(0) **0** 89000
Byshovets 2

Quarter-Final

14/6/70 **URUGUAY** . . . .(0) **1** **USSR** . . . .(0) **0** 45000
Esparrago

SPAIN 1982
GROUP MATCHES – GROUP 6

14/6/82 **BRAZIL** . . . .(0) **2** **USSR** . . . .(0) **1** 68000
Socrates, Eder *Bal*

19/6/82 **USSR** . . . .(1) **3** **NEW ZEALAND** . . . .(0) **0** 19000
Gavrilov, Blokhin, Baltacha

22/6/82 **SCOTLAND** . . . .(1) **2** **USSR** . . . .(0) **2** 45000
Jordan, Souness *Chivadze, Shengelia*

GROUP MATCHES – GROUP A

Quarter-Finals

1/7/82 **USSR** . . . .(0) **1** **BELGIUM** . . . .(0) **0** 45000
Oganesian

4/7/82 **POLAND** . . . .(0) **0** **USSR** . . . .(0) **0** 65000

MEXICO 1986
GROUP MATCHES – GROUP C

2/6/86 **USSR** . . . .(3) **6** **HUNGARY** . . . .(0) **0** 16600
Yakovenko, Aleinikov, Belanov (pen)
Yaremchuck 2, Radionov

5/6/86 **FRANCE** . . . .(0) **1** **USSR** . . . .(0) **1** 36540
Fernandez *Rats*

9/6/86 **USSR** . . . .(0) **2** **CANADA** . . . .(0) **0** 14200
Blokhin, Zavarov

Second Round

15/6/86 **USSR** . . . .(1) **3** **BELGIUM** . . . .(0) **4** 32277
Belanov 3 (1pen) *Scifo, Ceulemans, De Mol, Claesen*

(After Extra Time)

ITALY 1990
GROUP MATCHES – GROUP B

9/6/90 **USSR** . . . .(0) **0** **ROMANIA** . . . .(1) **2** 42960
Lacatus 2 (1 pen)

13/6/90 **ARGENTINA** . . . .(1) **2** **USSR** . . . .(0) **0** 55759
Troglio, Burruchaga

18/6/90 **CAMEROON** . . . .(0) **0** **USSR** . . . .(2) **4** 37307
Protasov, Zygmantovich, Zavarov,
Dobrovolsky

WALES
SWEDEN 1958
GROUP MATCHES – GROUP 3

8/6/58 **WALES** . . . .(1) **1** **HUNGARY** . . . .(1) **1** 15343
J. Charles *Bozsik*

11/6/58 **WALES** . . . .(1) **1** **MEXICO** . . . .(1) **1** 15150
Allchurch *Belmonte*

15/6/58 **SWEDEN** . . . .(0) **0** **WALES** . . . .(0) **0** 29800

Play-Off

17/6/58 **WALES** . . . .(0) **2** **HUNGARY** . . . .(1) **1** 2832
Allchurch, Medwin *Tichy*

Quarter-Final

19/6/58 **BRAZIL** . . . .(0) **1** **WALES** . . . .(0) **0** 25923
Pele

WEST GERMANY
SWITZERLAND 1954
GROUP MATCHES – GROUP 2

17/6/54 **WEST GERMANY** . .(1) **4** **TURKEY** . . . .(1) **1** 28000
Klodt, Morlock, Schaefer, O. Walter *Suat*

20/6/54 **HUNGARY** . . . .(3) **8** **WEST GERMANY** . . .(1) **3** 56000
Hidegkuti 2, Kocsis 4, Puskas, Toth *Pfaff, Hermann, Rahn*

Play-Off

23/6/54 **WEST GERMANY** . .(3) **7** **TURKEY** . . . .(1) **2** 17000
Morlock 3, O. Walter, F. Walter *Mustafa, Lefter*
Schaefer 2

Quarter-Final

27/6/54 **WEST GERMANY** . .(1) **2** **YUGOSLAVIA** . . . . . .(0) **0** 17000
Horvat (o.g.), Rahn

Semi-Final

30/6/54 **WEST GERMANY** . .(1) **6** **AUSTRIA** . . . .(0) **1** 58000
Schaefer, Morlock, F. Walter (2pens) *Probst*
O. Walter

Final

4/7/54 **WEST GERMANY** . .(2) **3** **HUNGARY** . . . .(1) **1** 60000
Morlock, Rahn 2 *Puskas, Czibor*

SWEDEN 1958
GROUP MATCHES – GROUP 1

8/6/58 **WEST GERMANY** . .(2) **3** **ARGENTINA** . . . .(1) **1** 31156
Rahn 2, Schmidt *Corbatta*

11/6/58 **WEST GERMANY** . .(1) **2** **CZECHOSLOVAKIA** . .(1) **2** 25000
Schaefer, Rahn *Dvorak (pen), Zikan*

15/6/58 **WEST GERMANY** . .(1) **2** **NORTHERN IRELAND**(1)**2** 21900
Rahn, Seeler *McParland 2*

Quarter-Final

19/6/58 **WEST GERMANY** . .(1) **1** **YUGOSLAVIA** . . . . . .(0) **0** 20000
Rahn

Semi-Final

24/6/58 **SWEDEN** . . . .(1) **3** **WEST GERMANY** . . .(1) **1** 49421
Skoglund, Gren, Hamrin *Schaefer*

Third Place Play-Off

28/6/58 **FRANCE** . . . .(3) **6** **WEST GERMANY** . . .(1) **3** 32482
Fontaine 4, Kopa (pen), Douis *Cierlarczyk, Rahn, Schaefer*

CHILE 1962
GROUP MATCHES – GROUP 2

31/5/62 **WEST GERMANY** . .(0) **0** **ITALY** . . . .(0) **0** 65440

3/6/62 **WEST GERMANY** . .(1) **2** **SWITZERLAND** . . . . .(0) **1** 64922
Brulls, Seeler *Schneiter*

6/6/62 **WEST GERMANY** . .(1) **2** **CHILE** . . . .(0) **0** 67224
Szymaniak (pen), Seeler

Quarter-Final

10/6/62 **YUGOSLAVIA** . . . . . .(0) **1** **WEST GERMANY** . . .(0) **0** 63324
Radakovic

ENGLAND 1966
GROUP MATCHES – GROUP 2

12/7/66 **WEST GERMANY** . .(3) **5** **SWITZERLAND** . . . . .(0) **0** 36127
Held, Haller 2 (1 pen), Beckenbauer 2

16/7/66 **ARGENTINA**......(0) **0** **WEST GERMANY**.. (0) **0** 51419
20/7/66 **WEST GERMANY** ..(1) **2** **SPAIN**........... (1) **1** 51875
    Emmerich, Seeler   *Fuste*

Quarter-Final

23/7/66 **WEST GERMANY** ..(1) **4** **URUGUAY**....... (0) **0** 33751
    Held, Beckenbauer, Seeler, Haller

Semi-Final

25/7/66 **WEST GERMANY** ..(1) **2** **USSR**............ (0) **1** 43921
    Haller, Beckenbauer   *Porkujan*

Final

30/7/66 **ENGLAND**.........(1) **4** **WEST GERMANY** .. (1) **2** 87696
    Hurst 3, Peters   *Haller, Weber*

(After Extra Time)

MEXICO 1970
GROUP MATCHES – GROUP 4

3/6/70 **WEST GERMANY** ..(0) **2** **MOROCCO** .... (1) **1** 9000
    Seeler, Muller   *Houmane*
7/6/70 **WEST GERMANY** ..(2) **5** **BULGARIA** ..... (1) **2** 12700
    Libuda, Muller 3 (1 pen), Seeler   *Nikodimov, Kolev*
10/6/70 **WEST GERMANY** ..(3) **3** **PERU**............ (1) **1** 18000
    Muller 3   *Cubillas*

Quarter-Final

14/6/70 **WEST GERMANY** ..(0) **3** **ENGLAND**........ (1) **2** 24000
    Beckenbauer, Seeler, Muller   *Mullery, Peters*

(After Extra Time)

Semi-Final

17/6/70 **ITALY** ....(1) **4** **WEST GERMANY** .. (0) **3** 80000
    Boninsegna, Burgnich, Riva, Rivera   *Schnellinger, Muller 2*

(After Extra Time)

Third Place Play-Off

20/6/70 **WEST GERMANY** ..(1) **1** **URUGUAY**........ (0) **0** 104000
    Overath

WEST GERMANY 1974
GROUP MATCHES – GROUP 1

14/6/74 **WEST GERMANY** ..(1) **1** **CHILE** .... (0) **0** 83168
    Breitner
18/6/74 **WEST GERMANY** ..(2) **3** **AUSTRALIA** ...... (0) **0** 17000
    Overath, Cullman, Muller
22/6/74 **EAST GERMANY** ...(1) **1** **WEST GERMANY**.. (0) **0** 60200
    Sparwasser

GROUP MATCHES – GROUP B

Quarter-Finals

26/6/74 **WEST GERMANY** ..(1) **2** **YUGOSLAVIA** ..... (0) **0** 67500
    Breitner, Muller
30/6/74 **WEST GERMANY** ..(0) **4** **SWEDEN**........ (1) **2** 67800
    Overath, Bonhof, Grabowski   *Edstroem, Sandberg*
    Hoeness (pen)
3/7/74 **WEST GERMANY** ..(0) **1** **POLAND** .... (0) **0** 62000
    Muller

Final

7/7/74 **WEST GERMANY** ..(2) **2** **HOLLAND** .... (1) **1** 77833
    Breitner (pen), Muller   *Neekens (pen)*

ARGENTINA 1978
GROUP MATCHES – GROUP 2

1/6/78 **WEST GERMANY** ..(0) **0** **POLAND** .... (0) **0** 77000
6/6/78 **MEXICO** ....(0) **0** **WEST GERMANY**.. (4) **6** 46000
    D. Muller, H. Muller, Rummenigge 2
    Flohe 2
10/6/78 **TUNISIA**..........(0) **0** **WEST GERMANY** .. (0) **0** 35000

GROUP MATCHES – GROUP A

Quarter-Finals

14/6/78 **WEST GERMANY** ..(0) **0** **ITALY**............ (0) **0** 35000

18/6/78 **HOLLAND**.........(1) **2** **WEST GERMANY**.. (1) **2** 46000
    Haan, R. Van Der Kerkhof   *Abramczik 2*
21/6/78 **AUSTRIA** ....(0) **3** **WEST GERMANY** .. (1) **2** 20000
    Vogts (o.g.), Krankl 2   *Rummenigge, Holzenbein*

SPAIN 1982
GROUP MATCHES – GROUP 2

16/6/82 **ALGERIA**.........(0) **2** **WEST GERMANY** .. (0) **1** 42000
    Madjer, Belloumi   *Rummenigge*
20/6/82 **WEST GERMANY** ..(1) **4** **CHILE** .... (0) **1** 42000
    Rummenigge 3, Reinders   *Moscoso*
25/6/82 **WEST GERMANY** ..(1) **1** **AUSTRIA**......... (0) **0** 41000
    Hrubesch

GROUP MATCHES – GROUP B

Quarter-Finals

29/6/82 **WEST GERMANY** ..(0) **0** **ENGLAND**........ (0) **0** 75000
2/7/82 **WEST GERMANY** ..(0) **2** **SPAIN**........... (0) **1** 90089
    Littbarski, Fischer   *Zamora*

Semi-Final

8/7/82 **WEST GERMANY** ..(1) **3** **FRANCE** .... (1) **3** 63000
    Littbarski, Rummenigge, Fischer   *Platini (pen), Tresor, Giresse*

(After Extra Time – West Germany won 5-4 on penalties)

Final

11/7/82 **ITALY** ....(0) **3** **WEST GERMANY** .. (0) **1** 90000
    Rossi, Tardelli, Altobelli   *Breitner*

MEXICO 1986
GROUP MATCHES – GROUP E

4/6/86 **URUGUAY** ....(1) **1** **WEST GERMANY** .. (0) **1** 30500
    Alzamendi   *Alloffs*
8/6/86 **WEST GERMANY** ..(1) **2** **SCOTLAND** ...... (1) **1** 30000
    Voeller, Alloffs   *Strachan*
13/6/86 **DENMARK**........(1) **2** **WEST GERMANY** .. (0) **1** 36000
    J. Olsen, Eriksen

Second Round

17/6/86 **MOROCCO**........(0) **0** **WEST GERMANY** .. (0) **1** 19800
    Matthaus

Quarter-Final

21/6/86 **WEST GERMANY** . (0) **0** **MEXICO** .... (0) **0** 44386
(After Extra Time – West Germany won 4-1 on penalties)

Semi-Final

25/6/86 **FRANCE**..........(0) **0** **WEST GERMANY**.. (1) **2** 45000
    Brehme, Voeller

Final

29/6/86 **ARGENTINA**.......(1) **3** **WEST GERMANY** .. (0) **2** 114590
    Brown, Valdano, Burruchaga   *Rummenigge, Voeller*

ITALY 1990
GROUP MATCHES – GROUP D

10/6/90 **WEST GERMANY** ..(2) **4** **YUGOSLAVIA** ..... (0) **1** 74765
    Matthaus 2, Klinsmann, Voeller   *Jozic*
15/6/90 **WEST GERMANY** ..(2) **5** **U.A.E.** .... (0) **1** 71167
    Voeller 2, Klinsmann, Matthaus, Bein   *Mubarek*
19/6/90 **WEST GERMANY** ..(0) **1** **COLOMBIA** .... (0) **1** 72510
    Littbarski   *Rincon*

Second Round

24/6/90 **WEST GERMANY** ..(0) **2** **HOLLAND** .... (0) **1** 74559
    Klinsmann, Brehme   *Koeman (pen)*

Quarter-Final

1/7/90 **CZECHOSLOVAKIA**..(0) **0** **WEST GERMANY**.. (1) **1** 73347
    Matthaus (pen)

Semi-Final

4/7/90 **WEST GERMANY** ..(0) **1** **ENGLAND**........ (0) **1** 62628
    Brehme

(After Extra Time – West Germany won 4-3 on penalties)

Final

8/7/90 **ARGENTINA**.......(0) **0** **WEST GERMANY**...(0) **1** 73603
Brehme (pen)

YUGOSLAVIA
URUGUAY 1930
GROUP MATCHES – GROUP 2

14/7/30 **YUGOSLAVIA**......(2) **2** **BRAZIL**.........(0) **1** 5000
Tirnanic, Beck Neto

17/7/30 **YUGOSLAVIA**......(0) **4** **BOLIVIA**.........(0) **0** 800
Beck 2, Marifanovic, Vujadinovic

Semi-Final

27/7/30 **URUGUAY**........(3) **6** **YUGOSLAVIA**......(1) **1** 93000
Cea 3, Anselmo 2, Iriarte Seculic

BRAZIL 1950
GROUP MATCHES – GROUP 1

25/6/50 **YUGOSLAVIA**......(3) **3** **SWITZERLAND**.....(0) **0** 7336
Tomasevic 2, Ognanov

29/6/50 **YUGOSLAVIA**......(2) **4** **MEXICO**.........(0) **1** 11078
Bobek, Cajkowski 2, Tomasevic Casarin

1/7/50 **BRAZIL**..........(1) **2** **YUGOSLAVIA**......(0) **0** 142409
Ademir, Zizinho

SWITZERLAND 1954
GROUP MATCHES – GROUP 1

16/6/54 **YUGOSLAVIA**......(1) **1** **FRANCE**.........(0) **0** 16000
Milutinovic

19/6/54 **BRAZIL**..........(0) **1** **YUGOSLAVIA**......(0) **1** 21000
Didi Zebec

(After Extra Time)

Quarter-Final

27/6/54 **WEST GERMANY**..(1) **2** **YUGOSLAVIA**......(0) **0** 31000
Horvat (o.g.), Rahn

SWEDEN 1958
GROUP MATCHES – GROUP 2

8/6/58 **YUGOSLAVIA**......(1) **1** **SCOTLAND**........(0) **1** 9591
Petakovic Murray

11/6/58 **YUGOSLAVIA**......(1) **3** **FRANCE**.........(1) **2** 12217
Petakovic, Veselinovic 2 Fontaine 2

15/6/58 **YUGOSLAVIA**......(2) **3** **PARAGUAY**........(1) **3** 13103
Ognjanovic, Rajkov, Veselinovic Parodi, Aguero, Romero

Quarter-Final

19/6/58 **WEST GERMANY**..(1) **1** **YUGOSLAVIA**......(0) **0** 20000
Rahn

CHILE 1962
GROUP MATCHES – GROUP 1

31/5/62 **USSR**............(0) **2** **YUGOSLAVIA**......(0) **0** 9591
Ivanov, Ponedelnik

2/6/62 **YUGOSLAVIA**......(2) **3** **URUGUAY**........(1) **1** 8829
Skoblar, Garlic, Jerkovic Cabrera

7/6/62 **YUGOSLAVIA**......(2) **5** **COLOMBIA**........(0) **0** 7167
Galic, Jerkovic 3, Melic

Quarter-Final

10/6/62 **YUGOSLAVIA**......(0) **1** **WEST GERMANY**..(0) **0** 63324
Radakovic

Semi-Final

13/6/62 **CZECHOSLOVAKIA**..(0) **3** **YUGOSLAVIA**......(0) **1** 5890
Kadraba, Scherer 2 (1 pen) Jerkovic

Third Place Play-Off

16/6/62 **CHILE**...........(0) **1** **YUGOSLAVIA**......(0) **0** 66697
Rojas

WEST GERMANY 1974
GROUP MATCHES – GROUP 2

13/6/74 **BRAZIL**..........(0) **0** **YUGOSLAVIA**......(0) **0** 62000

18/6/74 **YUGOSLAVIA**......(6) **9** **ZAIRE**.........(0) **0** 31200
Bajevic 3, Dzajic, Surjak, Katalinski
Bogicevic, Oblak, Petkovic

22/6/74 **SCOTLAND**.......(0) **1** **YUGOSLAVIA**......(0) **1** 56000
Jordan Karasi

GROUP MATCHES – GROUP B

Quarter-Finals

26/6/74 **WEST GERMANY**..(1) **2** **YUGOSLAVIA**......(0) **0** 67500
Breitner, Muller

30/6/74 **POLAND**..........(1) **2** **YUGOSLAVIA**......(1) **1** 53200
Deyna (pen), Lato Karasi

3/7/74 **SWEDEN**.........(1) **2** **YUGOSLAVIA**......(1) **1** 37700
Edstroem, Torstensson Surjak

SPAIN 1982
GROUP MATCHES – GROUP 5

17/6/82 **NORTHERN IRELAND**(0) **0** **YUGOSLAVIA**......(0) **0** 25000

20/6/82 **SPAIN**...........(1) **2** **YUGOSLAVIA**......(1) **1** 48000
Juanito (pen), Saura Gudelj

24/6/82 **YUGOSLAVIA**......(0) **1** **HONDURAS**.......(0) **0** 25000
Petrovic (pen)

ITALY 1990
GROUP MATCHES – GROUP D

10/6/90 **WEST GERMANY**..(2) **4** **YUGOSLAVIA**......(0) **1** 74765
Matthaus 2, Klinsmann, Voeller Jozic

14/6/90 **YUGOSLAVIA**......(0) **1** **COLOMBIA**........(0) **0** 32257
Jozic

19/6/90 **YUGOSLAVIA**......(2) **4** **UAE**............(1) **1** 27833
Susic, Pancev 2, Prosinecki Jumaa

Second Round

26/6/90 **SPAIN**...........(0) **1** **YUGOSLAVIA**......(0) **2** 35500
Salinas Stojkovic 2

Quarter Final

30/6/90 **ARGENTINA**.......(0) **0** **YUGOSLAVIA**......(0) **0** 38971
(After Extra Time – Argentina won 3-2 on penalties)

FRANCE 1998
GROUP MATCHES – GROUP F

14/6/98 **YUGOSLAVIA**......(0) **1** **IRAN**............(0) **0** 30392
Mihailovic

21/6/98 **GERMANY**........(0) **2** **YUGOSLAVIA**......(1) **2** 40775
Tarnat, Bierhoff Mijatovic, Stojkovic

25/6/98 **USA**.............(0) **0** **YUGOSLAVIA**......(1) **1** 39000
Komljenovic

Second Round

29/6/98 **HOLLAND**.........(1) **2** **YUGOSLAVIA**......(0) **1** 35000
Bergkamp, Davids Komljenovic

ZAIRE
WEST GERMANY 1974
GROUP MATCHES – GROUP 2

14/6/90 **SCOTLAND**.......(2) **2** **ZAIRE**.........(0) **0** 62000
Lorimer, Jordan

18/6/90 **YUGOSLAVIA**......(6) **9** **ZAIRE**.........(0) **0** 31700
Bajevic 3, Dzajic, Surjak, Katalinski
Bogicevic, Oblak, Petkovic

22/6/90 **BRAZIL**..........(1) **3** **ZAIRE**.........(0) **0** 36200
Jairzinho, Rivelino, Valdomiro

2 FREE ISSUES
when you
subscribe to
World Soccer

he No.1 International Football Magazine

World Soccer is the only magazine that reports on the international game in the detail that you want.
Follow your favourite teams in World Service, a detailed section with results and league tables from every soccer nation. Keep up to date on what's happening day to day in the World Soccer diary pages and enjoy sensational articles, news and features on the likes of Bergkamp, Ronaldo, Owen and Del Piero. **Heralded by Reuters as the "bible of the international game"** it provides more statistical coverage of international football than any other magazine.

Exclusive Offer

HERE'S WHAT'S ON OFFER...

- 20% DISCOUNT, save £5.76, equivalent to over two issues FREE on a one year subscription.
- A PRICE FREEZE throughout your subscription period, even if the cover price rises.
- FREE postage and packing.
- GUARANTEED DELIVERY direct to your door so you never miss a single issue.
- MONEY BACK GUARANTEE - if you're not 100% happy with World Soccer, you can cancel your subscription at any time for a full refund of the remaining balance.

AREA	1 YEAR		
	FULL PRICE	YOU SAVE 20%	YOU PAY
U.K.	£28.80	£5.76	**£23.04**
EUROPE	£35.00	£7.00	**£28.00**
USA	$75.15	$15.03	**$60.12**
REST OF WORLD	£45.00	£9.00	**£36.00**

UK & OVERSEAS SUBSCRIPTION PRICES

To order now and SAVE 20% call the Credit Card Hotline!
Please quote code: 24G to obtain the discount advertised

☎ Call +44 (0)1622 778 778
Lines open 7 days a week, 7am-7pm (UK times).

This offer is open to new subscribers only, and closes on 31st December 1999. Please allow up to six weeks for your first subscription issue. For enquiries, please call +44(0)1444 445555.